Representative Democracy in Flux

Deconstructive Narratives from a Legal and Constitutional Perspective

Edited by Martin Belov

Routledge
Taylor & Francis Group
LONDON AND NEW YORK

First published 2025
by Routledge
4 Park Square, Milton Park, Abingdon, Oxon OX14 4RN

and by Routledge
605 Third Avenue, New York, NY 10158

Routledge is an imprint of the Taylor & Francis Group, an informa business

The open access for this publication is financed by the European Union-NextGenerationEU, through the National Recovery and Resilience Plan of the Republic of Bulgaria, project No BG-RRP-2.004-0008.

British Library Cataloguing-in-Publication Data
A catalogue record for this book is available from the British Library

ISBN: 978-1-041-00596-4 (hbk)
ISBN: 978-1-041-00597-1 (pbk)
ISBN: 978-1-003-61067-0 (ebk)

DOI: 10.4324/9781003610670

Typeset in Galliard
by Apex CoVantage, LLC

This book and all chapters in it are produced as part of and funded by the European Union-NextGenerationEU, through the National Recovery and Resilience Plan of the Republic of Bulgaria, project No bg-rrp–2.004–0008.

Contents

Contributors

Jan Adamowski ORCID 0009-0005-3326-3063 is a PhD student in legal studies at the Doctoral School in the Social Sciences at the Jagiellonian University in Krakow, Poland. He holds an MA in law and is an associate at the Centre for Interdisciplinary Constitutional Studies and a contractor in the research project Protection of human rights in states of emergency: Theory and practice of the Visegrad Group countries, funded by the Polish National Science Centre. He was also a contractor in the research and didactic project Legislative omissions in the process of judicial application of law, funded by the Polish Ministry of Science and Higher Education, and a collaborator in the research project Rule of law and independent judiciary: Major challenges for Ukraine and Poland in the context of European Union integration, funded by the Foundation for Polish Science. He is a frequent speaker at academic conferences on constitutional law and the author of scholarly publications in constitutional law.

Antonina Bakardjieva Engelbrekt ORCID 0000-0001-5119-4851 is Professor of European Law at Stockholm University in Sweden and Chair of the Swedish Network for European Legal Studies. Her research is mainly within the area of European economic law and governance with a focus on European and comparative market law, consumer law, and intellectual property law. The research interest is directed toward processes of Europeanization and globalization and their influence on national law and legal institutions, as well as toward different legal systems' influence on each other ("legal transplants"). Other recurrent themes in Prof. Bakardjieva's research concern the fluid borderline between private and public law and the complex relationship between substantive law, on the one hand, and procedural law and institutions, on the other. She teaches courses on EU law, comparative law, market law, intellectual property law, and law and economics.

Martin Belov (editor) is Professor in Constitutional and Comparative Constitutional Law at the University of Sofia "St. Kliment Ohridski". He is Vice Dean of the University of Sofia "St. Kliment Ohridski", Faculty of Law.

Martin Belov has been visiting professor at UCD (Dublin, Ireland) (2024), University of Milano (Italy) (2024), University of Graz (Austria) (2024), EURAC (Bolzano, Italy) (2024), Reichman University, Harry Radzyner Law School (Herzliya, Israel) (2021–2023), Jagiellonian University of Cracow, Poland, (2024 and 2022), University Paris II Pantheon-Assas (2019), Goethe-University (Frankfurt am Main, Germany) (2019), University of Girona, Spain (2019), University "Pompeu Fabra" (Barcelona, Spain) (2019), Europa-University Viadrina (Frankfurt/Oder, Germany) (2017 and 2018), University of Bari, Italy (2018), European Law and Governance School, Athens (2017–2018 and 2020–2021), University of Södertorn (Stockholm, Sweden) (2017), Scuolla Superiore Sant'Anna (Pisa, Italy) (2016), University of Warsaw, Poland (2015), University of Lisbon, Portugal (2012), State University of Milan, Italy (2011), University of Cologne, Germany (2007–2009), etc. Martin Belov has been project researcher at the Max-Planck Institute for European Legal History, Frankfurt am Main, Germany (2010–2012) and visiting researcher at the Institute for Federalism, Fribourg, Switzerland (2014). He has specialized at the University of Oxford (UK) (2017), Max-Planck Institute for Comparative Public Law and International Law, Heidelberg, Germany (2009), and many other academic institutions. Martin Belov is member of the scientific boards of many academic journals. He has participated in numerous international research projects (including Horizon 2020 and Recovery Fund projects, the German Cluster of Excellence projects, etc.). He has published 24 books and more than 100 scientific papers and book chapters.

Guerino Fares is Full Professor of Administrative and Public Law at Roma 3 University, where he's also Lecturer of School Law, Constitutional Law, and Health Law. In the same university he's Director of Research Center on Innovation & Health, Director of Drug Innovation and Regulation Master, Director of Educator for Special Needs Master, and Deputy Director of Health-Pharmaceutical Law & Management Master. Moreover, he's Roma 3 University Rector's Delegate for the relationship with students in addition to Member of the ASA-Tre's (Roma 3 High School for Public Administration) Scientific Board, Italian Representative at HeaLab EuroNet (www.healab.net), Scientific Director of the Ius & Salus law journal (www.iusetsalus.it, www.rivistaiusetsalus.it), President of AIOP (Italian Association of Private Hospitals) Board of Arbitrators, and attorney at highest order courts.

Monika Florczak-Wątor ORCID 0000-0002-4324-5652 is a professor of constitutional law at the Jagiellonian University in Krakow, Poland, and serves as Director of the Centre for Interdisciplinary Constitutional Studies as well as Director of the Interdisciplinary Doctoral Programme "Society of the Future" within the Doctoral School in Social Sciences at the Jagiellonian University. She holds a PhD and Habilitation in Law, along with an MA in Law and Political Sciences. She is Deputy President of the Committee of Legal Sciences of the Polish Academy of Sciences and co-founder of the Central and Eastern European Chapter of the International Society of Public Law (ICON-S) and the Polish Association "Democracy in Practice". She is also a member of numerous academic associations and organizations, including the European Group of Public Law and the Legal Experts Group of the Stefan Batory Foundation. She has authored over 150 scholarly publications and is the principal investigator on several research projects funded by various academic institutions and agencies.

Ingeborg van der Geest https://orcid.org/0000-0002-9934-7412 is an assistant professor of legal argumentation and rhetoric at Vrije Universiteit Amsterdam, where she teaches courses in legal skills and methodologies. She has also lectured on argumentation and critical thinking at various institutions and for diverse professional audiences. Her research centers on legal argumentation, rhetoric, political discourse, and deep disagreement. She has published on topics including policy argumentation, argumentation and decision-making, populism, and communication skills.

Šejla Imamović ORCID 0000-0003-2121-9645 is a tenure-track assistant professor at the faculty of law of Maastricht University. Šejla's research and teaching interests are in European human rights law. She is mainly interested in the interaction between the European Union (EU) and the European Convention on Human Rights (ECHR). Recently, she has focused more on the ECHR legal system and the role of the European Court of Human Rights (ECtHR) in protecting and upholding human rights in Europe.

Bart van Klink https://orcid.org/0000-0002-7465-9292 is Professor of Legal Methodology at Vrije Universiteit Amsterdam, focusing on legal methods, legal skills, and legal theory. With over 30 years of teaching experience, he applies innovative methods to support critical thinking and responsible citizenship among students. His research explores the normative foundations of law, particularly in response to contemporary challenges such as populism and deep disagreements. He has published on topics such as academic legal education, the rule of law, and the role of utopian thinking in law.

Maria Victoria Kristan https://orcid.org/0000-0001-8014-8029 is an MSCA- Eutopia fellow at the University of Ljubljana (Slovenia). She has been a visiting scholar at the University of Roma Tre (Italy), holds a PhD in law from the Pompeu Fabra University (Spain), and a master's degree in global rule of law and constitutional democracy from the University of Genoa (Italy).

Matija Miloš https://orcid.org/0000-0002-3839-0273 is an assistant professor at the chair for constitutional law of the University of Rijeka, Faculty of Law.

Zoran Oklopcic ORCID 0009-0005-3791-3190 is Associate Professor at the Department of Law and Legal Studies at Carleton University, Visiting Professor at the Faculty of Law of the Union University in Belgrade, and Honorary Member of the Serbian Society for Social and Legal Philosophy. He holds an LLM in comparative constitutional law from Central European University in Budapest as well as an SJD from the University of Toronto Faculty of Law and was MacCormick Visiting Fellow at the University of Edinburgh School of Law, Junior Faculty at Harvard Law School's Institute for Global Law and Policy in Doha, Qatar, and Hauser Global Research Fellow at the NYU School of Law.

Jane Reichel ORCID 0000-0001-7509-4804 is a professor in administrative law and dean at the Faculty of Law, Stockholm University. Her research focuses on what globalization in general and Europeanization in particular mean for the public administration, its role within the state, and in relation to the EU and other organizations. Issues of interest concern how networks of authorities acting beyond the state are governed and controlled, and how administrative law ideals of efficient, transparent, and legally secure decision-making processes are achieved beyond the nation-state.

Mauro Zamboni ORCID 0000-0001-9002-4361 is Professor of Legal Theory at Stockholm University (Sweden), Senior Associate Research Fellow at the Institute of Advanced Legal Studies, University of London (UK), and Korea Legislation Research Institute Global Research Fellow (South Korea). His fields of interest are legislative studies and the relationships between law and politics (mostly from a legal theoretical perspective). He is also the general editor of the journal *The Theory and Practice of Legislation*.

Introduction[1]

Martin Belov

This book is devoted to representative democracy. It explores the key concepts, elements, and pillars of its institutional and axiological design. It presents some of the most important narratives related to representation and representative democracy. The book approaches representative democracy as both a holistic and layered narrative. It demonstrates that representative democracy is both a coherent intellectual product of Western modernity and a bulky phenomenon resembling a patchwork of institutions, principles, values, and imaginaries that can be dissembled into a range of narratives. These narratives have been merged into a convincing normative model during the 19th and 20th centuries by both constitutional theory and constitutional politics. Nevertheless, they are currently pressurized by the challenges of global post-modernity and the ongoing profound reshaping of the global (dis)order.

Representative democracy as an asymmetric and composite model and the only feasible form of democracy in constitutional history is a product of what Gunter Frankenberg defines as 'constitutionalism between magic and deceit.'[2] It must be deconstructed in order to properly understand its content beyond the fallacies of the cultural layers and political imperatives shaping its shell. It must also be reconstructed after it is explored in its historical, institutional, axiological, and imaginary dimension in order to be eventually adjusted to the imperatives and challenges of the global post-modernity of the 21st century.

The main focus of the book, however, is not only on representation and representative democracy as such, but rather on their crisis in the context of the constitutional polytransition that all constitutional orders are undergoing in the last decades. Hence, this book is a collective effort at exploring the phenomenon of representative democracy in flux.

1 This chapter is produced as part of and funded by the European Union-NextGenerationEU, through the National Recovery and Resilience Plan of the Republic of Bulgaria, project No. bg-rrp-2.004-0008.

2 Gunter Frankenberg, *Comparative Constitutional Studies: Between Magic and Deceit* (Edward Elgar 2018) 63–66.

DOI: 10.4324/9781003610670-1

The flux of representative democracy consists in the transition toward global algorithmic technocracy[3] triggered by the emergence of post-national, post-territorial, transterritorial, and aterritorial digital constitutionalism. It enhances the role of technocratic institutions and produces clear technocratic trends that render the institutional design of democratic representation and representative democracy increasingly dysfunctional. The institutional dynamics of this transition consist in the increasing role of some traditional elements of the constitutional design – the courts and the administration – but also of the steady power growth of other players that are beyond the institutional design of traditional, modern, Westphalian constitutional law.[4] These are the agents of global governance – the transnational corporations, the NGOs, and the other transterritorial players on the scene of post-sovereignty and post-democracy.[5]

Contemporary constitutional orders and their representative democratic institutional designs are experiencing the joint effects of constitutional polycrisis and constitutional polytransition.[6] Constitutional polycrisis consists in the multitude of overlapping crises – security, financial, migration, pandemic, ecologic, etc. – which have been mushrooming since the beginning of the 21st century and are producing a snowball effect of the permanent deconstruction of constitutional orders and their elements – rule of law, representative democracy, welfare state, sovereignty, etc. Constitutional polytransition is the phenomenon of multiple transitions that constitutional orders and representative democracies are simultaneously undergoing. The most important are the following transitions: from democracy to technocracy; from Westphalian to post-Westphalian and neo-Westphalian constitutionalism; from national to post-national constitutionalism; from territorial to post-territorial,

3 See Martin Belov, 'Rule of Law and Democracy in Times of Transitory Constitutionalism, Constitutional Polycrisis and Emergency Constitutionalism: Towards a Global Algorithmic Technocracy?' in Martin Belov (ed), *Rule of Law in Crisis: Constitutionalism in a State of Flux* (Routledge 2023) 21–47.

4 For the concept of Westphalian constitutionalism see Martin Belov, 'Three Models for Ordering Constitutional Orders' (2022) XIII(2) Pravni Zapisi 361–87; Martin Belov, 'The Challenges to Westphalian Constitutional Geometry in the Age of Supranational Constitutionalism, Global Governance and Information Revolution' in Martin Belov (ed), *Global Constitutionalism and Its Challenges to Westphalian Constitutional Law* (Hart Publishing 2018) 13–55; Martin Belov, 'Constitutional Nationalism and Constitutional Globalism on the Edge of Westphalian and Post-Westphalian Constitutionalism: The Bulgarian Case' in Marianthi Kalyviotou (ed), *Essays in Honour of Kostas G Mavrias* (PN Sakkoulas 2022) vol I, 221–51.

5 For the concept of post-democracy see Colin Crouch, *Post-Democracy* (Polity Press 2004) 1–144.

6 Martin Belov, 'The Conceptual Shapes of Constitutional Polycrisis: Deconstruction, Asymmetries and Post-Modern Anxieties of Constitutional Normalcy' (2023) 70 Irish Jurist, special issue Law in a Time of Crisis 393–410; Martin Belov, 'Rule of Law in Europe in Times of Constitutional Polycrisis, Constitutional Polytransition and Democratic Discontent' (2023) 3 Diritto Pubblico Comparato Ed Europeo 875–84; Belov, 'Rule of Law and Democracy' (n 3) 21–47.

transterritorial, and aterritorial constitutionalism; from sovereigntist to post-sovereigntist constitutionalism; from humanist to post-humanist and transhumanist constitutionalism; from physical to digital constitutionalism; and last but not least, from democratic to post-democratic and techno-authoritarian constitutionalism. The transition from democratic capitalism to technocratic post-capitalism produced by the simultaneous deconstruction of both neoliberal globalism and the welfare state also plays a very important role.

The deconstruction of the key normative ideologies and the dysfunctionality of the institutional design of representative democracies are triggered by several factors. These are the ongoing technological revolution, the globalization (paralleled by current attempts at global regionalization in the style of George Orwell's *1984*), and the clear tendencies toward technocratic elitism.

This collective monograph tries to explain the aforementioned crisis and transition producing representative democracy in flux through the prism of institutional analysis in context, but also via critical deconstruction of the imaginaries and narratives of representation, democracy, and representative democracy. The book is based on the following logic.

Part I is devoted to the imaginary foundations of representative democracy. It explores the imaginaries of representation and representative democracy as well as the non-democratic and post-democratic imaginaries of representation, including the imaginaries that shape the parliamentary and presidential variants of representative democracy.

Part II explores the impact of crisis, emergency, fear, and fear politics on representative democracy. It assesses the role of the COVID-19 pandemic for destabilizing the constitutional orders of representative democracy and the messages of fear delivered during this crisis. The detrimental effects of populism, fear politics, and fake news on representative democracy are also analyzed.

Part III focuses on the role of administration in the context of the current crisis of representative democracy. It explores several topical issues, such as agencification, transnational administrative networks, administrative legislative policymaking, the role of administration as political actor, and their impact on the future of representative democracy. The main task of this part of the book is to assess the democratic-technocratic (dis)balance and the trends toward technocracy, bureaucracy, and expertocracy.

Finally, Part IV offers a glimpse into the international, transnational, and global dimensions of representative democracy. It provides an analysis of democracy and the rights of representation in the case law of the European Court of Human Rights. It also offers a cosmopolitan, republican, participatory, and deliberative perspective summarized as a global democracy project eventually offered as an alternative to the current crisis of territorially entrenched representative democracy.

After briefly explaining the main goals of this edited volume and the logic that is underlying its structure, let's now briefly summarize the main claims of its separate chapters. This will allow for a more concrete glimpse into the particular scientific discourses in which the contributors to this collective monograph are engaged.

Chapter 1 of the book is devoted to the imaginaries of representation. Conceptually it is embedded in several discourses related to symbolic-imaginary constitutionalism, emotional constitutionalism, law-as-imagination, and constitutional imaginaries. Methodologically it is grounded in socio-legal studies of constitutional concepts.

The main claim of the chapter is that representation is not only legal, institutional, and normative but is also a socio-legal and imaginary phenomenon having axiological, volitional, and emotional aspects. Thus, representation and representative democracy are entrenched in constitutional conscious, but also in constitutional subconscious and unconscious being stretched between the legal, the real, and the imaginary. In that regard, representation and representative democracy as its wide-spread form in late Western modernity are largely dependent on imaginaries of representation that are elements of rational, but also of symbolic-imaginary, and emotional constitutionalism. The imaginaries of representation were initially detached from democracy. Later on, in the course of the development of modern constitutionalism and liberal democracy they were widely shaped as imaginaries of democratic representation. Since the beginning of the 21st century imaginaries of democratic representation are again challenged and partially replaced by non-democratic imaginaries of representation that are having both old and new forms.

The chapter starts with analysis of the imaginaries of representation as mixed rational-emotional narratives and symbolic proxies to constitutional insights. It demonstrates the link between the imaginaries of representation and emotional constitutionalism and shows representation, democracy, and representative democracy as objects of multinarrative symbolic-imaginary signification of meaning. Special attention is devoted to the analysis of representative democracy as a phenomenon that is stretched between the history of ideas, the normativity of patterns of socio-legal behavior, and the imaginary heritage of constitutional modernity.

The chapter outlines the key imaginaries of representative democracy in constitutional modernity. It demonstrates the general features of the imaginaries of representative democracy. It presents the most influential constitutional imaginaries of representative government and parliamentarism, namely: the imaginary of the Parliament as the temple of the nation being the secular God of modernity; the imaginary of the parliamentary government as a rational, logical, and systematic chess board; the imaginary of the Parliament as a utilitarian rational stock exchange; the imaginary of the Parliament as a mirror of the nation; and the imaginary of the Parliament as a national agora. It also exposes the place and role of the imaginaries of democratic representation in the overall scheme of constitutional imaginaries.

Chapter 1 also explores the imaginaries of representation beyond representative democracy. Three groups of such imaginaries are delimited. These are the populist, the elitist, and the technocratic imaginaries of representation.

The chapter critically assesses the process of emergence of non-democratic imaginaries of representation in the context of constitutional polycrisis and constitutional polytransition.

Chapter 2 deconstructs key normative ideologies of representative democracy exploring 'programmatic government beyond conceptual distinctions.' It is an effort at overcoming false dichotomies and at looking beyond the façade of established distinctions joint in dichotomic and trichotomic clusters. Its author aims 'to show what's wrong with the definitional approach to the conceptualization of (liberal) representative democracy' and 'what's gained when we resist the temptation to consider the problems of actually existing representative democracies through the lens of definitions.'

Zoran Oklopcic starts with an analysis of the concept of majority rule exploring both of its components - 'majority' and 'rule.' Thus, he demonstrates the different meanings implied in them and used for stigmatization of majoritarian versions of representative democracy. He critically deconstructs several normative ideologies of crucial importance for representative government, representative democracy, and parliamentarism. More precisely, he focuses on responsible, responsive, accountable, and majoritarian government.

The author shows the perils of misunderstanding both forms of accountable representative governments: parliamentary and presidential. More precisely, Oklopcic explores the use and misuse of majoritarian legitimation and delegitimation of parliamentary and presidential forms of government and the permutations of majoritarianism in both of them. He shows the variable manifestations of majoritarianism on the different phases of the constitutional process: the stages of election, leadership selection, legislative drafting, parliamentary control, etc.

A common effort of the first two chapters of this book is the attempt at outlining the imaginaries of representation behind Parliament. In Chapter 2 Oklopcic demonstrates that 'in the US context, Congress appears in three guises, as a diplomatic parley, a farmer's market, and an aristocratic court.' This is a context-specific attempt at exploring the normative imaginaries of representative assemblies.

Chapter 3, written by Matija Miloš, is devoted to symbolic representation. The central concern of his research is the representative role of law in different legal and political contexts and the representative role of the constitution seen through the perspective of symbolic representation. In his rich and multilayered analysis, the author outlines different concepts of representation and emphasizes the tension between them. His analysis implies tension between legalistic and formalist and socio-legal, dynamic, and substantial understandings of the constitution, the constitutional process, and the nature and forms of representation.

According to the author, 'there is a clear tension between presenting a constitution as a representational image and interpreting a constitution as a legal act.' This tension is illustrated through the prism of several constitutional and constitutionally relevant referenda in Croatia and the interplay between the people, the Constitutional Court, and the Parliament as key actors of the process of political and constitutional representation. Following Saward's understanding that the representative claim consists of five segments: the maker, the subject, the object, the referent, and the audience, Miloš explores these elements in the context of the Croatian referenda.

Miloš confronts the widely spread legalistic viewpoints of representation with critical deconstruction of the traditional schemes of representation centered around Parliament as the ultimate player in representative games. He shows the central role played by constitutional courts in shaping and reshaping the lines of representation mostly in favor of parliamentary representation and to the detriment of direct democratic claims for political representation. Thus, the interplay between the people, the Parliament, and the Constitutional Court is the real ground for dynamic determination of representation – political, legal, and symbolic.

The author considers constitutional and legislative drafting and amendment as a vehicle for political representation. Hence, he defines the constitution as a representational device. He explores the impact of representative games on the concepts of agency, hierarchy, stability, boundary, failure, and clarity, having in mind the still underestimated constitutional imaginary perspective. Thus, Matija Miloš's chapter is a valuable contribution to the scientific debates regarding the law as a resource of symbolic political representation as well as the phenomena of 'symbolic legislation,' 'symbolic constitutionalization,' 'communicative legislation,' and symbolic legislation in a positive sense. It shows how law can be used as a resource in constructing representative claims and shaping constitutional imaginaries.

In Chapter 4 Jan Adamowski and Monika Florczak-Wątor discuss the detrimental effects of the COVID-19 pandemic on representative democracy. They outline both the challenges that occurred for the pandemic emergency regimes and the negative perspectives stemming from them and shaping the constitutional future. The authors reaffirm a thesis that has been proven in the recent literature that the pandemic emergency had massive detrimental effects on both human rights and institutional design. According to them, three spheres of constitutional relations have been most pervasively impacted by the emergency regime: the general elections, the functioning of the parliaments, and the delegation of legislative power to the executive.

Adamowski and Florczak-Wątor identify how the measures adopted in response to the COVID-19 pandemic have permanently changed the functioning of representative democracy. Thus, they offer a contribution to the debate on the transformation of the emergency into normalcy and its structural impact on constitutionalism and constitutional law. They engage in the discussion on the proportionality and balancing of rights focusing mostly on the rights related to representative democracy, e.g., electoral rights. In that regard, they discuss the conditions for admissibility to postpone elections and evaluate the proportionality of the application of COVID-19-related restrictions to the electoral process that also impact the construction of legitimate representative democracy.

The authors explore the possible solutions in terms of voting techniques that could have allowed for balancing between the rights to life and health and the right to vote. They demonstrate the advantages and problems related to voting in polling stations, with a specific sanitary regime, postal voting, and internet voting in times of pandemic.

Special attention is devoted to the global pandemic as a challenge to the functioning of parliaments and representative democracy. Adamowski and Florczak-Wątor explore the impact of pandemic constitutionalism on the separation of powers and the performance of the different functions of Parliament. They critically assess the shift of powers toward the government in lawmaking and on 'other essential elements of parliamentary functioning during a global pandemic.'

In Chapter 5 Bart van Klink and Ingeborg van der Geest explore the crisis (mis)management and fear politics in the context of constitutional polycrisis. This is done from a particular perspective – the political rhetoric of fear in the time of the COVID-19 pandemic. In their account 'fear tends to become an ever-present feature of contemporary political discourse.' Thus, they explore the fear rhetoric of official stakeholders in the Netherlands – mostly the government and the ruling majority and opposition party MPs.

The authors raise the important and topical question, is there 'any room for appeals to fear and crisis in democratic political debates'? They explore this question by analyzing the political debate on the COVID-19 pandemic in the Netherlands. In doing so, they 'depart from two models of democracy: the model of deliberative democracy (Benhabib, Habermas and others) and the model of agonistic pluralism (Mouffe and Laclau).' The authors propose 'a rhetorical conception of democracy in which debate is encouraged and emotions play an important sustaining and supporting role.'

The central part of the analysis is devoted to the politics of fear. According to van Klink and van der Geest, 'politically speaking, it can be advantageous to invoke fear, because it may mobilize people and unite a social group.' However, as they properly underline, 'fear may be detrimental to democracy since it can be very difficult to engage in a rational exchange of arguments when the political debate is dominated by highly emotive language.'

The transformation of emergency into normalcy and the exception into rule is common threat of Chapter 4 and Chapter 5. However, in Chapter 5 van Klink and van der Geest focus more precisely on fear and the normalization of the state of exception. The main sources of data for the analysis are the main press conferences of the Dutch ministers and the debates in Dutch Parliament during the COVID-19 pandemic.

The authors critically assess the rhetorical means that have been put in practice during the COVID-19 pandemic by politicians for the purpose of creating an atmosphere of crisis and fear in society. They 'evaluate how these appeals to pathos, in particular fear, affects the democratic quality of the political debate.'

On the basis of the case study of the Netherlands, van Klink and van der Geest offer some conclusions regarding the relationship between fear and democracy. They explore 'on what conditions may appeals to pathos be permissible within a representative democracy?' Last but not least, they suggest what they define as 'rhetorical conception of democracy which allows for strategic maneuvering in political debates.'

In Chapter 6 Guerino Fares discusses the role of freedom of information in a representative democracy. Thus, his chapter is related to both previous Chapter 5 and Chapter 11, where Šejla Imamović explores the political rights that are fundamental for representative democracy in the case law of the European Court of Human Rights.

Fares explores the impact of fake news, post-truth politics, and the distorted use of information on the crisis of representative democracy in the digital age. The chapter devotes special attention to the role of digital platforms for distorting information and producing information asymmetries in the case of health crises. It critically assesses the transformations produced by the digital revolution on the processes of consensus building and trust, which are key assets of a legitimate governance and stable and efficient representative democracy.

Fares explores the relationship between democracy, politics, truth, and public opinion. After some general considerations he focuses on the definitional, epistemological, pragmatic, and political issues related to finding a proper balance between them. After presenting the two methods of spreading fake news (click baiting and astroturfing), he analyzes the relationship between privacy, protection of personal data, and fake news.

Before discussing the issues of disinformation in the context of health crises, Fares briefly presents the responses of the EU to fake news. He emphasizes the legal problems for regulating fake news without distorting the principles of proportionality and balance of rights. Fares rightfully points out that 'we cannot limit ourselves to a sanctioning approach.' Otherwise there is huge danger of censorship and distortion of the proper flow of scientific information. In his account, 'the fight against disinformation cannot be assimilated to an instrument of protected democracy: the early protection and repression of ideological dissent cannot, in fact, be reconciled with the constitutional guarantee of information pluralism.'

In Chapter 7 Mauro Zamboni explores the impact of globalization on law-making. He critically assesses the role of globalization for democratic legislation, investigating the rising role of the administrative agencies in law-making, which is pushing aside the Parliament as representative body that should be the central legislative body according to modern constitutional law and constitutional theory.

The chapter discusses key issues related to de-parliamentarization and de-democratization stemming from globalization, technocracy, and the crises of representative democracy. It demonstrates that globalization has profoundly changed not only the substance but also the forms, institutions, and procedures for law-making. Zamboni shows that the traditional separation of powers is no longer the accurate explanatory model but also emphasizes that the domestic players are not just victims of globalization. On the contrary, globalization increases the role of administrative agencies both beyond and within statehood. In his account, 'globalization of law has shifted the primary law-making responsibility among legal actors,' while 'the center of gravity for law-making seems to have moved toward the two other major legal actors: the public administration and the judiciary.'

Zamboni starts with exploring the conceptual problem of the impact of transplantation, transposition, reception, and migration of legislative concepts and ideas embedded in foreign, international, and supranational legal standards in the domestic legal order on the structure and functioning of representative democracy. He suggests the concept of 'administrative legislative policy' by outlining the 'the modalities and reasons behind the extensive use of public administration as the default mode for law-making at the national level.' He explores both the vertical and horizontal interactions between the national administrative agencies in the composite constitutional order of the EU.

The author analyzes what he defines as 'administrative legislative policy.' He outlines the main factors for the rising power of administrative agencies as legislators. According to him these are 'the prompt decision-making procedures, the inherent authoritative nature of the process, and the specific and cumulative organizational legal (and non-legal) expertise within the public administration.'

Zamboni devotes special attention to the main deficiencies of this model. According to him, despite the aforementioned advantages 'its extensive application in democratic forms of government raises significant concerns. These concerns pertain to accountability to the citizens affected by the administrative regulations, safeguarding fundamental rights, and the ability to innovate within the paradigms of the national legal discourse.'

The chapter concludes with concrete proposals for remedying the deficiencies of the administrative law-making model that is currently propelled by globalization and is gradually replacing representative democracy with technocracy. Zamboni suggests that

> it is crucial to establish clear and defined boundaries, preferably at the constitutional level, to restrain the regulatory power of the public administration . . . to expand and clarify in both the Constitution and all constitutionally relevant documents, such as decisions by higher courts, the areas subject to direct legislative authority[and thus to] explicitly limit political actors from delegating regulatory responsibilities to administrative authorities through framework legislation in specific domains.

The author emphasizes the role of courts and participatory democracy in limiting administrative discretion, although the former remedy may promote technocracy itself in the form of '*gouvernement des juges*.' Zamboni believes in the crucial role of the constitutional court and the ombudsman as safeguards of 'community's welfare rather than the interests of political actors in the Parliament.'

In Chapter 8 Jane Reichel explores the challenges to rule of law and representative democracy stemming from the European composite administration. The central question explored by Reichel is 'how this European composite administration for data is constructed within the representative democracies of the EU and its Member States. Is the European composite administration for data governed under the rule of law?'

The analysis is both conceptual and pragmatic. The chapter explores two aspects of the European composite administration in general and the data administration in particular. These are the governance tools for promoting coherent compliance and capacity building and individual decision-making. The analysis revolves around several key concepts. These are the European composite administration (for data), the European administrative space, the single market for data, and the administrative law beyond the state. It derives its conceptual conclusions on the basis of the analysis of the GDPR, the AI Act, and the EHDS Regulation.

The chapter consecutively explores several main topics. It starts with analysis of the executive powers in a representative democracy under the rule of law, the dilemma of coping with the transfer of competences from the nation-state to the European administrative space and the assessment of the functions of the executive power in a representative democracy. It continues with exploring the constitutional setting for EU agencies and the European composite administration and the legal basis of the EU administration in the EU Treaties.

The process of agencification and the role of EU and the national administrations with the EU leading to the rise of a European composite administration is explored both conceptually and with regard to the sector-specific field of data space and data protection. In that regard, the role and functions of the composite administration in the EU Strategy for Data and the building of an EU composite administration for data are presented. Moreover, an overview of the administrative entities under the GDPR, the AI Act, and the EHDS, the governance tools for promoting coherent compliance and capacity building, and the cooperative and composite elements in individual decision-making on administrative fines are thoroughly explored with view to assessing the future for the European composite administration for data.

Reichel admits that the role of the administration under the EU Treaties is unclear. Similarly to Mauro Zamboni, she finds the advantages of the agencies in 'their ability to draw on highly technical, sectoral know-how, the increased visibility they give to the sectors concerned (and sometime the public) and the cost savings they can offer for businesses.' She adds the advantage stemming from the concept of composite administration that the EU agencies perform a bridging function between the EU and the Member State administrations.

The author concludes that 'it is difficult to uphold administrative procedural safeguards such as the principle of good administration in a composite context' and 'the idea of the closed ecosystem of the state is no longer upheld.' She insists on the need of finding new principles of good administration that can secure democracy and rule of law in the context of administrative law and constitutionalism beyond statehood.

Chapter 9 is titled 'Coherence in diversity? Exploring the institutional dynamic of enforcement networks in the EU Internal Market.' According to its author, Antonina Bakardjieva Engelbrekt, since the beginning of the 1990s, when the EU stepped up its efforts to complete the Single Market, increasing emphasis has been placed on effective enforcement of commonly agreed legislative instruments and policies. Given the diversity of national regulative and institutional solutions, influential policy reports at the time called for a 'cooperative approach to enforcement,' identifying it as 'the single most important way of reinforcing mutual confidence between Member States and the Commission.' Such an approach was to be based on 'groups of contact points between the Member States and the Commission,' to deal with the application of internal market rules, and creating a 'permanent framework for administrative partnership.'

Indeed, moving on this track, in the years that followed, a veritable web of networks with different enforcement functions was rolled out, connecting national authorities and enforcement bodies with corresponding units of the Commission. Such networks nowadays exist in almost every policy area of the Internal Market and beyond. Moreover, new networks continue to emerge, most recently with the Digital Services Act package and its main legislative pillars – the Digital Services Act and the Digital Markets Act.

While the general notion of administrative network is well understood, the variety of networks in terms of constitutive units, tasks, structure, and modes of governance is overwhelming. In this contribution, Engelbrekt revisits the concept of network in social sciences and attempts to offer a taxonomy of networks in the context of the European Internal Market, paying special attention to the category 'enforcement network.' In a second step, she looks more closely at two enforcement networks of central importance for the Internal Market – the European Competition Network (ECN) and the Consumer Protection Cooperation Network (CPC-Net), mapping the institutional structure, constitutive units, and the distribution of decision-making powers within the respective network. Furthermore, the author explores the dynamic within the networks, identifying patterns of interaction vertically, between the Commission and national constitutive entities, as well as horizontally, between individual national enforcement bodies.

The aim is through comparing the structure and dynamic of the two networks to identify factors that enhance or reduce the potential of enforcement networks to ensure the effective application of Internal Market rules, and ultimately to bridge institutional diversity. Several questions appear pertinent for the analysis: Have the examined networks improved mutual understanding and mutual learning, or is the diversity of participating national entities a persistent source of fragmentation and inefficiency? Have the enforcement networks brought about empowerment of national enforcement bodies, or have they rather strengthened the position of the Commission? In what way, if any, have the enforcement networks influenced national institutional choices in the areas concerned? Can we see the networks as conduits of a gradually evolving convergent EU model of enforcement? Or have legitimate national institutional choices been unnecessarily sacrificed on the altar of uniformity? Are there robust mechanisms to ensure the accountability and legitimacy of enforcement networks? The more overarching task is to critically evaluate the role of enforcement networks and the way they influence the distribution of power in the multi-level institutional landscape of the Union.

In Chapter 10 Šejla Imamović engages with detailed analysis of the role of the European Court of Human Rights in protecting and promoting democracy on pan-European scale. The analysis is embedded in a range of conceptual debates, such as the twofold role of courts in representative democracy as its protectors and as actors of emerging transnational juristocracy, the possibility for the achievement of democracy through rule of law, and the advantages and issues of regional standards of democracy in Europe.

The author admits that judicial restraint is a core value in a democracy that requires a degree of deference to the elected government and legislature. Nevertheless, she admits that 'democracy means upholding the rule of law, which is in the hands of the judges at both national and European level.' The tension between the advantages of an extensive set of international standards of democracy and the risks of judicial activism aiming toward global judicial technocracy are implicitly conceptually framing the chapter.

The analysis commences with an outline of a concept of democracy in the European Convention of Human Rights system. It explores representative democracy as an element of the constitutional and political traditions and as a pillar of the constitutional orders of the Council of Europe Member States.

Šejla Imamović provides us with thorough exploration of the case law of the Strasbourg court on political rights that are directly related to representative democracy. She focuses mostly on the right to free and fair elections. The author presents the case law related to the active (the right to vote) and passive (the right to stand for elections) electoral rights. She also explores the jurisprudence of the ECtHR concerning the integrity of the election process as a whole. The chapter concludes with analysis of the ECtHR's contribution to protecting representative democracy.

Chapter 11 can be conceived as a radical criticism toward representative democracy as predominant form for ordering of the world society of states. Instead of a state-centered approach, with its territorially entrenched, hierarchical, and monolithic schemes of authority and legitimacy, Maria Victoria Kristan proposes a global deliberative and participatory model aiming at the achievement of the ideal of freedom as non-domination. Coming from a globalist and cosmopolitan radical democratic and republican perspective Kristan dismisses the predominant approaches to global democracy. She blames them for neglecting public participation and favoring state representation instead.

Kristan is interested 'how we can establish a concrete transition strategy from current governance structures to a participative global governance' and 'how we can find ways to ensure participation and make contingent, sporadic and spontaneous participation necessary, permanent and relevant.' She is convinced that the states shall still play a role in a global world order, mainly as bonds between the different layers of governance. However, she prefers to seek models of empowerment and legitimacy beyond hierarchy and domination capable to promote global democracy based on the idea of relative authority. In her account, 'relative authority acknowledges that in a global context, no single authority operates in isolation. Instead, the legitimacy and effectiveness of an authority are inherently tied to its relationships with other authorities.'

The appeal of this chapter is that the pluralistic, interdependent, and interconnected nature of authority today and 'the reality of disaggregated authority makes electoral democracy a less useful ideal than contestatory democracy, so the realities of global governance should prompt us to return to a rediscovered usefulness of deliberative democracy.' In that regard, she explores global democracy and the value of individual participation, the ways to legitimize global post-representative democracy, the modalities of the global individual influence, direction and ultimate popular control, the value of individual participation in a global democracy, the ways for enhancing democratic participation in global governance, and the possibilities for transition to a global participation.

To sum up, the last chapter of this book is a critical assessment of the capacity to build a global society on the basis of the constitutional and political heritage of representative democracy. It is challenging the concept of representation in the global context from a radical cosmopolitan perspective. Thus, it is an interesting addendum to the overall concerns about the future of representation and representative democracy expressed by all chapters of this volume.

Part I

The imaginary foundations of representative democracy

1 Imaginaries of representation

There and back again[1]

Martin Belov

1. Introduction

Representation is a durable and well-established institution and practice in all societies and political orders. This does not mean that it always functions well, but rather that it is a necessary prerequisite of legitimate political and, later on in the course of history, also of constitutional government. In some pre-modern societies, representation has been entrenched in non-democratic, quasi-democratic, or semi-democratic regimes and had usually theological, aristocratic, or monarchic content.[2] Since the beginning of modernity, the people were convinced to believe in different political imaginaries of representation in the official schemes of power, authority, and government. These political imaginaries later became legally institutionalized. Thus, they were upgraded into constitutional imaginaries. This process has unfolded differently in the different sociopolitical contexts but had also overall structural similarities.

Representation is a structural precondition for legitimate and efficient government. Nevertheless, it has not always been practiced as democratic representation – the form that was predominant since the second half of the 20th century. Regretfully, we are currently witnessing the reemergence of non-democratic, semi-democratic, and quasi-democratic forms of representation. Currently they have elitist, technocratic, and populist instead of monarchic, aristocratic in the traditional sense, and theological substance. Actually, this is not a return to premodern elitist representation. Instead, it is entry into a new phase of elitism mixing democratic, technocratic, and populist elements.

1 This chapter is produced as part of and funded by the European Union-NextGenerationEU, through the National Recovery and Resilience Plan of the Republic of Bulgaria, project No bg-rrp-2.004-0008.

2 See Hasso Hofmann, 'Der spätmittelalterliche Rechtsbegriff der Repräsentation in Reich und Kirche' (1988) 27(4) Der Staat 523–45.

DOI: 10.4324/9781003610670-3

There is a vast amount of literature exploring the reasons, factors, shapes, and outcomes of the crisis of representative democracy.[3] The scientific discourse is either preoccupied with its legal, institutional, and normative dimensions or exposes its socio-legal and political manifestations. Instead, the imaginary aspect of representative democracy and its increasing dysfunctionality in the context of constitutional polycrisis and constitutional polytransition is less researched.

This chapter aims at exploring the constitutional imaginary dimensions of the crisis of representation and representative democracy. It shall analyze the historical and conceptual trajectory of constitutional imaginaries in the course of contemporary constitutionalism. It will present their rise and establishment in modern constitutionalism and their role for stabilizing representative democracy as a universal and holistic model for national constitutional orders implemented also on the sub-national level in federations and on the supranational level in the EU. It will also explore their deconstruction and demise in the context of globalization, technological revolution, post-modernity, and post-democracy.[4]

The chapter will also explore the process of use and misuse of imaginaries of representation as part of the constitutional make-believe. It will be focused on imaginaries of representation in constitutional post-modernity and in times of constitutional polycrisis, constitutional polytransition,[5] technological revolution,[6] and emerging post-democracy. The research will expose the constitutional imaginary dimensions of the crisis of representative democracy and the process and tendency of (re)emergence of non-democratic imaginaries of representation.

Imaginaries of representation are not always and not necessarily democratic. In fact, representation started as a non-democratic practice and was formed as a democracy-detached concept. Thus, the pre-modern and early modern imaginaries of representation were initially and essentially non-democratic but also autocratic, elitist, aristocratic, theocratic, etc. Even in the course of constitutional modernity, when representation was intermingled with democracy,

3 See Martin Belov (ed), *Rule of Law in Crisis: Constitutionalism in a State of Flux* (Routledge 2023) 1–280.

4 For the concept of post-democracy see Colin Crouch, *Post-Democracy* (Polity Press 2004) 1–144.

5 Martin Belov, 'The Conceptual Shapes of Constitutional Polycrisis: Deconstruction, Asymmetries and Post-Modern Anxieties of Constitutional Normalcy' (2023) 70 Irish Jurist, special issue Law in a Time of Crisis 393–410; Martin Belov, 'Rule of Law in Europe in Times of Constitutional Polycrisis, Constitutional Polytransition and Democratic Discontent' (2023) 3 Diritto Pubblico Comparato Ed Europeo 875–84; Martin Belov, 'Rule of Law and Democracy in Times of Transitory Constitutionalism, Constitutional Polycrisis and Emergency Constitutionalism: Towards a Global Algorithmic Technocracy?' in Martin Belov (ed), *Rule of Law in Crisis: Constitutionalism in a State of Flux* (Routledge 2023) 21–47.

6 See Martin Belov (ed), *The IT Revolution and Its Impact on State, Constitutionalism and Public Law* (Hart Publishing 2021).

as will be shown later, imaginaries of representation beyond democracy (e.g., charismatic, populist, heroic, existentialist, and exceptionalist) continued to persist.

In the context of constitutional polycrisis and constitutional polytransition that have been unfolding during the last two decades, we are witnessing the reemergence of non-democratic imaginaries of representation. Nevertheless, they are not limited only to populist imaginaries that are clearly predominant and are already well explored in the literature.[7] Simultaneously, there are also other non-democratic imaginaries of representation that are gaining momentum, mostly in the constitutional law in action and the constitutional law in collective imagination rather than in written law. The novelty here is that they are not limited to authoritarian, identitarian, charismatic, and populist imaginaries, as in the previous ages. There are also elitist, technocratic, and paternalistic imaginaries that are trying to shape emotionally and intellectually the feelings and beliefs of representation in the age of globalization, technological revolution, and post-modernity.

That is why this chapter shall not be limited to research of the imaginaries of representative democracy. It will expose, analyze, and systematize them, but it will also go beyond and explore populist, technocratic, and elitist-paternalistic imaginaries of representation that set the scene of symbolic-imaginary constitutionalism at the beginning of the 21st century in the context of constitutional polycrisis and constitutional polytransition.

2. Imaginaries of representation as mixed rational-emotional narratives and symbolic proxies to constitutional insights

2.1 Imaginaries of representation and emotional constitutionalism

'Sometimes reality is too complex. Stories give it a form'.[8] This famous saying of Jean-Luc Godard demonstrates the natural tendency of people to feel, signify, and visualize complex social, political, and legal phenomena. It shows their need to imagine constitutional phenomena not only in rationally plausible ways but also in emotionally appealing ways. In that regard, one should

7 See, e.g., Jiri Priban, 'Constitutionalism, Populism, and the Imaginary of the Authentic Polity: A Socio-Legal Analysis of European Public Spheres and Constitutional Demoicratization' (2023) 50(S1) Journal of Law and Society 26–44; Paul Blokker, 'Political and Constitutional Imaginaries' in S Adams and J Smith (eds), *Social Imaginaries: Critical Interventions in a Paradigm-in-the-Making* (Rowman and Littlefield 2021); Paul Blokker, 'Populist Constitutionalism' in C de la Torre (ed), *Routledge Handbook of Global Populism* (Routledge 2018); Paul Blokker, 'Populism as a Constitutional Project' (2019) 17(2) International Journal of Constitutional Law; Jo-Anne Dillabough, 'Higher Education, Violent Modernities and the "Global Present": The Paradox of Politics and New Populist Imaginaries' (2021) 20(2) Globalisation, Societies and Education 178–92.

8 See <https://www.goodreads.com/quotes/514541-sometime-reality-is-too-complex-stories-give-it-form>.

also consider the statement of Dale Carnegie: 'When dealing with people, remember you are not dealing with creatures of logic, but with creatures bristling with prejudice and motivated by pride and vanity'.[9]

Hence, people need to be emotionally inspired, enchanted, and even amazed in order to not only understand but to voluntarily adhere to central constitutional concepts such as democracy, representation, and democratic representation. In the words of the Orwellian *Nineteen Eighty-Four* Big Brother, it is not enough to understand or just to obey the legal and constitutional order.[10] The people must also love it. Indeed, George Orwell's *1984* was authoritarian dystopia, but in all constitutional orders the degree of adherence to normative ideologies and constitutional architecture is maintained not just by rational means. They are fostered and promoted also via instruments for establishment and preservation of emotional belongingness that are shaping the constitutional imaginaries of the community, the social groups, and the citizen. Hence, representation must not just be rationally plausible and practically useful. It must also produce adherence and affiliation maintained by sustainable constitutional imaginaries.

Indeed, there are many instantiations when representation is practiced in a purely rational way. It is used for promotion and protection of interests and for pragmatic influencing of policymaking. This has been the case of representation in both pre-modern and modern parliaments and representative bodies. Nevertheless, apart from and in parallel to this pragmatic, interest-based, and rational aspect there is also an emotional dimension of representation. It consists in the affectual discourse of the feeling of being represented, wanting to be represented, imagining ways of representation, and signifying them on the plain of the collective imaginaries. Interests of representation are mixed with feelings, emotions, and imaginaries of representation. Representation as a tool toward a pragmatic goal is paralleled by representation as an imaginary and representation as an emotional relation. Imaginaries of representation are emotionally loaded stories signified through a range of forms of symbolic-imaginary, visual, and performative constitutionalism. They give form to constitutional power realities and serve as emotional and imaginary proxies to relational pragmatics of representation condensed into signifiers of meaning that appeal to both individual and collective patterns of behavior.

Hence, constitutional phenomena are perceived, remembered, and shared between the people in terms of stories or narratives shaping through words, texts, and images constitutional myths and mythologies, normative ideologies and ideas, constitutional codes, and constitutional taboos as main forms of symbolic-imaginary constitutionalism.[11] In other words, the process of constitutional communication is in fact a process of semiotic signification of

9 See Dale Carnegie, *How to Win Friends and Influence People* (Pocket Books 1998).

10 See George Orwell, *1984* (Signet Classic 1961).

11 See Martin Belov, *Constitutional Semiotics: The Conceptual Foundations of a Constitutional Theory and Meta-Theory* (Hart Publishing 2022) 107–97.

meaning through forms of symbolic-imaginary, visual, and performative constitutionalism reflected in emotional constitutionalism beyond the official textual, normative-institutional, and rational constitutionalism.[12]

Emotions play a key role in shaping our understanding of the world and the constitutional order with its constitutional design and conceptual underpinning in particular. However, emotions *per se* need to be joined in clusters and to be at least partially institutionalized in constitutional texts and textures in order to be preserved, transmitted, and shared and to produce legally relevant throughput. Thus, they are building elements of a broader phenomenon that is defined as constitutional imaginary.[13]

The affectual aspect of representation and the normative beliefs in the process of representation and its different manifestations and projections in valid law and in socio-legal practices can be properly perceived through the concept of imaginaries of representation. These imaginaries are the durable attitudes – both rational and emotional – of the people (or different social strata or segments) toward representation as holistic concept and its specific forms.

Signification of constitutional meaning[14] is also accomplished in a transtemporal manner. Preservation and translation of normative concepts, ideas, beliefs, and constitutional myths runs from the constitutional past through the constitutional present into the constitutional future. Thus, imaginaries, in order to sustain the test of time, must be emotionally appealing and rationally plausible also in a transgenerational manner.

2.2 *Representation, democracy, and representative democracy as objects of multinarrative symbolic-imaginary signification of meaning*

The proper exploring of imaginaries of representation requires the brief presentation of key concepts. They are the substance and target of signification in the collective constitutional imagination[15] and thus are the core of constitutional imaginaries of representation. These are the concepts of representation, democratic representation, and representative democracy as a multilayered phenomenon.

There are four main aspects, layers, or discourses of representation in general and democratic representation in the context of representative democracy

12 Belov, *Constitutional Semiotics* (n 11) 1–349.

13 More about constitutional imaginaries see Jiri Přibáň, 'Constitutional Imaginaries and Legitimation: On Potentia, Potestas, and Auctoritas in Societal Constitutionalism' (2018) 45(S1) Journal of Law and Society 30–51; Jiri Přibáň, *Constitutional Imaginaries. A Theory of European Societal Constitutionalism* (Routledge 2020) 1–251; Jan Komárek, 'Political Economy in the European Constitutional Imaginary – Moving beyond Fiesole' (*Verfassungsblog*, 4 September 2020) <https://verfassungsblog.de/political-economy-in-the-european-constitutional-imaginary-moving-beyond-fiesole/>.

14 See Belov, *Constitutional Semiotics* (n 11) 1–349.

15 For the concept of constitutional imagination see Martin Loughlin, 'The Constitutional Imagination' (2015) 78(1) Modern Law Review 1–25; Oliviero Angeli, 'Global Constitutionalism and Constitutional Imagination' (2017) 6(3) Global Constitutionalism 359–76.

in particular. These are the normative-institutional, socio-legal, theoretical, and symbolic-imaginary aspects. The normative-institutional aspect concerns the constitutional design of representation and representative democracy. The socio-legal aspect frames representation and representative democracy as social and political practice. The theoretical aspect contains the theories of representation, part of which are also the theories of representative democracy. Last but not least, the imaginary aspect defines representation and representative democracy in terms of constitutional imaginaries and constitutional imagination. It is the last aspect that is the object of analysis in this chapter.

The imaginaries of representation are embedded mostly in the theoretical and socio-imaginary discourses. The normative-institutional discourse contains normative ideologies and ideas, constitutional myths and mythologies, constitutional taboos, and constitutional utopias provided by the authoritative speakers of the constitutionally framed sociopolitical community. They are interpreted by the constitutional and political theorists as non-official and non-authoritative speakers of the community that, however, massively shape both the rational and the emotional aspects of the imaginaries of representation. The socio-legal imaginary discourse contains the imaginaries of representation spread in cloud constitutionalism[16] and the constitutional conscious, subconscious, and unconscious stretched between the imaginary and the real[17] and shaping the constitutional make-believe. However, they are developed and practiced in the socio-legal discourse on the basis of the constitutional design in the normative-institutional discourse.

Hence, the imaginaries of representation are related to and embedded in a conceptual power grid composed of several key explanatory paradigms. They are broadly framed by the overall concept of constitutional imaginaries, allocated on the plain of symbolic-imaginary constitutionalism, explained and ordered by constitutional epistemology, constitutional semiotics and constitutional anthropology, and resulting in constitutional make-believe and constitutionalism between magic and deceit.[18]

To sum up, the imaginaries of representation are narratives that allow the people to imagine and shape their own representative shadow or reflection in the institutions of public power. This shadow or reflection is stretching between the ideal, the imaginary, and the real and projecting itself into the plains of the textual, visual, performative, emotional, and symbolic-imaginary constitutionalism.

Drawing imaginaries of representation resembles the building of sandcastles on the shores of constitutional imagination. This is due to the fact that

16 See Belov, *Constitutional Semiotics* (n 11) and the following.

17 See Jacques Lacan, *Écrits* (WW Norton & Company 2007) 1–896; Jacques Lacan, *The Language of the Self* (Johns Hopkins UP 1956) 29–53; Cornelius Castoriadis, *The Imaginary Institution of Society* (Polity Press 1987) 160–65.

18 Gunter Frankenberg, *Comparative Constitutional Studies: Between Magic and Deceit* (Edward Elgar 2018) 63–66.

these imaginaries may endure for a very long time and then can be destroyed in a single strike in turning point situations such as Ackerman's 'constitutional moment'[19] or Schmitt's '*Ernstfall*'.[20] Imaginaries of representation are sediments in the abyss of the time-space continuum, which are both stable and fragile, evolutionary and fertile with revolutionary potential. They contain and signify established meaning, but can also be hollowed and filled with novel substance. Thus, imaginaries of representation are also chameleonic phenomena.

3. Representative democracy – between history of ideas, normativity of patterns of socio-legal behavior, and the imaginary heritage of constitutional modernity

Representative democracy is the pillar of constitutional architecture of the later phases of Westphalian constitutionalism[21] that is based on the normative ideologies of representation and democracy. Hence, representative democracy is conceptually embedded in the imaginaries of representation shaped in the course of constitutional modernity.

Representative democracy is a fundamental and complex phenomenon of constitutionalism. It is of pivotal importance for the constitutionally framed societies of the Global North since the 'long 19th century'.[22] Detailed rational justification of representative democracy has been developed for centuries by political philosophers and constitutional scholars. It has produced an intertwined web of reasoning that was underlying the logic of government in Western modernity and was also transplanted to non-Western contexts in the context of the 20th and early 21st centuries. Nevertheless, it would not have been such a successful transplant – ideological, axiological, or institutional – if not paralleled by convincing imaginaries mastering collective beliefs. Hence, the necessity to explore the imaginaries of representation in historic, socio-legal, and constitutional semiotic perspective.

That is why this chapter explores representative democracy as a dynamic, complex, and multilayered concept that is stretched between the history of ideas, the normativity of patterns of socio-legal behavior, and the constitutional heritage of modernity. Hence, imaginaries of representation are explained as the emotional-affectual core of representation and democracy.

19 See Bruce Ackerman, *We the People: Foundations* (Harvard UP 1991) 266.

20 See Carl Schmitt, *Der Begriff des Politischen* (Duncker & Humblot 1932) 30.

21 For the concept of Westphalian constitutionalism see Martin Belov, 'Three Models for Ordering Constitutional Orders' (2022) XIII(2) Pravni Zapisi 361–87; Martin Belov, 'The Challenges to Westphalian Constitutional Geometry in the Age of Supranational Constitutionalism, Global Governance and Information Revolution' in Martin Belov (ed), *Global Constitutionalism and Its Challenges to Westphalian Constitutional Law* (Hart Publishing 2018) 13–55; Martin Belov, 'Constitutional Nationalism and Constitutional Globalism on the Edge of Westphalian and Post-Westphalian Constitutionalism: The Bulgarian Case' in Marianthi Kalyviotou (ed), *Essays in Honour of Kostas G Mavrias* (PN Sakkoulas 2022) vol. I, 221–51.

22 See Eric Hobsbawm, *The Age of Revolution: 1789–1848* (Vintage 1996) 1–368.

Moreover, representative democracy is exposed as one of the most visible and important forms of 'constitutionalism between magic and deceit'.[23]

Representative democracy is a product of Western modernity. It is the result of the creative mixture of two concepts, models, and ideals of political government – democracy and representation. They never existed as a joint phenomenon before the invention of representative democracy by modern political and social philosophy and their implementation in the sphere of constitutional governance by the modern constitutional theory.

In fact, representation and democracy were antipodes. Representation was an elitist concept applicable to religious communities and monarchic regimes,[24] whereas democracy was rather a political ideal close to a political and constitutional myth.[25]

Democracy started its career in the history of political ideas exactly as a constitutional utopia that was pragmatically reduced to constitutional myth. Later it has been put in practice as an element of an 'invented tradition'.[26] It was serving as both a bridge between the past and the future and as normative ideology. It has been transformed into a constitutional model with concrete institutional design only in the advanced phases of modernization through constitutionalization exactly through its merger with the concept of representation.

Thus, representative democracy is maybe one of the most important examples of what G. Frankenberg defines as 'constitutionalism between magic and deceit'.[27] It was the result of a creative mixture of normative ideologies and constitutional mythologies that have different origins, axiologies, and pragmatics. Representation was initially a conservative and elitist concept used in the context of societies with radical non-egalitarianism – aristocratic, autocratic, and theistic regimes. It was a construct justifying the rule of monarchs, aristocrats, popes, and patriarchs. It was a tool for representation of class interest in the medieval assemblages of the privileged nobility.

In contrast, premodern ideals and versions of democracy were based on ideologies of radical egalitarianism, communitarian inclusion, and intense civic activism. Democracy was an exotic form of self-government practiced in historically or geographically remote destinations such as ancient Athens, the Alpine cantons of Switzerland, or the radical Protestant communities in the northeast colonies of the British Empire that later became part of the USA. While representation was a widespread model and praxis, democracy was 'invented tradition' that needed massive promotion through forms of

23 See Frankenberg (n 18).

24 See Hofmann (n 2); Otto Brunner, 'Vom Gottesgnadentum zum monarchischen Prinzip' in Otto Brunner (Hg), *Neue Wege in der Verfassungs- und Sozialgeschichte* (Vandenhoeck u Ruprecht 1968) 160–86.

25 See Monica Brito Vieira and David Runciman, *Representation* (Polity Press 2008) 29–63.

26 For the concept of 'invented tradition' see Eric Hobsbawm and Terence Ranger (eds), *The Invention of Tradition* (CUP 2012) 1–324.

27 See Frankenberg (n 18).

visual, emotional, and symbolic-imaginary constitutionalism in the course of modernity.[28]

Representative democracy is an element of the institutional design of modern constitutionalism. Thus, it has a normative-institutional aspect. It is a well-established practice with vast history in many societies. Hence, it is a socio-legal, historical, and empirical phenomenon. It is part of the constitutional heritage of Western modernity. Representative democracy has been transplanted globally in the course of different waves of modernization through constitutionalization and democratization.

Nevertheless, representative democracy also has a symbolic-imaginary dimension. This dimension can be coded and decoded, constructed, deconstructed, and reconstructed through the means of constitutional epistemology, anthropology, semantics, and semiotics. This is due to the fact that representative democracy is embedded in a set of constitutional myths, normative ideologies, and constitutional utopias. These forms of symbolic-imaginary constitutionalism became interrelated in the course of the development of constitutionalism as a broad process of conceptual and institutional amalgamation including legal, socio-legal, and imaginary dimensions.

The normative imaginaries of representative democracy were a result of different political philosophies, constitutional traditions, and local or regional experiences. Nevertheless, at a certain point of no return, allocated in the late 19th century, they were amalgamated into a semi-coherent project for modernization through the constitutionalization of power. This project, while claiming to be rational, logical, and systematic, was in fact largely dependent upon collective emotions, shared beliefs, and forms of socio-legal imagination spread in the community.

The constitutional imaginaries of representation, democracy, and representative democracy had a huge imprint on normative ideologies of modern constitutionalism. They were institutionalized in written and practiced constitutional law. Last but not least, they were preserved in the common constitutional anthropology and mentality of the constitutionally framed sociopolitical community in the form of 'cloud constitutionalism'.[29]

Representative democracy was conceptualized, designed, and imagined by the political philosophy and constitutional theory of early modernity as a system for the achievement of the common good through the common will. The parliament has been frequently imagined as a laboratory for the extraction and distillation of the common good as the normative standard of political behavior and the ultimate political goal through the use of the common will as an instrument for its achievement.

28 See also the excellent research of Nadia Urbinati on the tension between representation and democracy in light of the fallacies of the key authors in modern political philosophy and constitutional theory. See Nadia Urbinati, *Representative Democracy: Principles and Genealogy* (Chicago UP 2006) 1–326.

29 See Belov, *Constitutional Semiotics* (n 11) 289–96.

The integrative force of the parliament as an institution has been realized in early modernity. This is the reason why in some countries (e.g., England, France, and Spain) medieval aristocratic representative bodies have been transformed into forums for national representation, while in most of the other states where such pre-modern institutions did not exist they were created via transplantation and constitutional engineering. This was the formative age of the constitutional imaginaries of parliamentarism. They were the product of the ingenuity of the political philosophy and constitutional theory of Western modernity, many of which were taking the form of 'invented tradition'.

One of the remarkable advantages of parliaments was their capacity as platforms for representation and integration of interests. The parliaments were the most appropriate form for durable access to political power of the most influential sociopolitical players. Moreover, parliaments allowed for structured representation of interests and for their articulation in a deliberative, formal-procedural, rational, and peaceful manner. This structured representation with huge sociopolitical integrative force has been grounded on several autonomous but also interrelated constitutional imaginaries – mostly normative ideologies. They were the intellectual pillars of a new secular religion – the belief in parliamentarism as a source of sociopolitical eudemonia.

4. Key imaginaries of representative democracy in constitutional modernity

4.1 General features of the imaginaries of representative democracy

Representative democracy as norm and fact, as constitutional model and socio-legal practice, has been shaped, formed, and influenced by a range of constitutional imaginaries. These imaginaries do not form an uncontroversial system. Instead, they have been adjusted to each other in the course of time and practice for collective imagining the constitutional past, constitutional present, and constitutional future. Thus, after centuries of joint application and coexistence, they are felt, imagined, and practiced as part of conceptual unity with ideological, mythological, and utopian features. This imaginary unit forming the constitutional imaginary landscape of democratic representation serves as an imaginary normative framework for representative democracy as institutional model embedded in cloud constitutionalism and practiced on the basis of shared beliefs.

The imaginaries of representation and democracy that were merged into joint imaginaries of representative democracy in the course of the 'long 19th century'[30] and appeared to be stabilized during the 'short 20th century'[31] were products of different schools of thought, political philosophies, and historic

30 Hobsbawm, *The Age of Revolution* (n 21) 1–368.

31 Eric Hobsbawm, *Age of Extremes: The Short Twentieth Century 1914–1991* (Time Warner Books 1995) 1–627.

experiences. They were produced in different times by authors with rather divergent viewpoints on the best models of state, society, and the people and with different ideas of how the bulk of sociopolitical interests must be reflected in the state institutions and transformed into a state policy.

In other words, the imaginaries of representative democracy were not painted with a single stroke of the brush. Instead, they form a collective multilayered landscape – the constitutional-imaginary landscape of representative democracy framed by multitude of normative ideologies of Western modernity. Constitutional imaginaries of representative democracy were polyphony, which was gradually transformed into a symphony in accordance with the political imperatives of Western modernity. In that process of amalgamation, the controversies were suppressed and the inner logical, conceptual, and pragmatic contradictions were pacified through reconciliatory imaginaries and long practice of constitutional 'make-believe'.

As a result, representative democracy has been stretched between democratic and elitist, liberal and republican, technocratic and populist imaginaries of representation. Nevertheless, the predominant version of representative democracy is rooted in a mixed liberal democratic constitutional imaginary, whereas the populist, technocratic, and republican imaginaries played a more or less marginal role. The closest constitutional model behind this mainstream liberal democratic imaginary of representation is the concept of polyarchy suggested by R. Dahl.[32] It is the demise of liberal democracy in the age of constitutional polycrisis and constitutional polytransition at the beginning of the 21st century that gave rise to non-democratic and anti-democratic imaginaries – mostly elitist, populist, and technocratic ones.

In addition, these imaginaries were a bulky category, themselves represented by various semiotic means in the planes of symbolic-imaginary, visual, and performative constitutionalism,[33] triggering divergent constitutional emotions[34] and beliefs. Representative democracy has been imagined as a limited, responsible, and responsive government by discussion.[35] These are also the key normative ideologies framed by the overarching normative ideology of representative democracy. These normative ideologies can be partially autonomous, but have been intermingled in a joint composite concept by constitutional

32 See Robert Dahl, *Polyarchy* (Yale UP 1971) 1–257.

33 See Belov, *Constitutional Semiotics* (n 11) 107–241.

34 See Kathryn Abrams and Hila Keren, 'Who's Afraid of Law and the Emotions?' (2010) 94(6) Minnesota Law Review 1997–2074, SSRN <https://ssrn.com/abstract=2434251>; Andras Sajo, 'Emotions in Constitutional Institutions' (2016) 8(1) Emotion Review 44–49; Andras Sajo, 'Emotions in Constitutional Design' (2010) 8(3) I•CON 354–84; Susan Bandes and others (eds), *Research Handbook on Law and Emotion* (Edward Elgar 2021) 1–640; Amalia Amaya and Maximillian Del Mar (eds), *Virtue, Emotion and Imagination in Law and Legal Reasoning* (Hart Publishing 2020) 1–275.

35 See Georgi Bliznashki, *Principles of Parliamentary Government* (U of Sofia 'St. Kliment Ohridski' P 2010) 1–262 (in Bulgarian).

theory and political philosophy despite the fact that they can be even contradictory and altogether functioning not without tension.

Representative democratic imaginaries contain elements related to imaginaries of representation and imaginaries of democracy that produce joint imaginaries of representative democracy. They may also refer to the normative ideologies of parliamentarism as one of the widely implemented forms of representative government. The normative ideologies of parliamentarism were creatively mixed by the constitutional theory of the 20th and 21st centuries. Parliamentarism has been coined as responsive, responsible, limited, and discursive government.[36] This is despite the fact that the responsiveness of government makes representative democracy prone to populist (mis)use, the liberal concepts of limited government and responsible government contradicts the belief in the omnipotence of the 'secular God' – the nation as a sovereign, while the discourse ethics utopia – the representative democracy as a government by discussion – clashes with the factual normativity of power politics and *Realpolitik*.

Hence, there are several constitutional imaginaries supporting representative democracy that are both mutually reinforcing and in tension with each other. These imaginaries were products of the acceleration of the just mentioned normative ideologies into democratic-sovereigntist, liberal, representative, rationalist, utilitarian, and discursive ethics utopias existing separately or much more frequently in a form of imaginary mixture. The most influential constitutional imaginaries of representative government and parliamentarism are the imaginary of the Parliament as the temple of the nation being the secular God of modernity; the imaginary of the parliamentary government as a rational, logical, and systematic chess board; the imaginary of the Parliament as a utilitarian rational stock exchange; the imaginary of the Parliament as a mirror of the nation; and the imaginary of the Parliament as a national agora.

4.2. The imaginary of the Parliament as the temple of the nation being the secular god of modernity

Let's start with the first imaginary – the imaginary of the Parliament as the temple and the altar of the ultimate secular God – the nation. This secular God, with its different conceptual versions shaped by the constitutional and political theory, the constitutional history, constitutional anthropology, etc., possesses ultimate, supreme, demanding, and imposing common will capable of detecting and mastering an objective, absolute, and holistic common good. This imaginary aims at sustaining a nationalist-parliamentary utopia.

Hence, the first group of imaginaries of representation must secure the imaginary, aspirational, and emotional power of nationalism and parliamentarism as key ideologies of Western and especially of European modernity that

36 Bliznashki, *Principles of Parliamentary Government* (n 35).

have been developed in the course of the 'long 19th' and the 'short 20th century'. In fact, the imaginary of the Parliament as the temple and the altar of the nation has been of huge political importance, much more in the course of the 'long 19th' than in the 'short 20th century'. This is due to the fact that the ideological combat for the hearts and minds of the people against the '*Ancien régime*' with its monarchist and religious imaginaries and conservative, pre-constitutional, feudal-aristocratic, and religiously inspired normative ideologies has happened most intensely in that period. Subsequently, the 20th century was already time for regional and then global expansion of the new status quo of republican nationalism and parliamentarism later on shaped as liberal representative democracy.

The 'secular God' to which the Parliament serves as temple and altar can differ as well. This can be the '*la nation*' or '*das Volk*'. The nation ('*la nation*') may be defined in historic but also in republican-activist terms as community of beliefs capable of collective will (*volonté générale*) and collective action in pursuit of the common good. This is a community of people sharing a common political project. Alternatively, '*das Volk*' is more a community of destiny and less a community of political beliefs. It is an organic, historic, and usually heroic entity that, similarly to the Hegelian *Weltgeist*,[37] takes different manifestations in the course of its traveling throughout history. Nevertheless, it remains ontologically, axiologically, and teleologically unified and capable of holistic representation.

This is the nationalist-representative utopia sustained by parliamentary-representative imaginaries. These imaginaries are naturally embedded in nationalism as political ideology and republicanism as constitutional ideology and form of governance, although to an extent, paradoxically, they are not irreconcilable with a monarchical form of governance.

4.3 *The imaginary of the parliamentary government as a rational, logical, and systematic chess board*

The second constitutional imaginary of modern representative democracy is the imaginary of the parliamentary government as a rational, logical, and systematic chess board allowing for a predictable and perfected system of checks capable of sustaining limited, responsible, and rational government. This imaginary is the pillar of a liberal utopia. Representation is imagined as a pillar of the rational construction of the constitutional powerhouse. It is a tool for the production of order out of disorder. Limitation is in fact empowerment serving the ultimate aim of preservation of the rules of the game.

Game metaphors are part of this imaginary. They are produced by rational choice, public choice, and game theories being themselves the offspring of rationalism and institutionalism. Similar to a chess play, the power grid of

37 See Georg WF Hegel, *Phenomenology of Spirit* (OUP 1977) 1–640.

representation is stable, predetermined, rationally constructed on the basis of enduring logic. Thus, the players – both the represented and the representatives – must simply follow the logic and obey the rules in order to achieve systemic equilibrium. Hence, the imaginary of the constitutional chess board serves limited government and ultimately produces constitutional autopoiesis.[38]

This liberal imaginary is mixed with rationalist, institutionalist, and system theory utopias. It is a clear example of the emotional-imaginary bias of hyper-rationalism. It demonstrates the perils of the institutionalist excesses and the rationalist entrapment of constitutional modernity.[39] The reasonableness of public action; the rational modality of governance; the systematic character of the constitutional order, the complexity of which is reduced to rules and procedures; the predictability of the choices the constitutional actors and veto players[40] make, and their subsumption into a quasi-mathematical calculus are some of the key elements of the 'chess-board' imaginary of representative democracy.

Clearly, the 'chess-board' imaginary of representative democracy has many deficiencies. Symbolically, it seems capable of explaining symmetric representative orders based on biparty systems, but not asymmetric and pluralist ones characterized by multiparty systems. The 'chess-board' imaginary focuses on rationalist utopia and on the understanding of the constitution as a limitation to power and restraint to veto players. Thus, it ignores the inclusive, aspirational, and volitional aspects of representation enabling engagement beyond pure restraint. The rationalist overburdening of a systematic order is not permissive for detection of representational games beyond the system of valid law with their emotional, affective, and imaginary power.

4.4 *The imaginary of the Parliament as a utilitarian rational stock exchange*

The third imaginary conceives the Parliament as a utilitarian stock exchange where bargaining is the main modus for decision-making. It is based on a utilitarian constitutional utopia. In certain ways, it is similar to the liberal-rationalist 'chess-board' imaginary in its emphasis on the rational calculus of the political game and in its perception of constitutional politics as purely a rational, logical, systematic, and quasi-mathematical enterprise. However, it differs from it in one important aspect. The stock exchange and marketplace imaginary puts the emphasis on interests, bargaining, and utility instead of rules perceived as a neutral and interest-detached normative grid. Hence, while the chess-board imaginary accentuates restraint, neutrality, and maintenance of order, the stock

38 See Gunter Teubner and Diana Göbel, *Critical Theory and Legal Autopoiesis: The Case for Societal Constitutionalism* (Manchester UP 2019) 1–408.

39 See Belov, *Constitutional Semiotics* (n 11) 49–55.

40 See George Tsebelis, *Veto Players. How Political Institutions Work* (Russell Sage Foundation, Princeton UP 2002).

exchange and marketplace imaginary allows for imagining constitutionalism as a melting pot of interests and aspirations for power and benefit maximization.

In this context the Parliament is imagined as a marketplace where national, subnational (local and regional), and since the second half of the 20th century also international and supranational interests can be reconciled. Moreover, the national interest is balanced with and against party political, lobbyist, and other sector-specific interests. This understanding rests upon the almost axiomatic belief in the ultimate power of human reason conceived as an all-powerful epistemic and ordering device. The belief in rational and reasonable constitutional, legal, and political order is intertwined with the belief in the interests as the main driving force of constitutional politics and strategic and tactical policymaking. Thus, representative democracy is imagined mainly as a scheme for rational interest maximization, adjustment, and bargaining. This is a rationalist-utilitarian utopia shaped through imaginaries of the Parliament as an interest powerhouse maximizing the most benefits for most of the people.

4.5 The imaginary of the Parliament as a mirror of the nation

The fourth imaginary is the imaginary of the Parliament as a mirror of the nation. It is based on the normative belief in procedural and input legitimacy[41] and on trust in the achievability of unity in diversity.[42] To an extent, paradoxically, this imaginary can serve both nationalist and communitarian-multicultural utopias. The Parliament can be conceived as a mirror of the unified national society organized in a liberal-republican way or as a mirror of the pluralist and multicultural society structured in a communitarian way.

Indeed, initially the Parliament was conceived as the mirror of the nation as a volitional and homogeneous transtemporal community of destiny. It has to serve as an institutional reflection of the national capacity to mobilize, organize, and represent the people as a source of legitimacy of the state power in the course of the reformulation of the state in modern terms as territorial, national, constitutional, parliamentary, and democratic entity. Thus, the mirror imaginary has been powered by the ideals of the revolutionary world at the beginning of the 'long 19th century' and was intended as justification for the promotion of constitutional nationalism. Later on, however, the representative maxima 'unity in diversity' rephrased in terms of the mirror metaphor and imaginary has been put in practice also in the context of constitutional multiculturalism for shaping consociational democracies.

The Parliament as a mirror of the nation is in fact a complex and composite imaginary. It includes the metaphor of two worlds – one real and one

41 For the input legitimacy see Philip Kiiver, *The National Parliaments in the European Union: A Critical View on EU Constitution-Building* (Kluwer Law International 2006) 95.

42 See Gregory Conti, *Parliament the Mirror of the Nation: Representation, Deliberation, and Democracy in Victorian Britain* (CUP 2019).

imaginary – interrelated by the interplay of prototype and shadow, original and imprint. Both the mirror and the nation are imaginaries. Thus, we are confronted with the phenomenon of double signification of meaning. The citizens are first packed, framed, and imagined as a community that possesses common will and is capable of mastering its own destiny. Thus, the nation is usually imagined as a 'community of faith', 'community of origin', and 'identitarian community'. Then, the nation is represented in its political replica, imprint, or shadow – the political representation in the Parliament.

Hence, there are at least two phases of self-identification employed in the mirror metaphor. These are, first, the self-identification of the people with the nation as transgenerational and meta-personal project and second, the identification of the nation with its clear, proper, quasi-automatic replication through representation in the Parliament. Thus, the citizens are socially represented by the nation and legally represented by the parliament as national representative institution.

The mirror metaphor is based, as all constitutional imaginaries, on a mixture of rationality and magic.[43] The magic is multilayered. It consists, first, in the belief of the parallel coexistence of the people as a social fact and the nation as a normative concept that imposes new political shape and brings additional capabilities to the people as an assemblage of citizens.[44] Second, the Parliament is supposed to reflect both the people in singular and the people in plural. In other words, it must represent the interests of the single person, the most relevant social groups, and the nation as holistic and fully fledged coherent community capable of joint action.

Thus, the imaginary of the Parliament as a mirror is composed of the imaginaries of the mirror as pure reflection, the mirror as a transformative lens, and the mirror as a crack in reality serving as a channel for transition to an imagined reality – the realm of the secular God (the nation) ruling through common will for the sake of the achievement of the common good.

The mirror metaphor, when intertwined with imaginaries of sovereignty, serves as justification for the constitutional imaginaries of sovereigntist nationalism. During most of its career in constitutional modernity, representation has been mostly a sovereigntist concept. Sovereigntist representation was mostly structured around the principles of national, popular, and parliamentary sovereignty. Sovereigntist imaginaries of representation varied from authoritarian visions of Leviathan, theistic, and monarchic representation to oligarchic or democratic visions of representation based on national, popular, and parliamentary sovereignty and democratic representation.

43 See Frankenberg (n 18).

44 See Saskia Sassen, *Territory, Authority, Rights: From Medieval to Global Assemblages* (Princeton UP 2008) 1–512.

4.6 *The imaginary of the Parliament as a national agora*

The fifth imaginary is the imaginary of the Parliament as a national agora. It conceptualizes the Parliament as a forum of national deliberation. The national agora is imagined as a representative, inclusive, enlightened, and deliberative locus for staging the national debate. It is allowing for the communicative inclusion of the sociopolitical forces and for the discursive construction of a common public meaning negotiated via never-ending processes of mature and reasonable political communication.[45]

Hence, the imaginary of the Parliament as a national agora is a deliberative democratic utopia. It is grounded on the normative belief in the possibility for free and fair deliberation that is reasonable, efficient, and inclusive. The requirement for reasonableness and efficiency is similar to several imaginaries of democratic representation that have been explored previously. That is why it is exactly the belief in the capacity of communicative action to produce inclusive and thus representative debate, which is the essence of this deliberative democratic imaginary. This debate is supposed to produce decisions that shall be accepted by the constitutionally framed socio-legal community due to their input legitimacy.

4.7 *The imaginaries of democratic representation in the overall scheme of constitutional imaginaries*

Finally, it has to be mentioned that the constitutional imaginaries of representation are embedded in a broader imaginary framework. It consists of the imaginaries of the state as territorial container, the imaginary of the state as pyramid-like hierarchical order, the imaginaries of sovereignty as the political source of normative hierarchy, and last but not least, the imaginary or rather normative belief that the constitution can be a rational, logical, systematic, and written plan for ultimate ordering of the political order.

The imaginary of the state as territorial container sets the spatial framework of representation. It determines representative democracy as territorial democracy and follows its imperative that democracy requires closure.[46] All aforementioned imaginaries of representation – the imaginary of the Parliament as the temple of the nation, the imaginary of the parliamentary government as a chess board, the imaginary of the Parliament as a stock exchange, the imaginary of the Parliament as a mirror of the nation, and the imaginary of the

45 See Jurgen Habermas, *Theorie des kommunikativen Handelns Band I: Handlungsrationalität und gesellschaftliche Rationalisierung* (Suhrkamp 1995); Jurgen Habermas, *Theorie des kommunikativen Handelns Band II: Zur Kritik der funktionalistischen Vernunft* (Suhrkamp 1995).

46 Seyla Benhabib, *The Rights of Others: Aliens, Citizens and Residents* (CUP 2004) 266; David Jacobson, *Rights across Borders: Immigration and the Decline of Citizenship* (Johns Hopkins UP 1997).

Parliament as a national agora – follow that territorial logic of representation. Indeed, some of them might be adapted to the post-national, post-territorial, aterritorial, and global constitutionalism. However, until now, they have been practiced entirely in the context of territorial democracy imagining the state as closed or much less frequently as open territorial container.

The hierarchical and pyramidal structure of the legal and also of the constitutional order is one of the most durable and fundamental imaginaries of modern constitutionalism. It has a profound impact on the constitutional geometry of Westphalian constitutionalism in general and its ordering and explanatory schemes related to the sources of law (including the constitutional supremacy), the institutions of the executive and judicial power, the bicameralism, etc.[47] It also influences the structure of representation justifying the distinction between representatives and represented. Nevertheless, it has less relevance for democratic representation since it is based not on the principle of supremacy but on the principle of identity. In other words, representative democracy, apart from the ontological role of popular or national sovereignty as source of the constitutional order, is a binary concept of political self-identification based on symmetry instead of hierarchy.

The impact of the imaginary of the constitution as a rational, logical, systematic, and written plan for ultimate ordering of the political order on the imaginaries of representation has already been discussed. It has been mentioned that it is of special relevance for the imaginaries of representation based on excessive rationalism. These are mostly the imaginary of the parliamentary government as a chess board and the imaginary of the Parliament as a stock exchange.

Consequently, imaginaries of democratic representation have twofold specifics. They are focused on the Parliament as a national representative institution. In that regard, they are mostly imaginaries of parliamentary representation. Moreover, they are allocated in a network of constitutional imaginaries that shape their overall outlook and set their general conceptual framework. Due to space constraints I am not going to explore the imaginaries of representation related to the head of state. In fact, monarchic representation has been briefly mentioned in the context of the outline of the history of the idea of representation. In the context of transplantation of monarchic imaginaries in the republican context and their adjustment to the republican constitutional axiology and its institutional order range of imaginaries related to the president of the republic have also been developed. These imaginaries, e.g., the imaginary of the president as supreme leader, the imaginary of the president as republican monarch, the imaginary of the president as neutral moderator,[48]

47 See Belov, *Constitutional Semiotics* (n 11) 241–315.

48 See, e.g., Georgi Bliznashki, *Parliamentary Government in Bulgaria* (U of Sofia 'St. Kliment Ohridski' P 2009) 59–81 (in Bulgarian).

and the imaginary of the president as state notary,[49] deserve special attention and cannot be developed in detail in this chapter.

5. Imaginaries of representation beyond representative democracy: populist, elitist, and technocratic imaginaries of representation

5.1 Non-democratic imaginaries of representation in the context of constitutional polycrisis and constitutional polytransition

Representation has not always been democratic. In fact, democratic representation is an invention of Western modernity. It was properly functioning only in a relatively limited number of states and short historic periods under specific socio-legal circumstances. Thus, from a broader historic and geopolitical perspective, democratic representation seems to be the exception rather than the norm. In the pre-constitutional period – the time before the entry into constitutional modernity, which has lasted in some countries until the end of the 18th century, whereas in others it continued until the end of the 19th and the beginning of the 20th century – representation was an elitist, aristocratic, and even autocratic concept. This phenomenon has already been discussed in the previous parts of this chapter. Moreover, there are multiple signs of a possible demise of democratic representation producing implosion, deconstruction, and flux of representative democracy as a constitutional model of the Global North that has been exported and transplanted also elsewhere.

One of the biggest challenges of our time is whether we can preserve the heritage of democratic representation not only as a form and procedure but also as content and substance. We have to admit that representative democracy has been a mixture of rational and emotional elements possessing charismatic, rationalist, technocratic, and traditionalist features embedded in the context of mass democracy. We have to face also the divorce between democratic and technocratic, representative and democratic, charismatic and rational elements of representative democracy producing increasing mismatch between representation and democracy.

Hence, similarly to the rule of law and democracy, one can expect the emergence of 'thin' and 'thick' versions of representation. Indeed, all three constitutional principles, which are also pillars of modern liberal-democratic constitutionalism, are experiencing huge pressure and are gradually dismantled in the context of globalized, technocratic, and post-democratic post-modernity. In that regard, we witness processes of deconstruction, fragmentation, and crisis of these principles (being also normative ideologies of constitutionalism)

49 See, e.g., Roland Lhotta, 'Der Bundespräsident als "Außerparlamentarische Opposition"? Überlegungen zur Gewaltenteilung und Typologisierung des parlamentarischen Regierungssystems' (2008) 39(1) Zeitschrift für Parlamentsfragen 119–33.

that are producing rule of law, democracy, and representation in flux. They jointly lead to constitutionalism in a state of flux.[50]

The structural transformations of representation raise the question whether we can still speak of representative democracy or if representation will be again detached from democracy in post-modern, post-national, post-territorial, and post-democratic contexts. Another issue is whether such detachment will lead to a situation similar to the pre-modern forms of aristocratic, elitist, and theocratic representation or if we will witness new forms of post-democratic representation. Very important, but less exposed and explored, is the problem of the elements of symbolic-imaginary constitutionalism (normative ideologies, mythologies, utopias, etc.) that will shape the forms of post-democratic representation from a symbolic-imaginary perspective. It is important to analyze whether post-democratic representation shall be rooted in old or new autocratic ideologies or if new forms of constitutional imaginaries more adequate to the global algorithmic technocracy shall arise and be established. These are just a few of the most important topics this part of the chapter shall address.

There are two main factors for the implosion of the constitutional imaginaries of representative democracy. They are mutually related and produce a joint negative impact on Westphalian symbolic-imaginary constitutionalism. Thus, they are paving the way to post-Westphalian and neo-Westphalian constitutional imaginaries of post-democratic representation.[51]

The first factor is the deconstruction of the bulk of representative democratic constitutional imaginaries and the destruction of their appearance as a system that was created in the course of modernity. Constitutional polycrisis and constitutional polytransition are swirling these constitutional imaginaries. They are exposing the inner controversies that have always existed but were suppressed and remedied by rational, emotional, and symbolic-imaginary means producing their acceptance during late modernity.

Hence, we are currently facing imaginary disorder and dare need for reshaping the imaginary construct of constitutional post-modernity. The holistic visions of representation, democracy, and representative democracy are transformed into narratives.[52] The narrative character of post-modern constitutional imaginaries produces fundamental uncertainty. It questions the ability of the constitutional order to produce viable and convincing imprints in the collective imagination of the people creating holistic and normative visions of truth, e.g., imaginaries related to representative democracy.

50 See Belov, *Rule of Law in Crisis* (n 3).

51 For more about Westphalian, post-Westphalian, and neo-Westphalian constitutionalism, see Belov, 'Three Models for Ordering Constitutional Orders' (n 21) 361–87; Belov, 'The Challenges to Westphalian Constitutional Geometry' (n 21) 13–55; Belov, 'Constitutional Nationalism and Constitutional Globalism' (n 21) vol I, 221–51.

52 For constitutional law as narrative and for the constitutional narratives see Belov, *Constitutional Semiotics* (n 11) 80–93.

The second factor is the emergence of new constitutional imaginaries deriving their normative, formative, and convincing power from the context of post-modernity and post-truth in the post-territorial and post-national condition of the globalized constitutional disorder and the world risk society.[53] From a system theory viewpoint, the new constitutional imaginaries in general and those related to the representation in particular can be perceived also as a response to the ongoing fourth technological revolution that is massively and profoundly reshaping our legal, political, social, and moral orders.

There are three main groups of post-representative democracy imaginaries. They can be defined as populist imaginaries, elitist imaginaries, and technocratic imaginaries. Some of them are new, while others have been also used during constitutional modernity in parallel with the traditional imaginaries of representation. There are also imaginaries that were pre-modern but are being recycled, reconstructed, and put in practice anew. Finally, there are also genuinely post-modern imaginaries triggered by the determinants of the current constitutional moment[54] – globalization, technological revolution, post-modern situation, rise of elitism and technocracy, etc. Hence, the post-democratic imaginaries of representation are not a coherent system of forms of symbolic-imaginary constitutionalism. Instead, they are a divergent group of forms of collective imagination jointly or separately challenging the imaginaries of the modern liberal-democratic constitutionalism and its institutional framework – the representative democracy.

5.2 *Populist imaginaries of representation*

Populism is, in principle, detrimental for true, well-established, and well-functioning representative democracy. Nevertheless, populism is also frequently part of representative democracy. Populist messages to the people are delivered by both extreme and mainstream political parties and players. The principle of responsiveness of government serves as a gateway for populism. Thus, populist imaginaries are, up to a certain extent, part of representative democracy. Hence, the problem of populism is a matter of degree, extent, and scale. It may be supportive of legitimate government based on responsiveness and output legitimacy. However, it may also be destructive for the democratic framework based on rule of law and toxic for the maintenance of pluralist society based on toleration, reasonableness, and responsibility.

There have been important historic periods when populism and its supportive constitutional imaginaries were expanding beyond the scale permitting their coexistence with representative democracy. Clear examples are the interwar period and the first decades of the 21st century. This means that populism has always been part of the political game. Moreover, it has been practiced

53 See Ulrich Beck, *World Risk Society* (Wiley 1999) 1–192.
54 See Ackerman (n 19).

also by mainstream politicians in times of constitutional cohesion and peace. However, it expands in times of crisis and transition.

To a certain extent, populism is a side effect of the immune reaction against oligarchy, elitism, and technocracy. Thus, the paradoxical simultaneous rise of populist imaginaries, elitist imaginaries, and technocratic imaginaries can be explained. This is due to the fact that they are all an offspring of the same problem or disease – the deficiency, crisis, and even dismantling of representative democracy and the key fundamental consensuses that form its core. These are the consensus for the establishment of representative democracy combining representation with democracy, liberal democracy combining liberalism with democracy, and capitalist democracy combining market economy with welfare state. The deconstruction of these fundamental aspects of the constitutional consensus in the age of neoliberal globalization and fourth technological revolution produces deep discontent manifested also through post-representative democracy constitutional imaginaries.

Populist imaginaries have been widely explored in recent years in constitutional theory, political theory, and comparative constitutionalism.[55] The reason is the massive rise of populism as socio-political, legal, constitutional, and imaginary phenomenon. Apart from the debates on details and implications in various contexts there is an overall broad consensus regarding the general outlook and key features of populist constitutionalism and the populist constitutional imaginaries. Thus, my analysis will build upon the achievements of this research, looking at it from the prism and perspective of the populist imaginaries of representation.

The most important populist imaginaries can be structured into four main types. They can be defined as: coherent and holistic community imaginaries; identitarian, predestined, and charismatic leadership imaginaries; separative imaginaries; and salvation imaginaries. These imaginaries are usually practiced jointly and altogether produce a detrimental effect on representative democracy and its supportive constitutional imaginaries. Nevertheless, they have also independent content and meaning and are sometimes used also separately.

Coherent and holistic community imaginary is one of the most widely spread populist imaginaries. It suggests the existence of a coherent, cohesive, and holistic social group. This group has a common destiny, shared memories, and constitutional past, present, and future. The community has a common good and is traveling throughout history in pursuit of a common future. This community of destiny is typically defined as a nation. It is united by a common identity and is governed by exclusively majoritarian schemes of decision-making.

The coherent and holistic community imaginary seems to be applicable also to representative democracy. The existence of a nation and a community as the social substance of the state and its constitutional form is part of the concept of representative democracy, as previously mentioned in this chapter. What

55 See the literature cited earlier.

makes this imaginary populist-representative instead of representative democratic is the claim that the community of destiny is unchangeable throughout history, holistic, and representable only in an identitarian way. The will of this community cannot be fragmented into a range of interests that shall be subsequently represented in the Parliament and the other representative institutions. Instead, the will of the nation can be expressed and represented only in a majoritarian-identitarian way as single, indivisible, predetermined, and non-transferrable.

The community is substantially coherent, volitionally unified, and politically mobilized. Its will is indivisible the same way its common good is predetermined, quasi-eternal, static, and supreme. Hence, the 'community of destiny' layer of this imaginary is supplemented by other layers of communitarian-populist imagination. They include: the imaginary of the volitional community, the imaginary of the holistic community, and the imaginary of ontological community. Thus, the holistic-identitarian community is serving as a 'time capsule' through which its members travel from the constitutional past, through the constitutional present, to the constitutional future.

The second populist imaginary is the imaginary of the strong, identitarian, and charismatic leadership.[56] It suggests that the group interests and identity are expressed by a leader. This leader can be democratically elected, and his support may stem from immediate means of input legitimacy. Nevertheless, the leader may derive his position from other sources of power that are incompatible with even formal democracy but sustain non-democratic forms of representation. The leader can be appointed by theocratic aristocracy (e.g., the medieval forms of justification of power and some of their contemporary versions practiced, e.g., in Iran or the Vatican state). He can also be imposed by revolutionary elites being imagined as leader of both the revolutionary vanguard and the people (e.g., the case of Castro's Cuba and other charismatic dictatorships).

Thus, the imaginary of the strong charismatic leadership usually builds upon the imaginary of the coherent, holistic, integrated, and identitarian community. Both imaginaries are frequently mutually related and interdependent. This is due to the fact that the usually practiced way for representation of such coherent community of destiny is through a supreme leader. The combination of the two imaginaries aims at producing the belief that the leader is both democratic and autocratic. He is democratic because he is elected by the members of the community or stems from the will of an ultimate authority – religious or secular, e.g., revolutionary. Thus, the supreme leader is the focal point and climax of democracy-as-identity, democracy-as-natural God-like community, or democracy-as-revolution. At the same time, the leader is also autocratic because he has the ultimate choice over political decision-making on behalf of the constitutionally framed sociopolitical community. Thus, the

56 See, e.g., Cas Mudde and Cristóbal Rovira Kaltwasser, 'The Populist Leader' in *Populism: A Very Short Introduction* (Oxford Academic 2017).

identitarian politics is a product of the majoritarian will of the community expressed through its supreme leader. Conceptually, this construction can be justified through authoritarian theories of political existentialism, exceptionalism, and realpolitik. Clearest examples are Hobbes's *Leviathan*[57] and the theories of Niccolò Machiavelli[58] and Carl Schmitt.[59]

The peculiarity of this combined populist-identitarian imaginary is that the leader is both within and beyond the community. He is legally and formally embedded in constitutional procedures. Thus, he is enjoying rational[60] and input legitimacy, if they are generally stemming from at least formal democracy.

Such strategies for legitimation of the identitarian leader are necessary for the constitutional strand of features in the imaginary. However, this is not sufficient to feed the emotional-populist strand of the imaginary. In order to support also this rather metaphysical perception, the leader must be both part of the community, 'one of us', naturally embedded in the common origin and destiny of the nation, but also has to stand beyond the community as its natural and quasi-metaphysical leader. He must have specific volitional, charismatic, and at times also possibly traditional features that distinguish him from the rest of the people. These features must grant him special status that is both communitarian and supra-communitarian. Thus, imaginaries of natural leadership close to Nietzschean predestined heroism are mixed with radical democratic and communitarian imaginaries of identitarian belongingness and natural integrity via egalitarian inclusion and simplicity. Hence, the leader has to enjoy also output, charismatic, traditional,[61] or ecstatic and religious legitimacy, in case of revolutionary, authoritarian, or theocratic regimes.

The separative logic of populism is extensively discussed in the theory.[62] It consists of the separation between elites and the people, between good leaders and bad elites, and between the members of the community and external factors of policymaking. Populism rests upon the 'we-them', 'friend-enemy' distinction that, according to Carl Schmitt, is the key for the establishment and maintenance of the community, the polity, and the politics.[63]

These structural features of populist constitutionalism nourish the correspondent set of separative imaginaries. These are the imaginaries of the

57 See Thomas Hobbes, *Leviathan* (Penguin Classics 2017) 1–688.

58 See Niccolò Machiavelli, *The Prince* (Reader's Library Classics 2021) 1–107.

59 See Carl Schmitt, *Die Diktatur: Von den Anfängen des modernen Souveränitätsgedankens bis zum proletarischen Klassenkampf* (Duncker & Humblott 2023) 1–261; Carl Schmitt, *Politische Theologie: Vier Kapitel zur Lehre von der Souveränität* (Duncker & Humblott 2021) 1–72.

60 See Max Weber, *Soziologie: Weltgeschichtliche Analysen. Politik* (Kröner Verlag 1968) 151 and the following and John Patty and Elizabeth Maggie Penn, *Social Choice and Legitimacy: The Possibilities of Impossibility* (CUP 2014) 1–224.

61 Weber (n 60).

62 See, e.g., Marte Mangset and others, 'The Populist Elite Paradox: Using Elite Theory to Elucidate the Shapes and Stakes of Populist Elite Critiques' (2019) 34 Elites and People: Challenges to Democracy Comparative Social Research 203–22.

63 See Carl Schmitt, *Der Begriff des Politischen* (Duncker & Humblot 2018).

'others' – the minorities, the elites, the non-believers, the counterrevolutionaries, the range of external factors to the community, and 'the outsiders' that are frequently defined in the negative. Reversely, the imaginaries of the 'We' – the majority, the community, believers, the participants in the revolution, the identitarian leaders, and 'the insiders' – are shaped in an antipode way. Thus, the 'we-they' imaginaries actually form a symmetric dichotomic couple in the collective mindset. In both cases they are detrimental for the development of inclusive and liberal representative democracy.

Unfortunately, the separative imaginaries are widely used also by political players that pretend to be non-populist or even anti-populist. The increasing use of the 'we-them' distinction where 'we' are morally superior and politically better and 'they' are the morally inferior forces of evil, e.g., in the context of the 'war on terror' and all other strands of the constitutional polycrisis unfolding since the beginning of the 21st century show that this Schmittian approach to shaping the imaginaries of politics persists to be the leading one in both populist and seemingly non-populist political camps.

The salvation imaginaries stem from the messianic apprehension of leadership. Thus, they are related to all three previous groups of populist imaginaries. They presuppose a holistic and coherent community of destiny that needs to be saved from the misery of the constitutional present in the name of the constitutional past and for the sake of the constitutional future. Usually, the constitutional past is conceived as heroic and glorious, as tragic and oppressive, or very frequently as both. Furthermore, the salvation imaginaries require a savior. Hence, they are prone to identitarian, predestined, and charismatic leadership imaginaries. Finally, salvation suggests the existence of menace, peril, and threat stemming from an enemy. Thus, the imaginary of the enemy from whom the community should be saved and salvaged by the leader is the inevitable bond between separation and salvation populist imaginaries. Moreover, salvation in such context means representation. The community is represented in its desire to be saved by the identitarian messiah. Hence, there is intrinsic link between all these populist imaginaries. They jointly produce a mix of communitarian-identitarian-messianic-separation imaginaries of representation.

5.3 *Elitist imaginaries of representation*

Elitist imaginaries are the second group of post-democratic imaginaries of representation. They are thriving in connection with the mushrooming of conspiracy theories. In contrast to the populist imaginaries, some of which are reconcilable with specific versions of constitutionalism and democratic representation,[64] the elitist imaginaries are neither part of the constitution nor

64 See Blokker, 'Political and Constitutional Imaginaries' (n 7); Blokker, 'Populist Constitutionalism' (n 7); Blokker, 'Populism as a Constitutional Project' (n 7); Dillabough (n 7) 178–92.

of the valid law. They are mostly stemming from extralegal and meta-legal narratives with constitutional relevance that usually have no explicit legal standing. Nevertheless, these imaginaries have constitutional importance for constitutionalism as a socio-legal phenomenon fed by and resting upon collective constitutional emotions, beliefs, fears, and imagination.

Elitist imaginaries streamline with 'dark constitutionalism' as a form of constitutionalism resting upon fear politics.[65] The (un)constitutional politics of fear is an imminent part of the contemporary constitutional imaginaries. It is an element of constitutional polycrisis that is facilitated by constitutional polytransition. Constitutional fears impact the collective constitutional imaginaries of the constitutional past, constitutional present, and constitutional future.

Elitist imaginaries can be perceived as a post-modern version of premodern imaginaries. This is due to the fact that before the invention of representative democracy, democratic representation, and liberal-democratic constitutionalism representation had been an elitist phenomenon grounded on charismatic legitimacy and sacral imaginaries about the ontology and teleology of power. Supreme leaders were mediators between two worlds. They were community and political leaders representing the identity and unity of the society and divine leaders invested with sacred legitimacy to rule the world. Thus, pre-modern (and pre-constitutional) representation stemmed simultaneously from the will of the people and the will of God having joint communitarian-identitarian and sacred legitimacy.

The contemporary elitist imaginaries resemble the belief in the sacred origin of power of the elites. They mimic the imaginary of the divine, meta-legal, and meta-social ontology of the authority of the rules without giving it any form of justification. Thus, the post-modern elitist mythology is based on conspiracies of stolen, self-acquired, and abused power by hidden elites with esoteric entitlement to rule instead on official schemes for justification of the divine origin of public power. Constitutional mysticism and esoteric-elitist imaginaries are serving as a replacement of the lost transcendentality[66] due to the rationalist entrapment of modernity and the emotional-imaginary disenchantment of hyper-rationalism and their toxic effect on democratic representation.

Elitist imaginaries are totally inconsistent with the logic and justification of representative democracy. They cannot coexist with representative democratic imaginaries. They are toxic for the beliefs in democratic representation and destroy any form of democratic version of symbolic-imaginary constitutionalism. This is another difference between the contemporary, post-modern

65 For more about fear politics, see Frank Furedi, *Politics of Fear* (Continuum 2005) 1–208; Martin Belov, 'The Role of Fear Politics in Global Constitutional "Ernstfall": Images of Fear Under COVID-19 Health Paternalism' in Martin Belov (ed), *Populist Constitutionalism and Illiberal Democracies: Between Constitutional Imagination, Normative Entrenchment and Political Reality* (Intersentia 2021) 187–221.

66 Carl Schmitt, *Politische Theologie: Vier Kapitel zur Lehre von der Souveränität* (Duncker & Humblott 2021) 1–72.

elitist imaginaries and the pre-modern elitist imaginaries of monarchical or sacred representation. The latter are partially reconcilable with representative democratic imaginaries as the constitutional and parliamentary monarchies penetrated by the global religions.

5.4 *Technocratic imaginaries of representation*

In the last decades a range of technocratic imaginaries have appeared and gained momentum on the symbolic-imaginary scene of constitutionalism. They form the third group of post-democratic imaginaries of representation.

Similarly to elitist imaginaries, the rise of technocratic imaginaries is predetermined by the emergency constitutionalism, constitutional polycrisis, and constitutional polytransition that are unfolding during the last phase of neoliberal globalization and the fourth technological revolution. The increasing disturbances in the functioning of liberal democracy, the deconstruction of constitutional normalcy and its replacement with constitutional emergency,[67] and the multitude of crises and transitions that pave the way for global algorithmic technocracy altogether transform the well-ordered system of democratic representation into a 'shaken order'. The result is constitutionalism (including rule of law and democracy) in flux, which promote unprecedented levels of uncertainty, distrust, and insecurity with the capacity to trigger implosion of constitutional democracy and its replacement with global algorithmic technocracy.[68]

The distrust in the political elites is gaining momentum. It is gradually transformed into distrust in the constitutional infrastructure of the liberal-democratic constitutionalism with its representative democratic scheme for justification of the constitutional governance and for interest representation in complex societies. These tendencies are facilitated and promoted by the deconstruction of the fundamental constitutional consensus for safeguarding of fundamental autonomy and liberty and basic equality stemming from the marriage between liberalism and democracy, capitalism and democracy, and representation and democracy on normative-institutional, socio-legal, and constitutional imaginary levels.

The range of technocratic imaginaries is broad and complex. Moreover, they do not necessarily share common ontology, axiology, and teleology. Some of them possess added value for the system of liberal democracy, whereas others (in fact the majority) are structurally incompatible and functionally detrimental for the liberal-democratic constitutional order.

Some of the generally positive technocratic imaginaries that still produce detrimental effects for representation, democracy, and representative

67 See Belov, 'The Conceptual Shapes' (n 5) 393–410.

68 See Belov, 'Rule of Law and Democracy in Times of Transitory Constitutionalism, Constitutional Polycrisis and Emergency Constitutionalism' (n 5) 21–47.

democracy, are related to different variants of national, supranational, regional, or global technocracy. This technocracy usually relates to technocratic governance by courts and administrations, although it can also concern technocratic governance beyond constitutional law. Examples of the former are the imaginaries of the judiciary as ultimate safeguard of the constitutional order defined exclusively through the prism of rule of law and the imaginaries of administrative governance based on efficiency and impeccable problem-solving capacity. Judicial utopias and anti-utopias such as Montesquieu's 'gouvernement des juges', Ran Hirschl's concept of juristocracy,[69] or my idea of global judicial empire[70] are just some of the attempt at grasping the political role of courts as activist players in the constitutional power game.

Most of the court's related imaginaries are grounded on rule of law and human rights. Thus, they are by necessity also fed by rule of law and human rights–related constitutional imaginaries. The interplay between judicial governance, rule of law, and human rights is frequently embedded in different versions of liberalism as fundamental constitutional ideology. Thus, they are using freedom, liberty, and autopoiesis[71] as important axiological sources for activation of the constitutional imagination.

In fact, the very concept of autopoietic, self-ordering, nomocentric system is powerful constitutional imaginary. It is based on a mixture of liberal and system theory visions for the constitutional order.

The idea of the judiciary as ultimate source for self-refining and self-purification of the constitutional and political order is another important imaginary. In that liberal imaginary, the judge is supposed to be an independent and rational priest of the rule of law. He is supposed to be able to safeguard another liberal utopia – the belief of the practical possibility of 'rule of law instead of rule of men' that was launched in early modernity initially in the British and the US constitutional discourse.

The liberal rule of law– and courts-centered utopia is based on the conceptual preference for liberty and autonomy and for the principle of rule of law possibly sacrificing purely democratic axiology and sovereigntist, democratic, and egalitarian pragmatics. Thus, rule of law–based imaginaries centered around the judiciary are in deep tension with popular sovereignty, separation of powers, and democracy. They are detrimental for representative democracy because they are replacing political representation of interests with elitist technocratic representation of rights. In other words, representing politically active groups through democratic institutions is pushed aside by the technocratic interpretation of rights by hopefully benevolent, enlightened, rational,

69 See Ran Hirschl, *Towards Juristocracy: The Origins and Consequences of the New Constitutionalism* (Harvard UP 2007) 1–196.

70 See Martin Belov, 'Global Rule of Law Instead of Global Democracy? Legitimacy of Global Judicial Empire on the Edge between Westphalian and Post-Westphalian Constitutionalism' in Martin Belov (ed), *The Role of Courts in Contemporary Legal Orders* (Eleven 2019) 99–133.

71 Guilherme Vasconcelos Vilaça, 'From Hayek's Spontaneous Orders to Luhmann's Autopoietic Systems' (2010) 3 Emergent Order 50–81.

and socially engaged judicial elites. In these judicial imaginaries the institutional epicenter of the constitutional order are courts instead of parliaments, democratic representation is overshadowed by judicial decision-making, political process is shifted from parliamentary deliberation to the judicial procedure, political and democratic inclusion is replaced by judicial protection, and democracy is overshadowed by the presumed techno-democratic autopoiesis based on rule of law.

The rise of importance and political involvement of administration and bureaucracy on the national, supranational, regional, and global levels can be reflected in the collective constitutional consciousness through imaginaries of good governance. In contrast to the imaginaries of rule of law and judicial governance the imprints of bureaucratic-administrative imaginaries that are compatible with some positive version of constitutionalism in the constitutional imagination are rather scarce. Instead, most of them are related to different versions of technocratic paternalism.

Constitutional polycrisis and emergency constitutionalism produced several variants of technocratic paternalism. They were versions of traditional organic-paternalistic concepts enriched with markers, imaginaries, and ideas of technological society and embedded in the 'world risk society'. Consequently, several variants of bureaucratic-technocratic Leviathan have risen out of the different constitutional crises and emergency regimes starting from the 'war on terror', going through the financial and migration crisis, reaching its climax with the COVID-19 pandemic and going toward the perils of natural and ecological disasters and the risks of the algorithmic society and digital constitutionalism.

Hence, there are powerful versions of technological, post-modern, and global Leviathan. The first one was the security Leviathan. It was supposed to be protecting people from terrorism and organized crime. Then, we witnessed the emergence of the financial Leviathan. It was providing safeguards against different financial crises. The financial Leviathan was even protecting economies from the inevitability of the negative phase of the financial cycle through technocratic magic. The most visible, refined, and promoted form of such constitutional technocratic magic was the 'golden budget rule'. The utopia of financial stability and evasion of negative phases of the financial cycle related to public debt and budgetary deficit has been a powerful constitutional imaginary itself.

The COVID-19 pandemic has led to the birth of another very powerful version of technocratic paternalism. Its reflection in the collective imagination was the imaginary of the health Leviathan. The health or pandemic Leviathan was an omnipotent paternalistic state radically sacrificing liberty, freedom, autonomy, free will, and free choice for the sake of health protection and security.[72] The health Leviathan was an upgraded version of the security Leviathan.

72 See Belov, 'The Role of Fear Politics in Global Constitutional "Ernstfall"' (n65) 187–221; Alexandra Mercescu, 'The COVID-19 Crisis in Romania, or on How One Cannot Escape (Bad, Legal) Culture'

It was also mixed with the emerging digital Leviathan. Hence, the COVID-19 pandemic was a melting pot of paternalistic imaginaries. Some of these are traditional, e.g., the security and police state, while others are rather novel both in terms of manifestation and the depth of the intrusion in the personal sphere, the physical, and psychological autonomy.

The health Leviathan manifested itself through several imaginaries. They were constitutional with regard to their impact and importance and unconstitutional in terms of constitutional axiology and constitutional design. One of the most important imaginaries viewed the state as clinic or hospital and the society as medical sanitation camp. The most powerful imaginary that combines digital and health aspects is the imaginary of the state as panopticon.

One of the final versions of technocratic utopias is the digital Leviathan. It has different aspects ranging from global surveillance power to digital techno-oligarchy and data processing algorithmic technocracy. These utopias and their visions have been defined and explored in a neutral or generally positive sense as well as in a negative sense. Examples of the former are the theories of digital constitutionalism, algorithmic constitutionalism, AI constitutionalism, big data governance, etc. Imaginaries with largely negative connotations have been launched as part of several hypotheses for the direction of constitutional tendencies. The most challenging and critical among them are the 'surveillance capitalism' proposed by S. Zuboff[73] and the 'technofeudalism' launched by Y. Varoufakis.[74]

All these versions of technocracy and their constitutional imaginaries are hardly reconcilable with the system, design, axiology, and imaginaries of representative democracy. They have a double effect on representative democratic imaginaries. They deconstruct the belief in the feasibility of representative democracy in the current socio-legal context and dismantle many of the traditional representative democratic imaginaries, e.g., the imaginary of the nation as a community of destiny and secular God, the imaginary of the Parliament as a 'mirror of the nation' and efficient melting pot of interests, the imaginary of the Parliament as a deliberative forum of the nation capable of generating joint political decisions through political communication and public reason, etc.

Reversely, technocratic constitutional imaginaries demonstrate the value of representative democracy for the society in general and for personal autonomy and liberty, social equality, and political inclusion in particular. The shift from the imaginary of the Parliament as a temple of political liberty where the people can demonstrate their 'unity in diversity' with the different versions of

<http://exceptions.eu/2020/05/11/the-covid-19-crisis-inromania-or-on-how-one-cannot-escape-bad-legal-culture/?fbclid=IwAR3hTyciWCKiei2r9KFjHVN0KjGzx6aepFuZ9VYlnDz89Jr94dWUydAh_Y>.

73 See Shoshana Zuboff, *The Age of Surveillance Capitalism: The Fight for a Human Future at the New Frontier of Power* (Profile Books 2019) 1–704.

74 See Yannis Varoufakis, *Technofeudalism: What Killed Capitalism* (Melville House 2024) 1–304.

Leviathan and the replacement of the imaginary of the politically enlightened, rational, self-esteemed, and autonomous citizen with the citizen as a patient, obedient and patronized by uncontrollable technocracy, is a game changer in the history of constitutionalism. These shifts may be clear signs for the durable tendencies of post-democracy, post-liberty, and post-constitutionalism. However, they may be also a painful reminder of the importance of the liberal democracy and democratic representation. Thus, they may eventually reinforce traditional representative democratic imaginaries or produce new ones that are better adapted to the new reality of a globalized world risk society undergoing structural transition under the reformative pressures of the fourth technological revolution.

6. Conclusion

Representative democracy is in crisis. This is not a simple and short crisis, but rather a constitutional polycrisis with multiple dimensions and manifestations and with long duration leading to semi-permanency. It consists of multiple crises that are overlapping and are jointly producing huge dysfunctionality of the constitution and the institutional design and the normative order established by it. Constitutional polycrisis itself is partially a result of constitutional polytransition, the latter being a phenomenon denominating the multitude of transitions through which our constitutional orders are passing.

The shift of the forms of representation is paralleled by shifts in the ways they are conceptualized, apprehended, and experienced from emotional, cognitive, and affectual viewpoint. Thus, the range of constitutional imaginaries of representation is changing. The constitutional polycrisis and constitutional polytransition are promoting new imaginaries of representation. These are imaginaries that try to correspond to the global, post-democratic, increasingly digital reality in the context of post-modern deconstruction of truth.

Nevertheless, there is no automatic parallelism between the structural shifts of representative democracy and liberal democratic constitutionalism and the dismantling and reshaping of its supportive constitutional imaginaries. Hence, older beliefs sometimes prove to be of great endurance, whereas novel schemes are at times shaping our understanding of representation ahead of the socio-political and legal developments occurring in the constitutional, legal, and political order. Thus, antiquated and anticipated imaginaries are shaping the constitutional imaginary landscapes together with the mainstream imaginaries of democratic representation.

The interplay between representative democratic imaginaries and the post-representative democracy imaginaries – populist, elitist imaginaries, or technocratic – is another instantiation of 'constitutionalism between magic and deceit'. In that regard, constitutionalism is power game, legal game, but also emotional-affective game and, thus, a game of constitutional imaginaries. The battle for political control includes a fight for control over constitutional imagination and the constitutional conscious, subconscious, and unconscious.

Todays 'fight for law' (*Kampf um's Recht*)[75] is also fight for legal, political, and constitutional imaginaries and imagination, for the hearts and souls of the citizens.

There are signs of tendencies toward a post-representative administrative-technocratic governance. They are part of the overall trend toward a deconstitutionalized future. Hence, we may witness not just changes in the representation imaginaries that may shift from democratic to post-democratic forms. Non-democratic representation and its imaginaries – constitutional, pre-constitutional, or even anti-constitutional – have been the mainstream before the establishment of constitutional modernity and have persisted even during the 'long 19th century' and the 'short X20th century'. Trends toward post-democratic representation are also visible.

What is really challenging is that there might be imaginary representations embedded in post-representative society. In other words, we might be confronted with a brand-new claim of the power holders – to govern not just beyond democracy, liberal democracy, or representative democracy, but to rule without the need to make recourse to representation. Such claim is rather unique in history. It may be justified through (un)constitutional politics of fear. Fear instead of representation, fear management as a replacement of the representative bond between the people and the elites, fear as legitimation of technocratic governance that is not justified by democratic or even traditional autocratic, aristocratic, elitist, or theological schemes of representation may be the game changer of the game of political representation. Thus, dark constitutionalism grounded on politics of fear may produce new constitutional imaginaries for a post-democratic, post-representative, and post-truth society.

Hence, the mission of contemporary constitutionalists is to try to better understand the representative democratic imaginaries as a still predominant form of constitutional imagination. The proper knowledge of the democratic, pre-democratic, and post-democratic imaginaries of representation is of vital importance for sustaining representation, and its democratic forms as key legitimation strategies of government. The tendencies toward post-democratic and even post-representative governance can be understood and eventually remedied mainly on the basis of deconstruction and subsequent reconstruction of representative democracy as phenomenon of constitutional imagination with strong projections in symbolic-imaginary, visual, performative, and emotional constitutionalism.

75 See Rudolf Von Jhering, *Der Kampf Um's Recht* (Nabu Press 2010) 1–106.

2 Programmatic government beyond conceptual distinctions[1]

Zoran Oklopcic

1. Representative democracy: between dichotomies and trichotomies

To this day, most citizens of modern industrial societies think of 'Western democracy' as a pleonasm: If the system of government is truly a 'democracy' what else can it be but 'western'? What else can a 'Western' government be, if not a 'democracy'? What is still pleonasm to the citizens of present-day Western societies, to their future historians may look like an oxymoron. To some those future historians would be right not because Western democracies suddenly became so undemocratic in the second half of the 2020 that it no longer made sense to think of them as democracies, but because they've never been democracies in the first place. Rather than 'representative democracy', claims Frank Ankersmit, a far more accurate name the family of the regimes that the citizens of Western societies live under would be 'elective aristocracy chosen by the people'.[2]

To those who think of this system as exposed to the onslaught of populist, authoritarian, and other illiberal forces, however, this 'aristocracy' appears as something else: (1) an inherently fragile, yet precious achievement of Western societies; (2) an improved version of a system that proved unable to survive a prolonged economic crisis, attenuated class conflict, and unresolved national question, which collapsed under the onslaught of totalitarian movements; (3) the descendent of a system adopted by the countries that emerged from the collapse of Russian, German, and Austrian empires after the end of the First World War; (4) a system shaped by the lessons drawn from the collapse of parliamentary democracy in continental Europe between two world wars; and

1 This chapter is produced as part and funded by the European Union-NextGenerationEU, through the National Recovery and Resilience Plan of the Republic of Bulgaria, project No bg-rrp-2.004-0008.

2 Frank Ankersmit, 'What if Our Representative Democracies Are Elective Aristocracies?' in Hubertus Buchstein (ed), *Redescriptions: Yearbook of Political Thought, Conceptual History and Feminist Theory* (Verlag Münster) 25.

DOI: 10.4324/9781003610670-4

(5) an insistently liberal form of government, which properly emerged once majority rule became stigmatized under the name of majoritarianism.

What matters more than to pick a side in the contest of these conceptions is to notice a more profound difference between two kinds of thinking about democracy. The one, according to which democracy – together with two other historically existing forms of government monarchy and aristocracy – exists as a member in a trichotomy. And the other, which treats the multidimensional and never fully achievable ideal of democracy as the exact opposite to autocracy. While we think of autocracy as the rule of one and democracy as the rule of many, democracy may equally be understood as the rule of (only) one as well either as the rule of no one or as the rule of the one who rules in the name of the people as its only representative. Neither are democracies in a sense in which we know them: the first resembles anarchy, while the second autocracy. On a view that transcends these difficulties, democracy is the rule of everyone understood as an ongoing process of collective self-government in which everyone who so desires may take a part. Thus understood, democracy is not only the form of representative government that operates in conformity with the principle of majority rule, but also the one which ought to be seen as the embodiment of the ideals of popular sovereignty.

But this is not all. The meaning of representative democracy also hinges on what that democracy, a mental object, stands for: a mere form of government (which Churchill considered to be better than all the rest), or something more than just a form of government – something that American president Joe Biden recently equated with an entire 'way of seeing the world': a way of life that 'defines who we are, what we believe and why we do what we do' as – as Biden put it – 'Americans'. Unlike Churchill's, Biden's democracy is 'democratic' not because it has been sufficiently democratized, but because it is something for which 'too many' have sacrificed 'too much' for too long for it to be abandoned. Its institutions deserve to be revered, assisted, and defended, not just accepted as legitimate and obeyed, even though 'democracy' in question refers to something that cannot be critically evaluated. In that context, 'democratic' functions as an official call to arms: calling on those who already have a moral duty to obey the edicts of democratic institutions to support and assist them, as well as be ready to come to their defense not because they are legitimate, but because they are supremely valuable.

There is nothing wrong with Biden's conception of democracy—except that it would seem distinctly odd to anyone who wanted to know not what demoracy in the abstract is, but what democratic *governments* are, or could possibly be *for*.[3] Inspired by the latter understanding of democracy, this chapter

3 Democracies are oftentimes critiqued for their failure to 'deliver'. Is delivering a bonus, or is delivering in the description of democratic governments? Still, democracies that fail to deliver are no less legitimate than those that do. Were it any other way those who seek to make its organs more responsive to the manifest preferences of obvious majorities would probably be

aims to show what's wrong with the definitional approach to the conceptualization of representative democracy, or (to put it in more positive terms) to see what might be gained were we to resist the temptation to consider the problems of actually existing representative democracies through the lens of definitions.

2. Majority rule and counter-majoritarian institutions

A fitting beginning in that inquiry is the concept of the majority rule. While most of those who approach the notion of 'majority rule' as the self-standing object of scholarly attention tend not to interpret it as a descriptive reference to a situation in which actually existing majorities actually 'rule' most of those who use this term in the context of debates about the differences between liberal and illiberal, majoritarian and consensual, or Westminster and consociation democracy, oscillate between that view and a view that takes for granted not only the actual existence of majorities and the reality of their rule, but also of the minorities as those being ruled over on an ongoing basis, and over a longer period of time.

No similar ambivalence accompanies the notion of 'rule' that appears in 'the rule of law', which simply refers to the cluster of more specific and presumably intimately interconnected normative principles, which legal theorists have no problem articulating, defending, qualifying, and refining. In contrast with majority rule, one is yet to encounter those who'd with a straight face interpret the 'rule' in the 'rule of law' as a reference to an enduring state of affairs in which an actor called Law, like any other actor capable of ruling, rules over others over a longer period of time.

This is important because without clarity about the functions that the terms we use perform it becomes easier to do things that all of us should in principle oppose: give the cloak of general respectability to questionable specifics (so it will be less likely to occur to you that there is no logical connection between the ideal of 'the rule of law' and the rather specific notions of 'judicial independence', for instance) and devalue, reject, or malign perfectly reasonable, intuitive, or desirable propositions by pretending that the conventional names we use to allude to them more broadly actually refer to risky, dangerous, or misguided states of affairs – so that together with the baby water of 'majority rule' (qua, allegedly, the rule of the majority) you end up being morally blackmailed to, for no good reason, start seeing 'popular mandate', 'appeal to the people', or majoritarian decision-making' in bad light).[4]

---

described as radical reformists or institutional experimenters, not dangerous majoritarians or undercover authoritarians.

4 Bernard Manin, Adam Przeworski and Susan Stokes, 'Elections and Representation' in Adam Przeworski and others (eds), *Democracy, Accountability, and Representation* (CUP 1999) 1.

According to Juan Linz, 'the vast majority of the stable democracies in the world today are parliamentary regimes, where executive power is generated by legislative majorities and depends on such majorities for survival'. As a result, he didn't see a problem in the fact that a 'single disciplined party obtains the absolute majority of all seats . . . in what is close to a "winner-take- all" situation.'[5] For Arend Lijphart, the most typical example of this form of Westminster model of majoritarian democracy where an all-powerful 'one-party' cabinet governs with support of 'bare majority', thus keeping the large minority 'excluded' from power and 'condemned' to 'the role of opposition'. As the species of majoritarian democracy, the Westminster model refers to a 'government by the majority of the people', in which majorities govern and minorities oppose.[6] In contrast, consensual democracy is marked by the sharing, limiting and the dispersing of political power.[7] Lijphart embraced 'the consensus model of democracy' as its 'kinder' and 'gentler' version.

But what 'exactly' do such majorities 'win'?[8] If we're talking about parliamentary democracy – in which an idea like this at least makes some remote initial sense unlike in the United States – the winner wins the majority of the seats in the parliament and with it an opportunity to form the government. The only way for it to be logically possible for a minority to which you ostensibly belong to 'next time win the day' is by adding supporters that wouldn't alter its demographic makeup too much over the next four years, which in turn may only exist as a remote possibility if you live in a country with a two-party system where you've voted for one and the same party your entire adult life.

If so, it makes no sense to speak of majority 'winners' and minority 'losers'. The identity of electoral minority – just like the identity of an electoral

5 Juan L Linz, 'Presidents vs Parliaments: The Virtues of Parliamentarism' (1990) 1(4) Journal of Democracy 84–85.

6 Arend Lijphart, *Thinking about Democracy: Power Sharing and Majority Rule in Theory and Practice* (Routledge 2007) 31. In comparison to the cabinet in a parliamentary system, which functions as 'collective sounding boards', the one in a presidential system exists merely as a collection of 'underlings who head departments'. Bert Rockman, 'The performance of presidents and prime ministers and of presidential and parliamentary systems' in Kurt von Mettenheim (ed), *Presidential Institutions and Democratic Politics* (JHU Press 1997) 48. To Bingham Powell, 'the situation in which one party controls the presidency and the other controls the congress seems most comparable to the parliamentary situation of a majority coalition government', even though he admits the inherent difficulty of talking about 'the majority status of incumbent governments' in presidential regimes such as American (where voters must decide who is more responsible for good and bad outcomes that involve their interdependent powers'); Bingham G Powell, *Elections as Instruments of Democracy: Majoritarian and Proportional Visions* (Yale UP 2000) 57–58.

7 Arend Lijphart, 'Presidentialism and Majoritarian Democracy: Theoretical Observations' in Juan Linz and Arturo Valenzuela (eds), *The Failure of Presidential Democracy* (The JHU Press 1994) 92.

8 For Linz's acknowledgment of the conceptual problems associated with the notion of winner take all elections, see Juan L Linz, 'Presidential and Parliamentary Democracy: Does it Make a Difference' in Juan L Linz and Arturo Valenzuela (eds), *The Failure of Presidential Democracy* (The JHU Press 1994) 14.

majority can only be established retroactively – in light of the political composition of a majority that will have ended up supporting a new government in the parliament. Rather than being 'condemned', the parliamentary minority that finds itself in the role of opposition performs a function that is constitutive to the very idea of parliamentarism: to keep the government accountable, help improve the quality of legislation by actively participating in parliamentary debates, and, in so doing, prepare to step in as a new government should the existing one lose confidence in the next general elections.

Even when the government's program reflects the electoral promises of the ruling parties, at least three things remain sufficiently obscure(d) to make the idea of 'majority rule' plausible: (1) the extent to which electoral promises actually motivated the electoral choices of voters, including those of the electoral majority; (2) the extent to which those whose voting choice was motivated by electoral promises also interpreted those promises in a self-regarding/self-interested fashion; and (3) the extent to which those who voted for the parties of the governing majority continue to support them or their policies.

For those skeptical of majoritarianism, prime ministers can count on firm majority support in the legislature to overhaul infra-constitutional rules such as electoral laws in order to 'engineer an overwhelming parliamentary majority' that allow them to take over the courts in the next step, and soon thereafter the constitutional order as a whole. In contrast to the counter-majoritarianism of presidential democracy, parliamentary democracy 'allow[s] for perfectly legal institutional transformations that gradually establish authoritarianism' due to the relative weakness of its checks and balances.[9]

The question that remains unanswered by those who today see parliamentarism, not presidentialism as most likely to succumb to authoritarianism is: Why would prime ministers want to go in that direction? We've known why presidents in presidential systems would be inclined to become autocrats, but prime ministers? In a system that operates in conformity with the precepts of parliamentarism, doesn't parliamentary majority provide them with the power they need to see through their program? (The answer of liberal constitutionalists – 'because they are power-hungry' autocrats – is not only crude, but also counter-intuitive and in stark contrast with the sophisticated methods that they employ to seize absolute power. What those who affirm the superiority of the American system of checks and balances reject, according to Bruce Ackerman, is the notion 'that a single electoral victory is sufficient to vest plenary lawmaking authority in the victorious political movement'.[10]

In such a regime, a party that 'wins big' at one time may have to win n times more before it can gain 'plenary lawmaking authority'. This may be either

9 Max Steuer, 'Authoritarian Populism, Conceptions of Democracy, and the Hungarian Constitutional Court: The Case of Political Participation' (2022) 26(7) The International Journal of Human Rights 1207.

10 Bruce Ackerman, 'The New Separation of Powers' (2000) 113(3) Harvard Law Review 633, 650.

because the electoral majority, which the legislative majority reflects, is difficult to achieve, or it may be because the electoral system makes the translation of electoral majorities into legislative majorities more difficult. Or because the electoral system renders the possibility of translating electoral majority into a legislative majority conceptually impossible. This, in turn, may be due either to the norms that make the composition of the law-making organs, dependent on the factors other than election, or the norms that make the composition of the law-making organs dependent on the results of the elections. From the perspective of the majority of the electorate as a whole, such elections will appear not just staggered, but overlapping and partial. Rather than to simply deny the sufficiency of a single victory, such elections reduce the contestants' chances of winning big (enough), as well as their ability to predict what winning big enough might possibly mean when it comes to whom to support, whom to attack, and whom to defend. The point is not that the system staggered elections makes it more difficult to translate electoral into legislative majorities, or that it makes it more difficult to determine the composition or the magnitude of sufficiently numerous electoral majorities, but that it renders the ideal of majority rule in the American context unintelligible.

An electoral system that regulates the composition of the most important state organs according to different schedules and independently from the results of the elections is unable to specify time t, from which it would be, in retrospect, possible to determine whether party A only reached legislative majority at t+1 because it couldn't transform its electoral majority into a legislative one, or because it didn't even have an electoral majority to begin with. From the perspective of a system used for the purposes of leadership (selection in the executive) and of membership (selection in the legislature), the American system of government is majoritarian. From the perspective of law-making, it is neither counter-majoritarian nor complexly majoritarian but anti-majoritarian. Those who accept this conclusion might be happy to leave it at that. But those interested in the fate of representative democracy as a form of government which is either parliamentary or presidential need to confront the question which naturally present itself next: If the institutions that are distinctive of presidential democracy are not really counter-majoritarian, in which sense is parliamentary democracy, on the whole, 'majoritarian'?

3. Beyond (simply) representative government

Parliamentary government is treated as an instance of majoritarian democracy without distinguishing between the role that the principle of majority plays at different stages in the production of general legal norms (periodic reorganizations of government): (1) at the stage of election, i.e., the stage of the determination of the composition of the legislature, (2) the stage of the leadership – selection, which in the presidential systems is (a) the stage of the election of the chief executive, and which in the parliamentary systems is (b) the stage of the appointment or the election of the prime minister and his cabinet.

In *Reference Re Secession of Quebec*, majority rule appears as the 'key pillar of democratic governance', which mandates 'that public decisions are made by popular majorities . . . whose votes all count equally'. In defining Canadian democracy as 'a political system that transcends simple majority rule', the Supreme Court of Canada unwittingly affirmed its majoritarian character: what confers 'legitimacy on the efforts of the government of Quebec to initiate the Constitution's amendment process in order to secede by constitutional means' is not simply the will of the people of Quebec but the clear expression of a '*clear majority* of Quebecers that they no longer wish to remain in Canada'.[11] In contrast with most other liberal-democracies, however, Canadian constitutional order is (1) sensitive enough to register large-scale shifts in what David Easton referred to as 'diffuse support' for the 'regime as a whole' among the population of Quebec; (2) irritable enough to be 'triggered' to react by a credible indication about the extent of popular support for secession among the people in Quebec; (3) responsive enough to react to the expression of such desire by entering into constitutional negotiations, which may result in the significant restriction of Canada's spatial and personal jurisdiction, wouldn't have been possible had the Supreme Court, as an organ of in charge of interpreting its constitution not been as (4) liberal-minded enough about the meaning the foundational concepts of modern democratic state and liberal constitutionalism in comparison with the approaches taken by other liberal democracies in similar situations – as well as relatively more (5) relaxed about the possibility that a successfully negotiated independence of one province might not doesn't put an end to a nation-wide constitutional crisis, but rather provide an impetus for the next round of territorial fragmentation.[12]

11 *Reference Re Secession of Quebec* [1998] 2 SCR 217, para 92.

12 The expression 'popular majorities' might allude not only to the majorities that are representative of the will of a sovereign people, but also to the majorities that are indicative of something which is popular in, to pardon the pun, popular sense: as something which, as Pierre Bourdieu reminds us, occurs 'with appreciable frequency and over long durations'. On this view, un-popular is popular with a minus sign: something that is either almost impossible (or unwise) to ignore and that deserves to be cared about, because the consequences of not paying attention to the actions, functions, and transformations – of something that is otherwise expansive, frequent, or enduring – may be grave. This sense of the term seems to be implied in the scholarly references to 'decent measure of popular commitment' as something that a 'constitutional liberal democracy' must enjoy in order to survive; or 'sustained popular consent' as something without which, as Stephen Holmes reminds us, a liberal constitution cannot claim moral authority; or to 'long nascent aspirations for popular governance' that, in Samuel Issacharoff's view, might be endangered by outlawing political parties that enjoy a fair amount of popular support. See Pierre Bourdieu, 'You Said "Popular"?' in Alain Badiou and others (eds), *What Is a People?* (Columbia UP 2016) 36; Stephen Holms, *Passions and Constraint: On the Theory of Liberal Democracy* (The University of Chicago Press 1996) 10; Samuel Issacharoff, *Fragile Democracies: Contested Power in the Era of Constitutional Courts* (CUP 2015) 1. If so, the popular in popular government may be a reference not only to the government of the people, for the people, and by the people, but may also be a reference to a constitutive bet of certain forms of democratic government: that things that are well liked,

'Government' may also refer to what the occupants of those offices do.[13] On this view, 'government' is a reference to the totality of the activities of governing, which – in the basic sense of the word – seems closest to the activity of steering: i.e., to manipulating the instruments at one's disposal, in order to ensure that a governed vehicle stays on course, proceeds according to schedule, continues along the path, and within the safe bounds, which (on even closer inspection) includes the determination of destination and of the limits to tolerable, acceptable, bearable deviations.[14]

Like in amendment, the suffix **-MENT** in government (in '*gouvernement*') is an allusion to the activity of governing, in the same way in which the suffix -tion in administration alludes to the activity of administering. Like a pilot, a government governs by steering. But a pilot pilots . . . the ship. But what does the government govern? Figuratively, the ship of the state. What the government 'governs' is a ship that stands for a state, not the state. Or if you wish, a state-shaped ship. It is with this object of governing that we have to reckon with when we are presented with the notion of a representative government

highly regarded, and widely supported will by and large be popular because they will have deserved to be popular: not because they've been dumbed-down or rendered simplistic, but because they've been usefully simplified; not because they've been expressed in vulgar terms, but because they've been articulated in an honest and straightforward manner; not because they are cheap and crude, but because they are quickly accessible and easy to use; not because they are vulgar or plebeian, but because they can be enjoyed by everyone. In that sense, the 'popular' in popular government is not necessarily a reference to a system in which the people 'have' constituent power, or in which the authority of government 'originates' in the 'will' of the people, or to the fact that sovereignty ultimately 'belongs' to the people, as the author of the constitution. Rather, the 'popular' in popular government points to the heightened baseline responsiveness of political institutions. From that perspective, both monarchies and republics may in principle be seen as popular forms of government. Such government is popular because it strives to ensure popular support and crafts policies that reflect popular preferences, but makes no attempt to justify its existence with references to popular sovereignty. The popular character of popular government hinges not on its verbal commitment to the ideals of popular sovereignty, but on how it behaves when confronted with events that indicate that it might no longer be enjoying the support of the people at large. What makes a popular government popular, in more specific terms, is its readiness to interpret massive displays of popular dissatisfaction as a reason to test the degree of popular support it enjoys ahead of schedule, by holding fresh parliamentary elections, and accept the outcome, which would either renew its mandate to govern, or bring in a government supported by the majority of the people at large. A government that acts in such a way submits not to the 'will' of a sovereign people, but to the 'verdict' of the people at large. He government which is popular in that sense is not only a constitutive attribute of liberal democracy but is also the common denominator that allows us to speak of both republics as well as monarchies as authentically liberal-democratic forms of government, even though the latter cannot possibly be seen as the institutional realizations of the principle of popular sovereignty.

13 On government as the activity of government, in the mold of civitas and universitas, respectively, see Martin Loughlin, *The Idea of Public Law* (OUP 2004) 16–17.

14 For the elaboration of the concept of government, from the vantage point of steering; an activity that most resembles governing in its basic sense, see Karl Deutsch, *The Nerves of Government: Models of Political Communication and Control* (Free Press 1963) 182.

in its territorial state and face the notion of representative government. But a state-shaped ship is neither a government nor the state. Public administration, public service, as the extension of government, perhaps? Or with 'government' as the collective organ, of that service, in the shape of a territorial state?

To speak about organs – instead of bodies it speaks of a body that is organized, a body that is the outcome of organization, about a body that contributes to an organization, or a body that functions to an organization: the configuration of offices, whose occupants, in fulfilling their tasks produce results on an ongoing basis, and in conformity with expectations. To speak of those organs, as bodies, or of organizations as institutions is to make it less likely for others to ask: what do they do, how, and why? The thing that is made to function can be repaired or improved. The thing that cannot be repaired or improved is the one that appears to act but cannot or should not be made to serve a function. The one that can't is something inanimate that we've personified. The one that shouldn't is something that's alive: something that cannot be improved in order to make things better. To make things better is only possible by new institutions, for which to become possible the ones that exist must first die.[15]

'Responsible government consists of the responsibility of ministers to parliament. This may be called in a very loose and, again, ambiguous sense a parliamentary system, that is, a system based on the parliamentary support of government . . . designed as a control for the people . . . [not] by the people. . . . [While] A responsible government need not respond beyond its technical responsibility [a] responsive government is, instead, a government that is required to yield to demands . . . one can speak of a democratic party only when the emphasis shifts from responsibility to responsiveness'.[16] Responsible government became 'responsive' precisely because parties supplied the channels for articulating, communicating, and implementing the demands of the governed, which is what parties are for.[17]And in turn: a government 'is

15 Is democracy a 'form' or the 'system' of government? How are they different? Something is a system if it displays properties that do not belong to a separate consideration of its component elements and if it results from, and consists of, the patterned interactions of its component parts, thereby implying that such interactions make the system bounded. Giovanni Sartori, *Parties and Party Systems: A Framework for Analysis* (ECPR Press 2005) 39. In more detail, the foregoing implies (1) that there must be such an interdependence of parts or variables that the resulting relationships have an 'order', so that not just anything can happen; (2) that this order must tend to self-maintenance; and (3) that the self- maintenance in question includes the maintenance both of the boundaries and of the 'distinctive relationships of the parts of the system within the boundary' (Sartori (n 17) 41). For a distinction between 'self-destroying', 'non-viable', 'viable', and 'self-enhancing' systems, see Deutsch (n 16) at 249. For the sociologist's imagination of societies as systems, see P Rosenthal, *Words and Values: Some Leading Words and Where They Lead Us* (OUP 1984) 195.

16 Sartori (n 17) at 19.

17 Sartori (n 17) at 21. According to Bernard Manin, representative democracy is a 'system in which public policies and decisions are made subject the verdict of the people, i.e., to the 'retrospective appraisal' of the electorate, conceived as a 'judge'. Bernard Manin, *The Principles of Representative Government* (CUP 1997) 192.

representative in the narrow ("mandate") sense if it adopts the policies preferred by the specific majority by which it was elected . . . or it is representative in a broader ("top cycle") sense as long as it pursues the interests of any majority. . . . A government is "responsive" if it adopts policies that are signaled as preferred by citizens. . . . Governments are "accountable" if citizens can discern representative from unrepresentative governments and can sanction them appropriately, retaining in office those incumbents who perform well and ousting from office those who do not'.

Accountability is inseparable from the evolution of British parliamentarianism, which emerges as a direct corollary of the overarching political maxim 'no taxation without representation'. Those who are about to be taxed not only have a right to be represented, but also have a right to know whether government spends the raised funds the way it committed itself to, before it obtained the agreement of their representatives. Unlike the British prime minister, the American president is not really accountable to anyone. He can only be 'repudiated' (or indirectly 'shellacked' if his party suffers losses in the midterms that lead to its loss of control in the legislature).[18]

An accountable agent ought to be ready to articulate: the task(s) he performed on the principal's account; specific instruction(s) he received from the principal; concrete acts performed in the pursuit of those tasks; the extent to which those acts conformed with the instructions; the reasons for failure to perform the tasks undertaken; or the reasons to comply with the principal's instructions. As Waldron put it, 'individuals and minorities don't have the formal power to throw politicians out of office, [b]ut they may have a right to embarrass them with questions' – something, which in his view is 'often politically (and electorally) consequential', due to the 'reputational and "legacy" considerations' of elected politicians, not to mention 'pride, vanity, honor, distinction, and an awareness of one's place in history' of their nations.

Though such sentiments should never be underestimated, they do deserve to be put in their proper place, especially since it is all but manifest that the highest offices of the state long ceased to be seen as the final stops on a long journey toward the summit of sociopolitical order. Rather, it seems more reasonable to think of them as episodes that – in the context of a career that moves forward by meandering between public and private sector – may easily be surpassed by those that are more lucrative and satisfying. Waldron ignores this because he seems to assume that the situational barriers that foster accountability in the private sector – i.e., low when it comes to entry into but high when it comes to exit from profession – also exist in the context of electoral politics.

18 The main factor that contributes to the plausibility of accountability is the government's 'clarity of responsibility'. In that department, according to Powell, the US government fares extremely poorly, in good part due to the governing party cohesion'. Powell (n 8) at 67.

What 'accountability' might mean under circumstances where that assumption doesn't hold becomes obvious once we consider the fate of one George Osborne, who quickly leveraged the time spent as the chancellor of the exchequer in the cabinet of David Cameron, to gain a number of highly lucrative advisory positions in various financial institutions and commercial enterprises worldwide. As is the case with most high-ranking electoral losers in 'Western liberal democracies', Osborne suffered no reputational damage for the austerity policy that Cameron's government inflicted on the poorest segment of the British population. Instead, he was confronted with a hardly agonizing choice of whether to accept a lucrative consultancy gig in the private sector, take on a well-paid job in a nongovernmental sector, join a highly paid bureaucratic job in some international organization, or simply retreat to the level of local politics, maybe spend some time as a mayor, or a regional governor, and bide time plotting the triumphant return to the national stage.

Not only do political theorists overestimate the pull of the reputational considerations, but they also neglect the fact that at certain professional levels the difficulty of making the kinds of professional or career transitions that would allow one to escape reputational cost begins to diminish. In underestimating the attractive power of external incentives, they invariably underestimate not just the short-term effects of succumbing to them, which take the form of corrupt behavior and personal enrichment, but also the long-term ones that may not necessarily cause immediate material damage or financial loss to public interest, but which may eventually still prove to be far more harmful, extensive, and long-lasting.[19]

Languages such as Serbo-Croatian also lack a corresponding word for accountability. Instead of accountability, the closest reference to the responsibility is 'odgovornost', which depending on context may also be used as a reference to civil liability or criminal responsibility. Closest to accountability in that language is 'uračunljivost', a word that in English translates as *mens rea*, which as a specialist term belongs to criminal, not constitutional law. As is the case with 'accountability', distinctly Anglo-American 'rotation in office' and 'alternation in power' have no terminological equivalent in the vocabularies of non-Anglophone parliamentary democracies. There, the closest cognate to rotation and alternation is (for lack of a more artful word) removability of those in power (*'smjenjivost vlasti'*). From the perspective of this ideal, the purpose of the elections is not only to ensure that those who no longer enjoy the support of the people at large be removed from power, but also that they be replaced by those who do.

19 Example: drafting friendly private-sector legislation, which ends up depriving the state of significant tax revenue, which makes the state dependent on suboptimal services, which over time makes the state more incompetent, etc.

4. Accountable representative governments: parliamentary v. presidential

Though it's increasingly treated as the distinguishing feature of democracy as such, the functioning of accountability can hardly be imagined outside the realm of parliamentary government, especially if one envisions it as 'the system of committees', with the people as the committee of the state itself, the parliament as the committee of the people, and the government appearing as the committee of the parliament.[20] Visually, we may imagine the centripetal polity in a pyramidal shape, broad at the bottom and narrow at the top, with myriad connecting routes leading up, down, and across representative bodies stretching from the electorate at the base to the cabinet and prime minister at the apex. Led by the prime minister, parliamentary government 'directs the affairs of the country until its party support disintegrates [and] not merely execute and administer, as people who think in American terms are prone to assume'.[21] To speak of such government as remaining 'in power' as long it enjoys the confidence of the parliament is true but misses its central constitutional obligation: to act in accordance with a comprehensive, anticipatory, long-term, large-scale, and relatively detailed plan of action intended to benefit the people as a whole and which ought to be judged by the positive difference its implementation made in the life of the people. The program in question is the program of a government that in the interest of the people at large governs a country – not the one that we habitually, but counterintuitively, refer to as 'of', 'for', and 'by the people'. In parliamentary monarchies the content of such a program is typically presented to the parliament in speeches that the monarchs, in the name of 'their' governments, deliver 'from the throne' themselves.[22] In parliamentary republics, however, the content of similar speeches tends to be delivered either by a prime minister immediately after the appointment by a head of state or by a person who holds the title of the candidate for the position of the prime minister typically ahead of the parliamentary vote of confidence.

While the constitutions of parliamentary monarchies tend not to mention the purpose of the monarch's speech from the throne, in the majority of the

20 Carl Schmitt, *Constitutional Theory* (Duke UP 2008).

21 CJ Friedrich, *Constitutional Government and Democracy* (Revised edn, Blaisdell Publishing) 369.

22 For throne speech as 'a forum for agenda setting' and 'a direct means to signal its executive and legislative priorities and set the national agenda', see Will Jennings, Shaun Bevan and Peter John, 'The Agenda of British Government: The Speech from the Throne, 1911–2008' (2011) 59(1) Political Studies 74, 94. Unlike the annual addresses that the US presidents deliver on the 'state of the union', the aim of the prime ministerial speeches that precede the votes of confidence is not to convey a backward-looking appraisal of the country's overall condition ('the state of our union is strong!) but to s . . . degree to which government achieved its program, justify failures to do so far, and outline what remains to be done to fulfill the objectives envisaged in the existing plan of action, or use an opportunity to seek support for a modified one.

constitutions of contemporary parliamentary republics the programmatic character of a speech delivered by the candidate for the position of prime minister is made fully explicit. Such program is a sequential plan of activities, which involves ongoing anticipation, organization, regulation, invigilation, calculation, and adaptation, and whose implementation therefore cannot be reduced to the activity of legislation. From its perspective, liberal-democratic parliamentary republics have more in common with non-democratic developmentalist regimes such as Chinese than with the democratic ones such as American. Or: the program is more than the totality of government's policies. Its content reflects considerations about the effects of government's policies on each other, and their implications for relevant populations, the sequence of more specific actions intended to contribute to the realization of those policies, the anticipation of resources to be used for the purpose of their realization, and the mode of their provision, personnel decisions as well as modifications in the structure of government, including territorial reorganization or the establishment of brand new institutions.

In the US context, Congress appears in three guises, as a diplomatic **PARLEY**, a farmer's **MARKET**, and an aristocratic **COURT**. The first is a place where those that have been 'sent' to Washington by their constituents gather not as the representatives of the people, but as the ambassadors of their constituencies, whose task is to broker a mutually acceptable settlement, which – in the phraseology of American government – includes activities. The second is a place where the members of congress were explicitly 'sent' by the voters to 'work' in the interest of their constituents, and whose 'first and main duty', as James Bryce reports, is to 'get the most they can for their constituencies, either 'out of treasury or by means of legislation' (in by means of pork-barreling, log-rolling, and horse-trading). Finally, the third is a place where one goes to ask for, promise, and exchange favours, make plots, and spread gossip, not like the representatives of the people, but more like self-interested courtier-bureaucrats.[23]

Unlike in Britain – where both Parliament and the cabinet 'move in the full view of the people, who sit as arbiters, prepared to be judged in any controversy that may arise' – Congress is destined to descend into 'petty localism' since there will be no one vested with sufficient AUTHORITY to resist the 'mischief' of legislators. In contrast with the confidence that the head of government receives from the parliament, the pseudo-constitutional 'mandate' that the people allegedly bestow upon the American president as a winner in an electoral contest is merely a mandate to speak for the nation, not a mandate

23 For skepticism about the systemic character of the presidential-parliamentary divide, see Jose Antonio Cheibub and Zachary Elkins and Tom Ginsburg, 'Beyond Presidentialism and Parliamentarism' (2014) 44(3) British Journal of Political Science 515.

to govern.[24] In contrast to 'a popular prime minister [who] may carry Parliament . . . to effect some sweeping change',[25] the American president is compelled to do business with a 'restless' and 'unworried' legislature, oftentimes inducing him to use patronage as his last effective means of persuasion (ibid., 189), undermining the credibility of the idea of the president as the only authoritative mouthpiece of the people, and inevitably making him appear as (yet another) retail politician, shoring up his re-election prospects, by throwing it on swing-states and spending it on districts represented by loyal allies.[26]

The fact that throughout their term in office they operate under two mutually exclusive expectations – to implement the partisan agenda on the basis of which they won the election, yet embody and represent the people as a whole, without distinction – ends up exposing them to an ongoing temptation to portray the political opponents of the second as the enemies of the first. Such a system doesn't just encourage messianic posturing, but also incentivizes the candidacies of outsiders, who – in contrast to modern parliamentary regimes – are more likely to appear in the guise of mavericks and underdogs in the imaginary of presidential democracy.

The idea that a successfully adopted piece of legislation could ever count as an achievement 'simply in virtue of being adopted'; that this 'achievement' can be attributed to the head of executive alone; that the totality of such achievements can, should, or will be the measure of that official's overall 'success'; that there is a preciously memorable aspect of his achievements that will count as his legacy; or finally that the pursuit of that legacy may legitimately be prioritized at the expense of the projects that, at a particular point in time, are in the best interest of the people at large – remains completely alien to the logic of the parliamentary system of government. While he may plead, propose, exhort, demand, veto, appoint, and command, the American president must proceed in a piecemeal fashion, negotiate with Congress 'constantly and carefully', must be willing to compromise, and be ready to pare down policy priorities.[27] The root of the difficulties this actor has when it comes to 'accomplishing [his] agenda', or getting 'support to implement [his] policy'[28] lies not in a constitution that denies him not 'plenary lawmaking authority'[29] but

24 Fred Riggs, "Presidentialism versus Parliamentarism: Implications for Representativeness and Legitimacy" (1997) 18(3) International Political Science Review 253, 267.

25 James Bryce, *The American Commonwealth* (Liberty Fund 1995) 252.

26 See Douglas Kriner and Andrew Reeves, *The Particularistic President: Executive Branch Politics and Political Inequality* (CUP 2015). For presidential mandates and elections that shape the national agenda, see Patricia Conley, *Presidential Mandates: How Elections Shape the National Agenda* (Chicago UP 2001). For presidential 'program' in the American context, see Andrew Rudalevige, *Managing the President's Program: Presidential Leadership and Legislative Policy Formulation* (Princeton UP).

27 Robert Elgie, *Political Leadership in Liberal Democracies* (Bloomsbury Publishing 1995) 127.

28 Scott Mainwaring, 'Presidentialism in Latin America' (1990) 25 Latin American Research Review157, 162.

29 Ackerman (n 12) at 650.

plenary authority to outline a comprehensive plan of action, seek support for its terms, and – on the basis of the support received – take measures toward its implementation.

Rather than 'to attain great common ends by securing a good government', the main aim of the American Constitution is, as AV Dicey put it, to avoid the evils that any government might inflict on 'individual citizen[s]' or on 'pre-existing communities'. As a result, the problem of how to achieve 'harmonious and efficient action among those who devise it and implement it' doesn't even present itself, since the American Constitution renders the very idea of policy 'in the European sense' unintelligible.[30] Rather than the alternative, American presidentialism is better understood as the negation of British proto-parliamentarism – an 'antithesis to the "immature" form of parliamentary government'.

30 Bryce (n 27) at 476. For Kelsen, 'parliamentarism is the only realistic form in which the idea of democracy can be fulfilled within today's social reality' – with 'parliamentary majority principle' proving to be not only 'perfectly suited to preventing class rule', but also fully 'compatible with protection of minorities'. Hans Kelsen, 'On the Essence and the Value of Democracy' in Arthur Jacobson and Bernard Schlink (eds), *Weimar: A Jurisprudence of Crisis* (U of California P 2001) 96. As a result, he considered the presidential form of a republic as more autocratic than a 'republic with collegiate government' in which 'the democratic element is comparatively stronger'. Hans Kelsen, *The General Theory of Law and State* (Harvard UP 1949) 301. Since such republics almost invariably feature a parliamentary system of government, most contemporary scholars refer to them as 'parliamentary'.

3 Framing political processes through constitution-based symbolic representation

*Matija Miloš**

1. Introduction

During the COVID-19 pandemic, two terms had gained constitutional significance in Croatia: "pandemic" and "epidemic". The reason for the increased import of the two was not grounded only in the spread of the virus, but in the state's response to it. The governing majority in the Parliament consistently adopted human rights restrictions related to the virus as if they were not measures taken in extraordinary circumstances.[1] The Croatian Constitution provides that, in certain cases, one of them being natural disasters, the Parliament must adopt any human rights restriction with a qualified, two-thirds majority.[2] As the governing majority had refused to do this, a citizen-initiated referendum spearheaded by a political party of the opposition tabled the inclusion of two terms, "pandemic" and "epidemic", into the relevant constitutional provision. The expectation was that the addition would embody the will of the people by which the Parliament would be incentivized to adopt human rights restrictions with a two-thirds majority.

At the core of this conflict was a clash between two visions of vulnerability, which only partially had to do with the pandemic.[3] On the one hand was the

* This chapter is produced as part of and funded by the European Union-NextGenerationEU, through the National Recovery and Resilience Plan of the Republic of Bulgaria, project No bg-rrp-2.004-0008.

1 Đorđe Gardašević, '"Business as Unusual": Pandemic Concentration of Executive Powers in Croatia' (2021) 12 Pravni Zapisi 91 <https://scindeks.ceon.rs/Article.aspx?artid=2217-28152101091G>; Đorđe Gardašević, 'Pandemija i Ustav Republike Hrvatske' (2020) 6623 Novi Informator 1.

2 The Constitution of the Republic of Croatia, Official Gazette No 56/90, 135/97, 8/98 [pročišćeni tekst], 113/00, 124/00 [pročišćeni tekst], 28/01, 41/01 [pročišćeni tekst], 55/01 [ispravak], 76/10, 85/10 [pročišćeni tekst] and the Amendment to the Constitution of the Republic of Croatia, (citizen initiated referendum) Official Gazette No 5/2014 Decision of the Constitutional Court SuP-O-1/2014 (hereinafter: The Croatian Constitution) Art 17(1).

3 Sanja Barić and Matija Miloš, 'Mapping the Constitutional Terrain of Vulnerability in the COVID Pandemic' (2022) 43 Zbornik Pravnog fakulteta Sveučilišta u Rijeci 431 <https://hrcak.srce.hr/279918>.

DOI: 10.4324/9781003610670-5

idea that it is democracy, bolstered by fundamental rights, that is exposed to the vicissitudes of the pandemic and that the two-thirds majority is an important safeguard against its loss.[4] Those arguing against the requirement of a two-thirds majority essentially argued for the vulnerability of the executive power, vulnerability to scrutiny of the public mediated through the Parliament. For them, it was essential that the executive power has as much space for action as it would in any regular circumstance. Regularity and routine were goods to be preserved.[5] The constitutional amendment proposed through the citizens' initiative was an intervention into this dispute, supporting the first vision, the idea that an increased democratic consensus would help avert the vulnerability of individuals to the powers of the state.

When it declared the attempt to amend the Constitution unconstitutional, the Croatian Constitutional Court found that the amendment could not represent the informed will of the voters.[6] It is possible to read this finding narrowly, as a problem of legitimacy, where the unpredictable consequences of a referendum lead to the unconstitutionality of the question.[7] A more interesting take, and one I will explore here, is that cases like these pose a broader issue. They ask us to think about what it means to construct the law, here a constitutional amendment, as a vehicle for political representation.

In the most recent literature on "far-right newspeak", furthering illiberal aims using legal language has already been identified as a relevant problem.[8] These contributions demonstrate how legal concepts can be instrumentalized to further political projects that may to some extent, or completely, depart from ideals enshrined in a constitution. What I propose here is to study the use of the law, particularly the constitution, as a representational device. This is both narrower and broader than the exploration of how liberal discourse may be abused for illiberal aims. It is narrower because it focuses on cases in which the law is posited as a symbolic political representative. It is broader in that it is not restricted only to illiberalism but seeks to outline and investigate a practice that may be motivated by different interpretations of (il)liberalism. In the contemporary studies on illiberalism, it has already been noted that a

4 Gardašević, 'Pandemija i Ustav Republike Hrvatske' (n 2).

5 Marinko Jurasić, 'Omejec: "Na izvanredno stanje ne treba ni misliti, a kamo li ga zazivati!"' (*Večernji list*, 2020).

6 Decision of the Constitutional Court of the Republic of Croatia U-VIIR-2180/2022 of 16 May 2022.

7 Matija Miloš, 'Ustavnosudski nadzor jasnoće referendumskih pitanja' (2020) 20 Hrvatska i komparativna javnas uprava 128, 761 <https://hrcak.srce.hr/249224>.

8 See, in particular, Timea Drinóczi and Agnieszka Bién-Kacała, 'The Transition from Liberal to Illiberal Constitutionalism in Poland and Hungary: The Language of Rights and Equality' in A James McAdams and Samuel Piccolo (eds), *Far-Right Newspeak and the Future of Liberal Democracy* (Routledge 2024); Frank Wolff, 'When Legal Language Meets Apocalypse Anxiety: Democracy, Constitutional Scholars, and the Rise of the German Far Right After 2015' in A James McAdams and Samuel Piccolo (eds), *Far-Right Newspeak and the Future of Liberal Democracy* (Routledge 2024).

practice-based focus is valuable, as it allows a more detailed contextual interpretation.[9] By bringing our attention to the use of law in symbolic political representations, we may better understand how the use of legal language to support particular illiberal outcomes may in fact be a representational practice rather than only a perversion of legal interpretation. As a practice, symbolic political representation through law draws on (constitutional) legal imaginaries that may be used for both liberal and illiberal aims. In the broadest terms, they may be used to frame a political process, affecting its surroundings without necessarily intervening into its core. It is my ambition here to enable this form of reading of the constitution's representative role.

In the next part of this chapter, I will outline some of the cases where the law may be deployed as a representative sense (Section 2). I then focus on the constitution in particular, suggesting that its possible use as a representative device can be explored as a case of symbolic political representation (Section 3). The penultimate section of the chapter will focus on exploring how representative claims tailored from legal fabric may produce incidental effects due to the way they recreate a constitution's characteristics in a political claim (Section 4). In particular, I argue that such a claim may draw upon the notions of agency, hierarchy, stability, boundary, failure, and clarity intertwined with constitutional imaginaries.

2. The politically representative law

In order to begin exploring the representative role of the constitution, I first want to provide an outline of the scenarios that may involve the representative role of law. An understanding of how and when law may play the role of a political representation helps in clarifying the contribution of my argument to the already existing scholarship on "newspeak". Furthermore, it helps in recognising the relevance of the law's representative role in different legal and political contexts.

It should be noted at the outset that my argument deals only with cases involving claims that the law represents in a political sense. Political representation is a complex concept, but, for the purposes of this chapter, we may adopt Hannah Pitkin's definition, according to which "to represent" is to make something present that is in reality absent.[10] In this sense, representation may include all kinds of procedures that generate the presence of someone or something.[11] What is key, however, is that there must be an attempt to generate the presence of the represented in a political sense. Hence, a reading of the

9 Marlies Glasius, 'Illiberal Practices' in András Sajó, Renáta Uitz and Stephen Holmes (eds), *Routledge Handbook of Illiberalism* (Routledge 2022) 339.

10 Hannah Pitkin, *The Concept of Representation* (U of California P 1967) 8–9.

11 Jane Mansbridge, 'The Evolution of Political Representation in Liberal Democracies' in Robert Rohrschneider and Jacques Thomassen (eds), *The Oxford Handbook of Political Representation in Liberal Democracies* (OUP 2020) 18.

law that departs from any axiology, whether liberal or not, does not in itself fall within the scope of this chapter, unless it also involves a claim that the law is in some sense representative.

As events of high political significance often involve a legal change, referendums are conducive to claims that the law is representative. My example of the unsuccessful Croatian referendum on adding the terms "epidemic" and "pandemic" to the Constitution is a case in point. This referendum was not only a response to the much-criticised practice of adopting extraordinary human rights restrictions without a two-thirds parliamentary majority. The referendum organisers also wanted to resist an earlier decision of the Constitutional Court, in which the Court had provided the Parliament with the power to decide whether a human rights limitation is extraordinary or not.[12] The claim was that the referendum result, the constitutional amendment, represents the actual political will of the citizens. As such, the referendum was expected to persuade the parliamentary majority to yield and start adopting human rights restrictions with a two-thirds majority.

At the core of the dispute concerning the representative role of the amendment involved was a different understanding of what representation means. For the Constitutional Court, the representative process was a highly legalistic endeavour. Not only did the Court confine it to the Parliament and once again reiterated that the Parliament has the power to choose whether there are extraordinary circumstances that demand a two-thirds majority.[13] It also found that the voters were misinformed about the referendum's possible outcomes, as the referendum organisers did not explain the impact of the Court's earlier decision to the general public.[14] This is the very same decision that was one of the causes of the referendum initiative in the first place. By contrast, the three dissenting judges argued that the referendum campaign sufficiently informed the electorate. They have thus argued that the signatures provided by citizens in favour of calling for a referendum were sufficiently informed and that the referendum result would be representative of the voters' "constituent will".[15] However, as this was a minority position, the referendum was never held, although it has had no legal effect that should have made it unconstitutional.

Referendums involving the representative role of the law have been frequent in Croatia. Ten years prior to the failed referendum on adding the terms

12 Decision of the Constitutional Court of the Republic of Croatia U-I-1372/2020 and Ors of 14 September 2020, Official Gazette No 105/20, para 28.

13 Decision of the Constitutional Court of the Republic of Croatia U-VIIR-2180/2022 of 16 May 2022, Official Gazette No 61/2022, para 11.1.

14 Decision of the Constitutional Court of the Republic of Croatia U-VIIR-2180/2022 of 16 May 2022, Official Gazette No 61/2022, para 15.1.

15 Decision of the Constitutional Court of the Republic of Croatia U-VIIR-2180/2022 of 16 May 2022, Official Gazette No 61/2022, joint dissent of judges Kušan, Selanec, and Abramović, ch 2.

"pandemic" and "epidemic" to the Constitution, another citizen-initiated referendum amended the Constitution. The amendment included the definition of marriage as a union of a man and a woman into the fundamental act. The definition had existed earlier as part of the Family Law Act. Its introduction into the Constitution was organised by a conservative social movement.

Interpreting the constitutionality of the referendum, the Constitutional Court penned a passage that warns against a "systemic constitutionalisation", in which broad swathes of legislation are incorporated into the Constitution. Nonetheless, the Court found that exceptions to this are possible. According to the Court, if a piece of legislative matter is a "deeply rooted cultural and societal characteristic" it may be incorporated into the Constitution.[16] The identification of a "deeply rooted characteristic" is of course extremely controversial, as defining such characteristics and providing them with legal consequences is a political issue. It could be persuasively argued that they should remain outside the scope of the Constitution precisely so that they may be politicised through regular democratic processes. The Court, however, did not consider this, but found that defining marriage as a heterosexual union is a "deeply rooted characteristic" of Croatian society. The definition of marriage, in addition to being a part of the law, already codified as such in the Family Law Act, became representative of an imagined societal core.

Similar issues have emerged in other Croatian referendums that I will not explore in detail here. For instance, in some of the referendums that dealt with socio-economic matters, the problem was the representative quality of a legal change that aimed at a prohibition of a particular policy. The Court here had found that such a change is problematic as it would permanently lock out public policy options from the scope of the powers wielded by the Parliament and the executive. The Court reached this finding although it was not supported by law, but by its evaluation of the possible political impact of a referendum.[17] In a referendum that was about prohibiting the display of the script of a national minority, the problem was the attempt to make a piece of legislation represent the emotions invoked by those advocating for the prohibition. Although the Court found the advocated legal change unconstitutional, it did acknowledge the limited legitimacy of the emotional charge read into the referendum project.[18] This delayed the application of the relevant law to a part of the country particularly affected by the Homeland War and, by consequence, made the position of the Serb national minority more precarious.

16 Notification of the Constitutional Court of the Republic of Croatia concerning the citizen initiated constitutional referendum on the definition of marriage No SuS-1/2013 of 14 November 2013, Official Gazette No 138/2013, para 9.1.

17 Matija Miloš, *Ustrojstvo i učinak građanskih inicijativa u kontekstu koncepta predstavljanja* (Sveučilište u Zagrebu 2019) 240 <https://dr.nsk.hr/en/islandora/object/pravo%3A2153>.

18 Decision of the Constitutional Court of the Republic of Croatia in U-VIIR-4640/2014 of 12 August 2013, Official Gazette No 104/2014 (correction) paras 10.2 and 13.1.

It is unsurprising that referendums offer a chance to posit the law as a representation. On the most fundamental level, they are regularly juxtaposed to representative democracy.[19] As exceptions to political decision-making exercised by elected representatives, they are also perceived as exceptions from political representation that nonetheless must be politically relevant. Their precarious position calls for legal regulation, one that may also be used to discipline the use of referendums and prevent them from deviating from regular representative politics.[20] It is thus possible to claim that referendums involve a conflict over representation.[21] In such conflicts that heavily involve the law, it is only to be expected that the representative role of the law would come to the forefront.

Nonetheless, law may be interpreted as a political representation even in contexts that do not involve the voters or political decision-making as overtly as the referendum does. A (constitutional) court may be one arena for constructing such representations. At first glance, to make this claim is to ignore the standard role of a judge, being as they are empowered to interpret and apply the law and not involve themselves in political representation outside, possibly, election disputes. However, according to Minkkinen's interpretation, the judiciary cannot be isolated from political activity, particularly when it is interpreting fundamental rights. As he convincingly argues, human rights are never completely set down in law.[22] While restrictions on human rights are a regular topic of legislative activity, fundamental rights always transcend these limitations, and any legal codification for that matter. The political nature of fundamental rights may be heightened when the courts are empowered to strike down legislation, majoritarian decisions, as constitutional courts regularly are. Thus, there is in this respect nothing inherent to the judiciary and constitutional courts that would completely exclude them from propping up the law as a political representation.

Examples for representative images of the law produced in the (constitutional) judicial arena can be drawn from the literature on what Gargarella calls "dialogic justice". The debate revolves around the courts' enforcement of social, i.e. positive, rights.[23] The courts set the standards that the legislature

19 Leah Trueblood, 'Are Referendums Directly Democratic?' (2020) 40 Oxford Journal of Legal Studies 425.

20 Patrick Taillon, *Le Référendum Expression Directe de La Souveraineté Du Peuple? Essai Critique Sur La Rationalisation de l'expression Referendaire En Droit Comparé* (Dalloz 2012).

21 Matija Miloš, 'Reimagining Direct Democracy as an Intersection of Different Forms of Representation' (2020) 11 Pravni Zapisi 69 <https://scindeks.ceon.rs/Article.aspx?artid=2217-28152001069M>.

22 Panu Minkkinen, '"Enemies of the People"? The Judicary and Claude Lefort's "Savage Democracy"' in Matilda Arvidsson, Leila Brännström and Panu Minkkinen (eds), *Constituent Power. Law, Popular Rule and Politics* (Edinburgh UP 2022) 34, 39.

23 Roberto Gargarella, 'Dialogic Justice in the Enforcement of Social Rights: Some Initial Arguments' in Alicia Ely Yamin and Siri Gloppen (eds), *Litigating Health Rights: Can Courts Bring More Justice to Health?* (Harvard UP 2011).

must meet to ensure the fulfilment of its obligations under the constitution. The courts here need not be the only involved stakeholders. They may employ “complex remedies” involving other actors, such as civil society associations, that inform the court’s work and ruling.[24] In the process, courts effectively turn social rights into demands justified by the needs of those affected by the deprivation of interests protected by social rights. For example, courts in a variety of jurisdictions have formulated the minimum standards the state should meet in ensuring the right to water.[25] In this manner, those whose social rights are violated become represented before the political branches of power through the social rights made relevant by the courts.

This is not to say that other legal constructs may not be used as representations. Constitutional identity, for one, is not only a concept used by constitutional courts to construct what is inviolable in a constitution, but, particularly in the European Union, to engage in “constitutional dialogue”.[26] At its core, the dialogue is about a legal concept and, particularly in the European Union, it is plausible to claim that it can be exercised only insofar as it conforms to the Union’s constitutional identity.[27] However, it is also true that the construction of a constitutional identity of the Union is not without its pitfalls.[28] This, along with the practice of constitutional courts that deploy the argument not in the spirit of dialogue but as a political trump card, demonstrates that constitutional identities have a layer that can be interpreted as a practice of symbolic political representation.

If, however, legal concepts that escape complete legal codification open the space for symbolic political representation, the constitutional courts are not the only ones able to act in this space. With human rights in particular, other actors, such as civil society associations and individual citizens, may argue that such legal provisions represent in a political sense. This is because, at its core, to claim that a human right is being violated, is to claim that one is not an equal member of a political community.[29] Hence, the invocation of

24 Gaurav Mukherjee, *Complex Remedies in Social Rights Litigation* (Central European UP 2023) 29–30 <https://sierra.ceu.edu/record=b1447768>.

25 See, for example, Inga T Winkler, ‘The Human Right to Water’ in Stephen C McCaffrey, Christina Leb and Riley T Denoon (eds), *Research Handbook on International Water Law* (Edward Elgar Publishing 2019).

26 Federico Fabbrini and András Sajó, ‘The Dangers of Constitutional Identity’ European Law Journal <https://onlinelibrary.wiley.com/doi/abs/10.1111/eulj.12332?af=R>; Julian Scholtes, *The Abuse of Constitutional Identity in the European Union* (OUP 2023) 51–82.

27 Timea Drinóczi and Pietro Faraguna, ‘The Constitutional Identity of the EU as a Counterbalance for Unconstitutional Constitutional Identities of Member States’ (2022) 4 European Yearbook of Constitutional Law 57.

28 Jakob Gašperin Wischhoff, ‘A Plaidoyer Against the Sisyphean Endeavour to Imagine the Constitutional Identity of the EU’ (2022) 4 European Yearbook of Constitutional Law 25.

29 Eduardo Gill-Pedro, ‘Claiming Human Rights: The Reflexive Identity of the People’ in Matilda Arvidsson, Leila Brännström and Panu Minkkinen (eds), *Constituent Power: Law, Popular Rule and Politics* (Edinburgh UP 2022) 143; Elviro Aranda Álvarez, ‘Poder Democrático y

a fundamental right also involves a vision of the community of equal citizens that is then represented through human rights claims. The argument based on fundamental rights that has representative dimensions can thus be articulated in a bottom-up fashion in the public arena. An example of this are social movements directed towards reforms of existing law, which may include specific articulations of fundamental rights as a desirable path forward.[30]

The openness of representative arguments that involve the law is essential as, when open-textured constitutional norms are used for this purpose, they may help disturb legislation and associated relations of power that narrow the realization of constitutional promises.[31] At the same time, however, the representative potential of these provisions can be used to lock out alternatives. Constitutional provisions can be interpreted as political projections that ignore or negate any contrary legal substance and supersede all political alternatives to them. For instance, Sajó argues that the shifts towards illiberalism in some states are performed without constitutional amendments, often with a series of apparently technical changes to the law and with the aid of a "constant popular mobilization", achieved by specific representations of the nation and those that threaten it.[32] In Hungary in particular, the Fundamental Law of 2011 contains a substantial "ideological part" that refers to a wide variety of symbols attached to the effective ruler.[33] The place of "the people" in this regime is mediated through "manipulated" representations generated by those in power, involving "cultural stereotypes".[34] In short, a use of symbolic representations, sometimes associated with law and its interpretation, is noticeable in such states.

As Sajó argues, what is involved is an "emotional image, a kind of emotional constitutional representation for society as well as a new constitutional subject".[35] Insofar as liberal constitutionalism involves emotions as well, symbolic representations associated with them can be relevant in democracies that do not veer towards illiberalism.[36] Indeed, some form of symbolism is intrinsically tied to the notion of "the people" at the heart of any democracy, and the interpretative spaces it opens may be one of the reasons for the success

Derechos En Una Sociedad En Crisis' in Ignacio Gutiérrez Gutiérrez (ed), *La democracia indignada* (Editorial Comares 2014) 46.

30 George Meszaros, *Social Movements, Law and the Politics of Land Reform* (Routledge 2013).

31 Josep Maria Castellà Andreu, 'Las Enseñanzas Del Tiempo Transcurrido, o de Cómo La Democracia Representative Sigue Siendo Imprescindible' in Ignacio Gutiérrez Gutiérrez (ed), *La democracia indignada* (Editorial Comares 2014) 152.

32 András Sajó, 'The Constitution of Illiberal Democracy as a Theory About Society' (2019) 208 Polish Sociological Review 395, 398.

33 Sajó (n 32).

34 Sajó (n 32) 401.

35 Sajó (n 32) 409.

36 Sajó (n 32) 410.

of illiberal narratives.[37] Hence, to explore the case of symbolic representations channelled through law, or, rather, law as channelled into a symbolic representation, is to shed light on what Belov calls "symbolic-imaginary" constitutionalism,[38] made particularly relevant by illiberal democracies but not exclusive to them. It is to engage with the way different actors, from citizens in the exercise of their political rights, across (elected) politicians in the political branches of power to (constitutional) courts use the representative image of the law to reimagine politics. To better map the operation of this practice, I now turn to the concept of symbolic political representation.

3. The representative role of the constitution through the lens of symbolic representation

As the case of Croatian referendums teaches us, to use the constitution as a representation is not a process internal to the law, i.e. it cannot be identified with interpretation as a search for legally disciplined meaning. It is not limited to what Belov calls "textual constitutionalism".[39] The law is projected as a representative of a broader whole not restricted to it. The aim is to produce an extra-legal effect, sometimes despite the limited legal impact of the law concerned. This, in a nutshell, is a case of symbolic representation. To better understand its operation, we should first look at what symbolic representation entails (Section 3.1), then how such representation may draw from law as a resource (Section 3.2).

3.1 Symbolic representation as a political representation

In her seminal work on political representation, Hanna Pitkin differentiates between "acting for" and "standing for" representation. In the former case, a representative acts for the represented.[40] Where "standing for" representation is concerned, a representation emerges not from the actions of the representative but from their presence, describing the features of the represented or symbolising them.[41] Symbolic representation would usually be defined as "standing for" representation. As the brief overview of some of the Croatian

37 Zoran Oklopcic, 'The Illiberal Potential of the People' in András Sajó, Renáta Uitz and Stephen Holmes (eds), *Routledge Handbook of Illiberalism* (Routledge 2022) 221–22.

38 Martin Belov, *Constitutional Semiotics: The Conceptual Foundations of a Constitutional Theory and Meta-Theory* (Hart Publishing 2022) 118.

39 See more broadly on the different understandings of constitutionalism in Martin Belov, 'Constitutional Semiotics as a Post-Positivist and Post-Modern Approach to Constitution and Constitutionalism Based on the Linguistic, Visual and Emotional Turns' in *Research Handbook on Legal Semiotics* (Edward Elgar Publishing 2023) <https://www.elgaronline.com/view/book/9781802207262/book-part-9781802207262-15.xml>.

40 Pitkin (n 10) 113.

41 Pitkin (n 10) 60–111.

Constitutional Court's case law demonstrates, the law may be considered to "stand for" something else, as a symbol of something that transcends its limits.

To represent in this fashion, however, may be problematic. Pitkin argues that a symbol assumes a "natural connection" between what is represented and the representation.[42] It is meant to invoke particular "emotions and attitudes" in relation to the represented.[43] Symbolic representation as such does not necessarily require a rational, argument-based debate, as may be the case with acting for representation, since the symbol is able to single out and mobilise a particular public in any case.[44] For instance, the definition of marriage tabled in a referendum described earlier had as its aim the mobilisation of the conservative segment of the electorate against minority rights without having to make this explicit.

It may be an obvious point that, if the constitution's representative role is concerned, it is going to be a form of symbolic representation, being as it is that the law cannot "act for" another. However, in order for a law to be representative of something, its representative role must be constructed. This, in turn, requires symbol-making, it requires someone to posit the law as a symbol, to make it "stand for" the represented and, in doing so, to construct the relevant audience for this symbol.[45] The use of symbolic representation does not necessarily foreground these activities, but they still must exist in order for something to "stand for" in a representative sense.

If symbolic representation requires action, we need a way to think about the actions involved in the production and placement of symbols. The constructivist theories of representation, in particular Michael Saward's work on the representative claim, may be of use here.[46] At the core of Saward's approach is an interpretation that moves us away from what we have learned to identify with political representation in law: the election of representatives. Saward argues that representation should be explored as a "dynamic, shifting and elusive" interaction.[47] His theory is that of a "dynamic and creative" representation, one that is not necessarily constrained to institutional forms.[48] This approach is as such useful to explore the use of the law as an instrument of political representation.

42 Pitkin (n 10) 95.

43 Pitkin (n 10) 96.

44 Kristian Stokke and Elin Selboe, 'Symbolic Represention as Political Practice' in Olle Törnquist, Neil Webster and Kristian Stokke (eds), *Rethinking Popular Representation* (Palgrave Macmillan 2009) 66.

45 Gerhard Göhler, 'Political Representation - Reconsidered' in Paula Diehl and Alexandre Excudier (eds), *La 'représentation' du politique: histoire, concepts, symboles* (CEVIPOF - Centre du recherches politiques de Sciences Po 2014) 24.

46 Michael Saward, *The Representative Claim* (OUP 2010).

47 Saward (n 46) 1.

48 Saward (n 46) 3.

As Belov argues, to deal with "symbolic imaginary" constitutionalism, one needs to think of it as a bridge, a complex and composite bridge, between constitutional imagination and other "constitutional discourses".[49] Saward's theory of the representative claim lends itself to this project, as it is open to a multitude of ways one may imagine and posit the role of law as a representative, as well as its relationship to other constitutional discourses. It is a theory geared towards asking how the representative is "constructed", what representation "does".[50] As such, it allows us to open our thinking to a variety of institutional and extra-institutional actors who may attempt to posit the symbolic representation of the law and who participate in its making. It allows us to disassemble such claims and explore their operation, their interface with constitutional imagination on the one side and other interpretations of constitutionalism on the other. In this, we are empowered to explore what the claim of the law's representative role does. As any innovative theoretical enterprise, Saward's theory is subject to critique.[51] I do not claim that it is without its challenges, nor will I engage in a debate about its limitations in the abstract. Here I only want to borrow Saward's framework for exploring political representation.

In Saward's understanding, exploring representation requires us to focus on what he calls "the representative claim" rather than on institutional arrangements in which representation normally takes place. In a nutshell, the representative claim is an assertion made by an actor about a representative relationship that is received and evaluated by an audience. Each representative claim consists of five segments: the maker, the subject, the object, the referent, and the audience.[52] The maker is the creator of a representative claim. The subject is posited by the claim to represent something or someone. The object is that which is being represented, and it is a selection of some of the features of the represented. Everything that is outside the object, not contained in the representative claim, remains in the referent. Finally, the representative claim is directed to a specific audience.

The example of the referendum on the pandemic measures in Croatia may help illustrate how this theoretical framework may be mapped onto a situation related to this chapter. The organisers of the referendum (makers) presented an amendment to the law (subject) as a representation of the electorate's will to change how the human rights restrictions were adopted (object). The referent is the actual electorate, and the primary audience of the claim is the Parliament. The Constitutional Court's members engaged with this claim. The majority in the Court denied it any representative valence, restricting

49 Belov, *Constitutional Semiotics* (n 38) 126.

50 Saward (n 46) 10, 13, 32.

51 See, for instance, Howard Schweber, 'The Limits of Political Representation' (2016) 110 American Political Science Review 382.

52 Saward (n 46) 36.

representation strictly to the Parliament. In doing so, the majority in the Court actually designed a claim of their own, in which the Parliament (subject) was made representative of the electorate's will on the matter of human rights restrictions (object). The dissenter's view was, on the contrary, that the representative claim encapsulated in the constitutional amendment accurately represents the electorate.

This brief example demonstrates how Saward's representative claim theory helps us describe in more detail what occurs when someone attempts to construct the law as a symbolic political representation. It is important to underline that the theory is first and foremost a descriptive framework.[53] It is thus not my aim to claim that symbolic representation that has the law at its core is necessarily democratic or undemocratic, liberal or illiberal, but to provide a space to think more closely about the interface of symbolic representation and the law. This is valuable in that it does not necessarily condemn symbolic representation as undemocratic. Indeed, some have already argued that symbols can play an inclusive role in a democracy, representing the underrepresented and helping generate new spaces for them in political life.[54] The values often incorporated in a constitution, such as equality, may have a similar symbolic role, in addition to their instrumental value as enforceable legal structures. Furthermore, this approach can help in rethinking the role of constitutional law in the current circumstances. As "populist immediacy" is a growing phenomenon already touched upon in this volume, one that makes political life more a series of apparently unmediated events not necessarily reflected in a legal change, movements that in a sequence gradually transform a representative regime rather than a clean, momentous break with some imagined past, we need a framework to think about the law's symbolic role in these circumstances.

3.2 The law as a resource of symbolic political representation

In constitutional law and constitutional theory more specifically, "symbolic legislation" and "symbolic constitutionalisation" are already well-known concepts. Here I want to draw from those earlier contributions to explore how law may be used as a resource in constructing representative claims.

Let me begin with Marcelo Neves' excellent account of symbolic constitutionalisation. In his book, Neves investigates the symbolic role of constitutions, one that exists independently from the normative force of the law.[55] Hence, even where constitutions contain provisions that are not enforced and

53 Saward (n 46) 32.

54 Emanuela Lombardo and Petra Meier, 'Good Symbolic Representation: The Relevance of Inclusion' (2018) 51 PS: Political Science & Politics 327 <https://www.cambridge.org/core/product/identifier/S1049096517002451/type/journal_article>.

55 Marcelo Neves, *A Constitucionalização Simbólica* (Editora Academica 1994) 32.

may even at first glance be considered mere window-dressing, Neves argues that such constitutional elements may perform important symbolic roles. This symbolic influence may become far more important than the legal meaning of the law when the constitutions, faced with exceeding societal complexity, can no longer respond with a normative force. Thus, the theory Neves presents in his book is a theory of the political and broader social effects of the constitution.

Neves builds his theory in part on the German theory of symbolic law. This theory attributes a symbolic role to all law. Neves, like Luhmann, draws a difference between symbolic and instrumental effects of the law, dealing dominantly with the role of the former.[56] The theory Neves draws and ultimately departs from is the idea that all law is symbolic in that it provides a common point of identification, an ideal representation of institutions, integrating the society to which the law is applied.[57] According to Göhler, this understanding is a "second layer" of representation, on which what we normally take representative democracy to mean relies. This second, deeper layer emerges from common experiences of a polity, "functional and often unconscious values, which to some extent are not rational".[58] Göhler points to the idea of "existential representation" as the expression of this understanding of representation, an idea developed most famously by Eric Voegelin, Gerhard Leibholz, and Carl Schmitt.[59] As Loughlin argues, representation is in this view essential to the existence of the state's institutions.[60] Again, here the idea is that the symbolic representation stands at the foundation of a state, offering resources that bring together the institutions of the state into existence and bind the individuals within a state together.[61] There are in this sense clear parallels between this understanding of symbolic representation and Belov's symbolic-imaginary constitutionalism.[62]

Another concept relevant to the theme of this chapter is "communicative legislation" or symbolic legislation in a positive sense. The concept was developed in part as a critique of interpreting symbolic legislation as derelict instrumental law that ultimately produces symbolic effects along with certain negative instrumental effects, such as the confirmation of a "value system

56 Neves (n 55) 28–29.
57 Neves (n 55) 28.
58 Göhler (n 45) 22.
59 Göhler (n 45); Gerhard Leibholz, *Das Wesen Des Repräsentation* (Walter de Gruyter & Co 1960); Eric Voegelin, *The New Science of Politics. An Introduction* (Chicago UP 1987).
60 Martin Loughlin, 'Representation and Constitutional Theory' in Paul Craig and Richard Rawlings (eds), *Law and Administration in Europe. Essays in Honour of Carol Harlow* (OUP 2003).
61 Max Lerner, 'Constitution and Court as Symbols' (1937) 46 The Yale Law Journal 1290, 1298.
62 Belov, *Constitutional Semiotics* (n 38) 131.

defended by a particular group".[63] It is thus not identical to the way Neves used the symbolic legislation concept. The symbolic legislation in this sense also does not refer to sources of law that encapsulate foundational experiences of a polity. Instead, communicative legislation includes laws and parts of laws that have been intentionally crafted to foster communication and are expressive of higher values in a polity.[64] Unlike instrumental laws, which are often ridden with sanctions unless the law's addressees comply with it, communicative legislation relies upon broad, often value-based mandates that are supposed to frame an interaction within a community to which such legislation is directed.[65] This legislation is deployed when the legislature is faced with a complex or ideologically divisive subject matter and frames such matters in values of "a high moral standard".[66] It is thus considered preferable for the state to leave room for self-regulation of the law's addressees.

The concept of communicative legislation overlaps to some extent with the idea that there is a symbolic representation at the core of all constitutional orders. This is because the communicative legislation constitutes a community that is meant to develop its meaning and enforce it and also because it draws upon the values essential to a community.[67] However, unlike the symbolic representation of an "existential" character, the communicative community established by law is a matter of legislative design. While it may well express values at the core of a polity, the legislature sets up the framework to realize them, working from the perspective of textual constitutionalism more than that of a presupposed "existential core" of a state.

In the framework of this chapter, the different senses of the symbolic dimension of the law and its communicative role are useful in that they show how the law serves as a repository of meanings. Those making representative claims that involve the law must situate themselves in relation to these meanings. With communicative legislation in particular, the legislator creates a range of topoi, sources of arguments, that can be deployed in developing the meaning of the law.[68] The legislature here prepares the terrain for future representative claims involving the law. This is particularly significant for the constitution as a legal act, because constitutions often contain broad and aspirational norms.[69] With the symbolic representation at the core of a legal order, the way it is

63 Bart Van Klink, 'Symbolic Legislation: An Essentially Political Concept' in Bart Van Klink, Britta van Beers and Lonneke Poort (eds), *Symbolic Legislation Theory and Developments in Biolaw* (Springer 2016) 21.

64 Van Klink (n 63) 24.

65 Willem Witteveen and Bart Van Klink, 'Why Is Soft Law Really Law?' (1999) 14 RegelMaat 126, 128–29.

66 Witteveen and Van Klink (n 65) 138; Van Klink (n 63) 27.

67 Witteveen and Van Klink (n 65) 129.

68 Witteveen and Van Klink (n 65).

69 Sotirious A Barber, 'Fidelity and Constitutional Aspirations' (1997) 65 Fordham Law Review 1757.

imagined and presented may impact the spaces and the modes of deploying arguments from representation, including the arguments that present the law as a representational device. In this sense, the law is a resource that actors constructing representation can draw upon and not only a constraint. Because of this, however, it is possible to project interpretations that fly in the face of the instrumental facet of the law. The Croatian referendum on marriage is one such example in how it enabled the constitutionalisation of the term "marriage" based on what it represented, despite the express anti-discrimination structures contained in the Constitution.

When we think of the law as a resource, we may first think of how it helps bolster some actors in making representative claims rather than others. Indeed, there are some actors, particularly the bearers of institutional roles within a constitutional order, who are authorised to imagine and thus to project representative claims that encapsulate these imaginings.[70] For some of them, most notably constitutional courts, we expect that their expertise will prevent them from abusing this privileged position. Others, such as parliaments, may be held accountable for their work at elections. The symbolic representation of law as a foundation of representative politics may serve to establish some representations and challenge others. For instance, the idea that the parliament is the central representative of the electorate and the sole bearer of the legislative power may downplay claims formulated outside it.[71] Hence, the law in this sense does not only provide scaffolding for institutions but allows them, to some extent, to reshape the rhetorical terrain.

Secondly, the law serves as a resource in that representative claims may contain it, using it as a representation of an object. For instance, it can be claimed that a numerical threshold legally enshrined as a condition for a national minority to have their script displayed in public represents the presence of a vibrant minority community.[72] The claim here selects one aspect of an object, the number of members of a group in a certain locale, and projects it as a claim of political representation. Any representation must necessarily be a work of selection, where some features of the referent, here a group of citizens belonging to national minorities, are placed under the political limelight. Representative claims that forefront the law or are couched in its framework are no exception. If this is the case, however, we must ask what the specific effects of representative claims that draw upon the law, particularly the constitution, are, as the constitution may already incorporate selections of its own.[73] I turn to this in the next part of this chapter.

70 Belov, *Constitutional Semiotics* (n 38) 119.

71 Decision of the Constitutional Court of the Republic of Croatia in U-VIIR-1159/2015 of 8 April 2015, Official Gazette No 43/15, para 33.2.

72 See, for instance, The Croatian Constitutional Law Act on the Rights of National Minorities, Official Gazette No 155/02, 47/10, 80/10, 93/11, Art 12(1).

73 Jiří Přibáň, 'On Legal Symbolism in Symbolic Legislation: A Systems Theoretical Perspective' in Bart Van Klink, Britta van Beers and Lonneke Poort (eds), *Symbolic Legislation Theory and Developments in Biolaw* (Springer 2016) 118–19.

4. The imaginative dimensions of constitution-based representative claims: framing political processes

I have concluded the previous section of this chapter by suggesting that the law may be a resource for representative claims in two senses. First, it may empower and restrain the maker of a representative claim. The debate on the constitutionalisation of the right to abortion that is taking place in different jurisdictions may be read in these terms as a struggle to legally restrict the legislature from making unbound claims of representation about women's bodies. On the other hand, the law can also serve as a resource in that it can be turned into an actual representative, a symbol of something or someone else. This was the case with the Croatian referendums on marriage and the pandemic, with both being about a segment of the legal system representing a vital societal structure and the citizens respectively.

It is important to avoid a conflation between interpreting the law and using it as a political representation. When the law is recreated in the latter sense, the image projected is not necessarily in line with what a mind disciplined in law would produce. There would otherwise be little to gain by looking at the law through the lens of the representative claim. As the emerging scholarship on "right-wing newspeak" teaches us, those using legal language to represent may depart from its legal core.[74] These departures do not need to be illiberal. For instance, we may invoke the constitutional definition of the state as a welfare state in order to claim that it represents the interests of those who are homeless, even though there may be no immediate standing for a homeless person to sue the state. Were we to ignore this, the political dimension of the law-based representative claim, the insistence on the creativity and the flexibility of representation, would collapse into a search for legal meaning. On the contrary, a claim of political representation may attempt reading into the law meanings that would be either unconstitutional or constitutionally irrelevant but not necessarily illiberal.

There is a clear tension between presenting a constitution as a representational image and interpreting a constitution as a legal act.[75] As noted throughout the chapter, to emphasise the former may lead to warping or casting aside the law's binding frame. The tension becomes less obvious if there is an overlap between the maker's institutional power to interpret the constitution and the representative claim. Recall, for example, the case of representing the interests of another through judicial interpretation of social rights. The central problem is that a court must not take an openly political role. However, insofar as the representative claim is merged with the act of interpretation and it manages to present itself as a matter of an abstract constitutional principle within the

74 A James McAdams, 'Far-Right Newspeak and the Fragility of Liberal Democracy' in A James McAdams and Samuel Piccolo (eds), *Far-Right Newspeak and the Future of Liberal Democracy* (Routledge 2024) 10.

75 Robin West, 'The Aspirational Constitution' (1993) 88 Northwestern University Law Review 241, 244.

purview of the courts, it may be less likely to be seen as a representative act. The political dimension of the claim will more easily remain restricted to the legislature responding to the court's findings. Thus, the ability of the claim's maker to couch it in legal doctrine will be essential for its impact.

The tension between a constitution as a representation and a constitution as a legally binding act is not merely a matter of different roles assumed by the makers of representative claims. It reveals an underlying imaginative dimension of representative claims that invoke the constitution, one involving agency. To illustrate this, we may once more revisit the two Croatian referendums involving the claim that the Constitution represents in some sense.

Both in the case of the COVID-19 referendum and the marriage referendum, the ability of the different actors to act politically and be free from extraneous political influence has been at stake. In the COVID-19 referendum, the representative claims advanced by the referendum initiative and the Constitutional Court represented the political agency of "the people" differently. The majority in the Court identified the electorate with a legal creation that can only perceive the Constitution as a legal act. In consequence, the representative image of the Constitution can only display the imagination of the Constitutional Court. In contrast, the supporters of the initiative and the three dissenting judges identified "the people" with the notion of a democratic majority with the power to overrule the Constitutional Court by the amendment that represents them. Although the Constitution was at first glance the identical subject of both representative claims, its interplay with the referent of the claim, the people, was imagined differently. This difference was made manifest in the different images of the claim's object, the will of "the people". In the case of the marriage referendum, when the definition of marriage was framed as a core societal feature, the agency to politically challenge its status was limited while apparently empowering the electorate to include it into the Constitution.

The examples of the two representative claims demonstrate that the immediate point of the claim is not only to politically represent something or someone, but to draw from constitutional imaginaries to reframe a political process. In the case of the two referendums, the representative claims draw from two images of the constitution. One image reflects the constitution as it is conceptualised in constitutionalism stemming from the United States. The constitution is a sacrosanct formal structure superseding all politics and apparently exhausts all possibility of political agency beyond it.[76] In the other image, while the constitution still frames political projects, its meaning is ultimately responsive to the reasoning of the electorate and does not completely condition their agency. The interpretation grounded in this other image both acknowledges

76 See an exploration and critique of this interpretation of constitutionalism in Martin Loughlin, *Against Constitutionalism* (Harvard UP 2022).

the primacy of the institutions of the state in interpreting constitutional mandates while providing the space for political action to the electorate.

In both cases, to invoke the constitution as the subject of a representative claim both empowers and effaces the maker of the claim. The image of a constitution reflects a variable constitutional framing that can be expanded to become an all-encompassing structure of political and even societal processes, all the while remaining only an apparent core of a broader whole. Its invocation can offer the maker of the representative claim powerful resources to imagine and direct the course of political processes. At the same time, especially if the constitution is seen as an almost mechanical structure that operates independently of any one actor, a representative claim drawing from it can hide its maker from view. The resulting claim can imbue its context with impersonality, inevitability, and certainty grounded in the apparent legal character of the constitution even though the constitution's legal meaning may diverge from the representative claim.

The use of the representative claim to impact political agency and to enable its maker to alter the appearance of their presence did not emerge with illiberalism. It is part and parcel of legal constitutionalism, with its emphasis on the judicial reconstruction of constitutional norms.[77] Again, the institutional limits of the judiciary and constitutional courts limit the power of these actors to make representative claims. Other actors, particularly political actors broadly conceived, from citizens to their elected representatives, have more freedom in making representative claims and thus deploy the images of the constitution in the process. The challenge at this juncture is that some institutional actors may make such claims all the while completely identifying them with the interpretation of the constitutional norm. Such is currently the case in Croatia, where the president of the Republic has repeatedly refused to acknowledge the validity of the Constitutional Court's interpretation, advancing his own vision of constitutional meaning.[78] This fundamentally relies on the same logic of representative claims made by (constitutional) courts but does away with any tempering of this power through law.[79] Symbolic political representation then

77 Alexander Latham-Gambi, 'Political Constitutionalism and Legal Constitutionalism – an Imaginary Opposition?' (2020) 40 Oxford Journal of Legal Studies 737 <https://academic.oup.com/ojls/article/40/4/737/5939843>; Helle Krunke, 'Courts as Protectors of the People: Constitutional Identity, Popular Legitimacy and Human Rights' in Martin Scheinin, Helle Krunke and Marina Aksenova (eds), *Judges as Guardians of Constitutionalism and Human Rights* (Edward Elgar Publishing 2016).

78 '"Prezirem upozorenje Ustavnog suda, neću ga poštivati. Ne mogu mi ništa, imam lukav plan"' (*Jutarnji list*, 2024) <https://www.jutarnji.hr/vijesti/hrvatska/prezirem-upozorenje-ustavnog-suda-necu-ga-postivati-ne-mogu-mi-nista-imam-lukav-plan-15441117> accessed 25 April 2024.

79 On the concept of "tempering power" as the aim of the rule of law, see Martin Krygier, 'Illiberalism and the Rule of Law' in András Sajó, Renáta Uitz and Stephen Holmes (eds), *Routledge Handbook of Illiberalism* (Routledge 2022).

again impacts agency, using the imaginary of the constitution to restrict the scope of its legitimate exercise to select actors, ideas, spaces, and temporalities.

By impacting the conditions for political activity, the constitution-based representative claim of symbolic representation does not only frame political agency, but also allows a different depiction of broader contexts for the exercise of this agency. Here I want to point out five attributes that can be reimagined through the use of such a representative claim: hierarchy, stability, boundary, failure, and clarity. In what follows, I will briefly discuss each in turn, illustrating how, in advancing "the constitution" as the subject of representation, symbolic representation can influence the underlying architecture of politics. They should thus not be scrutinised only for their immediate content, but for the visions of the political terrain they presuppose.

To begin with, constitutions are closely intertwined with the idea of hierarchy. There is little need to belabour this point. It is common knowledge that constitutions are defined as highest sources of law, not necessarily codified, and that they may be accompanied by a civil religion of sorts. It is also common knowledge that a constitution's origin is identified with the constituent power to which the powers established by the constitution are subordinated. Both themes involve a hierarchy that places the constitution at the pinnacle of the state, law, and possibly society.

However, hierarchies are not simple nor undisputable creations. According to Kukovec, it is possible to identify a multitude of hierarchies, all of which rest on the dynamic of injury and recognition.[80] Similarly, a constitution may contain the imaginary potential for many different hierarchies based on the same dynamic. The idea of a constitution being a part or even a source of only a single hierarchy may be a part of a claim that places a particular interpretation of a hierarchical constitution ahead of its competitors. For the Croatian Constitutional Court, an assumption that the Parliament always has primacy in representation in relation to referendums is an example of such a hierarchy.[81] It ignores that there may be cases where it is perfectly legitimate and acceptable to allow primacy to a referendum. Under the right conditions, even human rights, usually not a recommended subject for a referendum, may be reinforced through referendums.[82] By ignoring these possibilities, the Court generates an all-encompassing hierarchical rule that allows it to downplay any

80 Damjan Kukovec, 'Hierarchies as Law' (2014) 21 Columbia Journal of European Law (Online Supplement) 131.

81 See Decision of the Constitutional Court of the Republic of Croatia in U-VIIR-1159/2015 of 8 April 2015, Official Gazette No 43/15 (n 71).

82 Xenophon Contiades and Alkmene Fotiadou, 'The People as Amenders of the Constitution' in Xenophon Contiades and Alkmene Fotiadou (eds), *Participatory Constitutional Change: The People as Amenders of the Constitution* (Routledge 2017) 17; David Kenny, 'The Risks of Referendums: "Referendum Culture" in Ireland as a Solution?' in *Constitutional Change and Popular Sovereignty. Populism, Politics and the Law in Ireland* (Routledge 2021).

representative claim beyond the Parliament without acknowledging any possible alternative.

Secondly, constitutions have much to do with the idea of stability.[83] The aim of a constitution as an artefact is to provide stable foundational norms for political processes.[84] The prerogative of stability may be ensured by conferring the interpretation of the constitution to the judiciary and transforming the constitutional meaning-making into a complex hermeneutic enterprise.[85] Constitutional stability is then identified with judicial interpretation and distance from democratic majorities. It is mediated by law and by the imagined difference between interpretation and change. The specific nature of constitutional change can be further reinforced by introducing special formal amendment rules.[86] Nevertheless, as the Croatian COVID-19 referendum controversy teaches us, the Constitutional Court's interpretation effectively amended the Constitution by adding to the powers of the Parliament. Meanwhile, the Court maintained an impression of stability by refusing the opposing vision of constitutional stability advanced by the referendum initiative.

Constitutions are closely related to boundaries. As Wolin explain, "boundaries signify the will to contextualize" and "contextualization signifies the domestication of politics", with the constitution being "the crucial boundary" in this domestication.[87] When we think of constitutions and boundaries, the ideas of a limited government, ensured by separation of powers and human rights guarantees, come to mind. However, an argument grounded in constitution can draw many different boundaries. The constitution can thus be imagined as a federation of boundaries, with different regimes of enforcement and change. For instance, a constitution may draw a boundary between a form and its content or, more precisely, between different interpretations of form and content. To claim that a particular issue represents a political question may situate it beyond the scope of judicial review, which covers only content of a legal nature. Furthermore, an argument grounded in the constitution may define boundaries between public and private spaces and between different temporalities. For instance, the controversy concerning a possible second referendum concerning Brexit also involved a temporal boundary of the first

83 Peter C Ordeshook, 'Constitutional Stability' (1992) 3 Constitutional Political Economy 137.

84 Mel A Topf, 'Foundation and Revolution: Hannah Arendt and the Problem of Legitimacy and Stability in Constitutional Consolidation' in Richard Albert, Menaka Guruswamy and Nishcal Basnyat (eds), *Founding Moments in Constitutionalism* (Hart Publishing 2019) 54.

85 Aharon Barak, 'Hermeneutics and Constitutional Interpretation' in Michel Rosenfeld (ed), *Constitutionalism, Identity, Difference, and Legitimacy* (Duke UP 1994) <https://www.degruyter.com/document/doi/10.1515/9780822396406-012/html>.

86 Richard Albert, 'Formal Amendment Rules. Functions and Design' in Xenophon Contiades and Alkmene Fotiadou (eds), *Routledge Handbook of Comparative Constitutional Change* (Routledge 2021).

87 Sheldon S Wolin, 'Fugitive Democracy' in Nicholas Xenos (ed), *Fugitive Democracy and Other Essays* (2016) 101–2.

popular decision, which had taken place before the terms of UK's departure from the EU were agreed upon.[88] A recent Croatian controversy concerning men who pray in public squares on a weekly basis, pleading for, among other things, the "chastity of women", involves a problem of defining the boundaries of form, content, and space.[89]

As acts that often contain normative priorities, constitutions are intrinsically related to imaginations of failure. At their core, constitutions may be a response to an earlier time that involved a failure, an experience against which the new constitution is written to ward off the repetition of the past.[90] This failure may then be imagined as a recursive threat that must be defended against. For instance, Croatia's constitution still prohibits the country's accession to any alliance of states that may re-establish Yugoslavia.[91] This provision is a symbolic representation of often quite nationalist sentiments that interpret the current constitutional framework in the light of (sometimes exaggerated) Yugoslavian failures. Furthermore, insofar as constitutions establish normative goals and aspirations, failures in their realization can be a part of defining constitutional failures. The difference between these interpretations may highlight some failures more than others. For instance, failures in realizing different rights may be depicted as having different normative weight.

Finally, constitutions may be drawn from to forefront the theme of clarity. Clarity is usually associated with the requirements of the rule of law. The legislature must adopt laws that are clear enough to its addressees.[92] At the same time, a minimum of clarity is at the root of the constitution in that constitutional issues are often differentiated from other matters, meaning that the constitution must be discernible, normally because the issues it covers are more fundamental to a polity. What the quality of clarity as discernment means, however, is in itself not clear. The gaps and abeyances of constitutions, for instance, can at the same time be interpreted as invitations for a juristic

88 Rana İzci Connelly and James Connelly, 'Brexit: We'll Cross That Bridge When We Come to It' (2018) 26 Marmara Journal of European Studies 1; Richard Bellamy, 'Was the Brexit Referendum Legitimate, and Would a Second One Be so?' (2019) 18 Euroepan Political Science 126; Sionaidh Douglas-Scott, 'Brexit, Article 50 and the Contested British Constitution' [2016] Modern Law Review <http://ssrn.com/abstract=2846530>.

89 'Molitelji opet s krunicom na Trgu, prosvjednici im poručili: "Moje tijelo, moj izbor"' (*Večernji list*, 2024) <https://www.vecernji.hr/zagreb/foto-video-muskarci-opet-klecali-s-krunicom-na-trgu-prosvjednici-im-porucili-moje-tijelo-moj-izbor-1766532> accessed 20 April 2024.

90 A Sajo, 'Emotions in Constitutional Design' (2010) 8 International Journal of Constitutional Law 354, 383 <https://academic.oup.com/icon/article-lookup/doi/10.1093/icon/moq009>.

91 The Croatian Constitution, Art 142(2).

92 Jeremy Waldron, 'Clarity, Thoughtfulness, and the Rule of Law' in Geert Keil and Ralf Poscher (eds), *Vagueness and Law: Philosophical and Legal Perspectives* (OUP 2016).

interpretation or for a political practice.[93] The interpretation of this apparent lack of clarity will depend on how the constitution and its overall clarity is reconstructed. In this sense, clarity can also be a theme that influences the perception of failure, boundaries, stability, and hierarchies involved in using the constitution as a representative device.

5. Conclusion

An attempt to construct the constitution as a symbolic political representation may seem indistinguishable from the "far-right newspeak" that is once more in vogue. In this chapter, I indicated that it is more accurate to think of the attempt to invoke the constitution in this fashion as a specific practice not restricted to illiberalism. As a practice, symbolic political representation may be used to counter its illiberal uses. The first step in doing so is to move beyond its surface layer and explore how it engages the imaginative resources of constitutions to reshape agency, hierarchies, stability, boundaries, failures, and clarity. By looking at these themes and how they impact the maker, subject, object, referent, and audience of a representative claim, we may examine how invoking the constitution does not necessarily provide an apparently clear answer to a political dispute, but how it may reshape the terrain for political struggles and how this reshaping may be challenged.

93 Martin Loughlin, 'The Silences of Constitutions' (2018) 16 International Journal of Constitutional Law 922 <https://academic.oup.com/icon/article/16/3/922/5165836>; Michael Foley, *The Silence of Constitutions: Gaps, 'Abeyances' and Political Temperament in the Maintenance of Government* (Routledge 1989).

Part II

Crisis, fear, and their impact on representative democracy

4 The global pandemic as a challenge to representative democracy

Jan Adamowski and Monika Florczak-Wątor

1. Introduction[1]

The COVID-19 pandemic was a global challenge that extended beyond health services, impacting the entire public sector and reshaping individuals' private lives. It also posed a significant challenge to the institutions of representative democracy. In response to the pandemic, countries around the world employed a variety of approaches, including the adaptation of existing legal frameworks to accommodate restrictions on social contact[2] and the creation of new legal solutions tailored to the specific needs of the pandemic. The effect of both has been a remodelling of the way in which many traditional institutions of representative democracy operate.

At the core of representative democracy is the election of officials by the people in order to entrust them to exercise power within specific representative institutions following their mandate.[3] The key elements of this system are general elections and parliaments. Conducting elections in alignment with the highest democratic standards and within legally defined time frames confers upon the newly elected parliament a strong democratic legitimacy, which is

1 This chapter is produced as part of and funded by the European Union-NextGenerationEU, through the National Recovery and Resilience Plan of the Republic of Bulgaria, project No bg-rrp-2.004-0008. Part 3 of the chapter presents the results of the research conducted as part of the research project funded by the Polish National Science Centre (Decision No DEC-2020/37/B/HS5/02756).

2 The first regional lockdown in Europe was introduced in northern Italy on 8 March 2020 (see Decreto del Presidente del Consiglio dei ministri 8 marzo 2020: Ulteriori disposizioni attuative del decreto-legge 23 febbraio 2020, n 6, recante misure urgenti in materia di contenimento e gestione dell'emergenza epidemiologica da COVID-19 (20A01522)). It was extended to the whole country on the following day (see Decreto del Presidente del Consiglio dei ministry 9 marzo 2020: Ulteriori disposizioni attuative del decreto-legge 23 febbraio 2020, n 6, recante misure urgenti in materia di contenimento e gestione dell' epidemiologica da COVID-19, applicabili sull'intero territorio nazionale (20A01558)).

3 Sadik Haxhiu and Avni H Alidemaj, 'Representative Democracy: Its Meaning and Basic Principles' (2021) 17 Acta Universitatis Danubius 76. For more on the history and theory of representative democracy, see Nadia Urbinati, *Representative Democracy: Principles and Genealogy* (Chicago UP 2006).

DOI: 10.4324/9781003610670-7

essential for representing the people and legislating effectively. In turn, transparent legislative procedures and open parliamentary sessions enable scrutiny by the electorate, thereby continuously strengthening the legitimacy of parliament on an ongoing basis.[4]

This chapter aims to analyse the impact of the global COVID-19 pandemic on the institutions of representative democracy. It identifies the main challenges that these institutions faced during the pandemic, along with the countermeasures implemented by European countries to mitigate these risks and prevent their recurrence. Additionally, this chapter examines how the measures adopted in response to the COVID-19 pandemic have brought lasting changes to the functioning of the institutions of representative democracy. By identifying both the challenges and the responses, this analysis provides a basis for anticipating the future development and operation of representative democracy, including under conditions comparable to those experienced during the global pandemic.

2. The global pandemic as a challenge to holding general elections

2.1 Preliminary remarks

Holding general elections during a pandemic is an organisational challenge for the state. The choice of the most optimal way, under the given conditions, for the nation to elect representatives who will be entrusted with the mandate to exercise power must take into account, on the one hand, the need to ensure the safety of those who will vote, including in terms of health,[5] and, on the other hand, the need to guarantee the maximum implementation of basic electoral principles, such as the principles of the universality and equality of elections, fairness and transparency. Significantly, the outcome of elections should not lead to public disapproval because of the way in which the vote was conducted; electoral procedures should build confidence in the institutions of representative democracy. Even under non-pandemic conditions, where general elections can be conducted in a 'normal' manner, their conduct may raise doubts that translate into limited confidence in their outcome. This was demonstrated, for example, by the Polish local elections held in 2014, in which

4 For more on representative democracy in modern times, see Nadia Urbinati, 'Representative Democracy and Its Critics' in Sonia Alonso, John Keane and Wolfgang Merkel (eds), *The Future of Representative Democracy* (CUP 2011) 23–29.

5 For the potential impact of general elections on the spread of COVID-19, see Erik Asplund, Toby S James and Alistair Clark, 'Voting During the Pandemic Covid-19' in Toby S James, Alistair Clark and Erik Asplund (eds), *Elections During Emergencies and Crises: Lessons for Electoral Integrity From the Covid-19 Pandemic* (International Institute for Democracy and Electoral Assistance 2023). <https://www.idea.int/publications/catalogue/elections-during-emergencies-and-crises> accessed 29 October 2024.

there were several issues with the electoral IT system[6] and a higher percentage of invalid votes than had been observed previously,[7] as well as by the Austrian presidential elections held in 2016, the second round of which was ultimately annulled by the Constitutional Court (*Verfassungsgerichtshof*).[8] In the United States, on the other hand, doubts about the fairness of the 2020 presidential election were such that, to this day, the results of that election are still being questioned by some citizens of that country.[9]

The challenges and risks posed by the COVID-19 pandemic had a significant impact on the electoral process as a whole. This required special measures to guarantee the safety and hygiene of electoral staff and polling workers,[10] to set stricter rules for campaigning[11] and for conducting the vote[12] and to facilitate the observation of elections by representatives of political parties and independent experts.[13] The risk of electoral violence was further exacerbated by the prevailing pandemic conditions.[14] However, all of these challenges and risks essentially addressed two fundamental issues: the need to ensure security, including health security in particular, and the need to guarantee the fairness and universality of elections. The most crucial challenge for the authorities during the pandemic was to act in a manner that would achieve one of these objectives without undermining the possibility of achieving the other.

6 See, e.g., Bartłomiej Michalak, 'Conclusions and Recommendations (Not Only) De Lege Ferenda After the Crisis in the Polish Local Elections of 2014' (2016) 20/A Bialystok Legal Studies 211.

7 See, e.g., Michał Pierzgalski, Maciej A Górecki and Paweł Stępień, 'Ballot Paper Design and Vote Spoiling at Polish Local Elections of 2014: Establishing a Causal Link' (2020) 34 East European Politics and Societies 611.

8 See *Erkenntnis* [2016] Verfassungsgerichtshof W I 6/2016-125.

9 See 'Most Say Fundamental Rights Under Threat: Partisan Identity Determines Which Specific Rights People Feel Are at Risk' (Monmouth University Polling Institute, 20 June 2023) <https://www.monmouth.edu/polling-institute/reports/monmouthpoll_us_062023/> accessed 29 October 2024.

10 Erik Asplund and others, *Elections and Covid-19: Health and Safety at Polling Stations* (International IDEA, 5 February 2021) <https://www.idea.int/news/elections-and-covid-19-health-and-safety-polling-stations> accessed 29 October 2024.

11 Erik Asplund and others, *Elections and Covid-19: How Election Campaigns Took Place in 2020* (International IDEA, 2 February 2021) <https://www.idea.int/news/elections-and-covid-19-how-election-campaigns-took-place-2020> accessed 29 October 2024.

12 Erik Asplund and others, *Elections and Covid-19: How Special Voting Arrangements Were Expanded in 2020* (International IDEA, 25 February 2021). <https://www.idea.int/news/elections-and-covid-19-how-special-voting-arrangements-were-expanded-2020> accessed 29 October 2024.

13 Erik Asplund and others, *Elections and Covid-19: International Electoral Observation in 2020* (International IDEA, 17 March 2021) <https://www.idea.int/news/elections-and-covid-19-international-electoral-observation-2020> accessed 29 October 2024.

14 Sarah Birch and others, *How to Hold Elections Safely and Democratically During the Covid-19 Pandemic* (The British Academy 2020). <https://www.thebritishacademy.ac.uk/documents/2632/How-to-hold-elections-safely-democratically-Shape-the-Future.pdf> accessed 29 October 2024.

2.2 *Popular voting*

The popular vote constitutes an essential component of any electoral process. Naturally, it is neither the sole element of the electoral process nor a sufficient element for the election to be considered democratic and fair.[15] The impact of the pandemic on the conduct of the popular vote was evident at many levels, including the level of decision-making by key policymakers on matters such as the scheduling of elections or determining their form. The main challenge in organising popular voting in a global pandemic is to facilitate the casting of ballots by all eligible voters. In particular, the solutions introduced should not restrict the participation in the elections of people from the so-called high-risk groups (e.g. the elderly).[16] Indeed, a reduction in turnout among a particular group of voters may lead to a distortion of the outcome of the election, which in turn raises questions about the correctness (and validity) of such an electoral process. Commonly adopted solutions to protect public health and guarantee the possibility of a popular vote were the postponement of elections and the use of alternative voting methods.

The humanitarian postponement of an election in a life-threatening emergency represents one of seven cases for not holding elections, as identified by Toby James and Sead Alihodzic.[17] By humanitarian reasons, the authors mean both natural hazards (where they explicitly mention 'epidemic' and 'pandemic' as examples) and technological or man-made hazards.[18] The postponement of elections in a 'normal' situation would, in principle, have to be considered undemocratic and contrary to the institution of a 'fixed term', which is characterised by predetermination.[19] In an emergency situation, however, such an action may be assessed quite differently.[20] It must not lead to legal chaos or a crisis of legitimacy for the authorities. For this reason, it is essential that any postponement of an election date has both an adequate legal basis and sufficient public acceptance.

15 See, e.g., Veronika U Hinz and Markku Suksi, *Elections Elements: On the International Standards of Electoral Participation* (Åbo Akademi UP 2003).

16 Matteo Picchio and Raffaella Santolini, 'The COVID-19 Pandemic's Effects on Voter Turnout' (2022) 73 European Journal of Political Economy <https://www.ncbi.nlm.nih.gov/pmc/articles/PMC8715663/> accessed 29 October 2024; Paul Gronke and others, 'How Elections Under COVID-19 May Change the Political Engagement of Older Voters' (2020) 30 The Public Policy and Aging Report 147.

17 Other cases include cancellation, emergency postponement, interim postponement, technical delay, death of a candidate and annulment (Toby S James and Sead Alihodzic, 'When Is It Democratic to Postpone an Election?' (2020) 19(3) Election Law Journal: Rules, Politics, and Policy 346).

18 See James and Alihodzic (n 17) 348–50.

19 In the United Kingdom, a slightly different concept of the parliamentary term has been adopted. It is based on defining only the maximal length of tenure. However, in 2011, the fixed term was introduced (see Fixed-Term Parliaments Act 2011), but in 2022, the maximal term was reinstated (see Dissolution and Calling of Parliament Act 2022).

20 James and Alihodzic (n 17) 348.

According to a report prepared by Erik Asplund et al., at least 80 national or regional elections were postponed worldwide between February 2020 and February 2022. In contrast, at least 160 elections were conducted.[21] However, it appears that decisions taken in this area did not always meet the two aforementioned requirements, namely those of legality and public acceptance. For example, the manner in which the 2020 Polish presidential election was postponed raised some doubts. In accordance with Article 228(7) of the 1997 Constitution of the Republic of Poland,[22] the postponement of parliamentary or presidential elections is permitted solely in the event of a declaration of one of three states of emergency: martial law, a state of extraordinary situation or a state of natural disaster. This is due to the fact that during a state of emergency and for a period of 90 days following its conclusion, the holding of parliamentary and presidential elections is prohibited, and the terms of office of these bodies are extended for this period. However, as no state of emergency was declared in Poland due to the pandemic caused by the SARS-CoV-2 virus, there were no legal grounds to postpone the presidential elections scheduled for May 2020, let alone cancel them. Ultimately, however, no state of emergency was declared, and neither a constitutional amendment extending the presidential term by two years[23] nor the preparation of postal elections was successful. Consequently, the elections were formally held on 10 May, but no votes could be cast.[24] Therefore, a second election was held on 28 June 2020. The cancellation of planned elections or their postponement to a date other than the one resulting from the electoral calendar without an appropriate legal basis is a serious threat to democracy and the rule of law, and the Polish example serves to confirm the validity of this thesis.

However, the way for the authorities to respond to pandemic problems may be not only to cancel or postpone the elections, but also to change the voting method to one that is more adapted to the specific conditions. In such a situation, governors have three main voting methods at their disposal: voting at polling stations, postal voting and online voting.[25] Furthermore, hybrid solutions combining these different methods, additionally complemented by

21 Erik Asplund (ed), *Global Review of COVID-19: Impact on Elections* (International Institute for Democracy and Electoral Assistance, 1 December 2022) <https://www.idea.int/news-media/multimedia-reports/global-overview-covid-19-impact-elections> accessed 29 October 2024.

22 Constitution of the Republic of Poland of 2 April 1997, Journal of Laws No 78, item 483, as amended.

23 Draft Law on Amendments to the Constitution of the Republic of Poland (No 337/2020/IX term of the Sejm).

24 See Resolution of the National Electoral Commission on the declaration of the impossibility to vote for candidates in the election of the president of the Republic of Poland (No 129/2020).

25 See, e.g., Robert Krimmer, David Duenas-Cid and Iuliia Krivonosova, 'Debate: Safeguarding Democracy During Pandemics. Social Distancing, Postal, or Internet Voting: The Good, the Bad or the Ugly?' (2021) 41 Public Money & Management 8.

alternatives to the traditional ones, such as proxy voting, early voting or voting at home or in an institution, are also possible.[26] These particular voting methods are sometimes the only possible option for vulnerable people, such as the elderly or people in quarantine, to participate in elections. They do not raise major concerns when they are alternative methods that complement traditional voting methods. The issue arises only when these alternative methods are imposed as exclusive voting methods, replacing those previously used by voters, which require a direct presence at polling stations. Indeed, immediacy breeds trust, which can be challenging to establish when, in the electoral process, the voter is compelled to rely on technology that is beyond their control or on intermediary voting institutions that are under the control of those in power.

For these reasons, in the context of a pandemic, the objective should be to facilitate the ability of voters to cast their ballots at designated polling stations, while ensuring the implementation of a specific sanitary regime to safeguard their health. Although contingent upon the implementation of specific health countermeasures, this approach is the most proximate to the customary vote that has been taken in the majority of countries outside the pandemic period. This solution necessitates neither the creation of new infrastructure, as would be the case with internet voting, nor requires the adaptation of existing infrastructure, as would be the case with postal voting. However, there are two significant risks. The first relates to the potential for a disproportionate turnout among certain demographic groups, which could subsequently lead to an inaccurate representation of the election results.[27] This is because a voter's decision to participate in an election must, at least potentially, involve the acceptance of an increased risk of disease. It seems that the countermeasure to this potential risk could be the introduction of alternative voting methods and special arrangements at polling stations, as mentioned earlier. Secondly, in democratic countries, holding general elections often requires the functioning of both permanent electoral bodies (the professional electoral administration) and polling workers, which, in some cases, operate as *ad hoc* electoral commissions.[28] These commissions are responsible, among other things, for conducting the poll, counting the votes and declaring the results of the election, each in its own circuit or constituency. Therefore, it is the members of these

26 'Alternative Voting Methods and Arrangements' (Organisation for Security and Cooperation in Europe: Office for Democratic Institutions and Human Rights, 12 October 2020) <https://www.osce.org/odihr/elections/466794?fbclid=IwAR0Xa1LmFOnTwUinaL9p-D9XU5IMgWUyBU_ShYugE139FdkOXSjSnto3i74> accessed 29 October 2020; Asplund and others, 'Elections and Covid-19' (n 13); Asplund, James and Clark (n 5) 85–95.

27 Krimmer, Duenas-Cid and Krivonosova (n 25) 9.

28 To illustrate, in the Polish parliamentary elections held on 15 October 2023, 31,073 constituency electoral commissions were established with a total of 262,525 voters as members (see Report of the National Electoral Commission on the elections to the Sejm of the Republic of Poland and to the Senate of the Republic of Poland held on 15 October 2023).

voluntary (non-professional) electoral commissions, even if they are remunerated, who are particularly vulnerable to disease in the event of a pandemic due to their social interaction with a large number of individuals. In light of these considerations, those responsible for determining the format of the elections should give due consideration to the issue of establishing such commissions, given the dearth of individuals willing to assume the responsibilities associated with their work. This could, in turn, render the holding of elections unfeasible. The combination of a lack of citizen interest in working for electoral commissions and a genuine concern for their own safety and well-being may ultimately render the holding of elections under pandemic conditions unfeasible. This was precisely the situation in Poland during the presidential elections scheduled for 10 May 2020.[29] In the Warsaw district, for these elections, 750 constituency electoral commissions were required, comprising 3,835 members from among all willing voters. However, only 2,951 individuals applied, resulting in only 237 such commissions being fully appointed.[30]

The second mentioned solution, namely postal voting, in turn necessitates adaptations to the postal infrastructure in order to meet electoral requirements, both in legal and practical terms.[31] It is thus necessary to prepare appropriate legal regulations enabling citizens to cast their votes without being present at polling stations, with a guarantee that these votes will be taken into account in the overall result of the vote. Furthermore, personnel supporting the correspondence voting stage must be provided, for example, by organising appropriate training for postal operator employees. The necessary infrastructure must also be prepared, including ensuring universal access to postal boxes. Concurrently, the implementation of postal voting requires the involvement of two key entities: the independent electoral administration responsible for managing the election process and the postal operator responsible for delivering the election packages. On the other hand, excessive restrictions on the powers of the electoral authorities in favour of external, not necessarily independent, entities intermediating the delivery of electoral packages, may raise serious doubts as to compliance with international standards.[32] It should be noted, however, that today the very acceptability of the

29 Ultimately, the elections did not take place due to the impossibility of voting (see The Statement of the National Electoral Commission on the submission of candidates for members of territorial electoral commissions [2020] (ZPOW-571-32/20).

30 'W części miast w kraju brakuje wystarczającej liczby chętnych do obsadzenia komisji wyborczych' (*Polish Press Agency SA*, 29 April 2020) <https://www.pap.pl/aktualnosci/news%2C635169%2Cw-czesci-miast-brak-wystarczajacej-liczby-chetnych-do-obsadzenia-komisji> accessed 29 October 2024.

31 See, e.g., Birch and others (n 14) 10–13.

32 'Alternative Voting Methods and Arrangements' (n 26) 13; see also 'CCPR General Comment No 25: Article 25 (Participation in Public Affairs and Right to Vote) The Right to Participate in Public Affairs, Voting Rights and the Right of Equal Access to Public Service' (*Refworld*) Art. 20 <https://www.refworld.org/legal/general/hrc/1996/en/28176> accessed 29 October 2024.

use of postal voting as an alternative voting method is sporadically questioned. Indeed, it should be borne in mind that in many European countries, postal voting had been established and used in practice before the outbreak of the COVID-19 pandemic, albeit on a smaller scale than under pandemic conditions. In some countries, postal voting was introduced as a default option, with election packets sent by post to all eligible voters (e.g. Switzerland[33]). In other countries, election packets are made available upon a voter's request made in advance (e.g. Germany[34]). In addition, there are countries where postal voting is permitted only for specific categories of voters, such as the elderly or people with disabilities (e.g. Poland[35]). This differentiated approach to postal voting in European countries was also evident during the pandemic. In certain cases, elections were conducted or attempted to be conducted exclusively via postal voting (e.g. the second round of local elections in Bavaria in 2020[36] or the presidential elections in Poland scheduled for 10 May 2020[37]). In others, the method was employed as a widely available but only as an alternative voting method (e.g. the first round of local elections in Bavaria in 2020[38]) and, in still others, the possibility of using postal voting was not only an alternative and complementary method, but it was also selective, as it was accessible solely to certain categories of voters (e.g. during the presidential elections in Poland on 28 June 2020).[39]

The third solution, namely internet voting, requires the establishment of a dedicated electoral infrastructure.[40] Consequently, the implementation of this solution in the event of an emergency on an *ad hoc* basis is challenging without prior preparation.[41] In addition to the creation of an online infrastructure, it is essential to foster voter confidence in this form of voting. Notable examples

33 See Bundesgesetz über die politischen Rechte 1976, Art. 8; see also Magdalena Musiał-Karg, 'Alternative Voting Methods on the Example of Postal and Electronic Voting in Switzerland' (2016) 20 Bialystok Legal Studies 13, 15–18.

34 See Bundeswahlordnung 1985, Art. 25.

35 See Art. 53a of the Electoral Code Act of 5 January 2011, Journal of Laws of 2023, item 2408, as amended.

36 Arkadiusz Radwan and Sonia Horonziak, 'Wybory korespondencyjne w Bawarii 29 marca 2020 r. a COVID-19. Analiza empiryczna na tle debaty o zasadności organizacji wyborów w czasie pandemii' (2022) 9 Public Policy Studies 115, 120.

37 Art. 2 of the Act of 6 April 2020 on special principles for conducting general elections for the President of the Republic of Poland ordered in 2020, Journal of Laws of 2020, item 827.

38 Radwan and Horonziak (n 36) 120.

39 Art. 2 of the Act of 2 June 2020 on special principles for the organisation of general elections for the president of the Republic of Poland ordered in 2020 with the possibility of postal voting, Journal of Laws of 2020, item 979.

40 Magdalena Musiał-Karg, 'Implementation of Electronic Voting and the Matter of Security' (2015) 22 Politologia: Annales Universitatis Mariae Curie-Skłodowska 119; Slamet Risnanto and others, 'E-Voting: Technology Requirements Mapping' (2022) 11 TEM Journal 1282.

41 For the Lithuanian example, see 'Lithuanian Government Backs Online Voting, but with Caveats' (*lrt.lt*, 22 June 2020) <https://www.lrt.lt/en/news-in-english/19/1190786/lithuanian-government-backs-online-voting-but-with-caveats> accessed 29 October 2024.

of European countries that have adopted online voting include Estonia[42] and Switzerland.[43] However, these countries did not implement this solution in the wake of the COVID-19 pandemic; rather, they have been using it for approximately two decades.

Other special voting arrangements were also used during the pandemic. One of these was proxy voting. While this solution undoubtedly contributes to increasing the number of votes cast, it also carries two significant risks. Firstly, it can result in a distortion of the election results in relation to the actual preferences of the electorate. This is because the decision of which candidate to vote for is made by the proxy, rather than the entitled voter, and may even be contrary to the wishes of the entitled voter.[44] Secondly, in the event of widespread proxy voting, the pressure to grant such proxies, especially from vulnerable people, could not be ruled out.[45] Such a scenario could also lead to a distortion of the election results. It is therefore recommended that this solution be applied selectively, especially during non-pandemic periods, and that the law should define not only who is permitted to grant a proxy, but also who is eligible to serve as a proxy.[46] An additional potential solution is the introduction of early voting. The period during which early voters are permitted to cast their ballots and the criteria of eligibility may vary from one state to another. This solution may be particularly advantageous during pandemic periods, even if it only takes the form of multi-day voting.[47] This is due to the fact that it avoids the aggregation of all eligible voters at polling stations on a given day. However, this necessitates the establishment of polling stations where early voting is possible, as well as the guarantee of the secrecy of the votes cast in this manner. It is also noteworthy that the practice of adding the votes cast in this way to those cast on the main election day, or collecting them in one ballot box so that it is impossible to distinguish between them, is worthy of further consideration.[48] One further special voting arrangement is home- or institution-based voting. This involves the voter casting their vote

42 Michael R Alvarez, Thad E Hall and Alexander H Trechsel, 'Internet Voting in Comparative Perspective: The Case of Estonia' (2009) 42 PS: Political Science & Politics 497; Wolfgand Drechsler and Ülle Madise, 'E-Voting in Estonia' (2002) 6 Trames: Journal of the Humanities and Social Sciences 234; Piret Ehin and others, 'Internet Voting in Estonia 2005–2019: Evidence From Eleven Elections' (2022) 39 Government Information Quarterly <https://linkinghub.elsevier.com/retrieve/pii/S0740624X2200051X> accessed 29 October 2024; Magdalena Musiał-Karg, 'The Theory and Practice of Online Voting: The Case of Estonia (Selected Issues)' (2011) 29 Athenaeum: Polish Political Science Studies 180.

43 See Jan Gerlach and Urs Gasser, *Three Case Studies From Switzerland: E-Voting* (Berkman Center for Internet & Society 2009) Berkman Center Research Publication No 2009-03.1; Musiał-Karg, 'Alternative Voting Methods' (n 33) 18–21.

44 'Alternative Voting Methods and Arrangements' (n 26) 20.

45 'Alternative Voting Methods and Arrangements' (n 26).

46 See 'Alternative Voting Methods and Arrangements' (n 26) 21–23.

47 'Alternative Voting Methods and Arrangements' (n 26) 27.

48 'Alternative Voting Methods and Arrangements' (n 26) 29–30.

at their current location using, for example, mobile ballot boxes.[49] However, this method may raise concerns about the adequacy of ensuring that all voters are able to cast their votes freely and secretly. Nevertheless, it seems worth considering in a pandemic setting, particularly for those in quarantine or for those who have been hospitalised.[50]

2.3 *Other essential elements of conducting a general election during a global pandemic*

The global pandemic compelled a series of modifications at various stages of the broader electoral process. These challenges were evident from the outset of the electoral process, including the registration of candidates and the associated obligation to collect the legally required number of signatures for endorsement. It is worth noting, in this regard, that Iceland adopted an innovative solution to facilitate online endorsements.[51] Another challenge that registered candidates had to overcome was how to conduct their campaigns in the new electoral environment. This was largely due to the restrictions imposed by blockades and assembly bans, which forced the use of the media and the internet as the principial channels for campaigning.[52] It was also a challenge to conduct independent, international election observations. In this regard, the literature has examined four potential avenues: relinquishing observation, conducting it in a traditional manner, enlisting the assistance of foreign national residents in the country in question or, alternatively, conducting it virtually and through a partnership.[53] Each of these solutions presents a distinct set of specific benefits and potential risks. There is also no doubt that the pandemic facilitated closer cooperation between independent election observers who faced similar problems in different countries in conducting elections under emergency conditions that differed significantly from those of a normal state.[54]

49 'Alternative Voting Methods and Arrangements' (n 26) 31; Asplund and others (n 11).

50 'Alternative Voting Methods and Arrangements' (n 26) 35; Asplund, James and Clark (n 5) 93.

51 'Rafræn skráning meðmælenda fyrir forsetakosningar opnuð' (Government of Iceland, 17 April 2020) <https://www.stjornarradid.is/efst-a-baugi/frettir/stok-frett/2020/04/17/Rafraen-skraning-medmaelenda-fyrir-forsetakosningar-opnud/> accessed 29 October 2024.

52 Erik Asplund, Alistair Clark and Toby S James, 'How Election Campaigns Took Place During the Pandemic' in Toby S James, Alistair Clark and Erik Asplund (eds), *Elections During Emergencies and Crises: Lessons for Electoral Integrity From the Covid-19 Pandemic* (International Institute for Democracy and Electoral Assistance 2023) <https://www.idea.int/publications/catalogue/elections-during-emergencies-and-crises> accessed 29 October 2024; Asplund and others (n 11).

53 Birch and others (n 14) 20–25.

54 Birch and others (n 14) 25–26.

3. The global pandemic as a challenge to the functioning of parliaments

3.1 Preliminary remarks

The COVID-19 pandemic also had a significant impact on the functioning of parliaments around the world. On the one hand, it was necessary to enable parliaments to perform their basic legislative and oversight functions. On the other hand, the implemented solutions had to be in accordance with the general security rules introduced at the time in many countries, such as the ban on mass assemblies. The adaptation of parliamentary procedures to align with the relevant sanitary requirements proved to be a significant challenge, not only in terms of technical implementation, but also in light of the necessity for a rapid and far-reaching legislative response to the changing health situation in some countries. In these instances, it was the government, rather than parliament, that was responsible for implementing relevant measures. This constituted an emergency solution that was an exception to the principle of the separation of powers. It thus required an appropriate legal basis, frequently at the constitutional level. This emergency arrangement emphasised the necessity for flexibility in crisis management and cooperation between authorities during global health emergencies.

3.2 Law-making

In contemporary democratic states, parliaments directly elected by the people are the most democratically legitimated institutions, and thus they exercise legislative authority.[55] In states based on a parliamentary system, they also exercise political oversight over the government. Nevertheless, this does not preclude the active involvement of the government or individual ministers in the legislative process, particularly in drafting primary legislation[56] or issuing secondary legislation. It is noteworthy that the legislative process in parliament typically involves multi-stage procedures, largely due to the institution of 'readings' and, in the case of certain parliaments, its bicameral structure. While this solution is to be commended in terms of its potential impact on the quality of law-making, it may prove to be a hindrance in exceptional circumstances, necessitating a rapid and decisive change in the normative state. Consequently,

55 In some constitutions, legislative power is explicitly stated to be exercised by parliament in conjunction with the head of state, as in the case of Belgium and Iceland (see La Constitution Belge 1831, Art. 36; Stjórnarskrá lýðveldisins Íslands 1944, Art. 2) or by the government, as in the Dutch example (Grondwet voor het Koninkrijk der Nederlanden 1814, Art. 81).

56 For example, as Chris Watson pointed out, in the United Kingdom in the post-war period, in the majority of parliamentary sessions, at least 75% of the bills were introduced by the government (Chris Watson, 'Acts and Statutory Instruments: The Volume of UK Legislation 1850 to 2019' (House of Commons Library 2019) CBP 7438 6–7 <https://researchbriefings.files.parliament.uk/documents/CBP-7438/CBP-7438.pdf> accessed 29 October 2024).

some European constitutions permit the executive to enact legislation under specified conditions, often reserving the right to parliamentary review of issued acts. A more extensive involvement of the executive in law-making also occurred in Europe in the wake of the COVID-19 pandemic.

European countries have, to varying extents and on different legal bases, delegated broader legislative powers to the executive in connection with pandemics. The constitutions of certain European countries vest their governments with the authority to enact primary legislation following specified conditions. Such arrangements may prove useful in certain circumstances, such as during a pandemic when the need for the swift implementation of countermeasures may arise and the legislative process in parliament may be impeded. In this context, four main approaches can be distinguished. The first is the empowerment of the government to issue primary legislation due to the declaration of a state of emergency (*de jure* sphere). The second is the empowerment of the government to issue primary legislation due to the occurrence of extraordinary circumstances (*de facto* sphere). The third is the delegation of primary legislative powers on the basis of a parliamentary decision. The fourth is the delegation of secondary legislative powers on the basis of a primary legislation act issued by the parliament. Consequently, the initial three solutions, which are based on disparate rationales, culminate in the formulation of 'government primary legislation', which is, however, an exception to the principle of the separation of powers. This type of legislation was particularly useful during the pandemic when the rapid adoption of countermeasures was necessary and the standard legislative process was impeded.

Governmental primary legislation is a response to a situation in which extraordinary circumstances make it necessary to modify or suspend normal legal mechanisms. Indeed, the idea of a state of emergency is not a legal 'description' of reality, but involves the creation of a temporary 'legal regime' characterised by certain deviations from the ordinary rules of operation of a democratic state. However, these deviations are necessary to prevent or mitigate the effects of natural (e.g. natural disasters) or man-made (e.g. internal or external threats) events. A classic example of such an exception is the delegation to the executive of certain legislative powers statutorily reserved to the parliament.[57] The specific arrangements adopted may result in constitutions providing for one or more states of emergency.[58] In practice, the conditions for

57 See, e.g., Andrej J Zwitter, 'The Rule of Law in Times of Crisis: A Legal Theory on the State of Emergency in the Liberal Democracy' (2012) 98 Archiv für Rechts- und Sozialphilosophie 95.

58 For example, the Czech and Polish Constitutions distinguish between three different emergencies. The Czech Republic defines these as a state of war, a state of national threat and a state of emergency (see Ústava České republiky 1992, Art. 43; Ústavní zákon o bezpečnosti České republiky 1998, Arts 5–7), while Poland specifies martial law, a state of an extraordinary situation and a state of natural disaster (Constitution of the Republic of Poland, Arts 229–31). On the other hand, for example, in Latvia or Luxembourg, there is only one state of emergency:

their introduction and their impact on the population may vary from country to country.[59] According to a report prepared by Maria Diaz Crego and Silvia Kotanidis in December 2020,[60] constitutional states of emergency for the COVID-19 pandemic were adopted in 10[61] of the 27 Member States of the European Union. Significantly, however, as the cited studies show, only the constitutions of three Member States[62] did not provide for the introduction of a state of emergency (either *de jure* or *de facto*[63]), whereas the constitutions of 17 Member States[64] provided for a state of emergency that could be introduced (sometimes with additional conditions) in relation to the COVID-19 pandemic.

It is also noteworthy that several countries have opted to introduce special statutory states of emergency (regimes). This group includes countries whose constitutions did not provide for an appropriate state of emergency in the context of a pandemic (e.g. France[65]) as well as countries whose constitutions provided for an appropriate state of emergency but it was not declared

---

a state of exception and a state of crisis respectively (see Constitution du Grand-Duché de Luxembourg 1868, Art. 48; Latvejis Republikys Satversme 1922, Art. 62).

59 According to Arts 228–34 of the 1997 Constitution of the Republic of Poland, the differences between martial law, a state of an extraordinary situation and a state of natural disaster include not only the grounds for their imposition, but also the manner of their declaration, their permissible duration and the scope of the rights and freedoms that may be restricted under special provisions.

60 Maria Diaz Crego and Silvia Kotanidis, 'States of Emergency in Response to the Coronavirus Crisis: Normative Response and Parliamentary Oversight in EU Member States During the First Wave of the Pandemic' (European Parliament Analysis Office 2020) EP Study 659.385 10–18 <https://data.europa.eu/doi/10.2861/892605> accessed 29 October 2024.

61 I.e. Bulgaria, Czechia, Estonia, Finland, Hungary, Luxembourg, Portugal, Romania, Slovakia and Spain.

62 I.e. Austrian, Belgian and Danish Constitutions.

63 An example of a country where the difference between a *de jure* state of emergency *(requiring* an official declaration) and a *de facto* state of emergency (requiring only exceptional circumstances) is obvious: France. The Constitution empowers the president of the republic to exercise exceptional powers (*pouvoirs exceptionnels*) 'in the event of a serious and imminent threat to the institutions of the Republic, the independence of the Nation, the integrity of its territory or the fulfilment of its international obligations, as well as in the event of disruption to the proper functioning of the constitutional public authorities' (La Constitution française 1958, Art. 16). It also allows the Council of Ministers to declare a state of *siege* (*état de siege*). The first power is an example of a de *facto* state of emergency, while the second is an example of a *de jure* state of emergency.

64 I.e. Croatian, German, Lithuanian, Maltese, Netherlandish, Polish and Swedish Constitutions.

65 According to the French Constitution, there are two constitutionally defined states of emergency: a state of exception, which empowers the president of the republic to exercise exceptional powers (*pouvoirs exceptionnels*) and a state of siege (see La Constitution française Arts 16, 36). However, the emergency law (Loi d'urgence pour faire face à l'épidémie de covid-19 (1) 2020 (No 2020-290)) introduced a state of health emergency (*état d'urgence sanitaire*). In accordance with the jurisprudence of the Constitutional Council (*Décision* [2015] Conseil constitutionnel No 2015-527 QPC; *Décision* [2016] Conseil constitutionnel No 2016-535 QPC), such a state may be established and regulated by the legislature.

(e.g. Poland[66]). The rationale for such actions can be understood in two ways. Firstly, constitutional states of emergency are frequently perceived as temporary and interim measures designed to respond to a current problem in a prompt manner. The objective of such measures should be to remove the problem and stabilise the situation as quickly as possible. In contrast, the pandemic caused by COVID-19 was a long-term condition that at times required the implementation of more flexible statutory regimes. Statutory regimes, however, unlike constitutional regimes, are generally indefinite and may be extended repeatedly. This, in turn, gave rise to concerns about their abuse and the circumvention of the limitations of constitutional regulations. The experience of numerous countries during the COVID-19 pandemic demonstrated that statutory states of emergency were not an effective substitute for constitutional states of emergency. In emergency situations, the application of constitutional regulations, which have a guaranteed character for citizens, should be rigorous and not flexible. Some European countries, such as Hungary[67] and Portugal,[68] decided to combine the constitutional and statutory regimes, which seems to be a more justified solution than the one adopted in Poland, where the constitutional regime was replaced by the one created in the statute and modified *ad hoc* according to the then-current needs and expectations.

Some European constitutions empower governments to implement 'exceptional' measures, not on a legal basis (i.e. a declaration of a state of emergency), but based on factual necessity (i.e. the occurrence of an extraordinary situation). This arrangement permits the government to implement temporary legislative measures without prior authorisation from parliament or a declaration of a state of emergency. The government may take immediate legislative action in circumstances it deems extraordinary. This solution allows the government to respond swiftly while requiring specific parliamentary scrutiny. In principle, special decrees with the force of a statute issued in this way should be forwarded to parliament for approval as soon as possible, as failure to do so renders them null and void (often from the outset). Notable examples of countries that have adopted this solution include Greece,[69] Italy[70] and

66 In accordance with the Act of 5 December 2008 on Prevention and Control of Infections and Infectious Diseases in Humans, Journal of Laws of 2023, item 1284, a state of epidemic emergency was declared in Poland, followed by an epidemic state.

67 K Binder and others, 'States of Emergency in Response to the Coronavirus Crisis: Situation in Certain Member States' (European Parliamentary Research Service 2020) 6–7 Briefing PE 649.408 <https://www.europarl.europa.eu/RegData/etudes/BRIE/2020/649408/EPRS_BRI(2020)649408_EN.pdf> accessed 29 October 2024; Crego and Kotanidis (n 60) 12.

68 N Bentzen and others, 'States of Emergency in Response to the Coronavirus Crisis: Situation in Certain Member States III' (European Parliamentary Research Service 2020) 9–10 Briefing PE 651.972 <https://www.europarl.europa.eu/RegData/etudes/BRIE/2020/651972/EPRS_BRI(2020)651972_EN.pdf> accessed 29 October 2024; Crego and Kotanidis (n 60) 13.

69 Syntagma tis Elladas 1975, Art. 44.

70 Costituzione della Repubblica Italiana 1947, Art. 77.

Spain.[71] The constitutions of these countries similarly define the circumstances in which the government has the power to legislate. The Greek Constitution requires the existence of 'extraordinary circumstances of urgent and unforeseeable necessity', the Italian Constitution stipulates the existence of 'a case of necessity and urgency' and the Spanish Constitution necessitates the existence of 'cases of extraordinary and urgent necessity'. The procedure for approving government decrees issued under this procedure is also analogous. In the case of Greece, decrees must be approved within 40 days, in the case of Italy, within 60 days and in the case of Spain, within 30 days.

The government's authority to issue regulations with the force of a statute may necessitate neither the occurrence of *de facto* emergency circumstances nor the introduction of a *de jure* state of emergency. Such authorisation may also be based on an appropriate parliamentary decision. An example of a country that has adopted such a solution is France. According to Article 38 of the French Constitution of 1958,[72] the government may request parliamentary authorisation for a limited period of time to issue ordinances (*ordonnances*). These acts may regulate matters that are normally reserved for statutory regulation and are intended to implement the government's programme. They are issued by the Council of Ministers (*Conseil des ministres*),[73] after consultation with the Council of State (*Conseil d'État*), but they cease to have effect if a bill for their approval is not submitted to the parliament within the time frame set by the authorisation. This procedure was used during the pandemic to enact the Emergency Act 2020–290,[74] which authorised the government to issue ordinances regulating certain matters related to COVID-19 countermeasures.

In contrast, the parliamentarian primary legislation approach involves entrusting the legislative process to parliament while empowering the government to implement secondary legislation. Accordingly, this solution assumes the maintenance of the ordinary legislative process, even in extraordinary circumstances. As Maria Diaz Crego and Silvia Kotanidis have pointed out, this approach has been applied in 14 of the 27 Member States, including those where a statutory regime has been introduced and those where no state of emergency has been declared.[75] In the absence of constitutional provisions allowing for the introduction of a state of emergency or analogous statutory regime in response to a pandemic, this approach may be considered appropriate. Nevertheless, this solution could be seen as an implicit delegation of primary legislative powers. Some European countries' constitutions delineate a clear distinction between primary legislation enacted by parliament and secondary legislation delegated to the government. This distinction is reflected in

71 Constitución española 1978, Art. 86.

72 La Constitution française.

73 The Council of Ministers consists of both ministers and the president of the republic, who chairs its sessions.

74 Loi d'urgence pour faire face à l'épidémie de Covid-19 (1).

75 Crego and Kotanidis (n 60) 11–14, 28–29.

the requirement for 'detailed' delegations, which exclude legislative 'blanks'.[76] The rationale behind this distinction is that secondary legislation should be of a 'technical' rather than a 'substantive' nature.

3.3 *Other essential elements of parliamentary functioning during a global pandemic*

According to a report compiled by the Inter-Parliamentary Union,[77] a range of various measures were introduced by countries worldwide in order to adapt the activities of parliaments to cope with the conditions of the pandemic. Among these measures were remote and hybrid parliamentary and committee sessions and voting, as well as parity restrictions on the number of parliamentarians attending sessions. Nevertheless, certain solutions, particularly those related to remote voting, have been regarded as incompatible with constitutional regulations. An example of this is Austria, where constitutional provisions require the physical presence of at least one-third of the members of each chamber of parliament for the enactment of a law.[78] Consequently, the only possible solution was to reduce, by means of a political agreement, the number of MPs in attendance at parliamentary sessions during the pandemic.[79] In contrast, the Latvian parliament has developed a bespoke digital platform, *e-Saeimas*, for remote parliamentary meetings and voting.[80] A comparable infrastructure was established in Poland to enable remote parliamentary sessions, which were, however, conducted in a hybrid format.[81] However, as Ringolds Balodis and Edvīns Danovskis correctly observed, such a solution cannot fully replace on-site parliamentary debate, which involves not only the speeches of parliamentarians but also behind-the-scenes discussions that facilitate finding common solutions.[82] Piotr Uziębło, in turn, identified two additional issues related to remote parliamentary sittings under Polish solutions. Firstly, in accordance with the Standing Orders of the Sejm, the decision to hold a remote session is

76 For example, Art. 92(1) of the 1997 Constitution of the Republic of Poland stipulates that the specific authorisation for issuing a regulation (secondary legislation) shall specify the organ appropriate to issue the regulation and the scope of matters to be regulated as well as guidelines for the content of such an act.

77 'Country Compilation of Parliamentary Responses to the Pandemic' (Inter-Parliamentary Union, 25 March 2020) <https://www.ipu.org/country-compilation-parliamentary-responses-pandemic> accessed 29 October 2024.

78 Bundes-Verfassungsgesetz 1920, Arts 31, 37.

79 'Country Compilation of Parliamentary Responses to the Pandemic' (n 77).

80 'E-Saeima' (*saeima.lv*) <https://www.saeima.lv/lv/likumdosana/saeimas-sedes/e-saeima/> accessed 29 October 2024.

81 See, e.g., Piotr Kędziora, 'Zdalny tryb pracy Sejmu i jego organów w czasie stanu epidemii' (2022) 38 Acta Iuris Stetinensis 123.

82 Ringolds Balodis and Edvīns Danovskis, 'Functionality Problems of Collegial Government Institutions During the COVID-19 Pandemic and Solutions for the Future' (2021) 14 Journal of the University of Latvia Law 197, 202.

made by the Marshal of the Sejm, and this decision cannot be altered by either the Presidium of the Sejm or the Sejm itself. The Marshal's discretion, which is not obliged to maintain political independence, may result in a restriction of the opposition's rights.[83] Secondly, there are restrictions on the maximum duration of parliamentary speeches, which, in the lack of opportunity for backstage debates, may further limit the effectiveness of parliamentary discussions.[84]

Another significant challenge confronting representative democracies during the pandemic was to guarantee that parliamentary meetings were accessible to the public. In normal circumstances, the media plays a key role in reporting on parliamentary proceedings. However, during the pandemic, journalists' access to parliament buildings may have been severely restricted.[85] It is therefore reasonable for parliamentary staff to provide coverage of proceedings, which can also be considered good practice outside pandemic periods.[86]

4. Conclusions

The COVID-19 pandemic posed a significant challenge to representative democracy, requiring the adaptation of both the electoral process and the operating rules of national parliaments to emergency conditions. The extraordinary measures implemented during this period tested the resilience of democracy, the rule of law and public confidence in government and legislation.

The organisation of elections had to balance the imperative of upholding the principles of universality, equality, fairness and transparency with the necessity of protecting the health security of voters and electoral staff. The pandemic affected many aspects of the electoral process, including the timing and manner of voting. It became crucial to ensure that all citizens, especially vulnerable groups, could safely participate in the elections. A range of solutions was adopted by individual countries, from postponing voting dates to implementing alternative methods such as postal voting, online voting, or proxy voting. Each of these options brought specific advantages and challenges, especially regarding the integrity and fairness of the election.

The pandemic also impacted other aspects of the electoral process, such as signature gathering and campaigning. Adapting to these new circumstances required the development of innovative approaches, such as online campaigns

83 Piotr Uziębło, 'Nowelizacje regulaminu Sejmu w czasie pandemii w 2020 roku. Zapewnienie efektywności działania izby czy próba ograniczenia praw opozycji?' (2021) 34 Acta Iuris Stetinensis 131, 136.

84 Uziębło (n 83) 138–39.

85 See, e.g., Esther Luigi, 'State of COVID-19 Measures in Parliaments' (European Parliament: Directorate for Relations with National Parliaments Institutional Cooperation Unit 2021) Spotlight on Parliaments in Europe, No 33, 3 <http://www.epgencms.europarl.europa.eu/cmsdata/upload/30b463c9-4566-4a59-88bb-515322b86e46/No.33_State_of_COVID-19_measures_in_Parliaments_150221.pdf> accessed 29 October 2024.

86 See, e.g., Uziębło (n 83) 140–41.

when traditional in-person events were no longer feasible. Ensuring that independent international experts could observe elections during the pandemic posed another notable challenge.

The functioning of parliaments worldwide was also significantly affected by the COVID-19 pandemic. Ensuring the continuity of their functions, such as law-making and government oversight, while meeting public health requirements was critical. Adapting parliamentary procedures to comply with health standards presented substantial technical and legislative challenges that required rapid responses. In many cases, governments introduced emergency measures, sometimes without a solid legal basis.

The pandemic has also reduced the legislative power of parliaments, thereby affording executive bodies a more prominent role in the process of law-making. A common approach involved empowering the government to enact primary legislation during a declared state of emergency (*de jure* sphere) or in response to extraordinary circumstances (*de facto* sphere). Parliaments frequently delegated both primary and secondary legislative powers to the government, leading to what is known as 'government primary legislation'. These measures were essential when the normal legislative process was disrupted.

The COVID-19 pandemic required various adjustments to the daily operations of national parliaments, such as remote and hybrid sessions for both parliamentary and committee meetings, limiting the number of attendees and implementing new voting methods. Innovative tools, like dedicated platforms for remote meetings and voting, were introduced to support parliamentary work even beyond the pandemic. One major challenge was maintaining public access to sessions, as journalists had limited access to parliamentary buildings due to COVID-19 restrictions. Broadcasting parliamentary debates proved to be a valuable solution, with many countries continuing this practice even after the pandemic subsided.

5 Crisis, fear, and rhetorical democracy

Appeals to pathos in Dutch political debates on the COVID-19 pandemic[1]

Bart van Klink and Ingeborg van der Geest

1. Politics of fear

In times of crisis, politicians often appeal to fear. Since we are moving worldwide from one (health, climate, migration, financial, economic and so on) crisis to another, fear tends to become an ever-present feature of contemporary political discourse. Fear is generally seen as a primal emotion.[2] It signals that something essential to human existence is at stake: the property, safety, health or even the life of an individual, one's loved ones, a nation or some other collective. In the current climate debate, apocalyptic visions abound; according to many climate experts and activists, humanity is on the brink of extinction. As Doeland claims, extinction is inevitable and the best we can do as humans is to find a good way of dealing with our finality.[3] Politically speaking, it can be advantageous to invoke fear, because it may mobilise people and unite a social group by distancing it from other groups inside or outside society, deemed strange and dangerous (for instance, Muslims, asylum seekers or elites). At the same time, fear may be detrimental to democracy since it can be very difficult to engage in a rational exchange of arguments when the political debate is dominated by highly emotive language.

Fear is usually seen as a threat to representative democracy in liberal societies. In her recent analysis of populism in the Israeli context, Illouz argues that fear, together with disgust, resentment and love (in the form of national pride), may undermine democracy and democratic institutions:

> The mixture of these emotions forms the matrix of populism because they generate antagonism between social groups inside society and

1 This chapter is produced as part of and funded by the European Union-NextGenerationEU, through the National Recovery and Resilience Plan of the Republic of Bulgaria, project No bg-rrp-2.004-0008.

2 Martha C Nussbaum, *Political Emotions: Why Love Matters for Justice* (The Belknap of Harvard UP 2013) 320.

3 Lisa Doeland, *Apocalypsofie: Over recycling, groene groei en andere gevaarlijke fantasieën* (Ten Have 2023).

DOI: 10.4324/9781003610670-8

> alienation from the institutions that safeguard democracy, and because they are, in many ways, oblivious to what we might call reality.[4]

As she argues, Netanyahu's politics of fear continued and normalised the state of exception and created a sharp division between conservative and Orthodox Jews on the one hand and progressive and moderate religious Jews and Palestinians on the other hand. This contravenes the main tenet of liberalism to avoid fear as much as possible.[5] Nussbaum also warns that fear can 'distract us from general sympathy' and undermine people's 'commitment to the common good'.[6] However, she acknowledges that fear is a useful, even essential emotion since it prompts us to avoid danger.

This raises the question if there is any room for appeals to fear and crisis in democratic political debates. In our chapter, we explore this question by looking at political debates on the COVID-19 pandemic in the Netherlands. We offer a rhetorical analysis of some of the main press conferences, delivered by Dutch ministers during the COVID-19 pandemic, and debates on this issue in Dutch Parliament. During the recent pandemic, both the Dutch government and anti-government politicians and activists tried to create an atmosphere of crisis and fear in society by using rhetorical means. On the one hand, the government invoked the spectre of a serious health crisis that called for drastic measures, such as social distancing, a temporary lockdown and even a curfew. Factually but not officially, a state of exception was created for an indeterminate period of time. On the other hand, populist politicians from the extreme right wing turned the COVID-19 debate into a battle between the elite and the (common) people. In alarming terms, they warned that our liberal society would soon degrade into an authoritarian regime.

To begin with, we describe and compare the rhetorical strategies and means – such as metaphors, hyperboles, rhetorical questions and (other) appeals to pathos – used by politicians to create an atmosphere of crisis and fear in society (Section 2). Subsequently, we evaluate how these appeals to pathos, in particular fear, affect the democratic quality of the political debate (Section 3).

In our evaluation, we depart from two models of democracy: the model of deliberative democracy and the model of agonistic pluralism. In the model of *deliberative democracy*, defended by Benhabib, Habermas and others, political decisions are only valid if all those affected can agree with them after a thorough process of deliberation. Ideally, the decision-making procedure

4 Eva Illouz, *The Political Life of Populism: How Fear, Disgust, Resentment, and Love Undermine Democracy* (Polity Press 2023) 162.

5 Illouz refers here to Shklar's characterisation of liberalism as 'the political regime which abhors fear', Illouz (n 4) 21.

6 Nussbaum (n 2) 320, 376 respectively.

results in a rational consensus and not mere agreement. In this ideal speech situation, not much room is left for appeals to pathos, because they may distort the rational exchange of arguments. Mouffe criticises this model, since it ignores what she considers to be essentially political in political decisions, that is the distinction between us and them.[7] Instead, she advocates, together with Laclau,[8] the model of *agonistic pluralism*, which acknowledges the constitutive role of power struggles. In this model, appeals to pathos are welcomed, because they express cries for justice that otherwise, in a so-called rational debate, may be ignored.

Building on our case study we will draw some tentative conclusions on the relation between fear and democracy: on what conditions may appeals to pathos be permissible within a representative democracy (Section 4)? As a supplement to the two opposing models, we argue for a rhetorical democracy in which debate is encouraged and emotions play an important supporting role. Finally, we explain why we think that some restraint on the use of pathos is needed in political debates (Section 5).

2. Pathos in COVID-19 debates: a case study

In our case study, we conducted a rhetorical analysis of the Dutch political debate surrounding the COVID-19 pandemic, focusing specifically on the use of pathos, particularly appeals to fear. Pathos, one of the three modes of persuasion outlined in Aristotle's rhetorical framework, plays a crucial role in influencing an audience's emotions. While *logos* pertains to logical reasoning and rational argumentation, and *ethos* relates to speaker's credibility, *pathos* engages the audience's feelings, making it a powerful tool for evoking a wide range of emotions, including fear, anger and sympathy. Fear, as a fundamental emotional response to perceived threats, can serve as a strategic mechanism in political discourse. Appeals to fear can be used to highlight potential dangers, compel audiences to take them seriously, influence behaviour and mobilise groups who may seek to avoid or escape perceived risks.

2.1 Method

In this case study, we examined the use of pathos in political discourse on COVID-19 in the Netherlands. We conducted a qualitative rhetorical analysis to uncover the means and strategies employed in COVID-19 debates. Our corpus consisted of press conferences held by the Dutch government

7 Chantal Mouffe, 'Deliberative Democracy or Agonistic Pluralism' (1999) 66(3) Social Research 745.

8 See, for example, Ernesto Laclau and Chantal Mouffe, *Hegemony and Socialist Strategy: Towards a Radical Democratic Politics* (Verso 2014).

and the subsequent parliamentary debates. Between March 2020 and February 2022, there were 39 press conferences, each lasting about half an hour, featuring prepared speeches by the prime minister and the minister of public health, occasionally joined by other ministers or a scientist, followed by half an hour of questions from journalists. Each press conference was followed by a parliamentary debate. We selected 10 press conferences and parliamentary debates that addressed significant COVID-19 measures, such as the lockdown and the vaccination certificate. The aim of the press conferences was not only to inform the media and the Dutch public, but also to garner maximum societal support for the COVID-19 measures. During the debates, the Members of Parliament discussed the proposed measures and the government's strategies.

Pathos can manifest in various ways, including the selection of specific topics or the adaptation of arguments to resonate with a particular audience. It may also pertain to the form of the message itself, in that a rhetorical figure or stylistic device is used to evoke an emotional response. For instance, a metaphor can create a vivid image that connects with the audience, while a hyperbole may exaggerate a situation for emphasis. Additionally, the use of exclamations or intensified phrasing can reinforce the message's impact. In our analysis, we examined both content and form to gain a comprehensive understanding of their contributions to pathos.

In all contributions, we found appeals to fear, most notably in the debates on controversial measures such as the curfew and the vaccination certificate. The instances vary in both content – the messages themselves – and form – the means used to evoke fear. We will discuss the results through examples divided into three categories: contributions from the government and coalition parties, moderate opposition parties and populist parties.

2.2 Government and government parties

In the press conferences and their contributions to the parliamentary debates, the government employed appeals to fear to emphasise that a crisis situation exists and that action is necessary. The public must be convinced of the seriousness and urgency of the situation, as well as the need for measures to gain control of the virus, and is urged to comply with these measures.

In the first two examples, the minister of public health evokes feelings of fear by describing the negative consequences of the virus: people become sick, require hospitalisation and infect others, particularly vulnerable individuals who may not be vaccinated yet. To support his predictions, he provides figures and statistics from experts, highlighting rapidly increasing numbers while using intensifying language, such as 'completely replaced', 'bad news', 'exponential growth' and 'at a rapid pace'. He also references the dire situations in other countries, where the virus has already had a dramatic impact. After outlining the seriousness of the situation, he proposes the intended measures – including a curfew, additional measures for the summer and vaccination – as the only viable solutions.

Example 1. **Minister of Public Health De Jonge (Press conference 20 January 2021):**

> But regarding that new British variant, its R number is higher: it is already at 1.3. And that variant is gaining ground on Dutch soil more and more rapidly. Currently, it accounts for 1 in 10 infections. And by February, it will already be half. And the OMT [Outbreak Management Team] expects that the British variant will have completely replaced the classical variant by March or April. And that is bad news. Even though we know we will not get sicker from the British variant, we also know that many more people will get sick. The current measures are not enough to get this new variant under control. We have seen it before: nothing is as treacherous as exponential growth. And even if you think: it will probably go faster than I think, it still goes faster than you think. We see in England and Ireland how dramatically it can get out of hand. . . . And that is also why we are now taking these additional measures. Based on lessons from other countries, the OMT believes that a curfew can reduce the reproduction number by 8 to 13 percent – and that is a considerable number of sick people you can prevent.

Example 2. **Minister of Public Health De Jonge (Press conference 9 July 2021):**

> And yet there is reason to intervene. First of all, the speed at which the Delta variant is spreading throughout Europe, including the Netherlands. We had anticipated an increase – because more contact means more infections – but this is truly unprecedented. Just last week, we were seeing around 500–600 new infections per day. And today, there have been 7,000 new infections reported. It is moving at a rapid pace. And yes, for now, it is primarily among young people between 18 and 25 years old. But young people have parents and grandparents, young people have aunts, uncles and teachers. And if we let it escalate at this rate, it is inevitable that people from other generations will become infected. And this group also includes people with weakened immune systems, which makes the vaccine less effective. Moreover, not everyone has been vaccinated. Altogether, it could affect as many as 3 million adult Dutch people, where the virus can thrive and cause harm.

In both excerpts under Example 3, the ministers emphasise the consequences of the virus for those who do not follow the advice to get vaccinated: you will end up in the hospital. And that is your own responsibility.

Example 3.

Prime Minister Rutte (Press conference 2 November 2021):

> Listen, I really believe that people should decide for themselves whether to get vaccinated or not. I often meet people, well, sometimes I meet

> people who say, 'I have not been vaccinated,' and then I say, 'Hey, it is your choice. But you know, what I do know is that the chance of getting the disease is almost 100 percent or very high, and you run a very real risk of ending up in the hospital. But apart from that, it is your decision.' So there is no vaccination coercion, no vaccination pressure, people should decide for themselves.

Minister De Jonge (Press conference 2 November 2021):

> Everyone who has not yet been vaccinated, and has not already had the infection themselves, is very likely to become infected with the coronavirus at some point. Among those people, thousands will become so ill that they need to be hospitalised.

In Example 4, the prime minister justifies the decision to relax the measures only to a limited extent with a reference to a post describing the dire situation at the hospital. Here he uses someone else's description as a rhetorical device (exemplar), in order to arouse fear of code black, and also to make people under the age of 60 aware of the dangers. The quote itself ends with a tricolon ('the fact is . . . the fact is . . . the fact is . . .'), further reinforcing the message.

Example 4. **Prime Minister Rutte (Press conference 13 April 2021):**

> Yesterday, on one of the social media channels, a message appeared that I think sums up exactly where we stand now. It came from a hospital administrator, who wrote that in the past few weeks, he had lived in two worlds: the world outside and the world within the hospital. Outside the hospital, he mainly saw people who were looking forward to enjoying themselves on terraces, at concerts, and simply being together again. While inside the hospital world, everyone is busy coping with the third wave and, I add, preventing code black – the moment when all beds are full and hospitals ultimately have to say 'no'. And what does this hospital administrator write? The following: 'You can comment on the infection figures and the R value, but the fact is that hospitals are again as full as during the first wave. The fact is that scheduled care has been almost completely scaled back. The fact is that every day people die in the ICU from Covid, including too often people under 60.' End of quote.

The members of the government parties act in a manner similar to that of both ministers. Example 5 illustrates how MP (Member of Parliament) Paternotte, from the social-liberal party D66, appeals to fear by mentioning alarming statistics and referring to the precarious situation in the United States. He also makes uses of a specific example of a patient who could not receive treatment – a situation, he argues, that no one would want to find themselves in. At the end of his contribution, he presents the test certificate as a necessary measure for the upcoming period, describing it as a 'small sacrifice'.

***Example 5.* MP Paternotte (coalition party D66) (Debate 18 August 2021):**

> According to the OMT advice, we could still have around 16,000 to 22,000 hospital admissions and about 2,200 to 2,400 ICU admissions from the 1.8 million people in the Netherlands who are not yet immune and who all have apparently chosen not to be vaccinated. If all of that happens at once, hospitals will be overwhelmed. I hope we do not get it all at once. If it is spread out very evenly over two years, it might not even need to happen, but you and I also see what is happening, for example, in some states in America, where everything was opened up again at once, while there was not enough vaccination. That would not be wise. They are now hoarding ventilators again. I saw a video with a man who said, 'I was in the hospital with my wife, who has breast cancer; she was supposed to stay for four days and needed all kinds of treatments, but after two days, she was sent away because a bed was needed again for someone who was not vaccinated and became a Covid patient.' That is an ethical dilemma that I hope we can prevent in the Netherlands. Unfortunately, the OMT has to acknowledge that if we want to prevent these kinds of things, we will still need some measures in place in the coming period. If you can limit that to access passes, so that in principle everything can be open, but sometimes people are asked to show that they are either vaccinated or tested, that seems like a small sacrifice to prevent us from experiencing the same thing we are seeing in too many places in America right now.

2.3 Moderate opposition parties

In the parliamentary debates, the moderate opposition parties attempt to cast the government's proposed measures in a negative light. In doing so, they appeal to fear by exploiting feelings of anxiety regarding the potential consequences of these measures. In Example 6, MP Van der Staaij, from the conservative Reformed Christian party, expresses concerns about the coronavirus certificate and the increasing coercion it implies by asking a series of rhetorical questions.

***Example 6.* MP Van der Staaij (SGP, Reformed Political Party) (Debate 3 November 2021):**

> A feeling of unease, also because time and time again the Cabinet has stated that there will be no vaccination coercion, directly or indirectly. And the entire Parliament declared: no coercion, no pressure. But now, plans are on the table to possibly require the Covid pass in work settings, in healthcare, and even to make it mandatory for sports activities and, under certain conditions, in retail. If all of this proves insufficient, a Covid pass in education may follow later, or the option to use a test certificate as an alternative to the vaccination certificate might be removed.

> This is causing a lot of concern among citizens. Where does this end? When will we ever stop with this Covid pass? What is actually the goal of this approach and when will that goal be achieved?

In Example 7, MP Simons from BIJ1, a far-left, anti-racist and progressive party, shares similar concerns but does not pose questions. Instead, she issues a firm warning that these measures pave the way for the violation of citizens' fundamental rights: bodily integrity, the right to self-determination and freedom of choice. She also stands up for vulnerable people, whom she believes are being overlooked and, as a result, are at risk.

***Example 7.* MP Simons (BIJ1) (Debate 18 August 2021):**

> For months, this Cabinet has repeatedly stated that it is against mandatory vaccination, coercion or pressure. Despite clarity from the side of Parliament, today during this debate it appears that it is not at all clear for the Cabinet what exactly is meant by coercion, pressure, or obligation, and that we also need to consider unforeseen situations in which you may still need to consider an obligation in certain professional groups. This once again shows that the Cabinet is preparing to challenge the bodily integrity, the right to self-determination, and freedom of choice of Dutch citizens. I have my own opinions on this, of course. I also have various opinions on the entire Covid strategy; that has become clear by now. That aside: today I have one motion to continue protecting the vulnerable groups in our society as much and as long as possible, because the Cabinet seems to systematically forget about them.

In the eighth example, MP Van Kooten-Arissen, from a progressive, pro-animal welfare and social justice party, expresses concern about the postponement of the second vaccination. She poses rhetorical questions and accuses the government of playing 'Russian roulette', clearly alluding to the dangers faced by citizens.

***Example 8.* MP Van Kooten-Arissen (vKA) (Debate 21 January 2021):**

> The postponement of the second vaccination is at least illusory safety. That can become seriously dangerous. Last week, I asked the minister not to delay the second vaccination. He confirmed the risks involved. There are significant risks. Why is the Cabinet playing Russian roulette with health? Why does the Netherlands think it knows better again?

2.4 Populist opposition parties

The populist parties are highly critical of the government's measures. They make blatant use of pathos in the form of fear appeals. They primarily focus on greatly magnifying the consequences through enumerations, hyperboles, rhetorical questions, metaphors, exclamations and other stylistic devices. These consequences refer to the physical and mental effects of the measures on citizens' health. Additionally, populist politicians argue that various fundamental rights are being compromised: freedom, privacy, bodily integrity, freedom of speech, an independent judiciary and individual sovereignty. All of this is said to lead to experimentation on citizens, a dystopian society, a situation of medical apartheid and 'a totalitarian nightmare'.

In Example 9, MP Wilders, leader of the far-right populist party Party for Freedom (PVV), addresses the government's original strategy of seeking immunity from the virus within society. The MP makes the alarming accusation that the government is experimenting with human lives.

***Example 9.* MP Wilders (PVV, Party for Freedom) (Debate 18 March 2020):**

> The house is on fire. We need to extinguish it now and stop pushing more people into that house. We need to ensure that no more people get sick. We need to ensure that no more people die from that dreadful virus. Due to the government's strategy – once again: contrary to the advice of the World Health Organization, contrary to what most countries in Europe are doing, and contrary to what most virologists, including Dutch ones, say should happen – more people are deliberately infected based on a theory of herd immunity, which is not even scientifically proven. That is playing with human lives. That is an experiment with human lives. Surely, we cannot allow that here, can we?

In Example 10, MP Van Haga, from the far-right populist party FvD, makes an extended comparison of the curfew to an absurd and dictatorial society, referencing Orwell's *1984*.

***Example 10.* MP Van Haga (FvD, Forum for Democracy) (Debate 21 January 2021):**

> In 1980, I first read books about dystopian and absurdist societies: *Brave New World* by Aldous Huxley and, of course, *1984* by George Orwell. At that time, I was under the impression that it would be impossible for any of that to come true. The year 1984 passed and we were still living in freedom without a megalomaniacal, all-determining government.
>
> Recently, I reread *1984*, and to my dismay, I must conclude that we are not far removed from the horror scenario depicted in it. Newspeak has become normal, the Ministry of Truth is operating at full capacity, and state propaganda goes unchallenged. Demonstrating is still allowed, but only if it concerns a topic that is appealing to the government. The all-powerful government takes care of us, but in such a way that we become increasingly less free. In less than a year, we have gone from being a convivial and liberal people to a fearful group of individuals who no longer shake hands, no longer hug each other, and wear completely

> pointless face masks. We have willingly accepted that the government imposed a lockdown on us, causing small business owners and freelancers to go bankrupt. And no one rebelled. And all of this for a virus comparable to a severe flu, and because of a Cabinet incapable of scaling up the number of ICU beds. And now, this caretaker Cabinet imposes a curfew on us, and still we do not rebel. More and more, we are losing our freedom. I understand that leftist parties are fine with all of this. I have seen with my own eyes how this went in East Germany, Russia, China, and Cuba. I can tell you, it is hell. The socialist utopia does not lead to collective happiness, quite the opposite. What perhaps surprises me most is that liberal parties support this curfew. How is it possible that a liberal party can agree to such a disastrous measure?
>
> . . . Secondly, locking people up leads to illness, depression, obesity, child abuse, bankruptcies, and sometimes even suicide. The government is traumatizing an entire generation with this. How does the minister envision this dictatorial measure in practice?

MP Van Houwelingen, also from the FvD, emphasises in the last example the danger of a disruptive impact of the coronavirus measures and fundamental rights, which may end up on the bonfire. The unvaccinated will be forced to take a vaccine due to the vaccination certificate and will ultimately be blamed for everything.

***Example 11.* MP Van Houwelingen (FvD, Forum for Democracy) (Debate 18 August 2021):**

> The disruption caused by lockdowns, economically, physically and psychologically, will weigh on us for years to come. Meanwhile, and this greatly concerns us, it seems that those who still manage to retain their common sense, the unvaccinated, will be blamed for all of this, because this autumn – according to the logic of the pandemic – everything will be locked down again. And yes, even though there is obviously no ground for this: the blame for that, we will see, will be placed on the unvaccinated. They are pressured into getting a vaccine, while very sinisterly the minister continues to deny this. According to him, it's not pressure if someone has to pay every time to gain access, but an incentive.
>
> It may be clear: all COVID-19 measures can and should, as far as FvD is concerned, be lifted immediately. Freedom, privacy, bodily integrity, freedom of speech, independent judiciary, our individual sovereignty: with Covid, it all ends up on the bonfire. We are heading towards a situation of medical apartheid and must liberate ourselves from this totalitarian nightmare as soon as possible.

The examples from our case study illustrate how Dutch politicians used pathos, specifically appeals to fear, in press conferences and parliamentary debates regarding COVID-19 measures. The government and government parties, moderate opposition parties and populist opposition parties employed various rhetorical strategies and means, which will be evaluated in the following section.

3. Two models of democracy

As appears from our rhetorical analysis, in the Dutch political debate on COVID-19 appeals to pathos occur frequently. On both sides of the political spectrum fear is invoked to gain support for their respective position: the government mobilises fear for one's own and other's health and, ultimately, death to legitimise the drastic measures taken, whereas politicians from right-wing opposition parties present these measures as a threat both to democracy and people's physical and psychological well-being. How should we evaluate these invocations of fear? Is there any room for pathos in democratic political debates?

In our evaluation, we depart from two opposing models of democracy: the model of deliberative democracy and the model of agonistic pluralism. These models are derived from contemporary political theories of democracy; however, as theoretical abstractions, they may not fully align with the actual positions of the political philosophers involved or account for the variations among their perspectives. For the sake of argument and clarity we use these models to evaluate the appeals to pathos in the COVID-19 debate. In the model of deliberative democracy, defended by Benhabib, Habermas and others, political decisions are only justified if all participants can agree with them after a thorough process of deliberation. Collective decision-making is legitimate and rational if the collective deliberation is carried out in a rational and fair manner. That means, in particular, that the participants can deliberate freely, without any external constraints, and on an equal basis:

> According to the deliberative model of democracy, it is a necessary condition for attaining legitimacy and rationality with regard to collective decision-making processes in a polity, that the institutions of this polity are so arranged that what is considered in the common interest of all results from processes of collective deliberation conducted rationally and fairly among free and equal individuals.[9]

So, the legitimacy of the decisions taken does not depend on substantial (for instance, ethical) considerations but primarily on formal grounds, namely the extent to which the debate conforms to certain discursive principles. As Habermas argues, all types of practical discourse are subject to the discourse

9 Seyla Benhabib, 'Towards a Deliberative Model of Democratic Legitimacy' in Seyla Benhabib (ed), *Democracy and Difference: Contesting the Political* (Princeton UP 1996) 69.

principle, holding that 'only those norms can claim to be valid that meet (or could meet) the approval of all affected in their capacity as participants in a practical discourse.'[10] In his view, formal decision-making in legislative bodies is subject to the democratic principle of legitimacy: 'only those statutes may claim legitimacy that can meet the assent of all citizens in a discursive process of legislation that in turn has been legally constituted.'[11] When taking decisions on law, four types of validity claims have to be met: (i) truth claims about the likely consequences of different legal options, (ii) moral claims about the rightness or justice of these options, (iii) claims about the authenticity of different options (considering the polity's shared values and history) and (iv) pragmatic claims about which option is the most feasible or efficient.[12] Ideally, the decision-making process results in a rational consensus among the participants and not mere agreement.

In this ideal speech situation, not much room is left for strategic manoeuvring[13] since this may distort the rational exchange of arguments. According to Martin, many proponents of deliberative democracy explicitly reject rhetoric.[14] Rhetoric is taken in its colloquial, negative sense, referring to improper ways of influencing participants by appealing to emotion or to personal authority. Appeals to emotion (pathos) are primarily seen as manipulation: 'Emotion . . . is presumed to be manipulative in so far as it bypasses reasons and invites participants to accept arguments on the basis of unexamined feelings and automatic responses to symbols that do not bear rational scrutiny.'[15] Similarly, appeals to authority (ethos) defy rational deliberation, since participants are expected to accept arguments on the basis of trust alone – trust in the expertise or other special qualities of the speaker. In a truly rational debate, participants should appeal to valid arguments (logos) only, that is arguments that meet the standards of universality, truthfulness and sincerity.

According to Mouffe, deliberative democracy offers an inadequate model of democratic politics.[16] To begin with, she rejects the distinction between substance and form or, more specifically, between ethical considerations and

10 Jürgen Habermas, 'Discourse Ethics: Notes on a Program of Philosophical Justification' in Jürgen Habermas (ed), *Moral Consciousness and Communicative Action* (MIT Press 1990) 66.

11 Jürgen Habermas, *Between Facts and Norms: Contributions to a Discourse Theory of Law and Democracy* (W Rehg tr, MIT Press 1996) 110.

12 See further James Bohman and others, 'Jürgen Habermas' in *The Stanford Encyclopedia of Philosophy (Summer edn, 2023)* <https://plato.stanford.edu/archives/sum2023/entries/habermas/> accessed 25 March 2024.

13 See Frans van Eemeren, *Strategic Maneuvering in Argumentative Discourse: Extending the Pragma-Dialectical Theory of Argumentation* (Argumentation in Context, John Benjamins Publishing Company 2010).

14 J Martin, 'A Feeling for Democracy? Rhetoric, Power and the Emotion' (2013) 6(3) Journal of Political Power 461, 464.

15 Martin (n 14) 463.

16 Mouffe (n 7). See also Chantal Mouffe, 'Politics and Passions' (2000) 7(2) Ethical Perspectives 146.

discursive principles on which the theory of deliberative democracy is based. In addition, she criticises the very idea of a neutral and rational debate. Following Wittgenstein, she argues that having agreement in opinion presupposes an agreement on the language used which, in its turn, presupposes agreement in form of life.[17] In Wittgenstein's view, speaking a language always is part of other cultural activities and practices and, therefore, a form of life.[18] A form of life consists of concepts individuals share to give meaning to their world, the language that they use to communicate together with their cultural practices and values.[19] Different forms of life entail different ways of seeing the world. If participants do not share a form of life, there is no rational debate between them possible. A purely procedural approach, as advocated by Benhabib, Habermas and others, cannot settle fundamental differences of opinion, since procedures are always connected to substantial ethical commitments. In Mouffe's view, there are no universally valid standards of rationality; what is considered rational depends on the substantive opinions participants have about what is right and just. Therefore, we have to give up 'the dream of a rational consensus'; we cannot escape our human form of life. Subsequently, Mouffe questions the possibility of the 'ideal speech situation', where participants communicate freely with each other without any constraints and reach rational consensus by exchanging arguments. In her view, consensus is always the product of dominant forces (the 'hegemony') that suppress other, minority voices. She characterises discourse itself, after Lacan, as 'authoritarian in its fundamental structure', 'since out of the free-floating dispersion of signifiers, it is only through the intervention of a master signifier that a consistent field of meaning can emerge.'[20]

In short, Mouffe rejects the model of deliberative democracy, since it ignores what she considers to be essentially political in political decisions, that is the distinction between us and them. Instead, she advocates, together with Laclau,[21] the model of agonistic pluralism, which acknowledges the constitutive role of power struggles. In her view, democratic politics is not meant to overcome the us/them distinction, as deliberative democracy aims to achieve by means of rational consensus, but to find a suitable way of dealing with this distinction. In a pluralist democracy, participants should not treat the 'other' as an enemy who has to be destroyed – which is, according to Schmitt, the ultimate consequence of the us/them distinction[22] – but as an adversary. An adversary is a 'legitimate enemy' with whom we disagree but whom we grant

17 Mouffe (n 7) 750.

18 In his later, posthumously published, work, Wittgenstein uses this notion occasionally, see for instance Ludwig Wittgenstein, *On Certainty* (Basil Blackwell 1969).

19 Philip Tonner, 'Wittgenstein on Forms of Life: A Short Introduction' (2017) 24(1) eLogos 14 <https://e-logos.vse.cz/pdfs/elg/2017/01/02.pdf> accessed 25 March 2024.

20 Mouffe (n 7) 751.

21 Laclau and Mouffe (n 8).

22 Carl Schmitt, *The Concept of the Political* (George Schwab tr, Chicago UP 1996) 26–28.

the right to defend her or his ideas (Mouffe 1999, p. 755). What we share with the adversary is an 'adhesion to the ethico-political principles of democracy' (ibid.). However, disagreement remains about the interpretation and the application of these principles to concrete cases. According to Mouffe, this disagreement cannot be overcome by means of rational deliberation but requires conversion. Wittgenstein also believes that an appeal to logos cannot settle disputes among individuals who do not share a form of life.[23] As he states: 'At the end of reasons comes persuasion. (Think what happens when missionaries convert natives.)'[24] Conversion appeals to emotion rather than to reason; it is a kind of persuasion that works, as Martin says,[25] on judgement affectively. In this model, appeals to emotions are welcomed, because they express cries for justice that may otherwise, in a so-called rational debate, be ignored or suppressed. In an interview from 2013, Mouffe argued that democracy is in need of emotion and confrontation: 'an emotional engagement for more justice is not problematic at all.'[26] As she explains:

> Contrary to the model of 'deliberative democracy', the model of 'agonistic pluralism' that I am advocating asserts that the prime task of democratic politics is not to eliminate passions nor to relegate them to the private sphere in order to render rational consensus possible, but to mobilise those passions towards the promotion of democratic designs.[27]

These two models paint a rather black and white picture of what democracy is and how democratic debates should be carried out, whereas of course in reality often grey tones can be found. In the theory of deliberative democracy, emotions are not rejected fully. Gutmann and Thompson, for instance, criticise the Kantian distinction between emotion and reason and offer an Aristotelian account of deliberation which does not treat emotion as the enemy of reason.[28] Generally speaking, however, reason reigns over emotions: it is the ratio that decides which feelings may enter the democratic debate and in what way. Ultimately, emotions have to be translated into reasons that are acceptable for all participants. Conversely, agonistic pluralism does not reject some kind of rational control entirely. Mouffe, for instance, does welcome emotions to the extent that they increase the agonism between the various political fractions. Emotional interventions may help to articulate and bring to the fore differences in interests and value orientations. In her view, however,

23 Tonner (n 19) 17.
24 Wittgenstein (n 18) 612.
25 Martin (n 14) 473.
26 See <https://www.mo.be/en/article/democracy-need-emotion-and-confrontation> accessed 25 March 2024.
27 Mouffe (n 7) 755–56.
28 Martyn Griffin, 'Deliberative Democracy and Emotional Intelligence: An Internal Mechanism to Regulate the Emotion' (2013) 31 Studies in Philosophy and Education 517, 522.

they should not be used to feed antagonism between fractions, that is a sharp friend-enemy distinction that may end in war and attempts to annihilate each other. Mouffe has a preference for the positive emotion of hope, as part of a left-wing politics, since '[h]ope is rooted in justice, in equality'.[29] She dismisses the negative emotion of fear, as promoted by right-wing populist politicians. So proponents of both models do, on certain conditions, give room to emotions in the political debate. What divides them is that deliberative democracy, in order to reach a rational agreement, has to limit and suppress emotions, whereas agonistic pluralism gives them full stage since they may help to reveal hidden disagreements.

Abstracting from these nuances, we will first show how these models appreciate differently the various appeals to fear in the Dutch COVID-19 debate. In Section 4, we will give our own evaluation by using and combining some elements from both models.

From the viewpoint of deliberative democracy, the government and government parties have used pathos mostly in an appropriate manner. The government presents evidence which demonstrates that there is a serious crisis that calls for immediate action. The audience has to be convinced the controversial measures proposed, such as a lockdown or a curfew, are necessary. For that purpose, the government discusses the actual and potential consequences of the virus. In Examples 1 and 2, Minister of Public Health De Jonge refers to the fast-growing number of infections in the UK and Europe. Hospitals threaten to become overcrowded, as Prime Minister Rutte states (Example 4). Rising figures from scientific experts are cited to substantiate this claim. Within the deliberative democratic framework, the urgency of the situation has been demonstrated sufficiently. There is no need, however, to dwell too much on individual cases and potential threats. So it may be said that the government appeals too much to pathos, when it claims that people are dying in the ICU on a daily basis. The exemplar presented by Paternotte, member of the coalition party D66, is merely a sentimental illustration of how serious the infection can be in a concrete case (Example 5). What matters above all, from this perspective, is what measures have to be taken, given the gravity of the situation. A rational debate has to be held in which the available options are discussed and balanced from various – legal, ethical, pragmatic – perspectives.

In the contributions of the moderate opposition parties, even more strategic manoeuvring can be detected. Van der Staaij (SGP) invokes fear as he represents worried citizens and questions whether there will ever be an end to the utilisation of the coronavirus certificate (Example 6). Simons (BIJ1) points to possible violations of fundamental rights, such as the right to bodily

29 Gie Goris, 'Democracy in Need of Emotion and Confrontation: Interview with Political Scientist Chantal Mouffe' (*Mo*, 2013) <https://www.mo.be/en/article/democracy-need-emotion-and-confrontation> accessed 25 March 2024.

integrity and the freedom of choice (Example 7). In her plea for an earlier implementation of the second vaccination, Van Kooten-Arissen (vKA), accuses the government of playing 'Russian roulette with health' (Example 8). The interventions from populist opposition parties do not contribute to a rational debate at all. Wilders (PVV) paints a rather distorted picture of the Dutch crisis response, as if the government carries out immoral experiments with people's lives (Example 9). In alarming terms, Van Haga (FvD) states that the curfew will have severe consequences such as obesity, child abuse and suicide, without any empirical support. According to Van Houwelingen (FvD) we are moving to 'a situation of medical apartheid' (Example 11). Moreover, no suggestions are given for how to deal with the crisis situation, since COVID-19 is not conceived as a serious threat; according to Van Haga (FvD), it merely is 'a severe flu' (Example 10). Instead, unfounded claims, argumentative fallacies and hyperboles are presented that are meant to discredit any of the measures proposed by the government.

Building on the model of agonistic pluralism, a very different appreciation of the debate can be given. From this perspective, the government together with the government parties appear to be the hegemony which uses, or rather abuses, the crisis to extend its power. Appeals to pathos are meant to frighten the citizens, so they are willing to comply with the measures taken. The moderate opposition parties offer some resistance, but very weak and only on minor points; they pose no real threat to the government's hegemony. Real resistance comes from the populist parties that are engaged in the debate with full passion. There is a deep disagreement between the government and the populist opposition: opinions diverge fundamentally, to begin with on the gravity of the situation and, subsequently, on the necessity of the measures taken. Therefore, a rational debate is not possible and consensus can never be reached. The rhetorical means used make very clear what the populist opposition parties fear the most: a backsliding into authoritarian ruling, socialist style. As Van Haga puts it:

> More and more, we are losing our freedom. I understand that leftist parties are fine with all of this. I have seen with my own eyes how this went in East Germany, Russia, China, and Cuba. I can tell you, it is hell.
> (Example 10)

The rhetoric effectively reinforces the populist distinction between us (the right, speaking on behalf of the 'common' people) and them (the elite, still associated with the left). In terms of Mouffe, the other is not treated as an enemy who has to be destroyed, but as an adversary with whom it remains worthwhile to communicate somehow, but mainly on an emotional level. Moreover, the populist opposition seems to adhere to what she calls 'the ethico-political principles of democracy', including equality (which is implied in the resistance against 'medical apartheid') and freedom (in the sense of free choice).

4. Rhetorical democracy

As we have shown, the two models of democracy assess the appeals to fear in the Dutch political debates on the COVID-19 pandemic very differently. Generally speaking, the model of deliberative democracy is very critical of the way politicians from the extreme right mobilise fear to protest the measures proposed by the government. The fear that they appeal to is the danger of a backslide into authoritarian ruling. They mainly recur to pathos as means of persuasion, without offering much evidence for the possible consequences alluded to. The model of agonistic pluralism, by contrast, may evaluate appeals to pathos from the populist opposition in more positive terms. These appeals can also be understood as an expression of legitimate concerns about how the government restricts basic freedoms in its fight against the virus. Moreover, through an abundant use of pathos, the us/them distinction is reinforced, that is between citizens who cherish their freedom and want to make their own choices and the political and medical elite that abuses the health situation to control people.

In this section, we give our own evaluation of the debate by using and combining some elements from both models. In line with the model of deliberative democracy, we deem the exchange of arguments in democratic discussions very important. In a democracy, it can be expected from politicians that they not just spread around opinions but substantiate these opinions by means of convincing arguments and evidence. The model of agonistic pluralism tends to downplay these appeals on logos, because it considers an exchange of arguments among individuals who do not share a form of life fruitless. In our view, politicians should not give up on reason too easily and continue their efforts to convince others of their point of view. A 'form of life' is not a static entity but may develop and change through encounters with other opinions and in the light of new experiences, if participants are willing to suspend or to call into question at least some of their beliefs. This is part of what may be called the *ethos of democracy*, which involves a flexible and critical attitude towards one's own beliefs. We do not deny, as Fogelin argues (after Wittgenstein), that there may indeed be deep disagreements among participants that are very difficult, if not impossible, to solve through reason. If a shared background of beliefs and preferences is lacking, it can be 'pointless' to enter the language game of argumentation.[30] But we believe that it is crucial, in the light of the great existential challenges facing humanity nowadays, that we try to find new ways to deal with disagreements, however deep and fundamental these may seem. For that purpose, Heidlebaugh argues for a 'rhetoric of the possible', which builds on inventive rhetorical technai, devised by sophists like Gorgias. One of these techniques is *commonplacing*, which aims at destabilising fixed positions and creating new commonplaces between opposing points of view.

30 Robert Fogelin, 'The Logic of Deep Disagreements' (2005) 25(1) Informal Logic 3, 7.

Commonplacing consists of 'pulling together concepts into a common place (a place of identity or similarity) or removing them from a common place'.[31] Heidlebaugh describes this process as follows:

> The proper use of language, then, is to suggest new possibilities and to compel belief in them, rather than to attempt to represent some sort of stable essences . . . in fact, the very ambiguities and instabilities of language make possible the disruption of old meanings. Invention may be seen as a process of using those ambiguities to create similarities where none had been seen to exist or differences where none had been apparent.[32]

Following Mouffe, we consider the constraints deliberative democracy places on collective decision-making too strict and not realistic. We agree that in political debates a rational consensus among all participants often is an unattainable goal. It may not even be a desirable goal when it is reached at the cost of suppressing minority voices. Moreover, emotions do not have to be banned altogether from political discourse. Rhetorically speaking, emotions can have an important signaling function: they highlight interests that matter to the participants involved.[33] As neuroscientific research shows, anxiety may stimulate immediate learning and may even create conditions for deliberation by stalling habits. The model of deliberative democracy tends to downplay appeals to pathos, because they would distort the rational exchange of arguments. However, pathos may also support logos by bringing to the fore arguments that otherwise would be neglected or not heard. Contrary to Mouffe, we do not think that emotions should be used to maximise the us/them distinction. In our view, the model of agonistic pluralism stresses too much the element of *agon* in politics. Politics is turned into a permanent struggle for power, without any promise of redemption. The ultimate goal of political decision-making in a democracy is not so much to continue the fight, but rather to bring it to a peaceful resolution which (at least most of) the participants can live with. The parties involved eventually have to find, after long and thorough processes of collective deliberation, some kind of agreement, compromise or work around that brings the conflict to a temporary halt. That means that appeals to emotion in our view are allowed in political discourse, if they are used in a responsible way: not to replace arguments but to support and reinforce them; not to distinguish us from them but to draw attention to issues that are relevant

31 Nola J Heidlebaugh, 'Invention and Public Dialogue: Lessons from Rhetorical Theories' (2008) 18 Communication Theory 27, 42.

32 Heidlebaugh, 'Invention and Public Dialogue' (n 31); a more extended description of the 'rhetoric of the possible' can be found in Nola J Heidlebaugh, *Judgment, Rhetoric, and the Problem of Incommensurability* (U of South Carolina P 2001).

33 As discussed in Griffin (n 28) 526 and Martin (n 14) 468 respectively.

both for us and for them; not to polarise for the sake of polarisation but to find together workable solutions for urgent social problems.

As a supplement to the models of deliberative democracy and agnostic democracy we advocate, with Martin, a *rhetorical democracy*.[34] In a rhetorical democracy, debate is encouraged and emotions play an important supportive role. As Martin argues, '[a] rhetorical democracy . . . is one where feelings are brought to the fore, not held back, so that they are productively contested and challenged'.[35] All rhetorical means of persuasion – in the domains of logos, ethos and pathos – are allowed as long as they contribute to a well-functioning process of democratic decision-making and, ultimately, to good decisions. Pathos has to be used responsibly, not to exclude others, but to promote an open debate on urgent social problems. An appeal to emotion has always to be accompanied or followed by an appeal to logos, in which arguments and evidence are provided for the position taken. In our view, it does not matter what kinds of emotion – fear, anger, desperation, hope, solidarity and so on – are invoked. It all depends on how pathos is used, for what purpose and in what context. According to Illouz, fear is 'the ally of the right because it enables people to live in what Carl Schmitt calls states of exception'.[36] It 'provides compelling motivation to repeatedly name enemies as well as invent them, to view such enemies as fixed and unchanging, to shift politics from conflict resolution to a state of permanent vigilance to threats, even at the price of suspending the rule of law'.[37] In her view, moral emotions such as compassion and fraternity are more suited for a decent society. Nussbaum considers fear to be one of 'compassion's enemies',[38] since it can undermine people's commitment to the common good. This may be true but is, in our view, no reason to exclude fear altogether from public discourse. In a situation of danger, it is perfectly reasonable to appeal to fear, as Nussbaum acknowledges.[39] In her view, the fear for the safety of one's loved ones should be retained in a decent society.

Whether a situation really is dangerous is, of course, a matter of individual judgement, and individuals can differ fundamentally and vehemently on this matter, as became apparent during the pandemic. As a consequence, a normative (linguistic or other) assessment of the debate is never neutral but involves an appreciation of the gravity of the situation and the necessity of the measures taken. In our rhetorical analysis we too have to take a stance in this politically

34 Martin (n 14) 472.

35 Martin (n 14) 474.

36 Illouz (n 4) 49. However, Wodak claims (with a reference to Altheide) that fear is used nowadays on both sides of the political spectrum, both by liberals and conservatives, see Ruth Wodak, *The Politics of Fear: What Right-Wing Discourses Mean* (Sage 2013) 13.

37 Illouz (n 4) 162–63.

38 As stated in Nussbaum (n 2) 320, the triad of fear, envy and shame constitutes 'compassion's enemies'.

39 Nussbaum (n 2) 320, 375.

charged discussion: are the rhetorical means employed by both sides fitting, considering the situation at hand and the measures proposed? In classical rhetoric (see, for instance, Aristotle's *Poetics*[40]), this is called the principle of *decorum*: the use of style has to be appropriate to the subject, situation, speaker and audience. According to Jakimov (2022, p. 5), representative democracies should aim at achieving affective alignment, that is 'congruence between the representative and those they represent in terms of the way they are moved (impressed upon) and move (impress) others (affective presence)'.[41]

Applied to the Dutch debates on the COVID-19 pandemic, it is evident that the Dutch government, like every government worldwide, faced a critical health crisis threatening the lives of many, particularly the elderly and vulnerable people. Such a grave situation necessitates a serious approach to the subject, raising the question of how to effectively address this existential threat. In this case, we believe that an appeal to emotion is not only permitted but also appropriate, to make people aware of the threat and to persuade them to comply with the measures proposed. The authorities involved, as speakers, have to show the audience that they take the situation seriously, both on a rational and an emotional level. At the same time, spokespersons of the opposition parties are entitled to present a different assessment of the situation and to express their worries about the measures proposed. However, if they do so, they must provide arguments why they assess the situation differently and reject the measures.

In our evaluation of the debate, we both build on and depart from the two models of democracy discussed earlier. In line with the model of deliberative democracy we believe that the government and government parties have used pathos, generally speaking, in an appropriate manner. We also agree that the contribution of the populist opposition parties to the debate was not very constructive. The reduction of the coronavirus to a mere 'severe flu' (Example 10) does not do justice to the serious consequences the virus has had and continues to have on people's lives. The Dutch government may be accused of limiting basic freedom too much, but in no way can it be compared to a socialist (or communist) state, as Van Haga (FvD) suggests (Example 10). These are examples of what Dryzek calls 'ugly rhetoric'.[42] In times of crisis, it is not helpful to maximise the us/them distinction; instead we have to find, despite our differences of opinion, ways of working together. That does not mean that everything the government proposes must be taken for granted – on the contrary. For that reason, we appreciate more positively the strategic manoeuvring from the moderate opposition. Members of the

40 George Whalley (tr), *Aristotle's Poetics* (McGill-Queen's UP 1997) 56, s IIV.2.

41 Tanya Jakimow, 'Representation through Affective Correspondence: The Force of Feelings and Their Consequences for Representative Democracy' (2022) 44 Emotion, Space and Society 1.

42 John S Dryzek, 'Rhetoric in Democracy: A Systematic Appreciation' (2010) 38(3) Political Theory 319, 333.

moderate opposition parties can be said to offer valuable input for the debate: they express legitimate concerns about the scope of the measures proposed (Example 6), possible violations of fundamental rights (Example 7) and the timing of the measures (Example 8). Both Van der Staaij (SGP, Example 6) and Simons (BIJ1, Example 7) question, for good reasons, whether the choice to be vaccinated really is as free as Prime Minister Rutte claims (Example 3). Moreover, the government itself does not shy away from some strategic moves itself: the numerous scientific figures and numbers it presents do not appeal to logos only but can also be taken as an appeal to pathos, since they show that the virus is spreading rapidly – not really a reassuring message. Against the model of deliberative democracy, we think strategic manoeuvring in debates is acceptable to stress the gravity of the situation and the need to take action. However, we would not go as far as the model of agonistic pluralism to support the excessive appeals to pathos by the populist parties. In our view, these appeals do not contribute to a constructive debate; they only serve to portray the involved parties as anti-establishment.

5. Civilisation and its discontents

In this chapter, we have advocated a rhetorical conception of democracy which allows for strategic manoeuvring in political debates. We have tried to find a middle way between two opposing models of democracy: on the one hand, deliberative democracy, which reduces political debate to a purely rational exchange of arguments and on the other hand, agonistic pluralism, which turns politics into a permanent struggle full of passion. We do believe, with Mouffe, that emotions may play an important role in political debates. As Aristotle already acknowledged, persuasion is not only a rational affair; it also involves trust in the speaker (ethos) and an emotional alignment with the audience (pathos). Rhetoric is an integral part of political discourse. An appeal to pathos may be helpful to foreground certain interests and to motivate people to accept the measures proposed and to act accordingly. However, as we argued earlier, an appeal to pathos is in itself never decisive but has to be accompanied or followed by an appeal to logos.

It may be claimed, however, that our conception still is rational, perhaps too rational, particularly in the face of an acute crisis situation. It is true that we intend to bring emotions under some sort of rational control. If claims are made, fueled by emotions, we require additional arguments that support these claims: Are the reasons given convincing? Is there any evidence for these claims? Are the sources referred to reliable? Although we may not succeed in convincing each other, we should not give up trying to create some common ground in what seems to be an instance of deep disagreement or at least to forge an acceptable compromise or a work-around.

When faced with the pandemic, authorities had to find a difficult balance between protecting public health and securing freedom. In hindsight, it may be said that the Dutch government, like many other governments, put too much weight on public health, building on a too narrow conception of health. In the name of public health, fundamental freedoms, such as the freedom of religion and the freedom of association and privacy, were restricted or suspended temporarily, which also had a negative impact on mental health of especially young people. At the same time, not acting would have put the lives of many more people, in particular older and vulnerable ones, at great risk.

Emotions can help to call attention to certain interests, but they can also drive a wedge between two opposing groups. In her latest book *Doppelganger*, Naomi Klein contends that the assertions propagated by Covid deniers and conspiracy thinkers were dismissed by mainstream liberals due to their exaggerated rhetoric.[43] Consequently, the majority readily acquiesced to the imposition of freedom restrictions in Canada and the US. 'The result is a troubling dynamic', as Klein writes.

> Rather than being defined by consistently applied principles – about the right to a democratically controlled public square, say, and to trustworthy information and privacy – we have two warring political camps defining themselves in opposition to whatever the other is saying and doing at any given time.[44]

The same may apply to the Dutch political debate on the pandemic. Opposition representatives, who voiced their concerns with an overabundance of emotion and relied on argumentative fallacies, were disregarded by the Dutch government and mainstream media. In retrospect, it may be said that at least some of their concerns were justified: not all measures taken, such as the curfew, appeared to be necessary and infringed too much on civil liberties.[45]

In order to keep political debates civilised and constructive in a representative democracy, it is necessary that appeals to pathos are used in a moderate and responsible way. According to Freud, civilisation – the regulated world of culture, law, religion and society – arises from the learned repression of individual instinctive drives. Civilisation or culture comprises 'the whole sum of the achievements and the regulations which distinguish our lives from those of our animal ancestors and which serve two purposes – namely to protect men against nature and to adjust their mutual relations'.[46] For the sake of self-preservation and, more generally, the preservation of the species, people are forced to live and cooperate with other human beings. Freud characterises the process of civilisation as the eternal struggle between *Eros* and *Thanatos*.

43 Naomi Klein, *Doppelganger: A Trip into the Mirror World* (Allen Lane 2023).

44 Klein (n 43) 93.

45 The Dutch Safety Board has given a critical evaluation of the Netherlands' crisis response in three separate reports, see <https://onderzoeksraad.nl/en/onderzoekserie/corona-response/> accessed 25 March 2024.

46 Freud often uses the terms 'civilisation' and 'culture' interchangeably, see Sigmund Freud, *Civilization and Its Discontents* (James Strachey tr, Norton 1989) 42.

Civilisation serves *Eros*, the life drive that brings people together. Contrary to this stands *Thanatos*, the death drive aimed at destruction, which manifests itself in aggressive behaviour. To make peaceful co-existence possible, people must learn to control and suppress their aggressive and sexual desires. This means that they must refrain from immediate gratification of needs. In Freud's view, civilisation is based on repression and sublimation of primary human needs. Sublimation is the process by which instinctive drives and energies are transformed into non-instinctive and socially acceptable behaviour.

The repression or 'reversal' of primary instincts inevitably results in discontent. As Freud suggests, civilised individuals partially sacrifice their happiness for a sense of existential security. If this discontent is not addressed – such as through sublimation – serious psychological disorders can arise. While sublimation can yield higher-order pleasures, these still serve as substitutes for the fulfilment of primary instinctual impulses. Thus, discontent is the price paid for living together in a civilised society. However, as the rise of armed conflicts around the world indicates, people appear increasingly unwilling to pay this price.

6 Fake news and democracy

A lesson from the COVID-19 pandemic[1]

Guerino Fares

1. Freedom of information, democracy, fake news: an introduction

Traditionally, in Western democracies the right to express one's thoughts is considered instrumental to the correct formation of public opinion, to the conscious exercise of citizens' political rights and, ultimately, to the proper functioning of democracy. In this context, a new challenge to democratic systems has been launched by the so-called fake news which tends to manipulate politics and social media. This is a phenomenon that affects entire communities, putting at risk the fundamental right to sound information, necessary to form free and critical thinking and to exercise the rights connected to democratic citizenship. These rights are often threatened by the distorted use of information which, even on scientific topics, fuels such confusion that everything can be true and false at the same time: in this regard, we speak of post-truth politics.[2]

The impact of technology on information can produce disinformation, impacting electoral processes and, more generally, relations between citizens and states. But disinformation has a broader and more global reach, as demonstrated by the examples of Brexit, the US presidential elections, COVID-19 and the war between Russia and Ukraine.

The problems related to communication on the web have a significant impact on both individual subjective rights and collective rights, such as security, public order and peaceful coexistence.[3] Aiming to undermine the pillars of democracy, fake news jeopardizes its functioning for electoral purposes or to contest the established order, sometimes inciting violence to

1 This chapter is produced as part of and funded by the European Union-NextGenerationEU, through the National Recovery and Resilience Plan of the Republic of Bulgaria, project No bg-rrp-2.004-0008.

2 S Giusti and E Piras (eds), *Democracy and Fake News: Information Manipulation and Post-Truth Politics* (Routledge 2021) <https://www.routledge.com/Democracy-and-Fake-News-Information-Manipulation-and-Post-Truth/Giusti-Piras/p/book/9780367479541.

3 See WHO, Risk Communication, Weekly Epidemiological Record, No 7, 2016, 91.

DOI: 10.4324/9781003610670-9

support anti-political projects, which can also lead to subversion and terrorism. Between democracy and bad information there's a strong and dangerous connection. Disinformation practices are often disguised as credible sources or personal opinions, infiltrating information channels and diverting the perception of reality. By exploiting people's vulnerability, fake news can direct public consensus toward extreme ideologies, dividing communities and weakening the social composition.

Fake news is not only accused of adulterating the genuine process of idea formation by misleading voters. "Hoaxes" based on false or unverified news have polluted the scientific debate during the coronavirus pandemic, destabilizing minds and increasing concern and confusion among populations. This problem raises particular social alarm,[4] since the spread of fake news occurs through automated tools and social media, thus managing to influence public opinion and individual beliefs, as well as significantly influencing collective and political decision-making processes. In this regard, we talk about "disrupting democracy", to describe the dark side of the role of technology in the democratic system.[5]

Nowadays, information influences the geopolitical framework and the very survival of states on a global level. Think of the growing diffusion of the warfare model known as hybrid warfare, namely, a flexible and mixed military strategy that includes conventional warfare, irregular warfare and other actions such as disinformation, cybercrimes, attacks on economies, sabotage of energy sources, espionage, acts of terrorism, propaganda and attempts to interfere with the foreign electoral result. Fake news is an important part of hybrid warfare, capable of putting the cohesiveness of our democracies at high risk.

There is therefore a need to first clarify the key concepts and then regulate social media by introducing certain rules, adequate sanctions, global governance mechanisms and effective techniques for preventing and combating fake news. New procedural obligations for actions involving freedom of expression should be established. The legal framework should simultaneously ensure transparency of sources, privacy of users, responsibility of those guilty of disinformation, pluralism of ideas and public and private ethics.

Measuring precisely the impact of disinformation on public opinion and on political and social life is not easy. The analysis of the democracy-truth-public opinion connection would require a real understanding of the transformations produced by the digital revolution on the processes of creating consensus. The impact of fake news on public opinion and on democratic processes requires, upstream, an investigation from a philosophical-political point of view of the relationships between politics and truth and between democracy and truth.

4 See A Ezra Waldman, 'The Marketplace of Fake News' [2018] Journal of Constitutional Law, Philadelphia 845.

5 Bertelsmann Foundation, *Disrupting Democracy: Point, Click, Transform* (Bertelsmann Foundation 2018).

However, on a legal level, taking a first step forward is possible if the basic notions are defined and the initiatives taken so far to deal with this phenomenon are analyzed.

An inappropriate notion and use of disinformation can be counterproductive and become a way to limit freedom of thought and public debate. The so-called information disorder[6] must also be considered, i.e., the dissemination of news, not necessarily false, through methods suitable for equally polluting the information ecosystem.[7] Therefore, great caution is needed in qualifying fake news as an autonomous legal category that includes unlawful behavior.[8]

The ambiguity of the concept, and its blurred boundaries, were also underlined by the "High Level Group of the European Commission" on fake news and online disinformation. In its report published in March 2018, it found that the term fake news has now been distorted in the public debate and is not adequate to describe in a complete and exhaustive way an increasingly complex phenomenon.

The definition of fake news raises several questions: What news does it include? Is it necessary to prove the intent of the diffusion or even just guilt is enough?[9] The "Code of Practice on Disinformation" from the European Commission provides a sufficiently clear and exhaustive definition of "fake news":

> Disinformation is verifiably false or misleading information created, presented and disseminated for economic gain or to intentionally deceive the public. It may have far-reaching consequences, cause public harm, be a threat to democratic political and policy-making processes, and may even put the protection of EU citizens' health, security and their environment at risk.[10]

The problem of definition is certainly linked to the methods of creation and diffusion of fake news, as well as to the identification of those responsible.

6 R Bracciale and F Grisolia, 'Information Disorder: Technological Accelerators and Social Dynamics' (*Federalismi.it*, 2020), 63; C Wardle, 'First Draft's Essential Guide to Understanding Information Disorder' (October 2019) <www.firstdraftnews.org>.

7 DO Klein and Joshua R Wueller, 'Fake News: A Legal Prospective' (April 2017) 20(10) Journal of Internet Law 6.

8 According to M Sullivan, 'It's Time to Retire the Tainted Term Fake News' (*Washington Post*, 8 January 2017), the same expression "fake news" is misleading and dangerous and it's time to shelve it.

9 On the importance of the will and the weaponization of context, see M De Cock Buning and others, 'A Multi-Dimensional Approach to Disinformation' (Report of the independent High-level Group on Fake News and Online Disinformation, Publications Office 2018) <www.data.europa.eu>.

10 European Commission, 'Tackling Online Disinformation' <https://ec.europa.eu/digital-single-market/en/tackling-online-disinformation>.

The concept of fake news includes different categories: (i) misinformation, when false content is accidentally spread by unaware users, convinced that they are disclosing content that corresponds to a real social interest; (ii) misinformation, when truthful information is published with the specific purpose of creating adverse consequences; and (iii) disinformation, when the content of the news spread is intentionally false and transmitted ad hoc to cause harmful consequences.

There are mainly two methods of spreading fake news.[11] The first is so-called click baiting, i.e., the publication of fake news with sensational photos and headlines aimed at arousing the user's curiosity, or by publishing previews of videos with different content than the real one. The second is so-called astroturfing, which is done by strategically distributing a specific news story across a variety of sources to give the impression that several of them are having a discussion. Both practices make false news appear to be true and accepted by an illusory majority based on non-existent knowledge, with the aim of profit or propaganda.[12]

Furthermore, the difficulty of identifying those responsible for fake news must be considered, as we must deal with a flow of globally disseminated disinformation from both immediate and mediated authors, perhaps located in foreign countries. In fact, fake news can originate from both real users and robots, as well as transmitted by individuals who even unknowingly spread it. Social platforms have suppressed the filter offered by information professionals and their guaranteed tools, allowing any subject, even those who according to the traditional scheme of the information report would have been mere users, to personally contribute to the production and dissemination of information: in this regard, we speak of information decentralization. Furthermore, there is a close relationship between privacy, protection of personal data and fake news. In this scenario cybersecurity, understood as the art of protecting networks, devices and data from unauthorized access or criminal use and the practice of ensuring confidentiality, integrity and availability of information, comes into play.

Regarding artificial intelligence, it is also worth mentioning the risk of data poisoning, which arises when learning algorithms are fed, even intentionally, with erroneous or compromised data in order to alter the contents produced by the algorithm itself and thus spread misinformation. Due to generative artificial intelligence and its ability to produce false content capable of influencing public opinion, the question has emerged of how much these technologies can undermine democratic processes, and to address this risk it is necessary to build a regulatory system aimed at mitigating and limiting the destabilizing

11 See A Information Society Project at Yale Law School and the Floyd Abrams Institute for Freedom of Expression, Fighting Fake News (Workshop Report 2017).

12 K Lerman, X Yan and XZ Wu, 'The "Majority Illusion" in Social Networks' (2016) 11(2) PLoS One <https://doi.org/10.1371/journal.pone.0147617>.

effects that new technologies can cause in the social fabric and in the political debate.

The undeniable concerns posed by fake news, also in relation to the aforementioned rights, led the European Union to intervene. In this sense, the European Union has published the report "A multidimensional approach to disinformation", the communication "Tackling online disinformation: a European approach" and the "Code of Practice on Disinformation". In particular, the Code attempts to provide a set of common principles capable of guiding the activities of private entities involved in the fight against the phenomenon of fake news, in order: (i) to guarantee greater transparency on the production and promotion of news; (ii) to ensure the credibility and diversity of information; and (iii) to create a cooperation system. In practice, both soft law acts (Commission recommendations) and hard law acts (as in the case of the "Digital Service Act") have been adopted to protect various public interests, combat hate speech and disinformation and mitigate the constitutional challenges raised from the private governance of communications networks.[13]

Alongside the first projects aimed at regulating communication on the web,[14] the Constitutional Affairs commission of the EU Parliament has prepared a specific study on "foreign institutions and interference", "defense of liberal democracy" and "integrity of European elections".[15] Indeed, European institutions can effectively contribute to reducing the problem of disinformation, adopting best practices and legal standards in order to protect everyone's right to freely construct their personality, identity and opinion.

2. Health crisis and disinformation

The legal regulation of fake news raises numerous issues, especially regarding the balance of rights. The advent of the digital revolution has led to an important evolution in the communication sector: greater speed, greater amount of information, the possibility for anyone to comment on the news and usable anywhere in the world (from a "one to many" to a "many to many" system).[16] Information through the web therefore appears fluid but makes it difficult to distinguish sources based on their authority.

The case of the right to health is emblematic. Inaccurate news campaigns have been developed that could endanger the health of users by causing an underestimation of the risks of the virus. Furthermore, conspiracy theories aimed at attributing responsibility relating to the origin or development of

13 E Llansò and others, 'Artificial Intelligence, Content Moderation and Freedom of Expression' (TWG Papers 2020) <www.ivir.nl>.

14 T Berners-Lee Launches Campaign to Save the Web from Abuse <https://www.benton.org/headlines/tim-berners-lee-launches-campaign-save-web-abuse>.

15 Fake News and Threats to Democracy: The European Parliament Takes Remedial Action <https://digital-strategy.ec.europa.eu/en/policies/online-disinformation>.

16 CR Sunstein, *#Republic: Democracy in the Age of Social Media* (Princeton UP 2017).

epidemics have spread. Analyzing the impact of the circulation of false news on the spread of viruses, we can speak of an "infodemic", i.e., the extraordinary and excessive diffusion of information, some of which is not always correct and accurate, which has made it difficult for people to find reliable sources and guidance, causing them to underestimate the real risks.[17]

After all, elections and crises are ideal contexts for the proliferation of disinformation and "fake news", also thanks to technological innovations (e.g., deepfakes). The main effect of this phenomenon on democratic politics is the erosion of trust between citizens and political decision-makers: where sometimes the former, as they lack any orientation, are unable to form an opinion and choose sources of information. In extreme cases, politics loses meaning for citizens and democracy is obscured by demagogy.

The delicate and increasingly widespread phenomenon of untruthful information has exploded in the last decade. The year 2016, marked by the referendum on Brexit and the US presidential elections, and consequently by very frenetic and polarizing electoral campaigns, has shown the importance of "fake news" and manipulated information in politics.[18] Attention to "fake news" has also been notable on the other side of the Atlantic, where the term is very often associated with Russia. During the recent coronavirus pandemic, fake news hit both the topic of vaccines and the so-called green pass, i.e., the pass issued to those who were vaccinated or immune to the virus. Fake news includes both fake news and news that is partially truthful but reworked in order to arouse or consolidate a specific belief or feeling in the community of users.

The spread of misinformation on social medias influenced the rate of vaccine hesitancy. The proliferation of wholly or partly false news, artfully constructed to encourage sharing across various networks, is a growing phenomenon on websites, forums, blogs, social networks, etc. The marketplace of ideas is in this case overwhelmed by irrelevant or completely false and unfounded news, spread thanks to a chain that, at least for online information, is based on a process characterized by a high level of disintermediation, which makes it difficult to identify sources and responsible for a news story.

There are various causes: (i) the irrepressible margin of uncertainty in scientific research and the difficulty of ascertaining scientific truths; (ii) the

17 WHO, Risk Communication, Weekly Epidemiological Record, No 7, 2016, 91; WHO, Munich Security Conference, 15 February 2020; BBC, 'WHO Says Fake Coronavirus Claims Causing "Infodemic"' (*BBC*, 13 February 2020); The Wall Street Journal, 'In the Coronavirus "Infodemic" Here's How to Avoid Bad Information' (*The Wall Street Journal*, 22 March 2020); People's Uncertainty About the Novel Coronavirus Can Lead Them to Believe Misinformation, Says Stanford Scholar (16 March 2020) <https://news.stanford.edu/press/view/32840>.

18 See H Allcott and M Gentzkow, 'Social Media and Fake News in the 2016 Election' (2017) 31(2) Journal of Economic Perspectives 213. See also H Byung-Chul, *Infocracy* (Polity 2022).

possibility that social networks and new technologies offer everyone to convey their ideas; (iii) the complexity of the relationships between politics and science, and between regulation and medical science in particular; and (iv) the aforementioned spread of the so-called infodemic, understood as the circulation of an excessive amount of information that is not always carefully examined, which makes it difficult to orient oneself on a given topic due to the difficulty of selecting reliable sources.

Philosophy has always sought the truth, Kant, Heidegger, Plato, Heraclitus, Demosthenes and other illustrious masters of thought having explored the relationship between freedom of expression and truth of facts. Regarding free expression of thought in democratic systems, Dostoevskij maintains that people, to be truly free, must be also left free to affirm that 2+2=5. Instead, according to Orwell freedom and democracy imply that a man must always and, in any case, recognize that 2+2=4. Dostoevskij's thesis better captures the essence of the freedom of speech: everyone must be free to say what they want, even if they talk nonsense. At the same time, freedom of speech has a strong impact on democracy since a bad information can undermine the democracy's hold.

It is true that the use of new technologies can fuel the viral spread of wrong, distorted, manipulative, if not downright violent and hateful news. But it is also true that the democratic system is based on freedom of thought as the free circulation of all ideas in the name of its intrinsic ability to produce the necessary antibodies, thus avoiding the risk of regulatory intervention that generates any form of censorship. In other words, the so-called minimum content of democracy is to be reconstructed starting from the right of citizens to freely form their own opinion through a free competition between organized political groups.[19]

Objective truth ends up being confused with the power of hidden persuasion that platforms exercise. Considering that the internet has not only become the center of a great engine of democracy, as a place where everyone's freedom of thought is welcomed and amplified, but has also profoundly changed the cultural, social, political coordinates and economic choices of large sections of the population. Both the lack of subjective knowledge, since the human being is limited on a cognitive level, and the objective lack, which induces, in the face of the bombardment of information, a substantial laziness in seeking the truth, ensuring that we end up accepting what we desire or what is more convenient for us, they play a central role in this match. Moreover, the intertwining of quality of information, science and participation hinders both the implementation and the request for policies aimed at maximizing collective well-being.

On the other hand, the epistemological conceptions of truth have highlighted how the latter is not an acquired fact waiting to be revealed but is

19 The balance between the form of State and social complexity, as well as between the role of the elite and political rights, was identified by N Bobbio, *The Age of Rights* (Polity 1997).

always the outcome or product of a process of research and approximation which, however, is inevitably conditioned by the subject who narrates the facts and exposes the results of the research: therefore, what must be protected through freedom of information is precisely the truth understood as a process of construction and refutation[20] to which each of us can contribute by drawing on a plurality of elaborate sources critically.

At the same time, it should not be forgotten that the freedom of expression of thought, as guaranteed by Western democratic constitutions, does not only cover objectively useful or truthful news, but rather all manifestations of thought. A general rereading of the meaning of freedom of expression of thought in the democratic constitutional state leads, at most, to valorizing the right to be informed, as a passive consequence of freedom. From this perspective, we can affirm the existence of a constitutionally protected interest in ensuring that the information circulating is transparent and truthful, to protect the recipient of the information itself.

If knowledge is not a mere perceptive phenomenon, divergence of views is the rule and not the exception; if there are no truths that are universally valid for everyone, if scientific truth is the result of a process of elaboration and continuous updating, and if the legal and social system wants to guarantee everyone's freedom to search for information and data to form an opinion, then establishing what is true and what is false is much more problematic than one might think. On the one hand, we can take for granted the fluctuation of scientific research, which is accompanied by the provisional nature of its assumptions, attested by the precautionary principle, and the complexity of the specialized technical language. On the other hand, the ontological lack of neutrality and objectivity of the postulates of science cannot legitimize an absolute skepticism that authorizes anyone to contest medical-scientific findings.

It is, therefore, necessary to identify regulatory mechanisms so that the power of the means of diffusion of thought and circulation of fake news does not cause a serious vulnerability to the free market of ideas, jeopardizing the protection of constitutionally guaranteed interests and rights. By leveraging the disorientation and concerns of the community in a time of health emergency, the propagation of information without scientific basis has led to the exploitation of people's needs and feelings, compromising the correct formation of public opinion and the very stability of the democratic order.

The topic of fake news introduces the debate on the role and responsibilities of social media and on the remedies for misinformation, considering that fake news spreads more easily and quickly than real news.

The main antidote remains, in my opinion, the cultural defense, which promotes scientifically based counter-information capable of authoritatively countering misinformation and so-called systemic bubbles, thus revitalizing

20 KR Popper, *Science and Philosophy* (Springer 2021).

the circuit of trust between scientific operators, political decision-makers and web users.

In this sense, the words of the US Supreme Court are very significant in the case *United States v. Alvarez* of 28 June 2012 eschewed the repressive option, favoring the dialogic approach also about disinformation. Finding that a law that punished those who falsely claimed to have earned a decoration was contrary to the First Amendment, the Court stated:

> The remedy for speech that is false is speech that is true. The response to the unreasoned is the rational; to the uninformed, the enlightened; to the straight-out lie, the simple truth. The theory of our Constitution is that the best test of truth is the power of the thought to get itself accepted in the competition of the free market of ideas. Any suppression of speech by the government can make exposure of falsity more difficult, not less so.

It's true that the use of social media with the related ease of access, lack of controls and easy dissemination of messages makes the issue of fake news particularly pressing; but it is equally true that the same circulation on social media can offer part of the solution through an easier and more immediate public "unmasking" of fake news, precisely by virtue of those same characteristics mentioned that encourage its diffusion.

Obviously, we cannot limit ourselves to a sanctioning approach, nor think that technology alone can solve the problems, nor delude ourselves into delegating to third parties, such as experts, the task of deciding the boundary between truth and lies, affirming the logic of dominant thought. The fight against disinformation cannot be assimilated to an instrument of protected democracy: the early protection and repression of ideological dissent cannot, in fact, be reconciled with the constitutional guarantee of information pluralism.

It is also necessary to avoid excessive accountability of social platforms and not to make the interest in democratic protection absolute to legitimize tools of ideological repression. Regulating the responsible functioning of platforms, renouncing any illusory claim to directly control the contents, may be the right objective. We must not, however, give in to the general paradox whereby freedom of expression finds its limit not so much in the protection of the rights of third parties, but rather in the misuse that would be made of freedom itself and therefore gives rise to a hypothesis of abuse of law. As is known, the scientific method cannot be reconciled with dogmatism, but on the contrary is nourished by the pluralism of opinions, which become, from time to time, hypotheses to be studied and validated. So, a system that truly wants to protect freedom of expression must also commit to protecting falsehoods.

After all, in liberal systems freedom of speech also protects opinions that are not true and doesn't require that people who express their thoughts must tell the truth, because even untrue news is protected. Nevertheless, truth and democracy are two closely linked values, in a both historical and philosophical perspective, considering the strong connection between quality of information and democracy's hold.

In the meantime, to correct information disorder, it makes no sense to propose a "new politics of truth", where the category of truth is transformed into democratic paternalism as a remedy for digital populism.[21] To fight misinformation governments may be increasingly empowered to control information based on what they believe to be true. Freedoms related to the internet, press and access to broader sources of information are already in decline and risk degenerating into a broader repression of information flows. Thanks to the expedience of the battle against *fake news*, the denial of the doctrine of the free market of ideas could produce the restoration of the single-class state, which cancels both the need for equal freedom annexed to pluralistic democracy and the very premises of the rule of law.

Nonetheless, there are numerous solutions proposed in the legal and mass media debate to deal with the malpractice of disinformation[22]: (i) the false news label; (ii) the accountability of the authors of false and unfounded news; (iii) the mechanisms of preventive censorship associated with forms of subsequent inhibitory and repressive control; (iv) the introduction of new types of criminal offense aimed at sanctioning the conscious dissemination of artfully misleading messages and news; (v) the creation of information channels validated by the relevant scientific community; and (vi) enhancing the principle of responsibility established by article 5, par. 2, of the GDPR, regarding the processing of personal data.[23]

In outlining the countermeasures with respect to the proliferation of fake news, two different approaches or operational models ultimately compete in the field: the first concerns public sanctioning intervention against certain conduct implemented by social networks, the second instead focuses on the self-regulation of online platforms by making them responsible so that they know how to identify and remove untruthful content. Further upstream, it

21 S Foà, 'Public Powers and the Fight Against Fake News: Towards the Effectiveness of Alethic Rights? (*Federalismi.it*, 2020) No 11, p 248, tries to outline the legal consistency of such a claims to truth, the degree of effectiveness and the ways in which public authorities (legislator, regulatory authority, public administration) can ensure their protection, especially in the face of the growing phenomenon of fake news on the net, checking whether a new "Social Cultural Right" could be invoked in the era of hyper-connection.

22 "Although disinformation exists since a long time, with the development of new technologies fake news have a significant impact even on the proper functioning of democracy and, therefore, it's theoretically acceptable that the legislature restricts – with due caution – the freedom of expression in order to limit as much as possible the risks of disruption of the public debate": P Passaglia, 'Fake News and Fake Democracy: A Convergence to Be Avoided' (*Federalismi.it*, 2020) No 11, p. 126.

23 The *EU Code of Practice on Disinformation* was signed and presented on 16 June 2022 as an act of self-regulation that provides, in addition to the removal of deceptive or misleading content, the role of the fact-checker having the task of guiding the managers of digital platforms both in the assignment of "green stickers" to news deemed to be true and in the identification of more reliable sources, to which the algorithms will have to ensure greater visibility.

would be very appropriate to avoid the stratification of transitory and close-by provisions, rather reducing the information asymmetry between regulatory authorities and citizens. In the absence of clear rules, a natural chilling effect linked to the fear of both legal and economic repercussions leads social providers to limit freedom of expression, renouncing their traditional role as neutral intermediaries and taking on the task of monitoring the contents published by users and their diffusion. Added to this is a further deficit in transparency and neutrality of the network, due both to the high number of data entered on the web and to the algorithmic profiling of news, which tends to accommodate user preferences (so-called information bubble).[24]

Further dysfunctions result: (i) gross errors, violent news and information distortions, the result of the biases of the algorithm programmers; (ii) de-responsibility of human moderators; and (iii) group polarization phenomena, i.e., the risk of information based on affinities with similar individuals with radicalization effects and renunciation of pluralism.

Technology can indeed help in identifying fake news, allowing the algorithm to understand the meaning of the text it analyzes and further contextualizing the content of the information. We must, however, accept the natural limits of technology, which are based on statistical-probabilistic foundations developed by an "anonymous" conscience, and which therefore remain a means and cannot become an end.

The phenomenon of information disorder cannot, therefore, be addressed exclusively with a technological approach, using algorithms for fact-checking or content moderation. Nor is it possible to entrust control entirely to the self-regulation of individual platforms that, as driven by economic interests, struggle to reclaim their role as neutral intermediaries, which was at the basis of the implicit statute of the network traditionally.[25]

In the contemporary democracies all pieces of the mosaic are to be considered: (i) right to free expression of thought; (ii) right to be informed; (iii) right to correct and genuine information; (iv) exercise of political rights; (v) democracy's hold; (vi) social media obligations; and (vii) trust between political decision-makers and citizen-voters.

3. Brief notes on the complex relationship between law and science

The public powers' claim to define false information is to be considered deceptive. The crucial challenge is to find out the conditions under which a positive framework inspired by the free marketplace of ideas and by the Kelsenian idea of pluralist democracy can be safeguarded. In any case, both the *anti-fake news*

24 D Palano, *Bubble Democracy: The End of the Public and the New Polarization* (Scholé 2020).

25 Foà (n 21) No 11, p 260, appreciates the "responsible" retreat of public control in favor of the self-regulation of network actors despite the lack of homogeneity of the policies followed by each of them.

measures provided by Western European states and the guidelines adopted by the European Union must be compared with the constitutional standard of protection of freedom of speech and the essence of pluralist democracy.[26] Therefore, a right balance, counteracting external attacks and, at the same time, guaranteeing freedom of expression, which is a founding pillar of our democracies, must be found.

As has been said,[27] even though the communication of science to the wider public has been a second-level priority for most scientists and institutions for a long time, in recent years the scenario has radically changed because social media is increasingly exposing science works, data and scholarly literature to a public never imagined before. Since the surge of fake news and conspiracy theorists may contribute to the discredit of science and researchers, research does not happen anymore behind closed doors of academia but rather in a publicly accessible arena. Therefore, science communication shouldn't be considered as a marginal part the work of a scientist, but rather a vehicle for making scientific facts accessible to the general public, by contributing to a better-informed society and more aware of the value of scientific research.

In this context, science is not univocal but is fueled by contrasts, censorship and struggles between orientations. Science is conditioned by the passage of time and the evolution of knowledge, which can be overcome and contradicted. Therefore, it is always difficult to establish what is true and what is false. Hence, the delicate chapter of the relationship between medical science and political and legal regulation opens: the theme of the science reserve is connected to the precautionary principle and the shared guidelines of the national and international scientific community based on the data and knowledge available in that specific historical moment.

Without adequate scientific input, the legislator and, more generally, the political decision-maker cannot make choices with a convincing and reasonable basis. For example, the state of scientific knowledge is crucial with a view to justifying in a rational and proportionate way the vaccination obligation for health workers, who occupy a position qualified by the principle of constitutional solidarity and by the mission of minimizing the risk to the health of patients, especially if frail and vulnerable, who meet them.

The question of whether the vaccination obligation is correctly and scientifically justified considering the authoritativeness of the studies and research carried out by the institutionally competent bodies in the field of health safety is fundamental. Imposing compulsory vaccination is an issue

26 E Lehner, 'Fake News and Democracy' (2019) 1 Media Laws Review 1, underlines that in terms of general theory, the debate involves, on the one hand, those who resolve Plato's paradox of freedom by referring to the limitations of power perspective and, on the other hand, those who claim the validity of the mentioned paradox, which can be clearly seen, among others, through the lines of Böckenförde's dilemma ("The secularized liberal state lives on assumptions that it is unable to guarantee").

27 C Colaiacomo, 'Scientific Fake News: Image Crisis for Research?' (*Federalismi.it*, 2020), No 11, p 188.

which, in addition to implying a delicate balance between fundamental values, that of self-determination and that of public health, affects the very relationship between science and law and, even more so, the relationship between knowledge – and, therefore, information and its opposite, disinformation – and democracy. In other words, it is science that indicates valid therapeutic options to legislators and individuals. At the same time, it could be appropriate to encourage the dissemination of information channels validated by the scientific community and suitable for combating the phenomenon of fake news. The reserve of science, which the public decision-maker must refer to when adopting health measures to deal with an epidemiological emergency, cannot erase the inevitable margin of uncertainty that characterizes scientific knowledge in the construction of truths that affirm themselves only over time, thanks to rigorous studies and experiments and subjected to the verification-falsification criterion, as well as to the control of judges.

The implementation of the precautionary principle therefore means that, whenever the risks induced by a potentially dangerous activity are not known with certainty, the action of the public authorities must translate into prevention in advance of the consolidation of scientific knowledge. In conclusion, it is worth reiterating the increasingly urgent virtuosity of the dialogue between jurists and scientists in the co-production of regulation with a technical-scientific content, according to a multidisciplinary approach that requires a careful balance between rights and scientific evaluations.

In conclusion, the principle of freedom of information and open debate between a plurality of opinions cannot put under discussion, being as an indispensable foundation of democracy. The issue of the creation and distribution of news is destined to become a decisive battleground for the future of our democracy. We must find the most suitable tools to check the source and truthfulness of each news. In making both technology and human beings responsible, public authorities will always have to find a balance between the need to regulate the contents produced by this technology and respect for the principles of plurality and freedom of opinion. Technology is built by humans and its use must protect human beings.

Part III

Agencification, transnational administrative networks, and the future of representative democracy

Democratic-technocratic (dis)balance and trends toward technocracy, bureaucracy, and expertocracy?

7 Administrative legislative policy in EU national communities

Assessing benefits and risks amidst the globalization of law

Mauro Zamboni[1]

1. Introduction

The globalization of law, though an inherently abstract concept, manifests as a phenomenon deeply ingrained in the daily lives of citizens within a national community. Legal categories and concepts originating from distant social, political, cultural, and economic contexts suddenly transform into obligatory regulations that individuals must adhere to. In this process of incorporating foreign legal constructs into a community's life, a pivotal role falls upon public administration and its officials. They act as the conduit for legal categories and values, transitioning from the external world, swiftly passing through national assemblies, and abruptly imposing themselves on individuals within a community. As pointed out by a legal scholar,

> Emerging forms of "complex sovereignty" break down the internal structural coherence of the State, replacing it with often autonomous regulatory agencies whose purpose is to meditate between the international and the local or national.[2]

1 This chapter is produced as part of and funded by the European Union-NextGenerationEU, through the National Recovery and Resilience Plan of the Republic of Bulgaria, project No bg-rrp-2.004-0008.

2 Kanishka Jayasuriya, 'Globalization, Law, and the Transformation of Sovereignty: The Emergence of Global Regulatory Governance' (1999) 6 Indiana Journal of Global Legal Studies 425, 437. Also Sabino Cassese, 'The Administrative State in Europe' in A von Bogdany, PM Huber and S Cassese (eds), *The Max Planck Handbooks in European Public Law: Volume I: The Administrative State* (OUP 2017) 57, 75. Eg Oksun Baek, 'The Constitutional Status and Roles of Public Agencies Participating in Legislation in the Global Domain – The Republic of Korea's Establishment of Technical Norms' in M Grahn-Farley, J Reichel and M Zamboni (eds), *Governing with Public Agencies – The Development of a Global Administrative Space and the Creation of a New Role for Public Agencies* (Poseidon Förlag 2022) 145, 159–62. But Alfred C Aman, 'Administrative Law for a New Century' in A Prakash and JA Hart (eds), *Globalization and Governance* (Routledge 2000) 267, 270.

DOI: 10.4324/9781003610670-11

In Western or Western-style democracies, constitutional documents often confer upon public administration the legal authority to "administer and implement" decisions made by parliaments through legislative provisions. This alignment with these normative requirements is crucial for garnering recognition as a legitimate player in supranational and international legal arenas.[3] However, reality reveals that the public administrations of nation-states have gradually expanded their legal prerogatives, sometimes subtly, surpassing the mere "implementation" of national legislative acts. Public agencies frequently operate within loosely defined legislative frameworks designed to incorporate, in a national legal context, the legal outcomes of globalization processes. This evolution transforms them from mere executive hands of legislative power into quasi-legislative entities. These entities give rise to regulatory provisions and regimes that, often operating at the fringes or outside of the borders set by national legislative assemblies, become the true agents of transformation for global legal categories into national law.[4]

This chapter seeks to investigate the phenomenon of democratic state public administrations transcending their traditionally assigned administrative functions and, influenced by the globalization of law, venturing into the realm of law-making. Specifically, by employing the concept of "administrative legislative policy" as the model for regulating various aspects of modern democracies, especially those susceptible to the impacts of globalization and its regulatory regimes, the study will examine this trend from two perspectives. First, the chapter aims to delineate the modalities and reasons behind the extensive use of public administration as the default mode for law-making at the national level. Furthermore, the use of this legislative policy model will be assessed, particularly concerning some of the legal pillars of a democratic state and the idea of participatory democracy.

After briefly outlining the framework of this chapter in Section 1, by focusing on the law-making activities of national public administrations in EU member states and by defining key terms, Section 2 delves into examining the impact of the globalization of law on national law-making. It particularly scrutinizes the roles of national legal actors such as legislative and administrative bodies. Sections 3 and 4 subsequently identify the advantages, especially concerning the efficiency of the law-making process, and the risks, particularly in relation to the foundational principles of a Western democracy, associated with administrative legislative policy. This policy model explicitly transfers regulatory power from national assemblies to public agencies through legislative drafting styles. Finally, in Section 5, corrective measures, primarily of a constitutional nature, are suggested to mitigate the risks for democracy associated

3 Eoin Carolan, *The New Separation of Powers: A Theory for the Modern State* (OUP 2009) 1.

4 Edward C Page, *Policy Without Politicians: Bureaucratic Influence in Comparative Perspective* (OUP 2012) 5–8. Eg Peter Grajzl and Peter Murrell, 'Allocating Law Making Powers, Self-Regulation v Government Regulation' (2007) 35 Journal of Comparative Economics 520, 529–34. Also Morten Egeberg and Jarle Trondal, 'Political Leadership and Bureaucratic Autonomy: Effects of Agencification' (2009) 22 Governance 673.

with the widespread use of administrative legislative policy, while retaining its benefits.

2. Why law-making by the public administration of EU member states matters (and exploring key definitions)

Before commencing the investigation, it is essential to undertake two preliminary steps: first, to highlight the significance of selecting this field, specifically the law-making by administrations in EU member states; and second, to clarify some key concepts employed in this study. Regarding the first step, the choice of law-making is rooted in the recognition that these processes play the pivotal role of creating the regulatory system known as law and of understanding then the very structure and ideas behind a legal system. However, as emphasized by Jeremy Waldron in the late 90s, legal scholars, irrespective of their standpoint, tend to predominantly focus on the final product (i.e., the law) and its connections with the surrounding environment (morals, economy, society, and culture).[5] The process by which a particular legal system arrives at the construction or introduction of a specific legal category is often neglected in systematic investigations from a legal scholarship perspective. Legal scholarship has exhibited limited interest in understanding how and why a legal system, particularly in the national system, incorporates a foreign "global" legal category into its law-making processes.[6]

Moving to the law-making by public administrations at the national level, this phase is crucial for comprehending the tangible consequences – both legal and otherwise – of the globalization phenomenon. The administrative bodies and their decisions stand as the public organs closest to the community, serving as the ultimate recipients of the changes brought about by globalization and its impact on the legal landscape. In essence, the law-making activities of public administrations at the national level play a fundamental legal role in shaping a national community. They are instrumental in understanding how the globalization of law affects this community, as these actors within the state apparatus are institutionally and legally endowed with the crucial task of translating "ambitious policy ideas into practice," thereby impacting the everyday lives of citizens.[7]

5 Jeremy Waldron, *The Dignity of Legislation* (CUP 1999) 1–2; Richard W Bauman and Tsvi Kahana, 'New Ways of Looking at Old Institutions' in R W Bauman and T Kahana (eds), *The Least Examined Branch: The Role of Legislatures in the Constitutional State* (CUP 2006) 1–2. Also Mauro Zamboni, *The Policy of Law* (Hart Publishing 2007) ch 2.

6 Eg Gordon Silverstein, 'Globalization and the Rule of Law: "A Machine that Runs of Itself?"' (2003) 3 International Journal of Comparative Law 427, 440–42.

7 Donald F Kettl and James W Fesler, *The Politics of the Administrative Process* (4th edn, CQ Press 2004) i, xviii. Eg Maria João Rodrigues, 'Improving Governance of the Lisbon Agenda: Conclusions of the Debate' in MJ Rodrigues (ed), *Europe, Globalization and the Lisbon Agenda* (Edward Elgar 2009) 310–12.

Given the considerable variations in the shapes and functions of public administrations across different realities, even within those adopting the same form of government, such as democracy, this study will specifically focus on the law-making conducted by public administrations in countries that are members of the European Union. This choice streamlines the investigation, as these countries share, to a large extent, the same type of legal system (civil law), constitutional ideal (liberal democracy), and conceptualization of the institutional role of the public administration (executive branch). Furthermore, by concentrating on EU member states, the study aims to identify common traits and tendencies among them, thus mitigating differences in how the globalization of law may impact diverse legal realities. These states not only participate in the same international legal environment (e.g., as full-fledged members of organizations like the UN and WTO) but also share a common supranational legal framework within the EU. The EU plays a pivotal role in the globalization of law, serving not only as a recipient of globalized legal concepts but also as an active producer in the global legal discourse. This role is particularly evident in its influence on member states, exemplified by the legal requirements of participatory democracy as outlined in Article 11 of the Lisbon Treaty.[8]

Due to space and clarity constraints, this study exclusively focuses on examining how globalization influences public administration at the national level. It foregoes delving into vertical interactions between domestic administrations and EU administrative bodies, as well as equally crucial horizontal interactions among various national administrations of EU member states. While this focus is certainly limiting, it nevertheless provides crucial insights into the law-making of public administration in democracies entrenched in the phenomenon of globalization. Importantly, the law-making of domestic administrations in EU member states is not merely a passive response to globalizing forces from the EU and from other member states; rather, national public agencies are integral legal and operational components of the entire EU administrative machinery. To comprehend their role and potential challenges in law creation, it becomes essential in order to understand the functioning of administrative law-making at the EU level, marking a fundamental, though not exclusive, step in grasping the dynamics within the broader context of globalization.[9]

8 Armin Von Bogdandy, 'The European Lesson for International Democracy: The Significance of Articles 9 to 12 EU Treaty for International Organizations' (2012) 23 European Journal of International Law 315, 323–26. Also Jean-Bernard Auby, 'The EU and Global Administrative Law' in PJ Birkinshaw and M Varney (eds), *The European Union Legal Order After Lisbon* (Kluwer Law International 2010) 57, 58–60; Martin Painter and B Guy Peters, 'Administrative Traditions in Comparative Perspective: Families, Groups and Hybrids' in M Painter and B Guy Peters (eds), *Tradition and Public Administration* (Palgrave Macmillan 2010) 19.

9 Hermann CH Hofmann and Alexander Türk, 'The Development of Integrated Administration in the EU and Its Consequences' (2007) 13 European Law Journal 253. Eg Torbjörn Larsson and Jarle Trondal, 'Agenda Setting in the European Commission: How the European Commission Structure and Influence the EU Agenda' in HCH Hofmann and A Türk (eds), *EU Administrative Governance* (Edward Elgar 2006) 11.

Transitioning to the second step of this introductory section, it is essential to elucidate certain central concepts utilized in this study. It is crucial to note that the ensuing definitions are not definitively established; instead, they adopt a non-logical, axiomatic nature, resembling postulates. Essentially, these are theory-specific assumptions open to questioning. Nonetheless, for the sake of discussion within the framework of this study, one may proceed under the assumption, without necessarily endorsing it, that these definitions are valid – or at the very least, plausible.[10]

Commencing with the concept of the *globalization of law*, or legal globalization, this term denotes the dissemination of legal models, encompassing legal categories and concepts. This process results in a tendency for various components of diverse legal systems to exhibit homogeneity.[11] As a consequence, a noticeable homogenization of legal issues and corresponding responses has become evident across a range of legal domains. This phenomenon is observable not only in traditionally "international" realms such as human rights and business law but also, more recently, in areas traditionally deemed the exclusive purview of national legislatures, including criminal law, taxation law, or, last but not least, administrative law.[12]

Regarding the concept of *law-making*, it is employed in a broad context within this discussion. Lawmaking encompasses the operational facets of the legal phenomenon, encompassing the mechanisms that render specific moral, economic, political, social, and other models directly pertinent in legislative or administrative forms within the legal sphere and among its participants. In this context, the adopted concept of law-making embraces both the "transcendental approach," where law-making is viewed as a process of "discovering and recognizing" models already present within a community, and the "rational approach," which perceives law-making as a process of "imposing" certain models created by lawmakers.[13] However, for *legislative law-making*, the focus is specifically on the process of translating non-legal ideals into sources of law, taking on the form and authority, or, as in the case of many administrative regulations, mimicking the statutory provisions.

Finally, *public administration* refers to the comprehensive machinery encompassing policies, rules, procedures, systems, organizational structures, personnel, and other elements funded by the state budget. This apparatus is entrusted with the management and oversight of the executive government's

10 Dieter Wunderlich, *Foundations of Linguistics* (CUP 1979) 149.

11 William Twining, *Globalisation and Legal Theory* (Butterworths 2000) ch 1. Also Elizabeth Hege Boyle and John W Meyer, 'Modern Law as a Secularized and Global Model: Implications for the Sociology of Law' (1998) 49 Soziale Welt -Zeitschrift Für Sozialwissenschaftliche Forschung Und Praxis 213, 217–27.

12 Eg Sabino Cassese and Elisa D'Alterio, 'Introduction: The Development of Global Administrative Law' in S Cassese (ed), *Research Handbook on Global Administrative Law* (Edward Elgar 2016) 1, 4–7.

13 Wojciech Cyrul, 'How Rational Is Rational Lawmaking?' in LJ Wintgens (ed), *The Theory and Practice of Legislation: Essays in Legisprudence* (Hart Publishing 2005) 93, 95–100.

affairs, engaging in interactions with various stakeholders in the state, society, and external environments beyond the state apparatus.[14] This interaction primarily involves the execution of laws and other regulations adopted or issued by legislatures, executives, and courts. It is important to note that the terms "public administration" and "public agencies," while often denoting entities with distinct extents and natures (with agencies frequently constituting part of the public administration), are used interchangeably in this study.

3. Globalization of law and the shift in law-making

If one defines globalization in terms of the circulation of legal models, the crucial role of law-making becomes evident in such a phenomenon – specifically, the transformation of values into legal categories. It is important to note that legal globalization has not only altered the content of the law in affected countries, introducing legal categories that may be perceived as "foreign" to local legal traditions and discourses. It has also significantly impacted the very process of law-making, particularly by reshaping the roles of the domestic legislative lawmakers.[15] In particular, the globalization of law has set in motion two forces that have dramatically altered, or in some cases brought to the surface, pre-existing changes in the traditional (and ideal) paradigm of a continental European democratic legal system. This paradigm traditionally entails the legislator creating the law, the judiciary adjudicating according to the law, and the administration implementing the law in everyday life.

The globalization of law has, first and foremost, widened the disparity between the creation of laws and their practical implementation by legal actors.[16] In contemporary times, legal models applicable within a specific legal system often originate from legislative processes occurring in foreign or distant countries and/or supranational entities. Notably, global legal categories are frequently articulated in vague terminology or terminologies intrinsic to the legal system of their origin. Consequently, their implementation within a local or national community necessitates a comprehensive process of redesign by implementing agencies, particularly the judiciary and administrative bodies. This transformative process is so extensive that, ultimately, it entails the

14 United Nations Development Programme, *Democratic Governance Group, Public administration Practice Note, 2003* (Bureau for Development Policy 2003) 5. *Cf* Andrew Massey, 'Civil Service Systems: Introduction and Scope of the Book' in A Massey (ed), *International Handbook on Civil Service Systems* (Edward Elgar 2011) 3–4. Also Haroon A Khan, *Globalization and the Challenges of Public Administration: Governance, Human Resources Management, Leadership, Ethics, E-Governance and Sustainability in the 21st Century* (Palgrave Macmillan 2018) 5–7.

15 Terence C Halliday and Bruce G Carruthers, 'The Recursivity of Law: Global Norm Making and National Lawmaking in the Globalization of Corporate Insolvency Regimes' (2007) 112 American Journal of Sociology 1135, 1138. Eg Paul Street, 'Stabilizing Flows in the Legal Field: Illusions of Permanence, Intellectual Property Rights and the Transnationalization of Law' (2003) 3 Global Networks 7, 13–14.

16 Twining (n 11) ch 1; Cf Neil Walker, *Intimations of Global Law* (CUP 2015) 47–48.

crafting of a new regulatory measure. This measure is intricately tailored to the local legal discourse, diverging from the original legal category to such an extent that the final outcome, i.e., the binding legal norm, is only loosely inspired by and based upon the original legal concept.

For instance, one should consider the legal concept of "equal pay for work of equal value," a globalizing paradigm within labor law aimed at fostering a genuinely gender-neutral pay equity working environment. However, its effectiveness can be compromised when translated into a national legislative principle. This is particularly true if the recipient legal system fails to anticipate the complete set of procedural and judicial mechanisms required for women or their union representatives to effectively realize the rights to equal pay. In such cases, the translated global legal principle may lose its binding force and become less effective in achieving its intended goals.

A second force has reshaped the ideal paradigm of the EU member states' legal system and has exerted a profound impact on the fundamental structure and role of the nation-state as the primary legislative authority. The globalization of law has played a pivotal role in diminishing the significance of the nation-state as the principal regulator, leading to a corresponding erosion of its primary regulatory instrument, namely, legislative law-making.[17] In this evolving landscape, the development of regulatory frameworks for critical domains has, to a significant degree, shifted away from state entities, finding new homes among non-state actors. For instance, environmental law is increasingly shaped by the influence of nongovernmental organizations (NGOs), while business law sees the emergence of regulatory models driven by collaborations among transnational corporations.

These forces, both signaling and amplifying law-making beyond the traditional realm of national assemblies and their legislation, are undeniably real. However, paradoxically, they have propelled legal actors, whether national or supranational, to the forefront of the law-making stage. Firstly, the globalization of law has not diminished the significance of domestic legal actors in the law-making process. As pointed out by Saskia Sassen,

> Legislative items, executive orders, adherence to new technical standards, and so on, will have to be produced through the particular institutional and political structures of each participating [to the globalizing process] state.[18]

17 Pierre Larouche and Péter Cserne, 'Introduction' in P Larouche and P Cserne (eds), *National Legal Systems and Globalization: New Role, Continuing Relevance* (TMC Asser Press 2013) 1–2; Ran Hirschl, *Towards Juristocracy: The Origins and Consequences of the New Constitutionalism* (Harvard UP 2007) 216. Also Commission of the European Communities, *European Governance – A White Paper on Governance, COM(2001) 428* (2001) 14 <https://ec.europa.eu/commission/presscorner/detail/en/DOC_01_10> accessed 13 April 2024. Eg Boaventura de Sousa Santos, *Toward a New Legal Common Sense: Law, Globalization, and Emancipation* (2nd edn, CUP 2003) ch 9.

18 Saskia Sassen, 'The State and Globalization: Denationalized Participation' (2004) 25 Michigan Journal of International Law 1141, 1156. Also Martin Shane, Thomas Saalfeld and Kaare

The centrality of legal actors becomes especially apparent when considering that the circulation of legal models invariably undergoes some form of sanction, either *ex ante* or *ex post*, by local or national legal entities. This form of approval, often referred to as "legalization" by various scholars, serves as a necessary (though not sufficient) condition for an ideal or value to attain normative force.[19] In Max Weber's terminology, this process grants a certain degree of "legal legitimacy," enabling the ideal or value to operate with the force and legitimacy typically associated with the tool of law in modern society.[20] Legislative bodies, judges, administration, and lawyers are still the central (although not exclusive) figures in this law-making process, allowing the transformation of global legal categories and concepts into legal categories and concepts with a legal status in their own (supranational or national) communities. The central role of legal actors does not, as often proclaimed by some researchers, consist of simply divulgating a legal pamphlet written abroad in their own country.[21] For the very transformative nature of the law-making process (both at legislative and judicial levels), legal actors play the central role of "rewriting" such a pamphlet in their own legal discourse, a re-writing affected by the then current social, economic, cultural, and legal situation of the addressees' community.[22]

Secondly, the globalization of law has shifted the primary law-making responsibility among legal actors. In the traditional, albeit possibly never fully realized, law-making model of a continental European democratic nation-state, the national assembly and its legislative measures held the dominant position in law-making. However, in the current landscape, the center of gravity for law-making seems to have moved toward the two other major legal actors: the public administration and the judiciary. Especially in legal areas most impacted by globalization, national parliaments are often perceived and, more often

W Strøm, 'Introduction' in M Shane, T Saalfeld and KW Strøm (eds), *The Oxford Handbook of Legislative Studies* (OUP 2014) 1, 3–5. Eg Sabino Cassese, 'Administrative Law Without the State? The Challenge of Global Regulation' (2005) 37 *New York University* Journal of International Law and Politics 663, 680–84.

19 Jürgen Habermas, 'Law as Medium and Law as Institution' in G Teubner (ed), *Dilemmas of Law in the Welfare State* (de Gruyter 1986) 203, 213–17; Ronald Dworkin, *Law's Empire* (Harvard UP 1986) vii. Also Martin Loughlin, *Sword and Scales: An Examination of the Relationship between Law and Politics* (Hart Publishing 2000) 229–35.

20 Max Weber, 'Politics as Vocation' in HH Gert and C Wright Mills (eds), *From Max Weber: Essays in Sociology* (Routledge 1991) 77, 95.

21 Paul Verbruggen, 'Gorillas in the Closet? Public and Private Actors in the Enforcement of Transnational Private Regulation' (2013) 7 Regulation & Governance 512, 523–26. Eg Robert A Kagan, 'Globalization and Legal Change: The "Americanization" of European Law?' (2007) 1 Regulation & Governance 99, 107–12.

22 Duncan Kennedy, *A Critique of Adjudication (fin de siècle)* (Harvard UP 1998) 152. Also Neil MacCormick, *Legal Reasoning and Legal Theory* (Clarendon Press 1997) 235–37; William Twining, 'Diffusion of Law: A Global Perspective' (2004) 36 The Journal of Legal Pluralism and Unofficial Law 1, 30.

than not, operate as mere rubber stamps for statutory provisions originating from distant sources. Under the influence of globalizing forces like the WTO or informal networks of political and economic powers, national legislators frequently incorporate globalized legal categories into upcoming legislation without providing substantive normative definitions or concrete measures for implementation. Using the previous example, a national legislator might introduce a comprehensive labor act stating simply that the principle of "equal pay for work of equal value" should be regarded as a paramount binding legal principle.

As a consequence, the intermediary agents, whether judicial or administrative, emerge as the true law-making actors in the entire process of translating global legal categories into national and local realities. The judiciary and the public administration assume a pivotal role in transforming the law in books into law in action, tasked with the fundamental responsibility of translating abstract "global" legal categories into concrete, binding measures that impact local communities.[23] This role became particularly evident during the Covid crisis and its impact on the EU member states. While national legislation tended to enact somewhat vague measures to counteract the spread of the disease – measures often derived from recommendations or legal solutions originating at the supranational or international level – the actual law-making, involving the production of binding measures regulating community life, was effectively delegated (albeit with varying levels of importance depending on the national legal and political contexts) to the public administration. The judiciary played a crucial role too in this process, especially in determining the external boundaries of the coercive measures.[24]

In summary, despite the globalization of law leading to a partial erosion of the law-making authority traditionally monopolized by the state, the state organization and its legal actors continue to play a central role in the law-making process. However, there is an observable trend, particularly among the member states of the EU, toward a shift in the primary actors involved in the law-making process – from predominantly legislative law-making to a more prominent role for administrative and judicial entities.

23 Elisia D'Alterio, 'Juridical Regulation in the Global Space' in S Cassese (ed), *Research Handbook on Global Administrative Law* (Edward Elgar 2016) 303; Olaf Dilling, Martin Herberg and Gerd Winter, 'Exploring Transnational Administrative Rule-making' in O Dilling, M Herberg and G Winter (eds), *Transnational Administrative Rule-Making: Performance, Legal Effects and Legitimacy* (Hart Publishing 2011) 1, 4–5 (in particular under points i and ii). Eg Jost Deöbrück, 'The Changing Role of the State in the Globalising World Economy' in PHF Bekker, R Dolzer, and M Waibel (eds), *Making Transnational Law Work in the Global Economy: Essays in Honour of Detlev Vagts* (CUP 2010) 56, 66–67.

24 Linda Hantrais and Marie-Thérèse Letablier, *Comparing and Contrasting the Impact of the COVID-19 Pandemic in the European Union* (Routledge 2021) ch 4.

4. Administrative legislative policy and its benefits

Shifting the focus to the public administration and its legislative function, one can readily observe that its augmented regulatory power does not occur in a vacuum. Despite the practical diminishment, legislative bodies such as national assemblies still maintain a central role. From a legal discourse perspective, the legislator remains at the apex of the national regulatory pyramid. By embracing a democratic form of government, the legal systems of EU member states introduce into the legal discourse the institutional impact of the national assembly as the highest legal entity representing the population of a specific community. Additionally, they carry with them a fundamental paradigm of this governmental structure, specifically the division of power and the inherent "default" law-making authority entrusted to the parliaments. Consequently, even though regulatory power of the legislative has been effectively diminished in numerous areas, there remains a need to legally justify and legitimize the expanding role of administration in law-making within the legal systems of continental European countries. Examining this necessity from the perspective of public administration, the need for legal legitimacy arises for the exercise of its law-making power. Typically, this legitimacy is conferred through one or several statutory acts that transfer the actual law-making authority to administrative agencies.[25]

Certainly, the content of these statutory acts can vary significantly, influenced by various factors such as the legal domain in which the delegation of law-making power occurs, the scope of regulatory power reallocation, the national characteristics of constitutional and administrative systems, and the overall traits of the national legal culture. However, irrespective of these variables, the delegation of law-making power to administrative bodies often assumes the form of a distinctive type of legislative policy, namely, the ***administrative legislative policy***.

Before delving into the meaning of such a specific legislative policy model, it is necessary to clarify that a *legislative policy* model represents a potential (and highly ideal-typical) model of regulation via legislation, designed to govern specific domains within a given national community. This typology is primarily founded not on the substance of legislative processes but on the allocation of responsibilities among the three principal actors traditionally involved in the regulatory process within a rule-of-law state: legislative, executive, and judicial actors, along with self-regulation.[26] In other words, the emphasis is on procedural aspects rather than the substantive qualities of legislative law-making. It is worth noting that each procedural model of legislative policy carries specific

25 Max Weber, *Economy and Society: An Outline of Interpretive Sociology* (U of California P 1978) 37.

26 Martin H Redish, *The Constitution as Political Structure* (OUP 1995) 140–41. Eg Juan J Linz and Alfred C Stepan, *Problems of Democratic Transition and Consolidation: Southern Europe, South America, and Post-communist Europe* (Johns Hopkins UP 1996) 14. Cf Tim Koopmans, *Courts and Public Institutions: A Comparative View* (CUP 2003) 247.

substantive implications for the legislative measures it generates, as will be explored shortly.[27]

One of the ideal-typical models of legislative policy can be characterized as "administrative," as it involves a shift in the production of regulatory regimes toward the executive actors within a legal system, specifically national and local public agencies. Whether due to internal factors, such as a high level of conflict within representative assemblies, or external reasons, like the need for a flexible law-making regime based on the nature of the area to be regulated, legislative bodies may delegate significant law-making authority to the administrative apparatus.[28] While public agencies are formally tasked with "implementing" statutory provisions, as it is common in most democracies, in reality, they have assumed the crucial role of "operationalizing" the general provisions established by national or local assemblies.[29] An example of this model of legislative policy can be observed in Swedish child law. This legal domain possesses a unique nature and history, with the legislative focus shifting since the 19th century from how adults (particularly those with legislative power) perceived children as functional to society. Instead, the emphasis has transitioned to focusing on children themselves and their perspectives. Consequently, the primary legislative policy direction has been to transfer the regulatory responsibility to specialized public agencies, where child psychologists often play a decisive role in understanding and translating "what children want and think."[30]

The "operationalization" of general principles outlined in legislation by public agencies is typically initiated already in the legislative drafting phase through the utilization of directional frameworks in statutory provisions. These frameworks often articulate, albeit vaguely, the general principles guiding the operations of public agencies and the intended direction of the regulatory regime.[31] As an illustration, Swedish child legislation is centered on the

27 Pauline C Westerman, 'Breaking the Circle: Goal-Legislation and the Need for Empirical Research' (2013) 1 The Theory and Practice of Legislation 395. Eg European Parliament, *Resolution of 4 September 2007 on Better Regulation in the European Union (2007/2095(INI))* (2007) point 17 <https://eur-lex.europa.eu/legal-content/EN/TXT/?uri=uriserv%3AOJ.CE.2008.187.01.0022.01.ENG&toc=OJ%3AC%3A2008%3A187E%3AFULL#CE2008187EN.01006001> accessed 13 April 2024.

28 Jürgen Habermas, *Between Facts and Norms: Contributions to a Discourse Theory of Law and Democracy* (The MIT Press 1998) 439; Giandomenico Majone, 'The Rise of the Regulatory State in Europe' (1994) 17 West European Politics 77.

29 Cornelius M Kerwin, 'The Element of Rule-Making' in DH Rosenbloom and RD Schwartz (eds), *Handbook of Regulation and Administrative Law* (Marcel Dekker 1994) 383, 385; Peter Cane, *Controlling Administrative Power: An Historical Comparison* (CUP 2016) 56.

30 Eg Pernilla Leviner, *Rättsliga dilemman i socialtjänstens barnskyddsarbete* (Jure 2011) 26–31.

31 Ronan Cormacain, *The Form of Legislation and the Rule of Law* (Hart Publishing 2022) 218–26; Rob van Gestel, 'The "Deparlamentarisation" of Legislation: Framework Laws and the Primacy of the Legislature' (2013) 9 Utrecht Law Review 106, 113–17. Also Helen Xanthaki, *Drafting Legislation: Art and Technology of Rules for Regulation* (Hart Publishing 2014) 269–75.

principle that every decision concerning minors should prioritize "what is best for the child." This overarching guideline provides public agencies with discretionary power, not only to ascertain the child's best interests, a determination often grounded in non-legal considerations, but more significantly, it affords administrative bodies the flexibility to operationalize this principle. This entails shaping the regulatory framework based on their discretionary interpretation of such a guideline.[32]

It is crucial to emphasize that the diverse entities comprising the institutional framework of modern democracies adhere to the doctrine of the separation of powers. Hence, the embrace of this administrative model of legislative policy signifies more than legislators simply being open to delegating a significant portion of their law-making authority to public agencies. It also requires a certain degree of collaboration, or at the very least, the absence of interference from the third actor in this arrangement: the courts. In essence, this model functions effectively when the exercise of discretion is endorsed by the courts, meaning that in case of disputes, the courts assume that the "creative" interpretation made by public agencies aligns by default with the (vague) letter of the statutory provisions.[33] The alignment of the courts with this shift from the legislative to the administrative branch may be rooted in tradition, such as the courts' belief that administration is essentially an extension of representative assemblies, or it could be based on more structural reasons, such as the courts' lack of expertise in matters of child psychology, leading them to rely on the "objective" experts operating within and for public agencies.

Given the foundational ideas underpinning the adoption of a legislative policy centered around the regulatory functions of the administrative apparatus, it is unsurprising that public administration tends to be perceived, either explicitly or implicitly, as the "default" law-maker when it comes to implementing global legal categories, particularly within the legal and political frameworks of the EU member states.[34] Several are the reasons for such preference and many

32 E.g., Johanna Schiratzki, *Barnrättens grunder* (6th edn, Studentlitteratur 2017) 33–42. Also Keith Hawkins, 'Law and Discretion: Exploring Collective Aspects of Administrative Decision-Making' (1998) 8 Education Law Journal 139, 141.

33 Tom Zwart, 'Overseeing the Executive: Is the Legislature Reclaiming Lost Territory from the Courts?' in S Rose-Ackerman and PL Lindseth (eds), *Comparative Administrative Law* (Edward Elgar 2010) 148–49; Guobin Zhu, 'Deference to the Administration in Judicial Review: Comparative Perspectives' in G Zhu (ed), *Deference to the Administration in Judicial Review: Comparative Perspectives* (Springer 2019) 1, 5–7. Also John Bell, 'Judicial Review in the Administrative State' in J de Poorter, E Hirsch Ballin and S Lavrijssen (eds), *Judicial Review of Administrative Discretion in the Administrative State* (TMC Asser Press 2019) 3, 5–6; Cass R Sunstein, *Designing Democracy: What Constitutions Do* (OUP 2001) 145–46.

34 van Gestel (n 31) 106. Eg Paul Schure and Amy Verdun, 'Legislative Bargaining in the European Union: The Divide Between Large and Small Member States' (2008) 9 European Union Politics 459, 467–78. Also Edoardo Chiti and Joana Mendes, 'The Evolution of EU Administrative Law' in P Craig and G De Búrca (eds), *The Evolution of EU Law* (3rd edn, OUP 2021) 339, 366–69.

of those are related to the specific legal and political contexts of the national legal system under observation. For example, the generally high level of trust in public agencies in Sweden positioned them, as the favored and explicitly chosen channel for legislative regulation during the Covid crisis. In Italy, on the other hand, the administration still played a central role in law-making, albeit more discreetly. This more hidden regulatory role played by public agencies in the Mediterranean country was influenced by the elevated level of conflict within the legislative arena and the traditionally significant role of the judiciary, particularly at the constitutional level. These factors prevented the enactment of legislation that explicitly and clearly delegated the entire regulation of anti-Covid measures to entities other than the legislative branch.[35]

However, when viewed comprehensively, it is still possible to identify several shared reasons across the diverse national communities of EU member states, explaining why the administrative legislative policy has emerged as the predominant approach for structuring law-making in addressing global issues with comprehensive solutions from a legal perspective. In this regard, public administration exhibits certain comparative advantages, both intertwined and overlapping, in comparison to other law-making actors, especially legislative bodies.

Firstly, the process of formulating regulatory measures, guided by policies or "official interpretations," is characterized by a notable swiftness. Legislative processes traditionally adhere to specific political and legal principles, necessitating the involvement of potential stakeholders, compliance with constitutionally mandated legislative law-making procedures, and the execution of a regulatory impact assessment. Consequently, in standard scenarios, legislative law-making tends to be inherently rigid, often stretching over several months, if not years. Contrastingly, the administrative regulatory process, as vividly illustrated by the response to the COVID-19 crisis in numerous European states, leans toward a more rapid and informal procedure. Public agencies navigate within the flexible confines of their "policy documents" and "recommendations," sometimes adopting approaches that may be viewed as questionable from a legal perspective. This flexibility allows them to operate within, and sometimes beyond, the rigid boundaries established by the constitutional frameworks of a national community.[36]

35 Julia Dahlqvist and Jane Reichel, 'Swedish Constitutional Response to the Coronavirus Crisis -The Odd One Out?' in MC Kettemann and K Lachmayer (eds), *Pandemocracy in Europe: Power, Parliaments and People in Times of COVID-19* (Bloomsbury Publishing 2022) 135, 141–43; Diletta Tega and Michele Massa, 'Fighting COVID 19 – Legal Powers and Risks: Italy' (*Verf Blog*, 2023) <https://verfassungsblog.de/fighting-covid-19-legal-powers-and-risks-italy/> accessed 13 April 2024. Compare Elena Griglio, 'Parliamentary Oversight Under the Covid-19 Emergency: Striving Against Executive Dominance' (2020) 8 The Theory and Practice of Legislation 49, 53–56.

36 van Gestel (n 31) 118. Eg Peter M Huber, 'Risk decisions in German Constitutional and Administrative Law' in G R Woodman and D Klippel (eds), *Risk and the Law* (Routledge

The informal nature of administrative law-making grants the state apparatus the capacity to respond swiftly and effectively to challenges and sudden changes in the surrounding reality. This adaptability proves particularly pivotal in the context of the globalized and globalizing legal discourse. In other words, the administrative regulatory process becomes a dynamic tool in addressing the intricate and swiftly evolving legal landscape, offering a level of responsiveness that may be challenging to achieve through the more structured and time-consuming legislative law-making procedures. As the globalized legal discourse continues to unfold, the ability to promptly adapt to emerging realities becomes a cornerstone in the effective governance of diverse and complex issues.[37]

Secondly, the essence of legislative law-making is characterized, particularly in a democratic context, by its inherently compromising nature. When endeavoring to integrate a global legal category into the national legal discourse, legislative bodies frequently find themselves engaged in internal negotiations and compromises, often driven by purely political and local interests. These considerations may be entirely detached from the context and operational scope of the pertinent legal category. Consequently, the legislative process often yields a final product – the legal act implementing the global legal category – that distorts or undermines the original rationale behind the global legal category.[38]

On the contrary, the public administration enjoys the structural advantage of operating internally as a hierarchical organization, where the directors and the highest instances, at least from a legal perspective, are not required, in their decision/law-making, to operate on a majority principle. Public agencies are organized as executive organs, and their primary legal objective is to operationalize decisions made by legislative bodies. In doing so, their chief criterion is to authoritatively implement measures that, in their judgment, best align with the "will of the legislator," within the frameworks established by the legal system and without necessarily requiring formal endorsement by the majority of the components within the public agency.[39] Given a considerable degree

---

2009) 23, 32–33; or Stéphanie De Somer, 'The Political Independence of National Regulatory Authorities: EU Impulse Versus National Restraint' (2015) 14 Revue du droit des industries de réseau 193.

37 Jerry Killian, 'The Missing Link in Administrative Reform: Considering Culture' in J Killian and N Eklund (eds), *Handbook of Administrative Reform: An International Perspective* (Routledge 2008) 44. Also Andrea Pradi and Elena Ioriatti, 'Comparative Law and Methodology Between Homogeneity and Complexity' (2023) 23 Global Jurist 237.

38 Mauro Zamboni, Globalization and Law-Making: Time to Shift a Legal Theory's Paradigm (2007) 1 Legisprudence 125, 139–40.

39 Tom Christensen, Per Laegreid and Kjell Arne Rovik, *Organization Theory and the Public Sector Instrument, Culture and Myth* (Routledge 2007) 99. Cf Linda F Dennard, 'The Maturation of Public Administration: The Search for a Democratic Identity' in GL Wamsley and JF Wolf (eds), *Refounding Democratic Public Administration Modern Paradoxes, Postmodern Challenges* (Routledge 1996) 293, 299.

of law-making latitude delegated by legislative bodies and the adoption of administrative legislative policy, public administration generally possesses the legal flexibility in its formulation of policies and recommendations to closely adhere to the original intentions of the "legislator" responsible for creating the global legal category – whether those intentions are defined by an international treaty, a EU directive, or the legal practices of arbitration tribunals.[40]

Thirdly, the globalization of law necessitates a high level of expertise in both legal and non-legal domains for an effective law-making. Complex and multifaceted issues arising in areas like e-commerce, environmental planning, or transnational corporations demand not only a comprehensive understanding from a legal perspective but also proficiency in non-legal aspects. Law-makers are tasked not only with comprehending these intricate issues, which often requires non-legal expertise, but also with formulating legal solutions to address challenging and global problems.[41] For instance, addressing the complexities of e-commerce demands specific knowledge about various forms of electronic payments prevalent in the hi-tech market and their corresponding security levels. Furthermore, expertise in legal matters such as copyright infringement, payment disputes, and consumer protection in the cyberspace realm and from international and comparative law perspectives becomes imperative in navigating this particular form of commerce.

In this respect, the national assemblies can offer a limited contribution: the parliaments are, per definition, expected of being capable to legislate on all matters concerning the life of a certain community. The process of drafting legislation varies depending on the system and circumstances, typically undertaken by either an in-house team of dedicated legislative drafters within the parliament or, in many cases, by external legal experts engaged specifically for the task of formulating a particular bill. However, inherent limitations exist in both approaches that often drive legislators toward adopting an administrative legislative policy.

In the case of national legislative drafters, when drafting is centralized within specific bodies, typically within parliaments, their expertise tends to be of a generalist nature, i.e., to encompass a broad and comprehensive legal knowledge across various topics or disciplines. While this breadth allows for a holistic understanding, it may lack the specific knowledge required for

40 Jocelyne Bourgon, 'Responsive, Responsible and Respected Government: Towards a New Public Administration Theory' (2007) 73 International Review of Administrative Sciences 7, 10.

41 Ulrich Sieber, 'Legal Order in a Global World: The Development of a Fragmented System of National, International, and Private Norms' (2010) 14 Max Planck Yearbook of United Nations Law Online 1, 3–32. Eg Peter Cserne, 'The Recodification of Private Law in Central and Eastern Europe' in P Larouche and P Cserne (eds), *National Legal Systems and Globalization: New Role, Continuing Relevance* (TMC Asser Press 2013) 73–74; or Susana Borrás, 'Three Tensions in the Governance of Science and Technology' in D Levi-Faur (ed), *The Oxford Handbook of Governance* (OUP 2012) 429, 434–35.

addressing technical issues and providing nuanced legal solutions in a particular area. Conversely, when drafting is institutionally decentralized and assigned every time to an ad hoc drafter within a ministry, a continuity issue may arise. Although such a legislative drafter brings expertise in the field to be regulated, the beneficial impact of their legal and non-legal knowledge typically concludes upon completion of the drafted legislation. When a new regulation within the same field is needed, a new set of legal experts within the ministry (or even a new ministry) is commonly engaged, resulting in a loss of the acquired knowledge.[42] This knowledge loss is particularly detrimental in areas highly affected by legal globalization, where technological innovations and evolving global situations constantly demand new regulatory solutions. For example, legislation governing real estate matters often endures for decades, if not centuries, while regulations related to aspects like e-commerce signature forms may have a shorter lifespan, given the rapid pace of technological developments.

The public administration system offers instead a form of (both legal and non-legal) expertise better suited for addressing the challenges inherent in a globalized world through law-making.[43] Notably, the expertise housed within public agencies is characterized by *specificity*, a necessity arising from the intricate nature of the legal issues at hand, and *continuity*, crucial for the cultivation of cumulative legal knowledge. In terms of specific competence, public agencies within the public administration are strategically designed to implement legislation within a particular domain of communal life, such as education, health, or telecommunications. Consequently, their organizational structure is tailored to necessitate a high level of expertise, encompassing both legal and technical aspects specific to the area to be regulated.[44] Furthermore, this organizational knowledge – defined as the collective understanding, information, and expertise held within the organization, specifically within the public agency – tends to accumulate over time and in response to various challenges,

42 Stefan Höfler, Markus Nussbaumer and Helen Xanthaki, 'Legislative Drafting' in U Karpen and H Xanthaki (eds), *Legislation in Europe: A Comprehensive Guide for Scholars and Practitioners by Country Guide* (Hart Publishing 2017) 145, 153–58. Eg Karine Gillberg, 'Legislation in France' in U Karpen and H Xanthaki (eds), *Legislation in Europe: A Country by Country Guide* (Hart Publishing 2020) 181, 196; or Wim JM Voermans and Sjoerd E Zijlstra, 'Education, Knowledge-Exchange and the Role of Professional Legislative Lawyers in the Netherlands' in F Uhlmann and S Höfler (eds), *Professional Legislative Drafters: Status, Role, Education* (Dike 2016) 39, 43–45.

43 Johan Christensen, Cathrine Holst and Anders Molander, *Expertise, Policy-Making and Democracy* (Routledge 2022) 26–29.

44 Giandomenico Majone, 'From the Positive to the Regulatory State: Causes and Consequences of Changes in the Mode of Governance' (1997) 17 Journal of Public Policy 139, 152. Also Kaifeng Yang and Lachezar G Anguelov, 'Trustworthiness of Public Service' in YK Dwivedi and others (eds), *Public Administration Reformation: Market Demand from Public Organizations* (Routledge 2014) 59, 64–65.

becoming then "organizational memory."[45] The career system, often hierarchical and featuring internal promotion mechanisms, means that legal experts within a public agency tend to dedicate decades to working within a specific area. This extended tenure allows them to develop a nuanced understanding of the regulatory landscape, its structure, and its functioning. Importantly, this wealth of knowledge is then transmitted to newly appointed legal experts, ensuring the continuity and depth of expertise within the organization.[46]

In conclusion, the administrative legislative policy stands out as the favored model for law-making in numerous EU member states. This preference is primarily attributed to three distinctive elements that set it apart from legislative bodies: the prompt decision-making procedures, the inherent authoritative nature of the process, and the specific and cumulative organizational legal (and non-legal) expertise within the public administration. Collectively, these factors contribute to the effectiveness of the administrative legislative policy, particularly when contrasted with legislative policies focused on the primary role of national assemblies, especially in regulating areas sensitive to globalization and its legal implications.

5. Public administration as the main regulator and participatory democracy: some issues

The adoption of an administrative legislative policy to address the challenges posed by the globalization of law to national legal systems offers several advantages, particularly in terms of legislative efficiency and effectiveness.[47] However, it is essential to recognize that these benefits should not divert attention from the fact that such a legislative policy choice directly challenges some foundational aspects of a democratic government and the role of law and legal actors within it. The extensive reliance on an administrative legislative policy may, in specific instances, pose a threat to certain fundamental components

45 Caroline Fischer, 'Public Servants as Competent Practitioners of Knowledge Management' in H Sullivan, H Dickinson and H Henderson (eds), *The Palgrave Handbook of the Public Servant* (Palgrave Macmillan 2020) 1, 12–15. Eg Karol Olejniczak and others, 'Discovering the Learning Mechanism' in K Olejniczak and S Mazur (eds), *Organizational Learning: A Framework for Public Administration* (Scholar Publishing House 2014) 20, 36–37. Also Linda Argote, *Organizational Learning: Creating, Retaining and Transferring Knowledge* (Springer Science and Business Media 2012) 85–113.

46 Max Weber, 'Domination' in M Rheinstein (ed), *Max Weber of Law in Economy and Society* (Simon and Schuster 1954) 322, 334. Also Christensen, Laegreid and Rovik (n 39) 24–25 and 103. Cf Gerald E Caiden, 'A Parabolic Theory of Bureaucracy or Max Weber through the Looking Glass' in A Farazmand (ed), *Bureaucracy and Administration* (CRC Press 2009) 111, 122–23.

47 Helen Xanthaki, *Drafting Legislation: Art and Technology of Rules for Regulation* (Hart Publishing 2014) 6–7; Helen Xanthaki, 'On Transferability of Legislative Solutions: The Functionality Test' in C Stefanou and H Xanthaki (eds), *Drafting Legislation: A Modern Approach* (Ashgate 2008) 1, 16–17.

or objectives of a participatory concept of democracy. In this context, *participatory democracy* is the idea that a democratic form of government fundamentally aims to ensure specific aspects of processes and procedures in governance, particularly within the realms of law-making, law-implementing, and law-applying, rather than solely focusing on the content or representativeness of the legal outcomes generated by these processes (such as an act, a court decision, or a decision of a public agency).[48] Applying this principle to the domain of law-making, the concept of participatory democracy emphasizes the importance of fair and transparent procedures, equal participation, and the protection of individual rights as fundamental criteria to be upheld during the law-making process.

If democracy is defined in these participatory terms, it is then possible to observe how the administrative legislative policy may raise some fundamental questions as to whether such policy may be adopted as extensively as it is usually done by the EU member states in the legal areas more sensitive to the globalization. In particular, at least when focused upon the European continental legal systems, it is possible to identify three major (and strongly intertwined) problems with the public administration taking the command of the law-making.

Firstly, one of the major drawbacks of having the administration directly regulate certain aspects of community life, as opposed to merely implementing legislation enacted by national assemblies, is the absence of *direct political accountability of the law-makers* toward the recipients of its actions. Direct accountability of the law-makers, in this context, refers to the ability to call upon a specific actor to justify and potentially face political consequences for their law-making actions directly in front of the addressees of those actions.[49] While this type of accountability for political actors operating in parliaments can, in many cases, appear to be problematic, the possibility remains to hold them accountable for their law-making, at least during each election period, through mechanisms such as voting. In contrast, when examining the public administration, its undemocratic structure, being a non-elective body within the state organization, tends to shift the accountability for their law-making regulatory measures at the horizon of the political landscape.[50] In other words,

48 Anna Gamper, 'Forms of Democratic Participation in Multi-Level System' in C Fraenkel-Haeberle, S Kropp, F Palermo and K-P Sommermann (eds), *Citizen Participation in Multi-Level Democracies* (Brill Nijhoff 2015) 67, 76–82. Also von Bogdandy (n 8) 329–33. Eg Gloria Golmohammadi, *Realizing the Principle of Participatory Democracy in the EU -The Role of Law-Making Consultation* (Stockholm UP 2023) 138–43.

49 Robert Behn, *Rethinking Democratic Accountability* (Brookings Institute Press 2001) 125. Also Ronald J Oakerson, 'Governance Structures for Enhancing Accountability and Responsiveness' in JL Perry (ed), *Handbook of Public Administration* (Jossey-Bass 1989) 114. Cf John Uhr, 'Accountable Civil Servants' in M Bovens, R Goodin and T Schillemans (eds), *The Oxford Handbook of Public Accountability* (OUP 2014) 226, 230.

50 Richard Mulgan, *Holding Power to Account: Accountability in Modern Democracies* (Palgrave Macmillan 2003) 61–63. Also van Gestel (n 31) 109; Jan Aart Scholte, *Globalization: A Critical Introduction* (Macmillan Press 2000) 261–82.

the member of a community can rarely make politically accountable in a direct away the public administration for its law-making, being their only (very vague option) of changing the political actors, in the hope that the latter will then make the public administration somehow more accountable (e.g., by changing the director of a public agency).

Secondly, a leaning toward an administrative legislative policy usually implies a lower level of ***justiciability***. Traditionally, in continental European legal systems, regulatory measures endorsed by legislative assemblies tend to be, to a greater or lesser degree, subject to potential control by other actors regarding their legality. Specifically, the institution of constitutional review (either in a diffuse or centralized form) allows judicial power to scrutinize and, if necessary, invalidate legislative provisions that violate the constitution or jeopardize the constitutional principles upon which a national legal system is based, ***in primis*** the protection of fundamental rights.[51] Conversely, in most cases, the justiciability of regulations and policies produced by public administration can only be challenged in ordinary or administrative courts. It is noteworthy that this possibility still maintains the potential for regulatory measures enacted by public agencies to be subject to judicial review, a form of oversight frequently enshrined within constitutional frameworks.[52] The issue lies in the fact that these types of courts, especially in continental Europe, tend to assess more in terms of "statutory validity" than constitutionality.[53] By "statutory validity," it is simply meant that ordinary or administrative courts are more inclined to evaluate the compatibility of administrative measures with the legal system provided by statutory provisions rather than with its constitutional architecture and discourse. This responsibility is typically reserved for constitutional courts and their constitutional review, a domain often limited by the constitution or constitutional practices to regulatory provisions enacted by national (or local) parliaments.[54]

The widespread use of an administrative legislative policy, coupled with this traditional limitation of constitutional review to statutory provisions, poses a significant risk. This type of review is the most crucial legal tool through which the state apparatus guarantees citizens the respect of fundamental rights, irrespective of the political or administrative climate created by the globalization

51 Albert HY Chen and Miguel Poiares Maduro, 'The Judiciary and Constitutional Review' in M Tushnet, T Fleiner and C Saunders (eds), *Routledge Handbook of Constitutional Law* (Routledge 2013) 97, 97–103.

52 Mads Andenas, '*EU Countries and the UK' in* G della Cananea and M Andenas *(eds), Judicial Review of Administration in Europe* (OUP 2021) 295, 300–2.

53 Andenas (n 52) 306; Jacques Ziller, 'The Continental System of Administrative Legality' in B Guy Peters and J Pierre (eds), *Handbook of Public Administration* (2nd edn, Sage Publications 2012) 323, 325–26. Also Brinton Coxe, *An Essay on Judicial Power and Unconstitutional Legislation, Being a Commentary on Parts of the Constitution of the United States* (Kay and Brother 1893) 339.

54 Alec Stone Sweet, 'Why Europe Rejected American Judicial Review: And Why It May Not Matter' (2003) 101 Michigan Law Review 2744, 2770. Eg van Gestel (n 31) 112.

and its legal consequences. In other words, the administrative legislative policy, by allowing the public administration a broader legal scope, may jeopardize the fundamental institutional principle of the separation of powers. Consequently, it diminishes the capacity of citizens to concretely realize the ideal of the rule of law – their ability, with the essential assistance of constitutional courts, to confine public powers' decisions within the boundaries of fundamental legal norms within the community.[55]

Thirdly, as highlighted earlier, the administrative legislative policy undeniably offers a procedural advantage when compared to legislative processes in national assemblies, particularly in terms of its generally faster and more responsive nature to the evolving needs of a community facing legal globalization. However, concerning the substance of the regulatory provisions swiftly generated by public administration, this same legislative policy tends to exhibit an inherent deficiency rooted in the institutional character commonly shared by the majority of public agencies across continental Europe. Public agencies, by nature, lean toward a more conservative stance than political actors. It is crucial to note that the term "conservative" here does not intend to impart a political connotation to the administrative apparatus. Instead, the conservative character of public administration merely denotes its institutional inclination to be path-dependent or legacy-dependent, adhering closely to established practices.[56] Put differently, due to various factors (beyond the scope of this discussion, such as the career system for personnel), public agencies in the EU member states tend to cling to established practices as much as possible when shaping regulatory regimes, even in the face of novel phenomena.[57]

It is indeed accurate that, in this regard, the administrative model of legislative policy can provide greater stability and continuity compared to a legislative policy that centralizes regulatory powers in the hands of elected legislative actors. The latter, originating from an elected parliament, often reflects the shifts in political majorities occurring with each term's election outcomes. However, when confronted with the challenges posed by the globalization of law, public administration tends to simplify these issues by viewing them as mere reformulations of previous concerns. Consequently, these challenges are addressed using non-innovative administrative regulatory solutions. In essence,

55 Gerald J Postema, *Law's Rule: The Nature, Value, and Viability of the Rule of Law* (OUP 2022) 116–17. Also Maxwell Cameron, *Strong Constitutions: Social-Cognitive Origins of the Separation of Powers* (OUP 2013) 169–70.

56 Ferd H Mitchell and Cheryl C Mitchell, *Adaptive Administration: Practice Strategies for Dealing with Constant Change in Public Administration and Policy* (Taylor & Francis Group 2016) 148–49; B Guy Peters and Martin Painter, 'Conclusion: Administrative Traditions in an Era of Administrative Change' in M Painter and B Guy Peters (eds), *Tradition and Public Administration* (Palgrave Macmillan 2010) 234. Also Max Weber, 'Bureaucracy' in HH Gerth and CW Mills (eds), *From Max Weber: Essays in Sociology* (Routledge 1991) 196.

57 Christopher Pollitt and Geert Bouckaert, *Public Management Reform – a Comparative Analysis* (OUP 2004) 33; Ellen M Immergut and Karen M Anderson, 'Historical Institutionalism and West European Politics' (2008) 31 West European Politics 345, 358.

although the administrative legislative policy may be more expedient (and, to some extent, more stable) than the political arena in addressing the novel regulatory challenges posed by the globalization of law, the same legislative policy tends, owing to institutional reasons rooted in the path-dependency of public agencies, to perceive true new problems and challenges within the current regulatory landscape as "usual challenges." These are often approached by reapplying previously established legislative categories and principles.[58]

In summary, although the administrative legislative policy undeniably provides advantages in terms of enhancing the efficiency of law-making to address regulatory challenges posed by globalization (such as quick decision-making procedures and specialized legal expertise), its extensive application in democratic forms of government raises significant concerns. These concerns pertain to accountability to the citizens affected by the administrative regulations, safeguarding fundamental rights, and the ability to innovate within the paradigms of the national legal discourse.

6. Some changes for a more democratic administrative legislative policy

Examining the advantages (Section 3) and risks (Section 4) associated with the extended use of an administrative legislative policy to integrate global legal categories into a national community, it becomes evident that striking a balance is crucial for a well-functioning legal system. This balance must ensure effectiveness in the law-making process while preserving fundamental democratic principles, primarily the rule of law. The increasing legislative role of the administration can be seen as a natural evolution for a community navigating the complexities of globalization. From a legal discourse perspective, globalization entails the shift of legislative power – once the domain of national assemblies – to international and regional entities. Consequently, as pointed out earlier, the public administration assumes the responsibility of translating the "law written in supranational books" into the "law in action" within a national community. As recently stated by B. Guy Peters and Jon Pierre, "[l]egislatures and political executives may pass all the laws they wish, but unless those laws are administered effectively by the public bureaucracy, little or nothing will actually happen."[59] However, acknowledging this inevitable expansion of the law-making power of public agencies necessitates consideration of potential legal, structural, and institutional changes. These adjustments are essential to

58 Mark C Suchman and Lauren B Edelman, 'Legal Rational Myths: The New Institutionalism and the Law and Society Tradition' (1996) 21 Law and Social Inquiry 903, 915; James G March and Johan P Olsen, 'Elaborating the "New Institutionalism"' in RAW Rhodes, SA Binder and BA Rockman (eds), *The Oxford Handbook of Political Institutions* (OUP 2006) 3. Eg Page (n 4) 161.

59 B Guy Peters and Jon Pierre, 'Introduction: The Role of Public Administration in Governing' in Guy Peters and J Pierre (eds), *Handbook of Public Administration* (2nd edn, Sage Publications 2012) 1–2.

enhance the quality and democratic character of national law-making, given the heightened role of the public administration. In essence, while recognizing the inevitability of the public administration wielding extended law-making powers to implement provisions from the international and supranational arena, it is crucial to establish clear and defined boundaries, preferably at the constitutional level, to restrain the regulatory power of the public administration.[60]

Firstly, there is a need to expand and clarify in both the Constitution and all constitutionally relevant documents, such as decisions by higher courts, the areas subject to direct legislative authority. To safeguard essential components of a democracy, constitutional law must explicitly limit political actors from delegating regulatory responsibilities to administrative authorities through framework legislation in specific domains.[61] For example, all constitutional charters in the EU member states already include provisions stipulating that the limitation of fundamental rights requires explicit support from a legislative act, often requiring a qualified majority from the parliament. Nevertheless, if the constitutional document explicitly states that a legislative provision is mandatory in all cases where a regulatory measure may "directly *or indirectly limit*" a fundamental right, this formulation will empower higher courts in particular to impede a risky use of the administrative legislative policy. The latter might not immediately violate a specific right but could potentially create conditions conducive to such violations, as evident in recent decades with various anti-terrorism legislations and their potential impact on personal integrity.[62]

The constitutional expansion of areas requiring detailed legislative drafting, as opposed to vague legislative frameworks, is pivotal. It ensures that, during exceptional circumstances that may necessitate a temporary restriction of fundamental rights, such limitations within a democracy are established through legislation by an accountable actor – namely, the parliament, directly responsible (through elections) to those affected by such measures. This stands in stark contrast to the present-day policy decisions, often characterized by a highly

60 Carol Harlow, 'Global Administrative Law: The Quest for Principles and Values' (2006) 17 European Journal of International Law 187, 190. Also Peter Strauss, 'The Place of Agencies in Government: Separation of Powers and the Fourth Branch' (1984) 84 Columbia Law Review 573, 580. Cf Joseph Heath, *The Machinery of Government: Public Administration and the Liberal State* (OUP 2020) 45.

61 Paul Craig, *EU Administrative Law* (3rd edn, OUP 2018) 112. Cf Eduardo Jordão and Susan Rose-Ackerman, 'Juridical Review of Executive Policymaking in Advanced Democracies: Beyond Rights Review' (2014) 66 Administrative Law Review 1, 4–6.

62 E.g., Queensland Government, *Human Rights Act 2019*, art 41 (4B) <https://www.legislation.qld.gov.au/view/whole/pdf/inforce/2020-09-21/act-2019-005> accessed 13 April 2024; or European Data Protection Board, *EDPB-EDPS Joint Opinion 03/2022 on the Proposal for a Regulation on the European Health Data Space* (12 July 2022) 6 at point 8 <https://www.edps.europa.eu/system/files/2023-04/22-07-12_edpb_edps_joint-opinion_europeanhealthdataspace_en.pdf> accessed 13 April 2024. Also Joana Mendes, *Participation in EU Rule-Making: A Rights-Based Approach* (OUP 2011) 61–70.

intrusive nature of law-making, produced by administrative agencies like the various national agencies for cybersecurity.

Secondly, it is imperative to enhance the nature of the justiciability of regulatory provisions generated by public administration. As mentioned earlier, in most European democracies, the vast majority of administrative acts, whether implementing or legislative, are generally subject to judicial scrutiny by ordinary and/or administrative courts. However, these courts, even at their highest levels, often lack the necessary knowledge and expertise to address constitutional issues, such as the compatibility of administrative decisions with the constitutional framework. Their competence primarily lies in assessing statutory validity – ensuring that administrative decisions and regulations conform to the system of ordinary legislation. To intensify judicial control over the law-making outcomes of administrative policies, it is essential to constitutionally guarantee to the citizens affected the opportunity to initiate, either directly or indirectly, a constitutional review process for regulations produced by the administration that may jeopardize the fundamental rights protected in the constitutional charter.[63]

For example, strengthening justiciability could involve a constitutional provision stating that constitutional review can be sought not only for legislative acts produced by the parliament but also for "decisions produced by the public administration *with a regulatory nature that may endanger fundamental rights*." While this formulation may leave certain aspects open-ended, such as delineating when an administrative act acquires a "regulatory nature" rather than merely executing a legislative provision, and when the endangering of fundamental rights may occur, it establishes a guiding principle for the constitutional court. This open formulation encourages the constitutional court, in its evolving jurisprudence, to recognize that certain outcomes of public agencies' actions merit constitutional review. It is only by ensuring a strengthened (or constitutional) justiciability of public administration actions that the cardinal principle of the rule of law, affirming that all public organs must operate in accordance with the law, can genuinely be upheld.[64]

Thirdly, considering the inevitable expansion of the regulatory role of public agencies as a potent instrument for integrating globalized legal categories into a national system, a series of institutional measures is required to enhance the institutional independence of public administration and its law-making processes. These solutions aim to mitigate the influences of other significant legal actors while simultaneously ensuring the accountability of its activities within a legal discourse framework. Such measures are crucial for a democratic

63 E.g., Venice Commission, *CDL-AD(2019)005, Principles on the Protection and Promotion of the Ombudsman Institution ("The Venice Principles")* (2019) Principle 19 <https://www.venice.coe.int/webforms/documents/?pdf=CDL-AD(2019)005-e> accessed 13 April 2024.

64 van Gestel (n 31) 120–21. Also Peter Cane, *Administrative Tribunals and Adjudication* (CUP 2009) 256–59.

form of government, especially in addressing the disruptions provoked by globalization, such as the rise of populist parties in the political arena.[65]

For example, to fortify the fundamental principle of the separation of powers, and to institutionally guarantee the autonomy of public administration and its agencies from political influence, constitutional provisions should explicitly state that, while implementing the legislator's will as expressed in ordinary legislation, the public administration must prioritize "*the general welfare of the community*."[66] Simultaneously, to ensure that public administration activities adhere to the rule of law, an effective oversight mechanism must be established. For instance, embedding an institutional figure like an *ombudsperson* in the constitutional framework, including a distinct career path, can guarantee independence from major institutional state actors. This figure should possess the authority, such as an effective legal power to initiate cases before the courts, to delineate boundaries and scrutinize the work of public administration in a legally rigorous manner.[67]

To summarize, although the utilization of an administrative legislative policy may enhance the effectiveness of the law-making process in the EU member states, the associated risks to certain fundamental legal principles of a democratic government necessitate the establishment of specific boundaries within the most authoritative legal document – the constitution of a national community. It is imperative not only to broaden the areas mandating detailed legislative acts constitutionally, thereby limiting the law-making discretion of public agencies; it is also crucial to explicitly incorporate provisions in the constitution outlining mechanisms for subjecting the actions and decisions of the public administration to legal scrutiny by two impartial entities – namely, the constitutional court and the ombudsman. These safeguards ensure that the endeavors of the public administration consistently serve the community's welfare rather than the interests of political actors in the parliament.

7. Conclusion

This chapter has delved into the impact of globalization on legal systems, particularly examining how this phenomenon has significantly transformed the law-making landscape in the national communities of the EU member states.

65 Andreas Lienhard, Peter Bieri and Anna Malandrino, 'The Role of Constitutional and Administrative Law in the Politics of Public Administration' in A Ladner and F Sager (eds), *Handbook on the Politics of Public Administration* (Edward Elgar 2022) 174. Also Woodrow Wilson, 'The Study of Administration' (1887) 2 Political Science Quarterly 197, 209.

66 Michael Decleris, 'Systemic Theory of Public Administration: Main Problems' in E Andreevsky, L Mehl and L Saint-Paul (eds), *Deuxième école européene de systemique* (AFCET 1992) 149–50. Also the classical work by Frank J Goodnow, *Comparative Administrative Law: An Analysis of the Administrative Systems, National and Local, of the United States, England, France and Germany –Volume 1 Organizations* (G Putnam's Sons 1893) 10.

67 E.g., Nick O'Brien, 'Ombudsmen and Public Authorities: A Modest Proposal' in M Hertogh and R Kirkham (eds), *Research Handbook on the Ombudsman* (Edward Elgar Publishing 2018) 34, 45–48.

Despite the practical diminution of regulatory power within legislative bodies, their legal status as the paramount representation in a democratic government necessitates a legitimate justification for the growing role of administration in law-making. This rationale often materializes in the form of statutory acts, transferring law-making authority to administrative agencies – a practice termed here as "administrative legislative policy." This policy emerges as a favored approach in the EU member states due to its adaptability in addressing challenges stemming from the globalization of law. Notably, its appeal lies in less time-consuming procedures, an authoritative structure of the decision process, and the specific cumulative expertise within public administration.

While recognizing that, due to these factors, administrative legislative policy may enhance efficiency and effectiveness in tackling global regulatory challenges, its widespread application in democratic governments such as those of the EU member states raises significant concerns regarding accountability, safeguarding fundamental rights, and the ability to innovate within national legal discourse paradigms. Specifically, the imperative need for clear constitutional boundaries to regulate the expanded law-making powers of public agencies should be considered pivotal. Consequently, three key recommendations are proposed to address constitutional challenges arising from the increasing legislative role of administration: the need to expand and clarify areas subject to direct legislative authority in constitutional documents, enhancement of justiciability (i.e., constitutional review) of regulatory measures taken by public agencies, and institutional measures ensuring the independence and accountability of public administration.

Regardless of the chosen solution, two clear starting points emerge as guidelines for upcoming maneuvers in the field of constitutional law in EU member states. Descriptively, owing to its efficacy in times of legal globalization, administrative legislative policy as the preferred tool to address the challenges of a modern European democracy appears to be a lasting phenomenon. The speed and expertise required by many global and supranational legal categories find a more suitable transfer mechanism in public administration, facilitating the incorporation of such categories into the local legal realities of national communities.

Given this reality, from a normative perspective, the constitutional charter should undergo a fundamental re-adjustment of its sections concerning the fundamental institutional actors of a national community. This restructuring involves establishing legal measures and institutions that, in response to the increasing law-making by public administration, ensure that such processes do not occur at the expense of the legal foundations of a modern Western-based participatory democracy – a model of government to which the states within the EU legally ought to aspire.

8 The role of European composite administration in the GDPR, the AI Act and the EHDS regulation – what about the rule of law?*

Jane Reichel

1. Introduction

With the European Strategy for Data, launched in 2020, the Commission has envisioned the EU as a leader in a data-driven society, where important societal benefits can be achieved by 'unleashing the data'.[1] The aim is to create a single market for data, allowing data to flow freely within the EU and across sectors, for the benefit of businesses, researchers and public administrations. A core feature of the EU vision for the data society and economy is that they should be human-centric, trustworthy and secure.[2] This vision is not new in itself – ever since the 1995 EC Data Protection Directive, the EU has built a regulatory framework for personal data with the dual aim to ensure the free movement of data within the EU internal market and to protect the individuals affected. It is famously stated in the preambles of both the Data Protection Directive and the GDPR, albeit with slightly differing wordings, that the processing of personal data should be designed to serve mankind.[3] As explained

* This chapter is produced as part of and funded by the European Union-NextGenerationEU, through the National Recovery and Resilience Plan of the Republic of Bulgaria, project No bg-rrp-2.004-0008.

1 A European Strategy for Data, COM(2020) 66 final, p 1.

2 Article 3.1(a) Decision (EU) 2022/2481 of the European Parliament and of the Council of 14 December 2022 establishing the Digital Decade Policy Programme 2030; Communication from the Commission to the European Parliament, the European Council, the Council, the European Economic and Social Committee and the Committee of the Regions, Artificial Intelligence for Europe, COM(2018) 237 final, 12; recital 3 of the Regulation (EU) 2022/868 of the European Parliament and of the Council of 30 May 2022 on European data governance and amending Regulation (EU) 2018/1724 (Data Governance Act) hereinafter DGA; Commission, 'A European Health Data Space: Harnessing the Power of Health Data for People, Patients and Innovation' (Communication) COM(2022) 196 final, 2, 3, 13 and 18.

3 Recital 4 of the preamble to Regulation (EU) 2016/679 of the European Parliament and of the Council on the protection of natural persons with regard to the processing of personal data and on the free movement of such data (General Data Protection Regulation) hereinafter GDPR; recital 2 in the preamble to Directive 95/46/EC of the European Parliament and of the Council on the protection of individuals with regard to the processing of personal data and on the free movement of such data, hereinafter Data Protection Directive.

DOI: 10.4324/9781003610670-12

by Jan Philipp Albrecht, at the time a Member of the European Parliament and one of the architects behind the GDPR, the GDPR is meant to serve as a starting point for international standards and a trustworthy digital market.[4] With the COVID-19 pandemic came a realisation of the importance of having access to relevant data in sufficient quantities, which became a catalyst for enhanced data sharing.[5] Also with the breakthrough of artificial intelligence (AI), the vision of a single market for data has gained further relevance.

According to the Commission, 'citizens will trust and embrace data-driven innovations only if they are confident that any personal data sharing in the EU will be subject to full compliance with the EU's strict data protection rules'.[6] In order to achieve this, the Commission identifies four central elements that are to be secured. First, the free flow of data. Second, that European rules and values in personal data protection, consumer protection and competition are guaranteed. Third, that rules for access to and use of data are fair, practical and clear, with clear and trustworthy data governance mechanisms in place. And fourth, that an open but assertive approach to international data flows is upheld, based on European values.[7]

European and national administrative agencies within the EU administrative space play a central role in achieving these goals. The importance of establishing independent supervisory authorities for the protection of personal data is explicitly recognised in both the EU Treaty on the Functioning of the European Union (TFEU), and the EU Charter for Fundamental Rights (EU Charter).[8] Building on the Data Protection Directive, the GDPR advances the administrative cooperation schemes involving national Data Protection Authorities (DPAs), and the European Data Protection Board (EDPB) at the EU level, which include the competence to issue guidelines and policy documents and to decide individual cases in composite administrative procedures, including decisions on administrative fines – which can be hefty.[9] The same pattern can be seen in several of the acts within the EU Strategy for Data that have been enacted in the years 2022–2024, such as the Data Governance Act

4 Jan-Philipp Albrecht, 'How the GDPR Will Change the World' (2016) 2 European Data Protection Law Review 287, 289. See further Anu Bradford, *The Brussels Effect* (OUP 2020) xiv; Paul M Schwartz, 'Global Data Privacy: The EU Way' (2019) 94 New York University Law Review 771, 817–18.

5 Angelica Fernandez, 'The Data Act: The Next Step in Moving Forward to a European Data Space' (2022) 8 European Data Protection Law Review 108.

6 A European Strategy for Data (n 1) 1.

7 A European Strategy for Data (n 1) 5; Jane Reichel, 'The European Strategy for Data and Trust in EU Governance: The Case of Access to Publicly Held Data' [2023] CERIDAP 129, 131. <https://doi.org/10.13130/2723-9195/2023-4-10>.

8 Article 16.2 TFEU and Article 8.3 EU Charter.

9 Hielke Hijmans, *The European Union as a Guardian of Internet Privacy: The Story of Art 16 TEU* (Springer 2016); Herwig CH Hofmann and Lisette Mustert, 'Data Protection' in Miroslava Scholten (ed), *Research Handbook on the Enforcement of EU Law* (Edward Elgar Publishing 2023) 461, 465–69.

(although without common rules on high administrative fines), the Digital Markets Act, the Digital Services Act, the Data Act, the AI Act and Regulation for a European Health Data Space (EHDS Regulation).[10,11] This developing composite administrative infrastructure can accordingly be expected to have important influences on policy issues, as well as having powerful tools to enforce policies. Furthermore, the data-driven society concerns basic constitutional values relevant for the state, society and the private lives of citizens, namely how general information and personal data are to be processed and in what technical environments.

In order to investigate the recent developments and their effects on the European composite administration as a political entity, three of the aforementioned acts will be studied more closely: the GDPR, the AI Act and the EHDS Regulation. The first two represent truly horizontal legislative acts, affecting large sectors of society. Whereas the GDPR lays down a general framework for the processing of personal data, the AI Act functions as a market surveillance act, setting out requirements on AI service providers.[12] The EHDS Regulation, for its part, regulates very sensitive categories of personal data – electronic health data – that are to be made available to both patients and health care providers, for the patient's own care (primary use), as well as to, among others, policymakers, regulators, researchers and official statisticians for the benefit of the public good (secondary use).[13] All three acts accordingly affect core features of the European and national societies.

The administrative infrastructure of these acts, involving both EU and national administrative entities, is built on a developing composite administration, stemming from both EU and national executive powers. As the executive

10 Regulation (EU) 2022/1925 of the European Parliament and of the Council on contestable and fair markets in the digital sector (Digital Markets Act); Regulation (EU) 2022/2065 of the European Parliament and of the Council on a Single Market For Digital Services (Digital Services Act); Regulation (EU) 2023/2854 of the European Parliament and of the Council on harmonised rules on fair access to and use of data (Data Act); Regulation (EU) 2024/1689 of the European Parliament and of the Council of 13 June 2024 laying down harmonised rules on artificial intelligence.

11 The EHDS Regulation has at the time of writing not yet been adopted by the EU legislator, but the final draft has been agreed upon by the Council and the European Parliament, Proposal for a Regulation on the European Health Data Space - Analysis of the final compromise text with a view to agreement, Interinstitutional File: 2022/0140(COD) Brussels, 18 March 2024. The numbering of the Articles in this contribution follows European Parliament, 'Corrigendum to the Position of the European Parliament Adopted at First Reading on 24 April 2024 with a View to the Adoption of Regulation (EU) 2024 of the European Parliament and of the Council on the European Health Data Space' (COM(2022)0197-C9-0167/2022-2022/0140(COD)) 27 November 2024 (EHDS). The Regulation is expected to be adopted in January 2025.

12 Commission Proposal for a Regulation of the European Parliament and of the Council Laying Down Harmonised Rules on Artificial Intelligence (Artificial Intelligence Act) and Amending Certain Union Legislative Acts, COM (2021) 206 final, 3.

13 Commission Proposal for a Regulation of the European Parliament and of the Council on the European Health Data Space, COM/2022/197 final, 1–2.

powers of the EU and the Member States are established within independent constitutional settings – the EU Treaties and the national constitutional frameworks, respectively – the constitutional foundation of the composite administration is regulated in separate legal contexts. The question can therefore be raised of whether this European composite administration for data is adequately construed to meet the constitutional requirements stemming from the representative democracies of the EU and its Member States. More concretely, how can the European composite administration fulfil the two basic tasks of the executive under the rule of law, to ensure that the aims and contents of the legislation are realised and that constitutional restraints of public powers are upheld? The overarching question can therefore be phrased as: is the European composite administration for data adequately construed to be able to fulfil the requirements for a public administration governed under the rule of law?

In order to answer this question, two aspects of the European composite administration for data will be analysed: the governance tools for promoting coherent compliance and capacity building, on the one hand, and individual decision-making, with a particular focus on the main deterrent tool, administrative fines, on the other. The first set of tools relates to the capacity of the administration to affect and define the regulatory policies within their respective fields, whereas the other includes more traditional implementation tools, albeit unusually powerful ones.

2. Executive powers in a representative democracy under the rule of law – coping with the transfer from the nation-state to the European administrative space

A central question for this contribution is what role public administration fulfils in the European composite administration when upholding executive functions beyond the scope of its founding constitutional basis, whether this be the EU Treaties or a national constitution. In this section, some thoughts on the functions of the executive power in a representative democracy will be presented as a background.

Two general points of departure can be identified. First, the public administration, as part of the executive power, has a role to ensure that the law is applied in an efficient manner, so that the policies of the democratically elected legislator can be realised in practice. Efficient governance structures should therefore be established, connecting both the European and national agencies that are to implement and enforce the policies in a uniform manner.[14] Second, it is generally accepted that in a democratic state under the rule of law, the exercise of public power is to be limited, applied in a law-bound and predictable manner, and within a framework of constitutional rules which ensure the

14 Miroslava Scholten, 'EU Enforcement Agencies' in Miroslava Scholten (ed), *Research Handbook on the Enforcement of EU Law* (Edward Elgar Publishing 2023) 152–53.

protection of fundamental rights.[15] This means that core constitutional and administrative principles are to be upheld. These may include the principle of legality, providing a legal basis for the exercise of public power, and substantive constitutional law requirements limiting administrative discretion, such as the principles of objectivity, impartiality and proportionality. They also include procedural requirements such as the principles of good administration and judicial protection, and the availability of accountability mechanisms, including judicial, budgetary and political.[16] These overarching and competing interests can be translated into efficiency and legal certainty in a broad sense, i.e., an interest to ensure that the aims and contents of the legislation are realised, and an interest to ensure that constitutional restraints of public powers are upheld. In the words of Rose-Ackerman, all modern states must confront the tension between competent, technical responses to policy mandates and efforts to assure the democratic accountability of the public administration.[17]

Nation-states have traditionally been seen as sovereign vis-à-vis each other when exercising public power, meaning that they may act independently.[18] The notion of sovereignty is closely linked to the principle of self-determination and the principle of territoriality, entailing that it is the task of each state and its administration to manage administrative issues concerning the state, its citizens and activities carried out within the state borders.[19] It has in the past been uncommon for national authorities to implement policies from foreign states or international organisations.[20] The law of the land is to be applied in administrative matters. The balancing act between the efficiency and legal certainty functions of the state bodies within a representative democracy is performed in the largely closed ecosystem of the state. The decision-making authority

15 See Carol Harlow, 'Global Administrative Law: The Quest for Principles and Values' (2006) 17 European Journal of International Law; Marco Macchia, 'The Rule of Law and Transparency in the Global Space' in Sabino Cassese (ed), *Research Handbook on Global Administrative Law* (Edward Elgar Publishing 2016) 212; The European Commission for Democracy Through Law (Venice Commission) Report on the Rule of Law, Study No 512/2009 CDL-AD(2011)003rev, 41.

16 Compare Hafsteinn Dan Kristjánsson, 'The Governing Idea of the Rule of Law' in Jane Reichel and Mauro Zamboni (eds), *Rule of Law 69 Scandinavian Studies in Law* (Stockholm Institute 2023) vol 69, 14 *et seq.*

17 Susan Rose-Ackerman, 'Administrative Law and Democracy' in Peter Cane and others (eds), *The Oxford Handbook of Comparative Administrative Law* (OUP 2020) 1074–75 <https://doi.org/10.1093/oxfordhb/9780198799986.013.58>.

18 Anne-Marie Slaughter, 'Sovereignty and Power in a Networked World Order' [2004] Stanford Journal of International Law 283–84.

19 Cedric Ryngaert, *Jurisdiction in International Law* (2nd edn, OUP 2015) 49; Herwig CH Hofmann, 'Dealing with Trans-Territorial Executive Rule-Making' [2013] Missouri Law Journal 423.

20 Henrik Wenander, 'Recognition of Foreign Administrative Decisions: Balancing International Cooperation, National Self-Determination, and Individual Rights' [2011] Zeitschrift für ausländisches öffentliches Recht und Völkerrecht 755, 762.

could be subjected to various forms of judicial, non-judicial, governmental and parliamentary accountability mechanisms within the ecosystem.[21]

These basic premises for the role of public authorities and the function of administrative law appear to have undergone a paradigm shift in recent decades. However, administrative law as a legal discipline has never – or at least not in the last centuries – been a matter exclusively for the closed ecosystem of the nation-state. As described by della Cananea, the traditional paradigm of administrative law as a province of the state has not – for all its importance – gone unchallenged.[22] Administrative law concepts and functions in European national legal orders have been open to influences from other European legal orders. Further, della Cananea points to a development beginning in the early twentieth century, whereby a role for administrative law beyond the states has emerged.[23] It is today widely recognised in legal doctrine that globalisation and Europeanisation have transformed administrative law, but also that the new role for administrative law is yet to be defined.[24]

As will be seen later, the uncertainties about the role of administrative law – and the administration as such – within the European administrative space have not prevented what seems to be an ever-increasing transfer of tasks, functions and administrative tools to the composite administrative structures of the EU agencies, networks and national competent authorities. It has been argued that there is a developing common understanding of basic concepts of constitutional and administrative law within the Council of Europe and the EU, at least if a practical approach is taken.[25] This is based not least on the general principles of administrative law stemming from both national law and essential European sources such as the European Convention of Human Rights and the EU Charter, as interpreted by the European Court of Human Rights and the European Court of Justice. Since the mid-1980s, the European

21 Hans-Gunnar Axberger, 'Rättigheter I' [2020] Svensk Juristtidning 759; Athanasios Psygkas 'Accountability' in Peter Cane and others (eds), *The Oxford Handbook of Comparative Administrative Law* (OUP 2020) 443, 447 <https://doi.org/10.1093/oxfordhb/9780198799986.013.28>.

22 Giacinto della Cananea, 'Administrative Law Beyond the State: The Influence of International and Supranational Organizations' in Peter Cane and others (eds), *The Oxford Handbook of Comparative Administrative Law* (OUP 2020) 357, 359 <https://doi.org/10.1093/oxfordhb/9780198799986.013.23>.

23 della Cananea (n 22) 360.

24 See, among others, Sabino Cassese, 'New Paths for Administrative Law: A Manifesto' [2012] I-CON 603; Eberhard Schmidt-Aßmann, 'The Internationalization of Administrative Relations as a Challenge of Administrative Law Scholarship' (2008) 9 German Law Journal 2061; Carlo Maria Colombo and Mariolina Eliantonio, 'The Changing Nature of the Public Administration: Innovations and Challenges for Public Lawyers' [2018] EPL 403–4.

25 Ulrich Stelkens and Agnė Andrijauskaitė 'Introduction: Setting the Scene for a "True European Administrative Law"' in Ulrich Stelkens and Agnė Andrijauskaitė (eds), *Good Administration and the Council of Europe: Law, Principles, and Effectiveness* (OUP 2020) 9–10, referring, amongst other, to EU Commission, *A New EU Framework to Strengthen the Rule of Law* (COM[2014]158 final) of 11 March 2014, 2.

Court of Justice has developed requirements for the Member States to apply certain minimum requirements in their administrative decision-making within the sphere of application of EU law.[26] Together with the case law on administrative procedural requirements for the EU institutions, this case law was codified in Article 41 of the EU Charter, within the right to good administration.[27] This common understanding is continuously deepened and strengthened as the European composite administration develops. However, as will be discussed in the following, the concrete delineation of administrative law tools and mechanisms remains underdeveloped in EU administrative law, and differs at the national level, from one Member State to another.[28]

3. The constitutional setting for EU agencies and the European composite administration

3.1 The legal basis of the EU administration in the EU Treaties

It should be noted that the role of the administration under the EU Treaties is unclear. For a long time, it was controversial whether the EU, as an international organisation, could be considered to have its own administration, and little attention was paid to the need for procedural rules for the EU institutions.[29] The question of whether the EU could be considered to have a constitutional basis was in itself a topic of debate until quite recently.[30]

Currently, unlike what is seen for the legislative and judicial powers, the Treaties do not identify a specific executive body. Instead, as will be discussed in the following section, the starting point has been that Member States implement the jointly agreed policies individually, as is customary in international organisations. Article 17 Treaty on the European Union (TEU), identifies that the Commission has executive functions, including to ensure the application of the Treaties, to execute the budget and to manage programmes. With the Lisbon Treaty in 2009, the position of the EU administration beyond the

26 Case C-222/86 *Unectef v Heylens* EU:C:1987:442; 5/88 *Wachauf v Bundesamt für Ernährung und Forstwirtschaft* EU:C:1989:321; C-260/89 *Elliniki Radiophonia Tiléorassi (ERT) v Dimotiki Etairia Pliroforissis* EU:C:1991:254.

27 Explanation on Article 41 – Right to Good Administration, Explanations Relating to the Charter of Fundamental Rights (2007/C 303/02) 29.

28 Herwig CH Hofmann and others, 'The General Principles of EU Administrative Law- an In-Depth Analysis' [2015] Revista Italiana Di Diritto Pubblico Comunitario 425–26; Marc Clement, 'Breach of the Right to Good Administration: So What?' [2018] ELTE Law Journal 19, 22; Päivi Leino, 'Efficiency, Citizens and Administrative Culture: The Politics of Good Administration in the EU' (2014) 20 European Public Law 681.

29 Sergio Alonso de León, *Composite Administrative Procedures in the European Union* (Universidad Carlos III de Madrid 2020) 75, 117.

30 Matthias Ruffert, *Law of Administrative Organization of the EU, a Comparative Approach* (Edward Elgar Publishing 2020) 12, referring to Opinion 2/13 [2014] EU:C:2014:2454, para 158.

Commission was at least indirectly recognised in the Treaties. Article 15(1) TFEU states that '[i]n order to promote good governance and ensure the participation of civil society, the Union's institutions, bodies, offices and agencies shall conduct their work as openly as possible'. The rule is thus aimed at the central EU institutions and EU agencies, as the 'bodies, offices and agencies' are referred to.[31] The fact that the EU agencies can enact legally binding decisions is indirectly reflected in Article 263(5) TFEU, i.e., the fundamental article of the Treaty that regulates the way in which legally binding EU acts can be subject to court control. The article simply refers to other EU legislation, the acts establishing the EU agencies, stating that the matter is regulated there.

The most important recognition of the role of the EU administration is found in Article 258 TFEU, which on the one hand fills out the aforementioned Article 15(1) and on the other hand gives the EU the legislative competence to adopt an administrative procedures act. In legal doctrine, it has long been advocated that the EU should adopt such an act. This suggestion gained political momentum after the fall of the Santer Commission in 1999 following allegations of fraud, mismanagement and nepotism.[32] The European Ombudsman issued a code of good administrative behaviour, which was adopted by the European Parliament in 2001.[33] In 2013, the European Parliament adopted a resolution calling on the Commission to adopt an administrative procedures act.[34] In parallel, the Research Network on EU Administrative Law (ReNEUAL) developed a model law for good governance in the EU, which has been published in the form of six books.[35] In 2016, the European

31 Compare the titles of two central books in the area, Merijn Chamon, *EU Agencies: Legal and Political Limits to the Transformation of the EU Administration* (Oxford Scholarship Online 2016); Miroslava Scholten and Alex Brenninkmeijer (eds), *Controlling EU Agencies: The Rule of Law in the Multi-Jurisdictional Legal Order* (Edward Elgar Publishing 2020).

32 Paul Craig, *EU Administrative Law* (OUP 2018) 36 ff; Henk Addink, *Good Governance: Concept and Context* (OUP 2019) 42 ff; Committee of Independent Experts (1999) First Report on Allegations regarding Fraud, Mismanagement and Nepotism in the European Commission; Reforming the Commission - White Paper. COM (2000) 200 final, vol I.

33 See in particular the European Ombudsman, *Report to the European Parliament Following the Own-Initiative Inquiry into the Existence and the Public Accessibility, in the Different Community Institutions and Bodies, of a Code of Good Administrative Behaviour (OI/1/98/OV)* (European Ombudsman 1998); European Parliament, *Resolution on the European Ombudsman' Special Report to the European Parliament Following the Own-Initiative Inquiry into the Existence and the Public Accessibility, in the Different Community Institutions and Bodies, of a Code of Good Administrative Behaviour (C5-0438/2000–2000/2212) (COS)* (European Parliament 2000).

34 European Parliament (2013) Resolution of 15 January 2013 with recommendations to the Commission on a Law of Administrative Procedure of the European Union (2012/2024(INL)); Hans Ragnemalm, 'Spelet om EU:s förvaltningslag - synpunkter från läktaren' in Thomas Bull, Olle Lundin and Elisabeth Rynning (eds), *Festskrift till Lena Marcusson* (Iustus 2013) 259 ff.

35 Paul Craig and others (eds), *ReNEUAL Model Rules on EU Administrative Procedure* (OUP 2017) also available on the ReNEUAL project's website.

Parliament adopted a new resolution, including a concrete legislative proposal based on the ReNEUAL's suggestions.[36] Since then, the process has stalled.[37] However, the EU has adopted administrative procedural rules in a large number of sector-specific acts, directed at both EU agencies and national competent authorities. As shown by Hofmann, Rowe and Türk, even though national law still constitutes the main locus for implementation of EU law, there is 'a clear trend in favours for a higher degree of Union-level constraint on the exercise of discretion by national administrative officials'.[38] The relevance of this trend will be discussed in Section 3.3.

3.2 EU agencies and the process of agencification

Despite the unclear legal basis for the EU agencies seen earlier, they have continued to grow in number and importance over the decades. Both the principle of conferred powers and the *Meroni* doctrine on limitations of delegation of treaty-based powers beyond the institutions set restrictions for which powers can be delegated to EU agencies.[39] In comparison to national agencies, EU agencies were originally endowed with very limited tasks. However, these have gradually expanded over the years.[40] The fact that the agencies continue to grow can be explained by efficiency arguments, as put forward in the 2001 White Paper on European Governance.[41]

The advantage of agencies is often their ability to draw on highly technical, sectoral know-how, the increased visibility they give to the sectors concerned (and sometimes the public) and the cost savings they can offer for businesses.

Perhaps even more importantly, the EU agencies form a bridge between EU and Member State administrations. The competent authorities within the Member States are usually closely organisationally connected to the EU agencies, as the competent authorities are generally represented in the organisation of EU authorities. For example, the heads of the national DPAs have a seat on

36 European Parliament (2016). Resolution on an open, efficient and independent EU administration (2016/2610(RSP)).

37 Joana Mendes, 'The EU Administrative Institutions, Their Law, and Legal Scholarship' in Peter Cane and others (eds), *The Oxford Handbook of Comparative Administrative Law* (OUP 2020).

38 Herwig CH Hofmann, Gerard C Rowe and Alexander H Türk, 'Synthesis and Assessment' in *Specialized Administrative Law of the European Union, a Sectoral Review* (OUP 2018) 639.

39 Article 5.2 TEU; case 9–56 *Meroni v High Authority of the European Coal and Steel Community*, EU:C:1958:7; Chamon (n 31) 136 et seq, 175 et seq.

40 Eva Ruffing and others, 'The European Administrative Space Over Time: Mapping the Formal Independence of EU Agencies' [2023] Regulation & Governance 1, 4 <https://doi.org/10.1111/rego.12556>.

41 European Commission, *European Governance - A White Paper*, COM (2001) 428 final, 20; Ruffert, *Law of Administrative Organization* (n 30) 88.

the Management Board of the EDPB.[42] As stated by Ruffert, 'the European administrative space cannot be governed by EU institutions alone'.[43]

There are currently around 35 EU agencies of differing kinds.[44] Many different categorisations have been suggested over the years.[45] In 2012, the European Parliament, the Council and the Commission concluded an agreement laying down a 'Common Approach'.[46] However, within legal doctrine, it is still held that the governance structure of the EU agencies remains in need of clarification.[47] Some general features can be distinguished. Due to the EU's lack of inherent powers of self-organisation, each EU agency is established via secondary law based on either the subsidiary general legal basis in Article 352 TFEU or – as with rules regulating national administrative infrastructures – under the substantive legal basis for the relevant sector.[48] EU agencies are usually permanent bodies, vested with personality under EU law, which enjoy independence to some degree and have at least some delegated powers.[49]

Information gathering and sharing are central features of many EU agencies.[50] Many agencies function as information hubs in sector-specific areas, assisting competent agencies at the national level and EU institutions, providing shared databases, managing structured forms of information exchange upon request, etc.[51] Also on the technical and administrative side, the EU has furthered its activities by establishing an agency – eu-LISA, the European Union Agency for the Operational Management of Large-Scale IT Systems in the Area of Freedom, Security and Justice – in charge of managing sector-specific databases, often encompassing sensitive personal data. These include the Schengen Information System (SIS), the Visa Information System (VIS), the European Travel Information Authorisation System (ETIAS) and the European Criminal Records Information System for Third-Country Nationals (ECRIS-TCN).[52]

42 Article 68.3 GDPR.
43 Ruffert, *Law of Administrative Organization* (n 30) 89.
44 Scholten and Brenninkmeijer (n 31) 3, with further references.
45 See for an inventory, Chamon (n 31) 18 et seq.
46 Chamon (n 31); Joint Statement of the European Parliament, the Council of the EU and the European Commission on decentralised agencies, with a Common Approach in Annex, 19 July 2012.
47 Scholten and Brenninkmeijer (n 31) 4; Ruffert, *Law of Administrative Organization* (n 30) 87; Chamon (n 31) 61.
48 Ruffert, *Law of Administrative Organization* (n 30) 94–95.
49 Ruffert, *Law of Administrative Organization* (n 30) 95–99; Ruffing and others (n 40) 18; Chamon (n 31) 10, 13.
50 Diana-Urania Galetta, Herwig GH Hofmann and Jens-Peter Schneider, 'Information Exchange in the European Administrative Union: An Introduction' (2014) 29 European Public Law 65–66, et seq.
51 Galetta, Hofmann and Schneider (n 50) 91.
52 See eu-LISA's web page <https://www.eulisa.europa.eu/About-Us/Who-We-Are>; Deirdre Curtin and Filipe Brito Bastos, 'Interoperable Information Sharing and the Five Novel Frontiers of EU Governance' (2020) 26 European Public Law 63.

3.3 *The role of the national administration with the EU and the rise of a European composite administration*

The role of the national administrations within the EU can be described as ambivalent. There are strong constitutional arguments to support the claim that the national administration remains the default forum for implementing and enforcing EU law. According to the doctrine of institutional and procedural autonomy, it is for the Member States to appoint public authorities competent to manage specific policy areas under EU law. In the absence of EU regulation, the Member States are to decide what procedures public authorities and courts are to apply, on the condition that they are effective and applied equivalently.[53] Article 291.1 TFEU declares that the Member States have the responsibility for adopting 'all measures of national law necessary to implement legally binding Union acts'. The EU does not have any independent competence to regulate the internal administrative structure of the Member States – it can only carry out actions to support, coordinate or supplement the actions of the Member States.[54] According to the principle of conferral, this means that the power to legislate in an area remains with the Member States.[55] Further, according to the principle of subsidiarity, EU may only use its competence where it can be shown, for a legislative act, that a proposed action cannot be sufficiently achieved at the national level and will be better achieved at the Union level for reasons of scale or effect.[56]

However, it must be submitted that these constitutional restraints on the EU's ability to develop common administrative infrastructures for EU and national administration have not prevented a development towards an at least partial European composite administration. Already from the very beginning of the establishment of the EU, it was recognised that administrative cooperation between the EU and its Member States was necessary, not least in the area of sharing administratively relevant data.[57] Further, as with the EU agencies, legislative competence to regulate national administrations can be found with sector-specific legal bases. It has accordingly become increasingly common with various forms of composite decision-making processes, in which both EU agencies and competent national authorities participate.[58]

53 33/76 *Rewe-Zentralfinanz eG and Rewe-Zentral AG v Landwirtschaftskammer für das Saarland*, EU:C:1976:167; 45/76 *Comet BVv Produktschapvoor Siergewassen*, EU:C:1976:191.

54 Articles 6 g and 197 TFEU.

55 Article 5.1 Treaty of the European Union (hereafter TEU).

56 Article 5.2 TEU.

57 An early example is the Administrative Commission on Social Security for Migrant Workers, established in 1958, see further Henrik Wenander, 'A Network of Social Security Bodies – European Administrative Cooperation Under Regulation (EC) No 883/2004' (2013) 6 Review of European Administrative Law 39, 47.

58 Craig and others (n 35) 50; de León (n 29).

One area where secondary law on complex decision-making procedures is common is financial market law.[59] A far-reaching example is the relatively new authority, the Single Resolution Board (SRB) from 2016, a central agency within a composite decision-making procedure to ensure the orderly resolution of a failing national bank.[60] The procedure further involves the European Central Bank, the competent authority of the Member States concerned, the Commission and, in some cases, the Council.[61] Composite decision-making procedures are also used for various types of authorisations, such as for pharmaceuticals and chemicals.[62] Another example of a complex decision-making process is when competent authorities are obliged to consult other competent authorities before making a decision. As will be described below, EU data protection law entails a far-reaching version of this procedure, in which the EDPB is mandated to enact decisions in cases where supervisory authorities cannot agree on the interpretation of the rules after a consultation process. Such a decision then binds the competent authority to enact the final decision in the case.[63]

Lastly, there are areas where there is no EU agency, such as competition, taxation, social security, migration and consumer affairs. In these areas, the competent authorities in the Member States usually cooperate through established networks. There may be close co-operation, with extensive exchange of information, which is the case as regards tax and social security. The Market Surveillance Regulation from 2019 coordinates market surveillance in a wide range of areas. In Sweden, 13 authorities are involved, including the Swedish Work Environment Authority, the Public Health Agency of Sweden, the Swedish Civil Contingencies Agency, the Swedish Environmental Protection Agency, the Swedish Post and Telecom Authority and the Swedish Transport Agency.[64] Throughout the EU, there are hundreds of competent

59 Jane Reichel, 'Ensuring the Principle of Good Administration in EU Financial Markets Law' in Carl-Fredrik Bergström and Magnus Strand (eds), *Legal Accountability in EU Markets for Financial Instruments* (Oxford University Press 2021) 137.

60 Regulation (EU) 806/2014 of the European Parliament and of the Council of 15 July 2014 establishing uniform rules and a uniform procedure for the resolution of credit institutions and certain investment firms in the framework of a Single Resolution Mechanism and a Single Resolution Fund.

61 Marta Božina Beroš, 'Some Reflections on the Governance Framework of the Single Resolution Board' (2018) 56 Journal of Common Market Studies 646, 651 et seq. <https://doi.org/10.1111/jcms.12645>.

62 de León (n 29) sections 4.4.4 and 4.4.6.

63 Articles 63–65 Regulation (EU) 2016/679 of the European Parliament and of the Council on the protection of natural persons with regard to the processing of personal data and on the free movement of such data (GDPR).

64 Regulation (EU) 2019/1020 of the European Parliament and of the Council of 20 June 2019 on market surveillance and conformity of products; SOU 2020:49 *En enhetlig och effektiv marknadskontroll [Uniform and effective market surveillance]*, 376.

authorities under the Market Surveillance Regulation.[65] As will be seen later, these authorities are also given tasks under the AI Act.

However, the institutional and procedural rules set out in secondary law are to a large extent formulated in the form of minimum rules, leaving ample room for the Member States to continue to handle the matters in accordance with national procedural traditions. As seen in Section 2, the Member States are obliged to respect the EU general principles when implementing EU law, including the right to good administration and the right to an effective remedy. Secondary law can therefore be interpreted as specifying how these obligations are to be realised under the relevant secondary act. However, the regulatory strategy has resulted in a piecemeal approach, often merely regulating the basic procedural rules covered by Article 41 of the EU Charter.[66]

4. The role and functions of the composite administration in the EU strategy for data

4.1 The building of an EU composite administration for data

As seen in the introduction, following the adoption of the 1995 Data Protection Directive, EU law had the dual aim of protecting the privacy of data subjects and promoting the free movement of personal data.[67] The enabling of economic and social progress and trade expansion has thus been connected to the need to respect for fundamental rights and freedoms of natural persons, most notably the right to informational integrity.

A central component of enforcement of these aims is the advanced administrative cooperative scheme between the national DPAs and the Article 29 Working Party Group, which the GDPR transformed into the EDPB.[68] The main centre for implementing the GDPR remains with the DPA, at the national level, in accordance with the doctrine of institutional and procedural autonomy.[69] However, the GDPR also serves to strengthen effective and uniform enforcement via two main categories of administrative tools: soft governance and coordinated and sometimes composite decision-making procedures

65 The Commission has published two lists of competent authorities under the Market Surveillance Regulation, one sorted by sector and the other by country <https://ec.europa.eu/growth/single-market/goods/building-blocks/market-surveillance/organisation_en> accessed 30 October 2024. The lists are 300 and 319 pages, respectively. However, it should be noted that the same authority can act as competent authority for several sectors.

66 Craig and others (n 35) 42 et seq.

67 This follows already from the titles of the two central acts, Directive 95/46/EC on the protection of individuals with regard to the processing of personal data and on the free movement of such data and Regulation (EU) 2016/679 on the protection of natural persons with regard to the processing of personal data and on the free movement of such data.

68 Article 29 of the Data Protection Directive; Article 58 GDPR; Hielke Hijmans, *The European Union as a Guardian of Internet Privacy: The Story of Art 16 TEU* (Springer 2016).

69 Hofmann and Mustert (n 9) 462.

for remedies, liability and penalties in individual cases, potentially leading to the enactment of high administrative fines. A central theme is thus combining a compliance-based approach with deterrents.[70] Accordingly, although the substantive data protection rules do not differ much between the Data Protection Directive and the GDPR, the cooperative approach to enforcement has brought about major changes. From being an area of law struggling with shortcomings in implementation and compliance, the GDPR is now one of the EU's flagship regulatory policies.[71]

The AI Act and the EHDS Regulation build on the composite administrative structure laid down in the GDPR, adding new layers of EU and national authorities with cooperative mandates. Although the national competent authorities retain the main responsibility to implement the EU data law in individual cases, the tasks are carried out in close collaboration with the other entities in the composite administration, creating a strong and partially independent European administration in its own right. Thus, the relationship between the GDPR, the AI Act and the EHDS Regulation might be seen as chronological, where the two new acts add an AI and health data dimension to the existing supervisory regime.[72] Accordingly, with the EU Strategy for Data, the GDPR and the European composite administration for data have been cast in the role as a guardian of efficiency and trust in relation to the developing data-driven society.[73]

Two aspects of the European composite administration for data are to be presented next: (1) governance tools for promoting coherent compliance and capacity building and (2) individual decision-making, with a particular focus on the main deterrent tool: administrative fines.

4.2 *An overview of the administrative entities under the GDPR, the AI Act and the EHDS*

4.2.1 *The GDPR*

An important aspect of the governance structure of the GDPR – differing from the other acts presented later – is that both Article 16 TFEU and Article 8 EU Charter require that compliance with data protection rules 'shall be subject to control by an independent authority'. The roles and functions of the DPAs

70 Hofmann and Mustert (n 9); Johanna Chamberlain and Jane Reichel, 'The Relationship Between Damages and Administrative Fines in the EU General Data Protection Regulation' (2020) 89 Mississippi Law Journal 667, 673.

71 Bradford (n 4) 7, 132 et seq.

72 Johanna Chamberlain and Jane Reichel, 'Supervision of Artificial Intelligence in the EU and the Protection of Privacy' (2023) 17 FIU Law Review 267, 274 <https://dx.doi.org/10.25148/lawrev.17.2.5>.

73 A European Strategy for Data (n 1) 1, 4; Reichel (n 7) 134.

thus have a constitutional basis.[74] These administrative ideals are concretised in Articles 51–67 GDPR. As mentioned earlier, the GDPR also introduces a new EU agency, the EDPB, that has taken over the role of the previous Article 29 Data Protection Working Party.[75] At the Union level, where Regulation 2018/1725 applies, this falls under the supervision of a European Data Protection Supervisor (EDPS), with a legal framework equivalent to those of the national DPAs.[76]

4.2.2 The AI Act

The AI Act sets out a rather complex governance structure for AI. First, the supervisory regime in the AI Act builds on and expands the regime set out in the GDPR, with many references to the rules and procedures therein, as well as supervisory tasks conducted by the EDPB, the EDPS and the DPAs.[77] Second, the AI Act introduces a large number of new administrative entities as well as conferring new tasks for existing entities, at both the EU level and the national level.[78]

At the EU level, a new EU agency is established – the European Artificial Intelligence Board or AI Board – in which the Member States are to be represented.[79] Further, the Commission has in a separate decision set up a European Artificial Intelligence Office, the AI Office, as an internal Commission function to ensure 'expertise and capabilities in the field of AI', for the implementation, monitoring and supervision of AI systems and AI governance.[80] Further, an advisory forum for stakeholders – industry, start-ups, small and mid-sized enterprises, civil society and academia – is to be established to provide technical expertise and advise the Board and the Commission.[81] A scientific panel of independent experts will also be instated.[82] The Commission is given quite

74 Chamberlain and Reichel, 'The Relationship Between Damages' (n 70) 671.

75 Articles 68–76 GDPR.

76 Chapters VI and VII, Articles 52–62 Regulation 2018/1725 of the European Parliament and the Council on the protection of natural persons with regard to the processing of personal data by the Union institutions, bodies, offices and agencies and on the free movement of such data.

77 See, for example, recital 10 of the preamble to the AI Act, declaring that the fundamental right to the protection of personal data is safeguarded in particular by (amongst others) the GDPR, providing the basis for sustainable and responsible data processing, including where data sets include a mix of personal and non-personal data. The recital further states that the AI Act does not seek to affect the application of existing Union law governing the processing of personal data, including the tasks and powers of the independent supervisory authorities competent to monitor compliance with those instruments.

78 Chamberlain and Reichel, 'Supervision of Artificial Intelligence' (n 72) 278.

79 Article 65 AI Act.

80 Articles 64 and 3(47) AI Act.

81 Article 67 AI Act.

82 Article 68 AI Act.

specific tasks, including an exclusive role as supervisor of general-purpose AI, discussed in Section 4.4.2.[83]

At the national level, the AI Act foresees the involvement of two types of administrative entities: notifying authorities and market surveillance bodies.[84] The notifying authorities are tasked with setting up and carrying out the necessary procedures for designation and notification of conformity assessment bodies and for their monitoring. These may be existing national accreditation bodies.[85] The tasks allocated to the market surveillance authorities are regularly conferred on existing competent authorities under the general Market Surveillance Regulation,[86] if they are not delegated to other sectoral surveillance authorities competent under EU law.[87]

4.2.3 The EHDS

The EHDS is drafted as an act specifying the conditions for processing health data under the GDPR in two situations, i.e., primary use of health data for a patient's own care and for health care services, and secondary use of health data for general-interest purposes.[88] As with the AI Act, the EHDS Regulation includes many references to rules and procedures set out in the GDPR, as well as supervisory tasks performed by the EDPB, the EDPS and the DPAs.

EHDS Regulation foresees the establishment of new administrative bodies for both primary and secondary use, and at both the European level and the national level. Within the pillar of primary use, each Member State is to designate a national contact point for digital health to ensure connection with other national contact points,[89] and a Digital Health Authority responsible for the performance of the tasks related to primary use.[90] For the second pillar, each Member State is to appoint a health data access body (HDAB), tasked with assessing applications for access to electronic health data.[91] Furthermore, at the EU level, the European Health Data Space Board (EHDS Board) is to be established, whose main task will be to facilitate cooperation and exchange of

83 Chapter V AI Act.

84 Article 70.1 AI Act.

85 Article 28(1, 2) AI Act, with reference to Regulation (EC) No 765/2008 of the European Parliament and of the Council of 9 July 2008 setting out the requirements for accreditation and market surveillance relating to the marketing of products.

86 Regulation (EU) 2019/1020 of the European Parliament and of the Council of 20 June 2019 on market surveillance and compliance of products; n 67 above.

87 Article 74(1, 3, 4 7, 8) AI Act.

88 Santa Slokenberga, 'Scientific Research Regime 2.0? How the Proposed EHDS Regulation May Change the GDPR Research Regime' [2022] Technology and Regulation, 2022, 135, 146 <https://doi.org/10.26116/techreg.2022>.

89 Article 23(2) EHDS.

90 Article 19 EHDS.

91 Article 55 EHDS.

information between Member States.[92] The Commission is also given specific tasks, including establishing a central platform for digital health, MyHealth@EU. This platform is to provide the services necessary to support and facilitate the exchange of electronic health data between the national contact points of the Member States.[93]

4.3 *Governance tools for promoting coherent compliance and capacity building*

4.3.1 *The GDPR*

As seen, the DPAs are the main locomotives in the supervisory regime for the GDPR; their primary tasks are to monitor and enforce the application of the GDPR.[94] However, there are 21 other tasks listed in the same article, which pertain to promoting the policies of the GDPR in a more general manner, such as promoting public awareness and understanding of the risks, rules, safeguards and rights in relation to processing, and promoting awareness among controllers and processors of their obligations.[95] One task stands out as a bit unusual for a public authority:[96]

> Each supervisory authority shall on its territory advise, in accordance with Member State law, the national parliament, the government, and other institutions and bodies on legislative and administrative measures relating to the protection of natural persons' rights and freedoms with regard to processing.

The DPAs, as national competent authorities with treaty-based independence, are accordingly tasked with advising their national parliaments and governments on what the EU data law requires of them.

The EDPB, on its part, has been mandated to support the DPAs in several ways, mainly by issuing guidelines, recommendations and best practices. Article 70 GDPR lists 25 tasks for the EDPB, among which almost half are related to guidance documents of different sorts, giving advice and opinions, and promoting cooperation, common training programmes and exchange of knowledge.

As will be discussed, this soft approach of the EDPB is combined with a function as an administrative final arbitrator in the composite decision-making procedure set out in the GDPR, which adds a certain weight to the guidance documents produced by the EDPB.

92 Articles 92 EHDS.
93 Article 23(1) EHDS.
94 Article 57(1) a GDPR.
95 Article 57(1) b, d GDPR.
96 Article 57(1) c GDPR.

4.3.2 The AI Act

One of the main aims of the AI Act is to enable the EU and its Member States to gain control over the fast development and to 'promote the uptake of human centric and trustworthy AI'.[97] Accordingly, the AI Act includes many governance tools to aimed at rendering AI services safe, without hampering beneficial innovation. The functions of the EU bodies under the Act – the AI Board, the AI Office, the advisory forum for stakeholders and the scientific panel of independent experts[98] – are mainly advisory, supportive and capacity building, to ensure that state of the art knowledge is available to the relevant administrative entities, the service providers and, to some extent, the public at large. As an example, the task of promoting AI literacy is laid on the AI Board,[99] the AI Office and the Member States when facilitating the drawing up of codes of conduct[100] and on the providers and deployers of AI systems themselves in relation to their staff.[101]

The national competent authorities – both notifying authorities and market surveillance authorities – are to be provided with adequate technical, financial and human resources, with a sufficient number of personnel with complex competences and expertise:[102]

> [A]n in-depth understanding of AI technologies, data and data computing, personal data protection, cybersecurity, fundamental rights, health and safety risks and knowledge of existing standards and legal requirements.

As noted in Section 3.3, the general Market Surveillance Regulation covers hundreds of competent authorities throughout the EU, on which the AI Act confers tasks to monitor sector-specific AI services.[103]

More concretely, three mechanisms to increase compliance among AI service providers may be highlighted. As the AI Act to a large extent builds on compulsory reporting schemes for AI providers, a large number of administrative tools are enacted to support the correct and uniform submitting of information, for example standardised forms for conformity assessments.[104] All in all, it can be foreseen that a massive amount of foremost technical information will be gathered and shared between European and national competent authorities.[105] Technical standards for CE markings are also to be developed,

97 Recital 1 of the preamble to the AI Act.
98 See Section 4.2.2.
99 Article 66 f AI Act.
100 Article 95(2) c AI Act.
101 Article 4 AI Act.
102 Article 70.3 AI Act.
103 See n 67.
104 Article 47 AI Act.
105 Chamberlain and Reichel, 'Supervision of Artificial Intelligence' (n 72) 281.

as well as code of conduct and guidelines.[106] Further, and quite innovatively, the AI Act introduces standardised regulatory sandboxes, to provide a controlled framework for providers of AI systems to develop, train, validate and test their AI systems, under the regulatory supervision of national competent authorities.[107] In providing the regulatory sandboxes, the national authorities are to offer AI service providers guidance, supervision and support in aspects such as fundamental rights, health and safety, testing, mitigation measures, as well as on issues regarding regulatory expectations and how to fulfil the requirements and obligations set out in the AI Act.[108]

4.3.3 The EHDS

An important aim of the EU Strategy for Data is to 'unleash the potential of data' for the benefit of relevant actors and, ultimately, society.[109] The EHDS Regulation contributes to this aim by setting out technical requirements on manufacturers of electronic health records to ensure the interoperability of health data[110] and to provide platforms at both the national and EU levels to ensure support and facilitate the exchange of electronic health data for primary use,[111] as well as secure processing environments for secondary use at both levels.[112] Both the Commission and the two new EU agencies, the Digital Health Authority and the EHDS Board, are tasked with supporting exchange of and access to data, and to build national capacity in various ways.[113] The competent authorities for secondary use at the national level, the HDABs, are also given a role as facilitators of access to health data. In relation to multi-country data applications, the HDABs are explicitly tasked with facilitating cross-border access, in close collaboration with each other and the Commission.[114] However, the Member States themselves – not the competent bodies – are given the general task to train and inform health professionals[115] and to promote and support health literacy for patients, with the aid of the Commission.[116] The latter task is described in a rather high level of detail, stating that 'awareness raising campaigns or programmes' are to include informing both patients and

106 Article 48 and 95 AI Act.
107 Articles 2 (55) and 57 AI Act.
108 Article 57(6) AI Act.
109 A European Strategy for Data (n 4) 26. See also Communication from the Commission to the European Parliament and the Council, A European Health Data Space: Harnessing the Power of Health Data for People, Patients and Innovation, COM(2022) 196 final 2, 3, 8, 13 and 18.
110 See the Proposal, Article 17 and Annex II.
111 Article 19 and 23 EHDS.
112 Article 57(1) a (i) and 73 EHDS.
113 Articles 19(2) j, 82, 94 (1) c EHDS.
114 Article 57(1) i EHDS.
115 Article 83 EHDS.
116 Article 84 EHDS.

the public at large about the aims of the EHDS and the rights, advantages, risks and potential gains to science and society that it entails.[117]

As with the AI Act, the Member States are to ensure that the HDABs are provided with the human and financial resources and expertise necessary.[118]

4.4 *Cooperative and composite elements in individual decision-making on administrative fines*

4.4.1 *The GDPR*

The GDPR offers a number of remedies for data subjects whose data protections rights have (allegedly) been infringed, including the right to lodge a complaint to the DPA, the right to an effective remedy against the DPA, the controller or the processor,[119] and the right to compensation.[120] Further, the GDPR offers the DPA an administrative deterrence tool to use vis-à-vis a controller or processor directly, in the form of administrative fines.[121] As was stated in the introduction, the fines can be quite substantial, up to EUR 20,000,000, or in the case of an undertaking, up to 4% of the total worldwide annual turnover of the preceding financial year, whichever is higher.[122]

It is an explicit aim of the GDPR that the level of protection of the rights and freedoms of natural persons with regard to personal data processing shall be equivalent in all Member States.[123] Article 83 GDPR sets out rather elaborate assessment criteria, which were interpreted by the predecessor to the EDPB, the Article 29 Data Protection Working Party, in guidelines issued in 2017.[124] The GDPR further contains a specific procedure for decision-making in matters with cross-border implications, a one-stop-shop mechanism where the DPAs collaborate in a composite decision-making process to enact a single decision covering activities in several Member States.[125] In short, the procedure

117 Article 84(2) EHDS.

118 Article 55(2) EHDS.

119 The controller is defined as the natural or legal person, public authority, agency or other body which, alone or jointly with others, determines the purposes and means of the processing of personal data, Article 2(7) GDPR. The processor is a natural or legal person, public authority, agency or other body which processes personal data on behalf of the controller, Article 2(8) GDPR.

120 Articles 77–79, 82 GDPR.

121 Article 83 GDPR.

122 Article 83(5), (6) GDPR.

123 Recital 10 of the preamble to the GDPR; Chamberlain and Reichel, 'The Relationship Between Damages' (n 70) 685.

124 Article 29 Data Protection Working Party, Guidelines on the application and setting of administrative fines for the purposes of Regulation 2016/679 (WP 253).

125 Articles 56.1, 60–65 GDPR. See further Hofmann and Mustert (n 9) 465–69; Hielke Hijmans, *The European Union as a Guardian of Internet Privacy: The Story of Art 16 TEU* (Springer 2016) 516; Chamberlain and Reichel, 'The Relationship Between Damages' (n 70) 673–75.

consists of three stages. In the first, the lead authority[126] and the other DPAs concerned are to cooperate with the aim of reaching a common understanding on how to handle the matter.[127] In the second stage, if the DPAs do not agree, the EDPB takes a leading role and issues an opinion.[128] In the third stage, the EDPB issues a dispute resolution, a draft decision for the relevant DPAs to implement by enacting final decisions in accordance with the requirements of the relevant national law.[129] As pointed out, this mechanism gives the EDPB the role as a final administrative arbitrator. However, the final decision enacted by the lead DPA can be appealed to the competent national court.[130] The aforementioned guidelines on administrative fines foresee that the EDPB can use its competence to enact a decision within the dispute resolution process in matters of administrative fines.[131]

This mechanism is intended to bridge the distributed model of implementing the GDPR described earlier, in accordance with the principle of institutional and procedural autonomy where the main implementation of EU law remains at the national level. Although this one-stop-shop mechanism is only available in matters with cross-border implications, it follows from the fluidity of data and the global features of the internet that such matters are common. The one-stop-shop mechanism, together with the guidance documents drafted by the EDPB, are accordingly effective tools for ensuring consistent application of the GDPR.[132]

However, in line with the basic principles for regulating national procedures within the sphere of application of EU law discussed in Sections 2 and 3.3, these one-stop-shop procedures provide only minimum rules, set out in general terms. For example, the GDPR does not contain any specific rules on how the DPAs are to ensure the right to good administration and the right to an effective remedy in relation to a complainant or a targeted data controller or processor. It merely states that the powers exercised by the Member States to enact administrative fines under the GDPR are to be 'subject to appropriate safeguards, including effective judicial remedy and due process, set out in Union and Member State law in accordance with the Charter'.[133] In its two-year evaluation of the GDPR, the Commission found that the current state of affairs – with significant differences between national administrative

126 Article 56 GDPR defines lead authority as the 'supervisory authority of the main establishment or of the single establishment of the controller'.
127 Article 60 GDPR.
128 Article 64 GDPR.
129 Article 65 GDPR.
130 Article 78.1 GDPR.
131 Article 29 Data Protection Working Party, Guidelines (n 124) 7.
132 Hofmann and Mustert (n 9) 462.
133 Article 83.3 GDPR. Compare the wording in recital 148 to the GDPR and Article 58 (4) GDPR; Chamberlain and Reichel, 'The Relationship Between Damages' (n 70) 690–91.

procedures – constituted an obstacle to effective implementation of the GDPR.[134] Following a resolution of the European Parliament, the Commission in 2023 proposed a new regulation laying down additional procedural rules relating to the enforcement of the GDPR.[135] Two aspects may be highlighted here: rules clarifying the position of the complainant in cross-border complaints, and rules describing the procedural rights of parties under investigation. The proposal defines the character of these procedures as non-adversarial, where the complainant and the parties under investigation cannot be seen as being in the same procedural situation. Rather, this is a procedure conducted by a DPA for fulfilment of its tasks under the GDPR.[136] Whereas the complainant can be provided a limited right to be heard via their national DPA, the investigated parties are to be heard by the lead authority itself, and have a right of access to files.[137] Further, the proposed regulation lays down more detailed rules on how the lead authority and the other DPAs are to collaborate.

4.4.2 The AI Act

As seen, the AI Act sets out a rather complex scheme for supervising AI services, adding an AI layer to the sector-specific market surveillance schemes already in place under EU law, as well as laying down procedures for how the Commission is to monitor general-purpose AI. Two aspects of the extra AI layer of supervision can be mentioned: the union safeguard procedure, in Article 81 AI Act, and the procedure for compliant AI systems that present risks, in Article 82 AI Act.

The first procedure gives a Member State and the Commission a possibility to raise objections to a market surveillance authority in another Member State, in a situation where the authority has taken a measure against an AI service.[138] According to the union safeguard procedure, the Commission may declare the measure taken by the market surveillance authority 'non-justified', whereupon the authority is to withdraw the measure.[139] The procedure is not in itself a novelty in EU market surveillance law, as it exists in several technically

134 Communication from the Commission to the European Parliament and the Council, Data protection as a pillar of citizens' empowerment and the EU's approach to the digital transition - two years of application of the General Data Protection Regulation (COM/2020/264 final) 6 et seq.

135 European Parliament resolution of 25 March 2021 on the Commission evaluation report on the implementation of the General Data Protection Regulation two years after its application (2020/2717(RSP)); Proposal for a Regulation of The European Parliament and of the Council laying down additional procedural rules relating to the enforcement of Regulation (EU) 2016/679 COM(2023) 348 final.

136 Recital 25 of the preamble of the proposed regulation.

137 Articles 11, 17 and 20 of the proposed regulation.

138 Articles 5, 79(5) and 81 AI Act.

139 Article 81(5) AI Act.

oriented acts.[140] The procedure resembles the GDPR one-stop-shop procedure described in Section 4.4.1, in that it allows for competent authorities and the Commission to react against a fellow competent authority and 'force' that authority to change its position in an individual case. Due to the very wide field of application of the AI Act, and the general speed and uncertainty of technical developments, it would be preferrable if the procedure were set out more clearly, for example as regards the role that the AI service provider is to have. The next procedure to be presented concerns high-risk AI systems which present a risk to the health or safety of persons, to the fundamental rights of persons, or to other aspects of public interest protection, even if they have been found to be compliant with the AI Act.[141] In this case, a market surveillance authority may place requirements on the AI system provider, which are to be fulfilled without undue delay. Here, too, the Commission is empowered to make the final decision on whether the measure taken by the national competent authority is justified.[142]

In regard to administrative fines, the AI Act sets out that the Member States are to lay down rules on penalties and other enforcement measures, including administrative fines. In comparison with the GDPR, which describes both specific investigatory competences for the DPAs and assessment criteria for setting fines, the AI Act is much less specific. On the other hand, Article 99 provides for extraordinarily high fines for non-compliance: up to EUR 35,000,000, or, if the offender is an undertaking, up to 7% of the total worldwide annual turnover for the preceding financial year, whichever is higher. In contrast to the GDPR, the AI Act does not give any guidance on what administrative procedural safeguards are to be applied vis-à-vis targeted AI service providers, but instead refers to the Market Surveillance Act, which lays down minimum rules.[143] However, it can be noted that the Market Surveillance Act does not contain any rules on administrative fines.

One relevant question is surprisingly absent from the AI Act, namely the division of competences between the DPAs under the GDPR and the competent authorities under the AI Act. According to Article 2(7), the GDPR is to be applicable to personal data processed in connection with the rights and obligations laid down in the AI Act, which would seem to mean that the supervisory mandate of the DPAs would also be applicable.[144] In such case,

140 See, for example, Article 43 Directive 2014/32/EU of the European Parliament and of the Council of 26 February 2014 on the harmonisation of the laws of the Member States relating to the making available on the market of measuring instruments; Article 41 Directive 2014/68/EU of the European Parliament and of the Council of 15 May 2014 on the harmonisation of the laws of the Member States relating to the making available on the market of pressure equipment.

141 Article 82.1 AI Act.

142 Article 82.4 AI Act.

143 Articles 79(2), (8) and 94 AI Act, referring to Article 18 Regulation (EU) 2019/1020.

144 See also recital 10 of the preamble to the AI Act.

delineation of the mandates between the DPAs and the market surveillance authorities would be needed. In some contexts, the AI Act even opens for a DPA to function as a competent authority under the AI Act. According to Article 74(8) AI Act, a Member State may choose to appoint the DPA to be the market surveillance authority responsible for monitoring certain categories of high-risk data.

4.4.3 *The EHDS*

Due to the more limited substantive sphere of application of the EHDS in comparison to the GDPR and the AI Act, the decision-making structure of the EHDS is more straight-forward. The primary use pillar is centred around the technical and legal condition for making health data interoperable throughout the EU, mainly for the benefit of patients seeking health care in other Member States.[145] The secondary use pillar involves a demanding, but well-structured procedure for third parties to access health data for any of the 15 permitted purposes defined in the Act. The parties involved are the data holders, the natural or legal person holding the health data which can be accessed under the act, the data users, the natural or legal persons who may lawfully access the health data, and the HDABs, which assess the applications for access and decides on permits.[146] The data subjects, the natural persons whose personal health data is processed, are not involved.[147] The assessment procedure is laid out in some detail, defining what information a data user must submit and what considerations the HDABs are to take into account.[148]

In contrast to the GDPR and the AI Act, the EHDS Regulation does not contain any formal composite procedures, where the competent bodies at the EU and national levels cooperate in the decision-making in an individual case. In the article defining the tasks of the HDABs, it is stated in the first section that '[e]ach health data access body shall contribute to the consistent application of this Regulation throughout the Union'. This is to be done by cooperating with other HDABs, the Commission and the DPAs under the GDPR.[149] A specific duty to cooperate is mentioned in relation to cross-border application for access to data, namely when a data user wants to access health data from more than one Member State.[150] However, the decision to issue the relevant permit rests with the competent body in each respective state.[151]

145 Article 2(2) d EHDS.
146 Articles 2(2) t and u, 55 EHDS; Ciara Staunton and others, 'Ethical and Social Reflections on the Proposed European Health Data Space' [2024] European Journal of Human Genetics 3 <https://doi.org/10.1038/s41431-024-01543-9a>.
147 Staunton and others (n 146) 3.
148 Article 68 EHDS.
149 Article 55(1) EHDS.
150 Article 67(3) EHDS.
151 Article 68(5) EHDS.

The HDABs are also given the power to enact sanctions towards data holders and data users that do not comply with the requirements regarding secondary use. In the Commission's initial proposal, the sanctioning tools were quite limited,[152] but in the trialogue, the EU legislator added a possibility to enact administrative fines modelled on the GDPR. The HDABs are accordingly conferred the power to impose fines up to EUR 20,000,000, or, in the case of an undertaking, up to 4% of the total worldwide annual turnover of the preceding financial year, whichever is higher.[153] Like the GDPR, the EHDS Regulation stipulates detailed assessment criteria for the HDABs to apply.[154]

Lastly, as with the AI Act, there is a need to delineate the competences falling on the competent authorities under the EHDS Regulation and the GDPR. Unlike what we saw for the AI Act, this is done in the EHDS Regulation. In the article laying down the enforcement tools of the HDABs, it is stated that if a finding of non-compliance involves a possible breach of the GDPR, the DPA is to be informed and provided with all the relevant information.[155] Further, as regards the possibility for Member States to introduce an opt-out mechanism from the processing of personal health data for secondary use, the EHDS Regulation allocates the supervisory responsibilities to the DPAs.[156] In regard to the right to file a complaint to a HDAB, the EHDS Regulation refers to the mandate of the DPAs in relation to their function vis-á-vis the opt-out mechanisms, and some further processing related to primary use of health data.[157]

5. What future for the European composite administration for data?

The question raised in this chapter is how the European composite administration can fulfil the two basic tasks of the executive under the rule of law, to ensure that the aims and contents of the legislation are realised, and that constitutional restraints of public powers are upheld. Two aspects have been analysed more closely, the governance tools available to the composite administrations to promote coherent compliance and capacity building and administrative tools for individual decision-making, with a particular focus on the main deterrent tool, administrative fines.

With the European Strategy for Data, the EU has taken further steps in creating a new arena for the European composite administration to define public policies in a cooperative manner, under the often vague and open-ended rules

152 Articles 41(4), 43(4)(5), 44(3) and 69 Commission Proposal for a Regulation of the European Parliament and of the Council on the European Health Data Space, COM(2022) 197 final.
153 Article 64(5) EHDS.
154 Article 64(2) EHDS.
155 Article 63(2) EHDS.
156 Article 65 EHDS.
157 Article 81(4) EHDS.

laid down by the legislator. As shown, the executive strategy of the GDPR, combining a compliance-based approach and with strong deterrents, has been transferred to the newly adopted legislative act as the ones in focus here, the AI Act and the EHDS Regulation. The compliance-based tasks include not merely technical standard-setting, but tasks for coherent compliance and capacity building in core areas of democratic policymaking, including collecting and making accessible information and personal data, defining prerequisites for research and technical development. The deterrents consist of a mandate to enact administrative decisions with un-precedented high fines.

The lack of a clear basis for the European composite administration in the EU Treaties means that its legal basis is drawn from a combination of EU and national constitutional frameworks, without a well-defined allocation of tasks and competences. Institutional and procedural responsibilities between the administrative entities within the cooperative administrative structures are at the same time often complex and vague. These shortcomings become even more challenging on the many occasions when entities are to cooperate beyond a sector-specific act. It is therefore difficult to foresee how this administrative organisational model can uphold the basic functions of the executive power in a representative democracy under the rule of law, as described in Section 2. Is it actually possible for the composite administration for data to ensure that the law is applied in an efficient manner, and to ensure that the exercise of public power is limited, predictable and performed in accordance with applicable legislation? This could be a challenge for public authorities within nation-based democracies, and could be expected to be more demanding in a constitutional model that is itself a newcomer in constitutional and administrative theory.[158] The doctrine of institutional and procedural autonomy has the advantage of clear allocation of constitutional powers: parliamentary, executive and judicial. However, enforcement in a cross-border context is ineffective and varied. In the composite administration, executive powers have migrated beyond the initial constitutional settings at the EU and the Member State level, respectively, but the democratic governance and control mechanisms have not undergone the equivalent development. As held by Ruffert, 'there are only piecemeal answers to the question of how representative democracy can be operationalised at the administrative level'.[159] Still, as seen, there is a clear trend, also beyond the composite administration for data, for EU law to place constraints on the exercise of discretion by national administrative entities.[160]

Although the close cooperation within the EU has connected EU and national administrations in many ways, taking the step to actually move the exercise of public powers in individual cases – to either vague and informal cooperation beyond the state or formal composite procedures involving several

158 Ruffert, *Law of Administrative Organization* (n 30) 12, 165.
159 Ruffert, *Law of Administrative Organization* (n 30) 165.
160 Hofmann, Rowe and Türk (n 38) 639.

different national and European authorities – is complicated and sensitive.[161] Administrative law is traditionally a tool for the nation-state to communicate with natural and legal persons within its jurisdiction, and having this tool regulated by an entity beyond the state could be interpreted as interference with national sovereignty.[162] On the other hand, informality does not provide sufficient legal certainty. Further, as is apparent from the three legislative acts analysed here, composite procedures are challenged by the multiplicity of the roles, functions and procedures among Member States. It is well recognised in legal doctrine that it is difficult to uphold administrative procedural safeguards such as the principle of good administration in a composite context.[163] The idea of the closed ecosystem of the state is no longer upheld. However, no basic legal principles for how new forms of administration are to be governed have been defined as yet.[164] The question may therefore be raised if it is legitimate to continue to develop a composite administration for data, with full knowledge of the difficulties that this administration has in abiding by the rule of law.

161 Rainer Arnold, 'The Relation Between Constitution and Global Administrative Law – Some Reflections' in Maria Grahn-Farley, Jane Reichel and Mauro Zamboni (eds), *Governing with Public Agencies: The Development of a Global Administrative Space and the Creation of a New Role for Public Agencies* (Poseidon Förlag 2022) 91, 112.

162 Matthias Ruffert, 'An Administrative Constitution for the EU?' in Giacinto Della Cananea and Martina Conticelli (eds), *Rule of Law and Administrative Due Process in Europe. Trends and Challenges* (Editoriale Scientifica 2020) 91.

163 Christina Eckes and Joana Mendes, 'The Right to Be Heard in Composite Administrative Procedures: Lost in Between Protection?' (2011) 36 European Law Review 651 et seq; Mariolina Eliantonio, 'Judicial Review in an Integrated Administration: The Case of Composite Procedures' (2014) 7 Review of European Administrative Law 65, 69 et seq; Filipe Britos Bastos, 'An Administrative Crack in the EU's Rule of Law' (2020) 16 European Constitutional Law Review.

164 Giacinto della Cananea, 'Administrative Law Beyond the State: The Influence of International and Supranational Organizations' in Peter Cane and others (eds), *The Oxford Handbook of Comparative Administrative Law* (OUP 2020) 358 <https://doi.org/10.1093/oxfordhb/9780198799986.013.23>.

9 Coherence in diversity? Exploring the institutional dynamic of enforcement networks in the EU internal market

*Antonina Bakardjieva Engelbrekt**

1. Introduction

Since the beginning of the 1990s, when the European Union stepped up its efforts to complete the Single Market, increasing emphasis has been placed on the effective enforcement of commonly agreed legislative instruments and policies. Given the diversity of national regulative and institutional solutions, influential policy reports at the time called for a "cooperative approach to enforcement", identifying it as "the single most important way of reinforcing mutual confidence between Member States and the Commission".[1] Such approach was to be based on "groups of contact points between the Member States and the Commission", to deal with the application of internal market rules, and creating a "permanent framework for administrative partnership".[2] In a follow up to the Sutherland report, the Commission charted a plan for implementing the approach through, among others, developing operational arrangements for cooperation and information exchange and organizing the work of competent officials designated in Member States "on the basis of networks".[3]

Indeed, moving along this track, in the years that followed, a veritable web of networks with different enforcement functions was rolled out, connecting national authorities and enforcement bodies with each other and with corresponding units of the Commission, or with specially created European

* This chapter is produced as part of and funded by the European Union-NextGenerationEU, through the National Recovery and Resilience Plan of the Republic of Bulgaria, project No bg-rrp-2.004-0008. Part of the research was conducted in the framework of a Torsten and Ragnar Söderberg Chair in legal science at Stockholm University.

1 See Recommendation 31, The Internal Market After 1992: Meeting the Challenge. Report Presented to the Commission by the High-Level Group on the Functioning of the Internal Market Presided Over by Peter Sutherland (Sutherland Report) SEC (1992) 2044, 28 October 1992.

2 Recommendation 31 (n 1); Recommendation 32.

3 Communication from the Commission to the Council and the European Parliament. The operation of the Community's Internal Market after 1992. Follow-up to the Sutherland Report, SEC (92) 2277 final, Brussels, 2 December 1992, para 22.

DOI: 10.4324/9781003610670-13

agencies.[4] Such networks nowadays exist in almost every policy area of the Internal Market and beyond. Moreover, new networks – and networks of networks – continue to emerge, most recently with the Digital Services Act package and its main legislative pillars – the Digital Services Act and the Digital Markets Act.[5]

Governance through networks is typically advanced as holding the promise of increased effectiveness of implementation and enforcement of agreed policies, mainly through enhanced mutual trust and greater coherence in enforcement practice. From a democratic perspective, networks are praised as a governance arrangement countervailing the shift of power to the supranational level and preserving the link to democratically elected national institutions.[6] The trade-off which notoriously informal network governance potentially entails with established principles of good administration, such as transparency, public access and accountability, are often considered offset by the advantages of greater possibilities for experimentation and learning from difference.[7] Further legitimacy is seen to be derived through involvement of a broader range of actors at the Member State level and a more deliberative decision-making process.[8]

While the general notion of network as a form of governance is well understood, the variety of networks in the EU Internal Market in terms of functions, legal basis, constitutive units and institutional design is overwhelming. In this contribution, therefore, (i) in a first step, I revisit the concept of 'network' in social sciences and in law and offer a tentative typology of existing networks in the EU governance landscape. (ii) Then, I look at the reasons for the rise of networks in general and of 'enforcement networks' in the context of the European Single Market, in particular. Likewise, I review briefly the interdisciplinary debate on the expected advantages and disadvantages of network governance. In a third step (iii) the chapter looks more closely at two enforcement networks of central importance for the EU Single Market – the European

4 Renaud Dehousse, 'Regulation by Networks in the European Community: The Role of European Agencies' (1997) 4(2) Journal of European Public Policy 246, 254; David Levi-Faur, 'Regulatory Networks and Regulatory Agencification: Towards a Single European Regulatory Space' (2011) 18(6) Journal of European Public Policy 810, 813.

5 See Regulation (EU) 2022/1925 of the European Parliament and of the Council of 14 September 2022 on contestable and fair markets in the digital sector (Digital Markets Act); Regulation (EU) 2022/2065 of the European Parliament and of the Council of 19 October 2022 on a Single Market for Digital Services (Digital Services Act).

6 Christian Joerges and Jürgen Neyer, 'From Intergovernmental Bargaining to Deliberative Political Processes: The Constitutionalisation of Comitology' (1997) (3) European Law Review 273. Cf. Anne-Marie Slaughter, 'The Real New World Order: The State Strikes Back' (1997) 76(5) Foreign Affairs 183; Anne-Marie Slaughter, *A New World Order* (Princeton UP 2004).

7 Charles Sabel and Jonathan Zeitlin, 'Learning from Difference: The New Architecture of Experimentalist Governance in the EU' (2008) 14(3) European Law Journal 271.

8 Joerges and Nyer (n 6); Christian Joerges, 'Deliberative Supranationalism – Two Defenses' (2002) 8(1) European Law Journal 133.

Competition Network (ECN) and the Consumer Protection Cooperation Network (CPC Network), tracing their history and the evolution of their respective policy fields and outlining the constitutive units and institutional design of each network. Proceeding from this largely descriptive account, in the sections that follow (v–vi) the performance and the dynamics within the two networks is studied, trying to capture the intensity and effects of interaction horizontally, across individual national enforcement bodies and vertically, in the relations between the Commission and national constitutive entities. This dynamic is analysed along four parameters (or logics): effectiveness, participation, horizontal and vertical empowerment (centralization). (vi) Finally, a sideways dynamic, in relation to other adjacent, more or less tightly related networks, is highlighted.

Through comparing the characteristics and dynamics of the two networks, the chapter seeks to put the expectations and misgivings in respect to enforcement networks to the test. The analysis is structured around the following questions: Can we identify features of the compared networks that enhance or, conversely, reduce the effectiveness of the networks and of enforcement coordination? What role does the diversity of national institutional solutions play in this regard? Have networks enhanced the engagement and ensured equal participation of national enforcement authorities? Do networks contribute to empowerment of national enforcement bodies and actors, or do they rather increase centralization and strengthen the position of the Commission and other supranational institutions? What impact, if any, do networks exert on the governance of adjacent policy domains? The more overarching task is to critically evaluate the effectiveness and legitimacy of enforcement networks and the way they influence the distribution of power in the multi-level institutional landscape of the Union.

2. Network governance: essential concepts and basic typology

Before embarking on an analysis of enforcement networks in the EU Internal Market, some central concepts and starting premises need to be clarified.

2.1 Essential concepts

The concept of 'governance' has developed in the social sciences (particularly political science) and is defined deliberately as wider than the well-established concept of 'government'. Governance refers broadly to any form of steering behaviour to achieve certain goals and solve societal problems.[9] Here belong classical forms of hierarchical governance through legislation, administrative

9 Colin Scott, 'The Governance of the European Union: The Potential for Multi-Level Control' (2002) 8(1) European Law Journal 59; Joanne Scott and David M Trubek, 'Mind the Gap: Law and New Approaches to Governance in the European Union' (2002) 8(1) European Law Journal 1.

rulemaking and control, but also judicial control and various 'soft' modes of steering, such as policy recommendations, guidelines, self-regulatory codes and private agreements. The term 'governance' was introduced in the social science discourse to capture an alleged trend of gradual transition from the previously prevailing strictly hierarchically organized control of society by the state and public administration and a shift to more horizontal, decentralized forms of steering, involving private actors and private-public interaction. This shift is seen as particularly prominent in the context of European integration, which has increased exponentially the number of players, their mutual dependencies and the complexity of decision-making across governance levels as shown compellingly by theories of multi-level governance.[10]

The other central notion, that of 'network', is even more ubiquitous and is used widely not only in social sciences, but also in natural sciences and in everyday life, albeit with different connotations. We speak of social networks, infrastructural networks, research networks, digital networks, network economy, etc. In social sciences, the concept 'network' has been used both to denote a type of analysis, employing quantitative as well as qualitative methods, but also to capture a distinct and arguably increasingly pervasive form of social and economic relations building on mutual interdependencies between seemingly autonomous and non-hierarchical units of governance.[11] In institutional economics, scholars like Coase and Williamson famously conceptualized markets and hierarchies as two distinct forms of organizing economic relations, the first relying on contracts, and the second on hierarchy, as represented by the firm. At the same time Williamson observed the existence of a whole panoply of intermediate forms of economic governance placed on a continuum between the two endpoints of atomistic markets and the firm.[12] Proceeding from this theoretical groundwork, economic sociologist Walter Powell conceptualized networks as a separate mode of economic governance, in-between markets and hierarchy, characterized by greater reliance on long-term recurring exchange, interdependence and mutual trust.[13]

Building on these insights, political scientists directed attention to so-called policy networks, starting with analysis at the national policymaking level and extending it to the transnational context, and in particular to the reality of

10 Gary Marks, Lisbeth Hooghe and Karen Blank, 'European Integration from the 1980s: State-Centric v Multiple-Level Governance' (1996) 34 Journal of Common Market Studies 341; Markus Jachtenfuchs and Beate Kohler-Koch, 'The Transformation of Governance in the European Union' [1995] Mannheimer Zentrum für Europäische Sozialforschung, Arbeitspapiere, Arbeitsbereich III, 8 <https://www.mzes.uni-mannheim.de/publications/wp/wp3-11.pdf> accessed 2 November 2024.

11 Renate Mayntz, 'Policy-Netzwerke und die Logik von Verhandlungssystemen' in A Héritier (ed), *Policy-Analyse, Politische Vierteljahresschrift (PVS)* (Springer 1993) vol 24, 39–56.

12 Ronald Coase, 'The Nature of the Firm' (1937) 4 Econometrica 386; Oliver Williamson, *The Economic Institutions of Capitalism* (Free Press 1985); Oliver Williamson, *Markets and Hierarchies: Analysis and Implications for Antitrust* (Free Press 1975).

13 Walter W Powell, 'Neither Market, nor Hierarchy: Network Forms of Organizations' (1990) 12 Research in Organizational Behaviour 295.

European integration. Following an oft-cited definition offered by Börzel, a policy network is conceived as:

> a set of relatively stable relationships of a non-hierarchical and interdependent nature which link a variety of actors, who share common interests with regard to a policy and who exchange resources to pursue these shared interests acknowledging that co-operation is the best way to achieve common goals.[14]

Within this broad definition, Börzel distinguishes between two main schools, analysing policy networks either as a form of interest intermediation or as a form of governance. The latter school conceives of networks as a governance form in which, unlike agencies, there is no principal or independent administrative and financial capacities.[15]

From a somewhat different perspective, scholars in international relations have focused on transgovernmental networks as a new form of global governance, different from both classical international organizations and from 'governance without government'. Transgovernmental networks are in this research strand conceived as networks of governmental officials, judges, regulators or parliamentarians that are "engaged in a common enterprise even as they represent distinct national interests."[16] Such networks are seen to result from the disaggregation of the state into functional sub-spheres and the pressing need of finding solutions to collective problems on the global stage. The concept is rather broad and extends to various forms of transnational cooperation, ranging from transnational committees of central bankers to informal ties between law enforcement agencies and legalized transnational administrative networks.[17]

While the policy networks literature tends to see networks as informal organizations, characterized by voluntary membership and flexible decision-making, it is widely acknowledged that in the EU governance landscape, networks are increasingly being institutionalized.[18] Thus, networks are set up as formal organizations on the basis of binding legal acts, with their legal personality, rules on membership and procedures. Eberlein and Newman speak of 'incorporated networks'.[19] This is evidenced by the existing regulatory networks,

14 See Tanja Börzel, 'Organizing Babylon – on the Different Conceptions of Policy Networks' (1998) 76 Public Administration 253–54.

15 Börzel (n 14).

16 Slaughter, 'The Real New World Order' (n 6) 195.

17 Slaughter, *A New World Order* (n 6) 184.

18 Levi-Faur (n 4) 813.

19 Burkard Eberlein and Abraham Newman, 'Escaping the International Governance Dilemma? Incorporated Transgovernmental Networks in the EU' (2008) 21 Governance 25; Phedon Nicolaïdes, 'The Political Economy of Multi-Tiered Regulation in Europe' (2004) 42(3) Journal of Common Market Studies 599.

connecting national regulators in the sphere of public utilities,[20] as well as by the enforcement networks in the focus of this contribution.

The interest in networks as a form of governance among legal scholars has been slow to emerge, probably due to the informal, sometimes 'soft law' nature of the instruments that steer network activity. However, in parallel with the growing formalization and institutionalization of governance networks, the attention to the phenomenon among lawyers has increased as well. First, a number of legal studies on subject-specific networks have analysed such networks from the perspective of the corresponding legal discipline, providing fine-grained account of the legal frameworks within which the networks operate. Here one can mention contributions on networks in the sphere of consumer, competition, telecommunication and data protection law and policy.[21]

A second strand of legal scholarship devoted to networks includes contributions of a more general theoretical character. The perspective is either a legal constitutional one, where the interest is in the distribution of competences between EU and national institutions, or an administrative law one, whereby the focus is on networks as part of the evolving European administrative space.[22] Scholars in the latter strand of research have criticized the very concept of 'network' as misleading since it, in their view, implies the absence of hierarchy, whereas the existing forms of EU and transnational administrative cooperation are all to a different degree formal, hierarchical and non-voluntary. Alternative concepts have been advanced, such as 'composite administration', 'shared administration' or 'European administrative space', as arguably corresponding better to the complex underworld of European administrative cooperation.[23]

The debate probably reveals the different starting premises and end goals of the disciplines of political science and law. Despite avowed commitment to interdisciplinarity, legal scholars still show preference for concepts that

20 See David Coen and Mark Thatcher, 'Network Governance and Multi-Level Delegation: European Networks of Regulatory Agencies' (2008) 28(1) Journal of Public Policy 49.

21 See, in particular, the monograph of Maartje de Visser, *Network-Based Governance in EC Law* (Hart Publishing 2009) on networks in competition law and telecommunications; cf. Imelda Maher, 'Regulation and Modes of Governance in EC Competition Law: What's New in Enforcement?' (2008) 31 Fordham International Law Journal 1713; for consumer law Cristina Poncibò, 'Networks to Enforce European Law: The Case of the Consumer Protection Cooperation Network' (2012) (35) Journal of Consumer Policy 175; for data protection Francesca Bignami, 'Trans-Governmental Networks vs Democracy: The Case of the European Information Privacy Network' (2005) 26 Michigan Journal of International Law 807.

22 For EU constitutional law see, for instance, Carl Fredrik Bergström, *Comitology* (OUP 2004); for EU administrative law perspective see Paul Craig, 'Shared Administration and Networks: Global and EU Perspectives' in G Anthony and others (eds), *Values in Global Administrative Law* (Hart Publishing 2011); Armin von Bogdandy and Philipp Dann, 'International Composite Administration: Conceptualizing Multi-Level and Network Aspects in the Exercise of International Public Authority' (2008) 9(11) German Law Journal 2013.

23 von Bogdandy and Dann (n 22) 2034.

"connect to normative bases and impart normative meaning".[24] While this preference is understandable, it can be argued that the concept 'network' with its versatility captures a broader variety of governance arrangements building on interconnected entities, beyond public administration. Importantly, the concept 'network' is by now well established in the legislative and regulatory vocabulary of the European Union.[25]

2.2 *A basic typology of governance networks in the EU*

The previous discussion lays bare the conceptual ambiguity surrounding the study of governance networks which arguably, at least partly, is related to the many shapes and guises that network-like organizations can take. Scholarly disagreement is thus often rooted in the fact that different strands of research focus on different 'species' of the more general 'genus' of governance network. To avoid misunderstandings, therefore, and to help navigate the complex landscape of network governance, drawing a very basic map over the most important categories of governance networks in the EU appears in order. Attempts at offering such taxonomy have been undertaken before, by scholars from different theoretical perspectives.[26]

Among the various criteria for distinguishing different categories of networks, the formal or informal character of a network seems most consequential. As pointed out, the policy network literature tends to focus on informal networks that connect both private and public actors within a discrete policy field or a regulatory regime. Such networks are characterized by a spontaneous, largely voluntary and organic process of creation. They are non-hierarchical and operate according to informal codes of practice. In contrast, formal networks are to a great degree institutionalized and legalized or incorporated.[27] They are founded by legislative fiat, through implementing acts of the Council or the Commission, have their official name, and formally defined functions and competences.

The other distinction of overarching character is the one between homogeneous and heterogeneous networks.[28] The notion of 'network' seems to presuppose similarity of the connected units. However, in the literature on policy networks, the difference between participating entities and actors in terms of their functions, private or public character and resources is identified as one main reason for mutual interdependence and an essential condition for the very emergence of networks. Therefore, heterogeneity of participating entities is seen as a distinctive feature of most policy networks. At the same time,

24 von Bogdandy and Dann (n 22) 2034.

25 Moreover, the concepts 'network' and 'composite, or shared administration' should not necessarily be seen as mutually exclusive Craig (n 22) 95 ff.

26 Börzel (n 14); Levi-Faur (n 4); Craig (n 22); Slaughter, *A New World Order* (n 6).

27 Ph Nicolaïdes (n 19); Eberlein and Newman (n 19).

28 See Börzel (n 14) 258.

scholars highlight the existence of homogeneous networks in which actors have similar interests and resources, for instance professional networks and so-called epistemic communities.[29] As regards transgovernmental networks, some degree of heterogeneity is always to be expected since the component units are embedded in different national institutional environments. Yet, many institutionalized transnational networks proceed from an assumption of certain equivalence and similarity of interconnected entities. Homogeneity is thus if not a defining characteristic, at least an ideal.

Further distinction between governance networks can be drawn depending on the private or public character of the networks and their constitutive units. In most cases, the private/public distinction is clear-cut. Establishing the public character of administrative agencies or courts, and respective networks, is hardly problematic; neither is the private character of networks of private standardization bodies.[30] However, the qualification may be more challenging in situations where private networks are endowed with public functions, or where networks connect individuals (for instance, judges) in their professional capacity, but not necessarily as representatives of their respective institutions.[31] Another ambiguous case constitutes hybrid networks that are conceived primarily as public in character, but that due to differences in institutional choice and design at the national level, have to include private entities as well, out of respect for institutional diversity.[32]

Within the category of public networks, further distinction can be drawn between networks linking entities at different levels of government (broadly speaking). The most extensively studied are the so-called administrative networks, connecting government officials or administrative agencies with corresponding peers across national boundaries.[33] More recently, however, scholarly interest has been directed at the emergence of networks in other spheres of governance, such as judicial networks, networks of parliamentary ombudsmen or even parliamentary networks.[34] In the judicial sphere, for instance, the EU has promoted the creation of a web of networks – connecting Supreme Courts, Judicial Councils and individual judges – which assume an ever-growing role

29 See Börzel (n 14) 258 with reference to Peter Haas, 'Introduction: Epistemic Communities and International Policy Coordination' (1992) 46 International Organization 1.

30 Fabrizio Cafaggi, 'Product Safety, Private Standard Setting and Information Networks' (2008) EUI Working Papers Law No 2008/17.

31 See, for instance, the Association of European Competition Law Judges <https://www.aeclj.com/about>.

32 See later, the example of the CPC Network.

33 Slaughter, *A New World Order* (n 6); Craig (n 22).

34 On judicial networks see Daniela Piana, *Judicial Accountabilities in New Europe: From Rule of Law to Quality of Justice* (Ashgate 2010); on networks of parliamentary ombudsmen see Carol Harlow and Richard Rawlings, 'Promoting Accountability in Multi-Level Networks' (2007) 13(4) European Law Journal 542.

in formulating common standards and best practices regarding judicial independence, effective administration of justice and judicial accountability.[35]

Furthermore, networks differ in their institutional design, i.e., the structure of the network and the relationship between its constitutive units. Structurally, the horizontal and vertical dimensions of a network are decisive, whereby the existence and the possible role of a network orchestrator or a principal are also of interest.[36] Networks have been originally perceived as a governance form characterized by the absence of a principal; hence revealing typically horizontal, flat and non-hierarchical structure. This is probably still an adequate description of informal networks. However, in the context of the increasing formalization and institutionalization of EU governance, networks are more often than not built upon the initiative of, or in close contact with, EU institutions, notably the Commission, and increasingly with 'networked' European agencies. Therefore, as highlighted by Craig, the particular role of the Commission, of the Court or other EU institutions and bodies, is of significance when analysing the institutional design and the dynamic in the network.[37]

Finally, a decisive criterion for grouping networks into different categories is the function of the network. Among the most typical functions assigned to networks are information, policymaking, policy implementation, regulation and/or enforcement. More recently, Harlow and Rawlings identified yet another distinct function for certain categories of networks, namely accountability networks. Examples of networks exercising such accountability function are some networks of judicial and ombudsmen bodies that have the task of strengthening the accountability of networks of regulators or of enforcers.[38]

In view of the considerable variation of governance network outlined (non-exhaustively) earlier, identifying carefully the type of network that is studied is essential for the sake of analytical precision. In this contribution, the focus is on enforcement networks as an institutionalized form of governance. At the same time, the analysis is cognizant of the broader uses of the concept in the literature on policy networks. Insights from this literature inform and inspire the investigation.

3. The rise of transgovernmental networks: globally and in the EU

The rise of regional and global networks that connect policymakers, governmental officials and regulatory bodies across national borders has early on been identified in social sciences.

35 On the role of these networks see Piana (n 34); Monika Claes and Maartje de Visser, 'Are You Networked Yet? On Dialogues in European Judicial Networks' (2012) 8(2) Utrecht Law Review 100.

36 On the distinction between horizontal and vertical networks see Slaughter, *A New World Order* (n 6).

37 See, e.g., Craig (n 22).

38 Harlow and Rawlings (n 34).

3.1 *Transgovernmental networks on the global stage*

According to a number of scholars, in the era of globalization that followed after the end of the Cold War, and especially with the advent of the digital society, transgovernmental networks have become an increasingly pervasive form of governance, different from classical intergovernmental cooperation and from looser forms of interaction between corporate and non-state actors on the global stage ('new medievalism').[39] In the influential account of Anne-Marie Slaughter, such networks are nowadays so ubiquitous that they represent a veritable "New World Order".[40] In this new order, expert bureaucrats, active at lower levels of rule-making, rule-implementation and rule-enforcement, build transnational communities that shape the governance of important sectors of economy and society, to a great extent beyond and besides the official channels of state representation in international relations. Slaughter conceives of the New World Order as a product of globalization; but also as a natural consequence of the functional differentiation (or dis-aggregation) of the state.[41] By highlighting the emergence of transnational administrative networks, she challenges the arguably reductionist narrative of globalization as leading to unconstrained hegemony of a neoliberal model of the economy, where free markets reign supreme. Her claim is instead that the state continues to be a crucial actor on the arena of global governance, but engages in novel ways, notably through functionally defined networks.[42]

3.2 *Network governance in the European Union*

For the European Community/Union, bureaucratic networks have been an even earlier occurrence, seen by many to form the very DNA of the European integration project. The phenomenon in its proto form can be traced back to the very conception of European integration. Ernst Haas famously defined integration as "the process of increasing the interaction and the mingling so as to obscure the boundaries between the system of international organizations and the environment provided by their nation-state members".[43] Building on this conceptualization, Lawrence Scheinman already in the 1960s studied different forms of close interaction between civil servants at the national and supranational levels, dubbing this interaction "bureaucratic interpenetration".[44]

39 Slaughter, *A New World Order* (n 6); Cf. Kal Raustiala, 'The Architecture of International Cooperation: Transgovernmental Networks and the Future of International Law' (2002) 43 Virginia Journal of International Law 1.

40 Slaughter, *A New World Order* (n 6).

41 Slaughter, 'The Real New World Order' (n 6) 195.

42 Slaughter, *A New World Order* (n 6) 5–6.

43 Ernst B Haas, *Beyond the Nation-State: Functionalism and International Organization* (Stanford UP 1964) 29.

44 Lawrence Scheinman, 'Some Preliminary Notes on Bureaucratic Relationships in the European Economic Community' (1966) 20 International Organization 750; Ernst B Haas,

This rather loose form of network-like cooperation, was later on followed by the expansive growth of policy networks in the 1980s and 1990s.[45] Scholars in the literature on policy networks have interpreted this expansive development as a response to the decline in the problem-solving capacity of national governments in a globalized world.[46] According to Jachtenfuchs and Kohler-Koch, "the proliferation of networks is a condition as well as a consequence of the growing differentiation of functional subsystems, the political emancipation of large corporate actors able to take strategic actions by themselves, and the increasing complexity of interdependence".[47]

Whereas the policy networks described earlier are typically informal networks, evolving in a non-hierarchical and spontaneous manner, in the EU, networks are increasingly being institutionalized and formalized.[48] A first wave of formalization is associated with comitology. As is well known, comitology is a summary term that refers to the widespread Council practice of setting up committees of Member State representatives to be closely involved in the implementation of Community/Union policies alongside the Commission. Such committees were not envisaged in the Treaties and emerged as a spontaneous institutional practice, but were gradually formalized through a series of Council decisions and other instruments, not least in response to the mounting critique of violating foundational constitutional principles, notably the principle of institutional balance.[49] Comitology committees have kinship with transgovernmental networks. However, they were, in their classical form, prompted by Member States' reluctance of leaving the implementation process entirely to the Commission, and thus by a sense of distrust, rather than by perception of trust and shared benefits from cooperation that are typically distinctive of networks.[50]

A much-observed move towards formalized and institutionalized networks was made with the setting up of a considerable number of so-called regulatory networks in the 1980s and 1990s. These were networks of national regulatory authorities in the area of public utilities, such as telecommunications, electricity, postal services and the like. They emerged as a result of the massive liberalization process in those regulatory domains at the time.[51] In the EU context,

'International Integration: The European and the Universal Process' (1961) 15(3) International Organization 366.

45 Mayntz (n 11); Beate Kohler-Koch, 'Catching Up with Change: The Transformation of Governance in the European Union (1996) 3(3) Journal of European Public Policy 359; Levi-Faur (n 4).

46 Kohler-Koch (n 45).

47 Jachtenfuchs and Kohler-Koch (n 10) with reference to Mayntz (n 11) 43.

48 Levi-Faur (n 4) 813.

49 Ellen Vos, 'The Rise of Committees' (1997) 3(3) European Law Journal 210; See Bergström (n 22).

50 See Bergström (n 22).

51 Coen and Thatcher (n 20); Renaud Dehousse, 'Delegation of Powers in the European Union: The Need for a Multi-Principals Model' [2008] West European Politic 789.

regulatory networks have been conceptualized as involving a multi-level delegation – first a delegation of economic regulatory functions from national governments to independent regulatory agencies and from Member States to the EU (the Commission), followed by double delegation to European Regulatory Networks.[52]

3.3 *The turn to enforcement and the rise of enforcement networks*

Still, the early 1990s marked a transformation of EU governance of qualitatively different proportions, with a conscious shift to network governance and importantly, advancing networks as a form of governance for the decentralized enforcement of EU law. Two main developments seem to have been crucial for this turn.

The first relates to the decisive steps taken by the Union in the beginning of the 1990s towards completing the Single Market, including crucially the dismantling of border controls. This implied greater reliance on the principle of mutual recognition and on the supervisory and enforcement authorities of the Member States. Consequently, the focus shifted from policymaking and law-making to enforcement of agreed laws and policies. As is well-known, decentralized enforcement in the EU has been based on the principle of national procedural and institutional autonomy. Although this principle has been progressively constrained by the doctrines of equivalence and effectiveness elaborated by the CJEU,[53] Member States have in principle been considered free to follow their own institutional choices and preferences; something that typically resulted in widely divergent institutional and procedural frameworks. Hence, ensuring coherent EU law enforcement at the national level and building mutual trust between largely diverse national authorities emerged as a paramount task for the Union. The cooperative approach to enforcement advanced in the Sutherland Report was put forward as an attractive way to meet exactly this challenge. The approach was indeed embraced by the Commission and by the Council.[54]

The second seminal development was the Eastward Enlargement of the Union, which was launched with the conclusions of the Copenhagen Council in 1993 and unfolded in the time span between 1993 and 2013. Whereas the Union had undergone several previous enlargements, the Eastward Enlargement was of such proportions that it posed unique structural and constitutional challenges for the Union. With the accession of 10 new Member States,

52 Coen and Thatcher (n 20); Levi-Faur (n 4).

53 See Michal Bobek, 'Why There Is No Principle of "Procedural Autonomy" of the Member States' in Bruno de Witte and Hand-W Micklitz (eds), *The European Court of Justice and the Autonomy of The Member States* (Intersentia 2011).

54 See Commission communication to the Council of 22 December 1993 "Making the Most of the Internal Market": Strategic Programme, (COM(93) 632 final); Council Resolution of 16 June 1994 on the Development of Administrative Cooperation in the Implementation and Enforcement of Community Legislation in the Internal Market, OJ C 179, 1 July 1994, 1.

the Union nearly doubled its size in terms of number of states, territory and population. More importantly, at the end of the process, it came to encompass economies and polities, which in their historical paths and institutional legacies differ considerably from the previous Member States.[55] This dramatically increases diversity of socio-economic, legal and institutional legacies and brings clearly a risk for diminished coherence and effectiveness of decentralized enforcement.[56]

Against this backdrop, the importance of the enforcement networks that are in the focus of this chapter looms large.[57] In the EU Single Market, enforcement networks are apparently employed as a mode of governance to alleviate what can be described as the risk of 'system entropy' associated with exponentially increased diversity in the decentralized enforcement of EU legislation.

3.4 *Normative expectations directed at enforcement networks*

The network occupies an intermediate position between the national sphere where implementation and enforcement of EU law takes place, and the supranational sphere in which EU institutions, the Commission, the EU authorities and the European Court of Justice act. Hence, the expectation is that by providing an infrastructure for exchanging information, best practices and cooperation on concrete enforcement files, enforcement networks will increase the effectiveness and coherence of the enforcement of Internal Market law.[58] On a more fundamental level, enforcement networks are anticipated to generate mutual trust between peer national enforcement agencies. The repeated and close cross-border contacts between officials from different national enforcement bodies are supposed to lead to enhanced knowledge and better understanding of the institutional traditions and frameworks of other Member States. Enforcement networks are thus seen as conduits for the much needed "binding trust", in the words of Kalypso Nicolaïdis, that should replace "blind trust" in the mutual recognition approach of Internal Market policies and generally in the process of European integration.[59]

55 Frank Schimmelfennig and Uli Sedelmeier, 'Governance by Conditionality: EU Rule Transfer to the Candidate Countries of Central and Eastern Europe' [2004] Journal of European Public Policy 661.

56 Fritz Scharpf, 'The Double Asymmetry of European Integration. Or: Why the EU Cannot Be a Social Market Economy' (2009) MPIfG Working Paper 09/12.

57 Miroslava Scholten, Michiel Luchtman and Elmar Schmidt, 'The Proliferation of EU Enforcement Authorities: A New Development in Law Enforcement in the EU' in Miroslava Scholten and Michiel Luchtman (eds), *Law Enforcement by EU Authorities: Implications for Political and Judicial Accountability* (Edward Elgar 2017); Miroslava Scholten, 'Mind the Trend! Enforcement of EU Law Has Been Moving to "Brussels"' (2017) 24(9) Journal of European Public Policy 1348.

58 Fritz Scharpf, 'Notes Toward a Theory of Multilevel Governing in Europe' (2000) MPIfG Discussion Paper 00/5, November 2000.

59 Kalypso Nicolaïdis, 'Trusting the Poles? Constructing Europe Through Mutual Recognition' (2007) 14(5) Journal of European Public Policy 682.

From an EU constitutional perspective, scholars studying network-like forms of governance have claimed their advantage in terms of democratic legitimacy of global and European policymaking. Examining comitology, Joerges and Neyer have conceptualized comitology committees as a way of preserving the influence of democratically elected Member State governments over the implementation process of EU law and policy, especially in areas of high social and political sensitivity, such as health and safety, agricultural policy and social policy. In a similar vein, Slaughter has argued that transnational networks provide a channel for democratic control over international and regional law and policymaking. Contrary to critics who are concerned about the democratic legitimacy and accountability of bureaucratic networks, Slaughter sees transgovernmentalism as a way for citizens to hold their governments to account not only for their domestic, but also for their transnational activities.[60]

Another, related benefit of network governance is its potential to engage a broader variety of actors in decision-making, especially in the European multi-level context. Grounded in Habermas's theory of deliberative democracy, Joerges has defended comitology also as providing a platform for exchange of views, in which a broader range of actors and Member State institutions are represented and where agreements are reached through participation and deliberation.[61] In a similar vein, Sabel and Zeitlin have praised new modes of governance in the European Union, including governance networks, as a way of 'learning from difference'. According to their theory of experimentalist governance, especially in areas of high scientific uncertainty and dynamic technological development, working with open-ended targets and goals and peer-review processes and benchmarking exercises allows for creative regulatory experimentation. Although diversity is seen by some as an inherent normative value of European integration,[62] from this perspective it is more instrumentally praised as providing a knowledge base for institutional experimentation.[63]

While these – at least potential – advantages of network governance are generally acknowledged, critics point to a number of imminent risks from a legal, constitutional perspective. The first and most fundamental critique that applies more generally to the transfer of decision-making powers to "non-majoritarian"[64] institutions, is the "inbuilt tendency" of such institutions to "reduce the influence of parliaments on the policy process".[65] The

60 Slaughter, 'The Real New World Order' (n 6) 185. For vehement criticism of this view, see Philip Alston, 'The Myopia of the Handmaidens: International Lawyers and Globalization' (1997) 3 European Journal of International Law 435.

61 Joerges (n 8).

62 See Joerges (n 8).

63 Sabel and Zeitlin (n 7).

64 Giandomenico Majone, *Regulating Europe* (Routledge 1996).

65 Jachtenfuchs and Kohler-Koch (n 10) 12.

notoriously informal under-legalized character of governance networks is furthermore seen to pose a threat to fundamental principles of democratic government and good governance, such as transparency and accountability. Thus, despite efforts to constitutionalize the process of comitology, comitology committees are still found to be poorly accessible, with comitology registers and rules on public access to information providing only limited remedy to the already diagnosed opaqueness of committee work.[66]

To meet such critique, proponents of network governance have advanced various normative principles that should guide transnational governance networks. Slaughter has formulated five principles for a "just New World Order", namely equal participation, legitimate difference, positive comity, checks and balances and subsidiarity.[67] Sabel and Zeitlin also emphasize the need for caution when designing institutions for experimentalist governance, in order to avoid the pitfalls of skewed and unbalanced participation.[68]

In light of these partly conflicting normative projections, in the following I will put some of these expectations and misgivings to the test by looking at the main characteristics and the dynamics of two major enforcement networks in the EU Single Market. The analysis will go along four vectors: effectiveness, participation, horizontal empowerment and centralization. Whereas effectiveness is usually considered as a source of 'output legitimacy', participation relates to theories of deliberative supranationalism and experimentalist governance. The analysis of horizontal vs. vertical dynamic seeks in turn to critically analyse potential redistribution of power between institutions and institutional levels, arguably unleashed by network governance.

4. Enforcement through networks in the EU internal market: the European competition network and the consumer protection cooperation network

The two enforcement networks that are analysed in this chapter are the European Competition Network (ECN) and the Consumer Protection Cooperation Network (CPC Network). These are probably the most prominent enforcement networks in the EU Internal (or Single) Market, having broad, horizontal, non-sectoral scope of operation. The networks were launched within the span of only two years: the ECN in 2003 and the CPC Network in 2004. They were established upon the initiative of the Commission, through formal EU legal acts; in the first case Council Regulation 1/2003[69] giving effect to the Treaty rules on competition, and in the second case Council and

66 Gijs Jan Brandsma, Deirdre Curtin and Albert Mejer, 'How Transparent Are EU "Comitology" Committees' (2008) 14(6) European Law Journal 819.

67 See Chapter 6 'A Just World Order'; Slaughter, *A New World Order* (n 6) 216–60.

68 Sabel and Zeitlin (n 7).

69 Council Regulation (EC) No 1/2003 of 16 December 2002 on the implementation of the rules on competition laid down in Articles 81 and 82 of the Treaty [2003] OJ L 1/1.

Parliament Regulation 2006/2004 on consumer protection cooperation,[70] later on replaced by Regulation 2017/2934/EU.[71] Thus, it is a question of formal, institutionalized or 'incorporated' networks.

4.1 Policy domain and legal basis

The two networks are tasked to coordinate the enforcement of EU law in two policy domains of fundamental importance for the EU Internal Market, namely competition policy and consumer protection policy. These domains have many intersections and are in a number of Member State jurisdictions treated as setting the framework of the social market economy and forming part of a broader area of market, or economic law.[72] There are, however, also significant differences between the two policy areas and the underlying EU competences.

1 EU competition policy as part of the European Economic Constitution

Competition policy constitutes since the beginnings of the European Communities, a foundational policy for European economic integration, widely regarded as one of the two main pillars of the Internal Market, the other one being the Treaty provisions on free movement. The main EU competition law rules are set out in primary law, the TFEU, and are thus of highest ranking in the normative hierarchy of EU law. This is one reason why many see competition law and policy as being not only of economic, but also of constitutional importance, forming part of the European Economic Constitution.[73] Importantly, competition policy in the EU Internal Market is one of only a few areas where the Union enjoys exclusive competence.[74] It has been called "the first supranational policy in the European Union".[75]

Whereas competition law sets out the normative foundations for an economically significant and complex policy area, requiring in-depth expertise, it is famously based on only a few Treaty articles, essentially Articles 101

70 Regulation (EC) No 2006/2004 on cooperation between national authorities responsible for the enforcement of consumer protection laws [2004] OJ L 364/1 (hereinafter the CPC Regulation).

71 Regulation (EU) 2017/2394 on cooperation between national authorities responsible for the enforcement of consumer protection laws and repealing Regulation (EC) No 2006/2004 [2017] OJ L 345/1; applying as of 17 January 2020 (hereinafter the New CPC Regulation).

72 See Ulf Bernitz, 'Market Law as a Legal Discipline' [1979] Scandinavian Studies in Law 55.

73 See David Gerber, *Law and Competition in Twentieth-Century Europe* (Clarendon Press 2001).

74 See Article 3(1) TFEU.

75 Lee McGowan and Stephen Wilks, 'The First Supranational Policy in the European Union: Competition Policy' (1995) 28 European Journal of Political Research 141.

and 102 TFEU, as well as the EU Merger Regulation.[76] This gives competition policy a clear focus and sharp delineation from other policy areas. Another distinctive feature is the horizontal character of the policy, with its legal rules and principles applying across all sectors of the economy.

What is particularly remarkable and relevant for the purposes of this chapter is that the Treaties accord the Commission substantial own direct supervisory and enforcement powers viz. individual undertakings, with the main principles originally laid down in Article 87 EEC Treaty and fleshed out through Council Regulation 17/62.[77] As is well-known, the Commission has through the years made intensive use of these powers and built a solid record of vigorous enforcement of EU competition law, sanctioning infringements and imposing fines of significant proportions.[78] The interpretation of the relevant legal rules has been the subject of an impressive volume of case law from the Court of Justice of the European Union (CJEU) and a considerable number of secondary law and soft law instruments, foremost Commission notices and guidelines. Moreover, the body of case law and the underlying legal and economic theory, have been at the centre of a vibrant scholarly debate in the disciplines of law and of economics. Institutionally, competition policy has from the very start of the European project, had its dedicated Directorate General (DG) Competition, which commands substantial resources and power.[79]

2 EU consumer policy: a policy with uncertain contours

In contrast, consumer protection policy was a relative latecomer to the European integration project. This is of course not surprising. The need for sustained public consumer protection policy caught the attention of policymakers first in the early 1960s, when the euphoria of post-war affluence had started to give way to growing awareness of the power imbalance in the relations between business and consumers. Since the original Treaties envisaged no competences for the Communities in the sphere of consumer protection, such competence had to be gradually carved out starting from the 1970s. The need for "strengthening and coordination measures of consumer protection" was first mentioned in the conclusions of the Paris Summit of Heads of State or

76 Council Regulation (EC) No 139/2004 of 20 January 2004 on the control of concentrations between undertakings [2004] OJ L 24/1.

77 See originally Articles 87 and 89 EEC Treaty (nowadays Articles 103 and 105 TFEU); EEC Council Regulation 17/62 implementing Articles 85 and 86 EEC Treaty [1962] OJ 13/204, replaced by Council Regulation (EC) No 1/2003 of 16 December 2002 on the implementation of the rules on competition laid down in Articles 81 and 82 of the Treaty [2003] OJ L1/1 (Regulation 1/2003).

78 Brenda Sufrin, Niamh Dunne and Alison Jones, *Jones & Sufrin's EU Competition Law* (8th edn, OUP 2023).

79 According to Wilks, the ECN is "very squarely centered on DG Comp", Stephen Wilks, 'Agencies, Networks, Discourses and the Trajectory of European Competition Enforcement' (2007) 3 European Competition Journal 437, 440.

Government of 19–21 October 1972. Later on, the Maastricht Treaty recognized consumer protection as a Union policy in its own right (Title XI EC Treaty, now Title XV TFEU). Article 129a EC Treaty set out the scope and instruments of consumer protection.[80] An upgraded version of this provision is now found in Article 169 TFEU, whereas Article 12 TFEU defines consumer protection as a horizontal EU policy.

Still, whereas the status of consumer policy has been systematically enhanced, it remains a competence shared by the Union and its Member States. Moreover, the role of the Union when exercising this shared competence is formulated in relatively weak terms as being to "*contribute* to protecting the health, safety and economic interests of consumers". Consequently, even today, the majority of legislative acts in the field of consumer protection are based on the internal market competence of the Union (Article 114 TFEU) and not on consumer protection as a self-standing competence.[81]

Another major difference with competition policy is the substantive scope of EU consumer law and policy. While enforcement of EU competition law concerns a clearly delineated substantive policy, the Union consumer protection *acquis* includes dozens of secondary legislative instruments extending to a wide variety of ever-expanding substantive policy issues only loosely connected by the concern for the consumer interest. As a consequence, the enforcement cooperation envisaged by the CPC-Regulation extends to over 29 pieces of legislation.[82] Most of the relevant legislative acts are directives based on a minimum or full harmonization approach. In addition, some instruments of mostly sectoral regulation take the form of directly applicable regulations. Furthermore, whereas some of these EU legislative acts, such as the Unfair Commercial Practices and the Unfair Contract Terms Directives, apply horizontally across all branches of the economy, others have sectoral character, for instance air passengers' rights, pharmaceuticals, foodstuffs or financial services. Related to this, is the character of the legal rules, which are classified differently in different national legal systems. The genealogy of consumer protection policy, especially in continental jurisdictions, has deep roots in civil law, foremost contract and tort law, which has influenced the systematic positioning of consumer law in university curricula and the self-identification of scholarly and professional communities. A public dimension of consumer policy has taken shape slowly and at varying pace in different EU Member States.[83]

80 On this development, see Thierry Bourgoignie, 'Consumer Law and the European Community: Issues and Prospects' in T Bourgoignie, D Trubek and L Trubek (eds), *Consumer Law and Federalism* (De Gruyter 1987).

81 See Article 4(2)(f) TFEU; cf. Jules Stuyck, 'European Consumer Law After the Treaty of Amsterdam: Consumer Policy in or Beyond the Internal Market?' (2000) 37 Common Market Law Review 367.

82 This is almost double the initial number of 15. For an updated list see Regulation 2017/2394, Annex.

83 See Daniela Caruso, 'The Missing View of the Cathedral: The Private Law Paradigm of European Integration' (1997) 3(1) European Law Journal 3.

Crucially, the Treaties do not assign the Commission any express own enforcement powers in the field of EU consumer law. Consequently, apart from some minimalist steps of encouraging cross-border injunctions,[84] EU consumer protection policy has followed the usual pattern of relying on the procedural laws, institutions and capacities of the Member States for the enforcement of EU law. This model of decentralized enforcement has been based, as outlined earlier, on the principle of national procedural and institutional autonomy and has resulted in widely divergent institutional and procedural frameworks of consumer law enforcement.[85]

Finally, in contrast to competition policy, the institutional positioning of consumer policy has been unstable, with the policy migrating between different directorates. Whereas initially, there was a separate Directorate General for Health and Consumers (DG SANCO), later on, consumer policy had its home with DG Justice and nowadays the responsibilities are divided between DG Justice and DG Internal Market. Indicative of this uncertain place of consumer policy is the fate of the executive agency that was tasked to ensure administrative support to the Union consumer policy programmes. For many years this was the Consumers, Health, Agriculture and Food Executive Agency (CHAFEA), which has undergone consecutive reshuffling and expansion of its mandate.[86] In 2021, following a new wave of rationalizations, the functions of CHAFEA were transferred to an even bigger agency – European Innovation Council and Small and Medium-sized Enterprises Executive Agency (EISMEA). Whereas previously consumer protection policy had its own dedicated programme, since 2021 it is part of a new composite Single Market programme with broad and rather disparate scope.[87]

In sum, this crisscrossing between different directorates and frequent reshaping of portfolios is hardly contributing to institutional continuity or raising the profile of this policy area.

84 See Directive 98/27/EC; nowadays replaced by Directive (EU) 2020/1828 on representative actions for the protection of the collective interests of consumers [2020] OJ L 409/1.

85 See BEUC (The European Consumer Organsiation), 'Strengthening the Coordinated Enforcement of Consumer Protection Rules: The Revision of the Consumer Protection Coordination (CPC) Regulation' (2022) <https://www.beuc.eu/sites/default/files/publications/BEUC-X-2022-135_Strengthening_the_coordinated_enforcement_of_consumer_protection_rules.pdf> accessed 2 November 2024.

86 A report on CHAFEA found that the frequent reshufflings impacted its governance structure negatively, generating problems of delineation between the policymaking responsibilities of the Commission and the administrative tasks of the Agency. See PPMI, CSES and Maastricht University, 'Study Supporting the Evaluation of the Operation of the Consumers, Health, Agriculture and Food Executive Agency (2014–2016)' September 2018, 14, 76–77.

87 Regulation (EU) 2021/690 of the European Parliament and of the Council establishing a programme for the internal market, competitiveness of enterprises, including small and medium-sized enterprises, the area of plants, animals, food and feed, and European statistics (Single Market Programme) [2021] OJ L 153/1. In this conglomerate programme, EU consumer policy with its many goals is described in one sub-paragraph, Article 3 (2)(d) and is granted EUR 198,500,000, including both economic interests of consumers as well as health and safety.

4.2 History of the networks

The proximity in the time of inception of the ECN and the CPC Network might suggest certain coordination and common thinking in the process of designing the two networks. However, there is no evidence to support such an assumption. In fact, when looking closely at the history of the networks, the differences seem more numerous than the similarities.

1 The ECN: a story of voluntary devolution of enforcement power

The ECN came about as part of a major reform endeavour, the so-called modernization package, aiming at increasing the effectiveness of EU competition law enforcement. The thrust of the reform was to carry through a transition from a model of almost full concentration of enforcement powers with the Commission to a new era of decentralized and coordinated enforcement, involving national competition authorities (NCAs). This transition was launched by Council Regulation 1/2003, the Modernisation Regulation. The reform was remarkable since it was carried out in the area where the Treaties, exceptionally, accord the Commission substantial own supervisory and enforcement powers, including powers of directly sanctioning individual undertakings. Yet, in a seemingly counterintuitive turn, with Regulation 1/2003 national competition authorities and national courts were empowered, and nowadays have the obligation, to actively apply the competition rules of the Treaty, in parallel to the Commission.[88]

To be sure, some form of cooperation between national NCAs and the Commission has always been part of EU competition law enforcement. Already the first Council Regulation 17/62 envisaged maintaining contacts with the authorities of the Member States and mandated the setting up of an Advisory Committee on Restrictive Practices and Monopolies (ACRPM) composed by national officials with corresponding competences.[89] The Commission was under the Regulation obliged to inform the ACRPM of any investigations and procedures it undertakes. Still, initiated analysts of the early phase of Community competition policy observe that there has been reluctance and even resistance to such cooperation on the part of the Commission.[90] Consequently, even in the mid-1990s, when, following the recommendations in

88 On the contrast with administrative and regulatory networks, which are arguably a result of Member States' efforts to avoid centralization of powers with an EU agency or the Commission, see Dehousse, 'Regulation by Networks' (n 4).

89 Article 10 Regulation 17/62 was expressly devoted to "Liaison with the authorities of the Member States".

90 This is explained by the fact that at the time, most Member States lacked active competition institutions and failed to recognize the importance of competition law policy. Conversely, Germany had strong views on the importance of a vigorous competition policy and was building up a powerful Federal Cartel Office (Bundeskartellamt, BKA). Hence, it was eager to impose its own visions of competition law and policy on the Community level, something largely resisted by the Commission, see Scheinman (n 44) at 755 and fn 10 and 15.

the Sutherland Report, the Commission published its first progress report on administrative cooperation, competition law was not treated as a priority area but under a heading "other areas".[91]

Yet by the mid-1990s the situation had changed dramatically and the almost exclusive position of the Commission in the enforcement of EU competition law had become untenable. On the one hand, the level of workload for the Commission, especially under a system of individual exemptions from the prohibition of Article 101 TFEU, managed exclusively by the Commission, were close to prohibitive.[92] Handling notifications was taking disproportionately large part of the Commission's time and resources, preventing it from developing a proactive competition law enforcement policy. Moreover, there was an acute awareness that the number of files would grow exponentially following the expected accession of 10 new Member States as a result of the Eastward Enlargement of the Union.

On the other hand, throughout the years, considerable expertise had accumulated in the Member States, partly by following closely developments of EU competition law and partly by voluntary adaptation of national competition law and practice to the EU competition law model.[93] Pursuant to seminal judgements by the CJEU, national competition authorities were recognized as enforcers of EU competition law and the Commission sought mechanisms to coordinate enforcement activities at the national and Union levels.[94] Moreover, during the 1990s, in the course of preparation of the Candidate Countries from CEE for accession to the Union, the Commission became closely entangled in the massive institution-building process in these states, which included setting up and shaping national institutions for the regulation of the market economy.[95] Whereas each country followed its individual path, the EU competition law model exerted strong attractive power, amplified by the leverage the Commission could use through the conditionality approach.[96]

91 See Report from the Commission to the Council and the European Parliament, Cooperation between administrations for enforcement of internal market law - a progress report, Brussels, 29. 01. 1996, COM(96) 20 final, 48–49.

92 On the notification regime, see Alan Riley, 'EC Antitrust Modernisation: The Commission Does Very Nicely – Thank You! Part 1: Regulation 1 and the Notification Burden' (2003) 24(11) European Competition Law Review 604.

93 Frans van Waarden and Michaela Drahos, 'Courts and (Epistemic) Communities in the Convergence of Competition Policies' (2002) 9(6) Journal of European Public Policy 913.

94 Commission Notice on cooperation between national competition authorities and the Commission in handling cases falling within the scope of Articles 85 or 86 of the EC Treaty [1997] OJ C 313/3.

95 Sven Norberg, 'Making a Virtue Out of Necessity and at the Same Time Strengthening European Competition Law Enforcement' (2007) 4 Europarättslig tidskrift 803; Hussein Kassim and Kathryn Wright, 'The European Competition Network: A European Regulatory Network with a Difference' (2010) Paper delivered at the 32nd EGPA Annual Conference, Toulouse, France, 8–10 September 2010.

96 See Antonina Bakardjieva Engelbrekt, 'Grey Zones, Legitimacy Deficits and Boomerang Effects: On the Implications of Extending the Acquis to Central and Eastern Europe' in Nils Wahl and Per Cramér (eds), *Swedish Yearbook of European Law* (Hart Publishing 2006) vol 1.

Under these circumstances, a process of rethinking of EU competition law enforcement was launched by DG Competition, setting up a so-called modernization group tasked with weighing different solutions and charting a sustainable way forward. As a result of this process, a novel decentralized model was launched through a so-called modernization package adopted by the Council and Commission in 2002.[97] The fundament of the reform, Regulation 1/2003, explicitly declares that it introduces "a system of parallel powers" (Recital 22), which is designed "to meet the challenges of an integrated market and a future enlargement of the Community" (Recital 1). The Regulation provided the basis for the setting up of the European Competition Network (ECN) tasked with nothing less than creating "a common competition culture in Europe". The 'nuts and bolts' of network cooperation were set out in soft law instruments, i.e., two Commission Notices and a Joint Statement by the Council and the Commission, giving additional weight to the ECN.[98]

In sum, the transition to decentralized enforcement was nothing imposed from the outside, but rather the result of a deliberative process within the Commission and a slow maturing of the view of a need for joint responsibility for the effective enforcement of EU competition rules. Given the powerful position the Commission enjoyed prior to the reform, and the relatively low level of bureaucratic interpenetration in the area of competition policy, it is understandable why experts called the reform a veritable "legal and cultural revolution".[99] The new mechanism is a remarkable example of a single and powerful supranational actor – the Commission, deciding itself to share its near-monopoly enforcement powers with national agencies.[100]

2 The CPC Network: a story of burst-entering the domain of enforcement

Like the Modernisation Regulation, Regulation 2006/2004/EU was largely the result of a Commission initiative. It was adopted on the basis of the internal market competence of the Union set out in Article 114 TFEU. In its preamble, the Regulation declared squarely that "[t]he protection of consumers

97 See Kassim and Wright (n 95) with reference to Norberg (n 95). Abolishing the requirement of notifications and individual exemptions on the basis of Article 81(3) EC Treaty was an important component of the reform.

98 See Commission Notice on cooperation within the Network of Competition Authorities, OJ C 101, 27 April 2004, 43–53; Commission Notice on the cooperation between the Commission and the courts of the EU Member States in the application of Articles 81 and 82 EC [2004] OJ C 101/54; Joint Statement of the Council and the Commission on the Functioning of the Network of Competition Authorities, Interinstitutional File 2000/0243(CNS) Brussels, 10 December 2002 (hereinafter Joint Statement). On the conscious choice by the Commission of a soft law instrument see Firat Cengiz, 'Multi-Level Governance in Competition Policy: The European Competition Network' (2010) 35(5) European Law Review 660, 663; cf. Wilks, 'Agencies, Networks, Discourses' (n 79) 442.

99 Claus-Dieter Ehlermann, 'The Modernization of EC Antitrust Policy: A Legal and Cultural Revolution' (2000) 37 Common Market Law Review 537–90.

100 Kassim and Wright (n 95) 10.

from intra-Community infringements *requires* the establishment of a network of public enforcement authorities throughout the Community" (my italics).[101] However, despite its categorical tenor, in fact the Regulation constituted a significant novelty in the regulatory landscape of consumer policy at the time. As mentioned earlier, the starting premise in consumer law and policy differed significantly from that of competition law and policy, assigning no central enforcement powers to the Commission whatsoever. Thus, the Regulation catapulted EU institutions into a domain previously considered to lie within the sphere of Member States' procedural and institutional autonomy.

More importantly, the idea of a network of public authorities presupposes quite logically the existence of such authorities in the Member States. However, at the time of inception of the CPC Network, public enforcement was not the preferred approach for consumer law enforcement in all Member States. In fact, many Member States lacked specialized public consumer protection authorities. Thus, while in the Nordic countries, already in the 1970s public bodies such as the Swedish Consumer Agency and the Consumer Ombudsman were set up with the task of implementing and enforcing relevant consumer protection legislation, in countries such as Germany, the Netherlands, Luxembourg and Austria, enforcement of legislation protecting consumer economic interests was entrusted primarily to consumer and business associations at the state or local level, relying on legal rules, procedures and remedies of a largely private law character.[102] In Germany, there has even been vocal opposition against creating new authorities and extending the reach of state bureaucracy in this policy area. Consequently, unlike the ECN, in the case of the CPC Network, it was not "simply" a question of connecting already existing public authorities with clearly defined enforcement powers, but of actually inviting, and even exerting pressure on, some Member States to introduce public enforcement of consumer law against long-standing national traditions in the field.

This challenge was acknowledged by the Commission, which was well aware of the existing divergences and the tenacity of national enforcement approaches. In its proposal for Regulation, the Commission pointed out that "each Member State ha(d) developed an enforcement system adapted to its own laws and institutions".[103] However, in a rather unusual manner, the Commission made a strong plaidoyer for a public dimension of consumer law enforcement and drew up a list of the advantages of public authorities as effective enforcers of consumer laws when compared to private consumer organizations. Public authorities were considered among others to have: "sufficient investigation powers; sufficient guarantee of confidentiality and professional

101 Recital 6, Regulation 2006/2004.

102 Commission Proposal for a Regulation of the European Parliament and of the Council on cooperation between national authorities responsible for the enforcement of consumer protection laws, COM(2003) 443 final, Explanatory memorandum, paras 30–31.

103 Commission Proposal for a Regulation, COM(2003) 443 final, Explanatory memorandum, para 12–13.

secrecy; proven efficiency and effectiveness of a public dimension to enforcement . . .; impartiality and accountability".[104]

This passionate defence of public enforcement can be seen as a rather bold break with the previously well-guarded principle of institutional and procedural autonomy.[105] To understand this development, it is once again helpful to look at the process of Eastward Enlargement of the Union, which influenced the choice between public and private enforcement of consumer protection laws in some indirect and intricate ways. Consumer policy had at the beginning of the 1990s just acquired the status of an EU policy area of its own right, which meant that in the negotiations with the Candidate Countries it was allocated a separate chapter (at the time, chapter 23) of the Community *acquis*. Since the Copenhagen accession criteria put special emphasis on ensuring the institutional conditions for effective application and enforcement of the *acquis*, in the course of Enlargement, the Commission had to outline an institutional dimension of EU consumer policy and translate it into detailed requirements viz. the Candidate Countries. In this process, the Commission acted vigorously to promote the setting up of public consumer protection authorities in the Candidate states. Given the strong leverage that the Commission could use through the instrument of accession conditionality, at the end of the accession process nearly all new Member States from CEE had their consumer protection authorities with tasks varying from market supervision to imposing sanctions and consumer advocacy.[106] Against this backdrop, Regulation 2006/2004 can be seen as a logical step in the same direction.

4.3 Constitutive units of the networks

A network is largely defined by the character of the interconnected units, or nods. One central dimension is the private or public character of the units and their place in the national system of government. Another is to what extent the prerogatives of the entities are clearly defined and focused on a distinct public policy area.

1 ECN: a network of strong public authorities with clear mandate

As to the first aspect, it is evident that the entities participating in the ECN are all public authorities. As stipulated by Regulation 1/2003, the ECN consists

104 See Commission Proposal for a Regulation, COM(2003) 443 final, Explanatory memorandum, para 34. For analysis of this shift see Bakardjieva Engelbrekt, 'Grey Zones' (n 96) 32–33.

105 Commission Proposal for a Regulation, COM(2003) 443 final, Explanatory memorandum, para 32.

106 See Antonina Bakardjieva Engelbrekt, 'The Impact of EU Enlargement on Private Law Governance in Central and Eastern Europe: The Case of Consumer Protection' in F Cafaggi and H Muir-Watt (eds), *The Making of European Private Law: Governance Design* (Edward Elgar 2008); Schimmelfennig and Sedelmeier (n 55).

of the Commission, as well as the competent authorities in the EU Member State. Following Chapter IV ("Cooperation"), Member States have an obligation to designate an authority responsible for the application of Articles 101 and 102.[107] Thus there are 27 NCAs connected through the Network. Despite inevitable differences in institutional set up, in most Member States competition authorities are powerful agencies, enjoying considerable degree of independence from the government.[108]

Concerning the allocation of powers between courts and public authorities, the prevailing number of Member States follow a so-called administrative model. The competence of deciding on termination of an infringement and imposing sanctions is assigned to an administrative agency, the decision being then subject to judicial review.[109] A limited number of Member States follow a so-called judicial model, whereby prohibition decisions or decisions imposing a fine can only be taken by a court, with the competition authority acting as a prosecutor before the Court.[110] Given these differences, the Regulation grants Member States explicitly the freedom to decide which of the authorities engaged in competition law enforcement – administrative or judicial – would form part of the network (Article 35(2) Regulation 1/2003). Eventually, however, all NCAs designated by the Member States are administrative authorities.

In terms of portfolio, all NCAs have enforcement of competition law (national and EU) as their main task. One common dilemma is whether the authority in charge of competition issues will focus exclusively on antitrust or whether it should also have responsibility for other policy areas, such as consumer protection, unfair competition, public procurement, state aid or other. The Commission has traditionally shown pronounced preference for a predominant, if not exclusive, focus of NCAs on competition law enforcement. This has become visible in the course of EU enlargement, when the Commission instructed Candidate Countries from CEE to create strong and focused competition agencies and advised vehemently against extending their portfolios to adjacent areas and thus diluting their competences.[111] This advice was not followed by all Candidate Countries. Moreover, some old Member States

107 See Recital 35, Article 11(1) and Article 35 Regulation 1/2003.

108 See <https://competition-policy.ec.europa.eu/antitrust-and-cartels/european-competition-network/national-competition-authorities_en> accessed 2 November 2024. See Giorgio Monti, 'Independence, Interdependence and Legitimacy: The EU Commission, National Competition Authorities, and the European Competition Network' (2014) EUI Working Papers Law, 2014/01, 10–11.

109 Internally, these agencies either exhibit a unitary structure whereby one body investigates and decides on a case or a dualist structure where the tasks are divided between an investigative body and a decision-making body.

110 See Notice, 2004/C 101/03, para 2.

111 Bakardjieva Engelbrekt, 'Grey Zones' (n 96); Katalin Cseres, 'Governance Design for European Private Law: Lessons from the Europeanisation of Competition Laws in Central and Eastern Europe' in Fabrizio Cafaggi and Horatia Muir-Watt (eds), *The Making of European Private Law: Governance Design* (Edward Elgar 2008) 138–39.

have designed their competition authorities with varied portfolios, either from the start or after consolidation and amalgamation of public authorities as part of austerity measures in the wake of the financial crisis in the 2010s.[112]

Still, irrespective of such institutional reshuffling, the task of enforcing competition law is usually central for the respective agencies, taking substantial part of their resources and defining their institutional identity.[113]

2 CPC Network: a heterogenous network with dispersed mandate

The CPC Network consists of "competent public enforcement authorities in the field of consumer law throughout the Union".[114] The Regulation defines as competent public authority, "any public authority established either at national, regional or local level and designated by a Member State as responsible for enforcing the Union laws that protect consumers' interests".[115] However, given the unclear contours of EU consumer policy and the broad subject matter covered by the Regulation, in combination with the institutional diversity of national enforcement systems, there is rarely one single public authority that is tasked with the enforcement of the whole panoply of relevant Union consumer laws. In some Member States, there exist central consumer protection authorities with broad ambit that covers most relevant legal acts within the scope of the Regulation. However, in the majority of Member States, enforcement tasks are spread over a range of public authorities with either horizontal, cross-cutting, or sectoral competence, located at the central, regional or local level.

This is acutely evident from the lengthy list of competent authorities made available by the Commission on its website.[116] No country has designated one single authority. In most cases, Member States designate a plurality of authorities, ranging between three and several dozens.[117] Under competent authorities for Germany, more than 70 authorities and bodies are announced on the

112 Cf. the Polish Agency for the Protection of Competition and Consumers (Urzad Ohrony Konkurencij e Konsumetow), the Italian Competition Authority (Autorita Garante del mercato e della concorenza). Cf. the example of the Netherlands Authority for Consumers and Markets, combining responsibilities for competition and consumer law with sectoral regulation in telecommunications, postal services, transport, healthcare and energy.

113 On the diversity in institutional designs see Kassim and Wright (n 95); cf. Maher, 'Regulation and Modes of Governance in EC Competition Law' (n 21).

114 Regulation 2017/2394, Recital 4.

115 See Article 3(6) Regulation 2017/2394. Thus, if a public authority has competences to apply strictly national laws, it would not be part of the CPC Network.

116 The various lists can be found on <https://commission.europa.eu/live-work-travel-eu/consumer-rights-and-complaints/enforcement-consumer-protection/consumer-protection-cooperation-network_en#documents> accessed 12 May 2024.

117 For instance, for the Netherlands, the competent authorities mentioned in the list are the Markets and Consumers Authority, but also: the Food and Consumer Product Authority; the Healthcare Inspectorate; the Authority for the Financial Markets; the Inspectorate for Environment and Transport and the Netherlands European Consumer Center.

list; the situation is similar for Spain obviously reflecting the federal character of the two countries. One report estimates the total number of competent authorities designated by all Member States under the Regulation at 300+.[118]

The way for coping with the overwhelming multitude and disparity of national bodies engaged in the system of enforcement cooperation is to oblige Member States to designate one public authority as a single liaison office (SLO) responsible for the application of the CPC-Regulation.[119] Thus, there are strictly 27 liaison offices in the Union, one per Member State, which constitute the crucial 'nodes', or the backbone of the CPC Network. Still, depending on the specific subject matter of individual files or of questions to be discussed in the Network, different public authorities may need to step in according to their competence and expertise.

The system with SLOs aims at ensuring some degree of equivalence and homogeneity in the CPC Network. However, when one looks at the list of SLOs, it becomes immediately evident that there are still substantial differences in the character of the entities expected to form the backbone of the CPC Network, both in terms of competences and institutional design. Out of the 27 SLOs, 11 are ministries, 9 are consumer authorities and the rest are Trade Inspections or agencies of mixed character. These authorities have different institutional position vis-à-vis their respective national government, ranging from considerable independence to forming part of the government. Apparently, within the system of public administration of many Member States, consumer protection is seen more as a policing activity, falling squarely within the scope of executive powers.[120] In those Member States where special consumer protection authorities exist, the way these authorities are structured, in terms of portfolios and functions is likewise widely divergent. This diversity is arguably so wide-ranging that the implications for the effectiveness of the Network are far-reaching; a point to which I shall return in the following.

The more fundamental problem for the coherence of the network has of course been the absence of a public authority in the area of consumer protection in certain Member States. This problem posed challenges and generated adaptation pressure at both the national and supranational level. As a result of the pressure, countries such as Austria and Luxembourg indeed introduced a public dimension in their consumer protection enforcement system.[121] Nevertheless, there remained countries, importantly Germany, that continued to

118 Ex-post evaluation of the Consumer Programme 2007–13 and mid-term evaluation of the Consumer Programme 2014–20 – Final report. Part 1 Mid-term evaluation of the Consumer Programme 2014–20, 2018 <https://op.europa.eu/en/publication-detail/-/publication/5e9ee253-22b0-11e9-8d04-01aa75ed71a1/language-en> accessed 2 November 2024.

119 See Article 4(1) Regulation 2006/2004; cf. Article 5(1) Regulation 2017/2394.

120 See Hans-W Micklitz and Fabrizio Cafaggi (eds), *New Frontiers of Consumer Protection* (Intersentia 2009).

121 See Studio Grimaldi, 'Study on Enforcement Authorities' Powers in the Application of Regulation 2006/2004/EC on Consumer Protection Cooperation. Final Report' (2016) September 2016, 10.

insist on preserving their preferred enforcement model relying predominantly on private consumer organiszations. The delicate question that emerged was how the Union should address this institutional aberration. Regulation 2006/2004 solved the dilemma by carving out a special 'German' exception. The national authorities acting as SLOs were allowed to delegate the duties of taking actual enforcement measures to so called designated bodies, which could be not only public but also private bodies, such as consumer and business associations. Thus, Member States lacking a public consumer protection agency were not required to establish one solely for the purposes of the Regulation. Fabrizio Cafaggi calls this hybridization of public and private law in transnational regulatory regimes.[122]

Summing up, in terms of constitutive units, while there is some degree of diversity in both networks, it is clear that the ECN stands out as a rather homogeneous network, whereas the CPC Network displays such heterogeneity that its capacity to act in a coherent manner appears problematic. A reasonable assumption is that to manage the diversity, the CPC Network would seek to develop compensation mechanisms of different sorts which is one important reason to look into the dynamic of network cooperation.

4.4 Institutional design of the networks

Both networks have as their main task to ensure effective and coherent enforcement of EU law and policy in their respective domain. They are expected to provide a framework for enforcement coordination through exchange of information, best practices and assistance in individual infringement cases. However, since the starting premises in the two domains are fundamentally different, the institutional design of each network reflects and accommodates these differences.

1 ECN: a centralized managed network

Despite the move to decentralized enforcement, the Commission still occupies a central place in the ECN. The Commission and the NCAs apply the same set of directly applicable rules of EU competition law, following the same jurisdictional criterion, namely infringements with effect on trade in the Internal Market of the Union. The Commission retains its role of enforcer of EU competition law, which means that the regime of enforcement cooperation builds on genuinely parallel powers. The institutional design of the ECN is therefore mostly concerned with ensuring a smoothly functioning mechanism for allocation of cases between the Commission and the NCA. The main

122 Fabrizio Cafaggi, 'New Foundations of Transnational Private Regulation' (2010) EUI Working Paper Series, RSCAS 2010/53, 19.

criteria for allocation are that cases should be handled by the authority best placed to investigate the case and that duplication should be avoided.[123]

The internal structure of the ECN includes four levels of organization: the Directors General meeting, the ECN plenary, horizontal working groups and sectoral sub-groups. Although there are no formally defined relations of hierarchy and subordination, still the structure resembles a pyramid.[124] Working groups are described as being "created organically" and working informally by consensus.[125] On the side of the ECN, and seemingly not being a formal part of the Network, the Advisory committee (ACMRP) continues its existence (Article 14 Regulation 1/2003) and is described as "essentially a consultative body". Since competition policy is an exclusive competence of the Union, there is no delegation of powers to the Commission. Hence, the ACMRP is not subject to the constraints and obligations which are valid for comitology committees.[126]

In sum, the ECN follows a model that has been dubbed "a centralised managed network". Commentators note that the Commission has retained powers that are not shared with the NCAs and is exercising a sort of monitoring over the latter.[127]

2 CPC Network: a decentralized network with hierarchical elements

In contrast to the field of competition law, the Commission has no direct enforcement powers of its own in the field of EU consumer law and is therefore not a full-fledged and equal member of the CPC Network. The CPC-Regulation establishes in essence a decentralized system of enforcement cooperation, in which the Commission is assigned coordinating and organizational tasks.

The EU consumer protection laws within the scope of the Regulation are foremost directives that are transposed into national law, and where Member States authorities have typically exercised discretion as to the forms and methods of implementation. Hence, the legal framework for consumer

123 Commission Notice on cooperation within the Network of Competition Authorities, OJ C 101, 27 April 2004, 43–53.

124 The structure is described in detail in the Commission Staff Working Paper accompanying the Report on the functioning of Regulation 1/2003 SEC(2009) 574 final, 29 April 2009, 73 (hereinafter Commission SWD Regulation 1/2003, 2009); cf. Kassim and Wright (n 95) 14.

125 Kassim and Wright (n 95) 14.

126 As Wilks puts it, "There is no need for the frustrations of comitology and the Council is effectively excluded from this policy area except when pressed for new regulations in areas like mergers, state aid and utility liberalisation." Wilks, 'Agencies, Networks, Discourses' (n 79) 439.

127 Cengiz (n 98) 661, 665. Cf. Stephen Wilks, 'Agency Escape: Decentralisation or Dominance of the European Commission in the Modernization of Competition Policy?' (2005) 18 Governance 431, 440.

law across Europe is not fully unified.[128] Instead, enforcement cooperation occurs through requests for mutual assistance and enforcement measures in cross-border infringement cases, whereby the requested national authority takes action based on its own substantive law. The Regulation envisages three main forms of exchange between participating national authorities: information requests (Article 6), information without request ('alerts') (Article 7) and enforcement requests (Article 8). Accordingly, the institutional design of enforcement cooperation is directed at setting the modalities for these mutual assistance requests. In addition, some possibilities for joint and coordinated actions are provided for.

The CPC Network is structured around a Committee (the CPC Committee), which is a 'comitology committee' typically set out to allow control by the Member States over the Commission's exercise of implementing powers.[129] The work in the Network is supervised by DG Justice and more specifically by the Enforcement and redress unit of its Consumer Directorate. Although the formal role of the Commission in the system is supposed to be limited, a closer look at the operation of the CPC Network shows that the Commission has a more central position than apparent at first sight and its role has arguably expanded with time. Following the general rules for Comitology Committees, and Article 3 Regulation (EU) No 182/2011 in particular, the CPC Committee's meetings are chaired by the Commission. The CPC Committee may set up working groups to examine particular issues. Like the Committee itself, also the working groups have to be chaired by a representative of the Commission and are under obligation to report back to the Committee.[130]

Summing up, despite the proclaimed ambition of decentralization and horizontal cooperation, both the ECN and the CPC Network display hierarchical elements with distinct place for the Commission. Still, the Commission appears to have much stronger capacity and authority to act as network manager and full-fledged enforcer in the domain of competition law than in consumer law enforcement.

5. Exploring network dynamics: enhancing effectiveness and participation?

Obviously, the setting up of the two enforcement networks in the beginning of the 2000s stirred up high expectations in their respective policy areas, but also triggered critical scholarly debate as to the potential gains or losses from the turn to network governance, in particular in the area of enforcement. With the networks having been in operation for more than twenty years now, there

128 See BEUC (n 85).

129 See Article 19 Regulation 2006/2004 with reference to Council Decision 1999/468/EC of 28 June 1999 [1999] OJ L 184/23; now Article 38 Regulation 2017/2394 with reference to Regulation (EU) No 182/2011.

130 Rules of procedure, CPC Committee, Article 6, Ref. Ares(2020)5494787, 14 October 2020.

is substantial empirical material as well as scholarly and institutional evaluations, that should allow an analysis of the performance of the networks. In this section I will trace the dynamics within the networks along the dimensions of effectiveness and participation. After all, these were the main expectations associated with enforcement network. Have the networks brought about the desired increase in effectiveness and coherence of enforcement? Have they allowed equal engagement and participation, and consequently have they contributed to mutual learning and enhanced mutual trust?[131]

5.1 *Effectiveness and participation in the ECN*

Some years after launching the modernization reform, the Commission published the first Report on the functioning of Regulation 1/2003, which was overwhelmingly positive about the cooperation within the Network and generally, the effects of the reform. According to the report, by the end of March 2009, more than 1000 cases have been pursued on the basis of the EC competition rules and more than 300 envisaged decisions announced by NCAs.[132] In the accompanying document to the Report, the Commission described Regulation 1/2003 as a "landmark change in the way the European competition law is enforced" and praised the ECN as "an innovative model of governance for the implementation of Community law by the Commission and Member State authorities".[133] In the next Report of 2014 on the occasion of the 10th anniversary of the modernization reform, the assessment remained unwaveringly positive.[134] The Commission boasted with "a considerable enforcement record, with more than 780 enforcement decisions applying the EU competition rules, underpinned by policy and horizontal work to enhance cooperation".[135] Between 1 May 2004 and 31 December 2012 NCAs had reported 1334 investigations and 646 envisaged decisions, while in that period the Commission reported 228 investigations and 88 decisions.[136]

131 See Slaughter, *A New World Order* (n 6).

132 Communication from the Commission, Report on the functioning of Regulation 1/2003 COM(2009) 206 final, 29 April 2009 (hereinafter Commission Report Regulation 1/2003, 2009); Commission SWD Regulation 1/2003, 2009 (n 124) 83.

133 Commission SWD Regulation 1/2003, 2009 (n 124) 89; Cengiz (n 98) 668.

134 Commission Communication, 'Ten Years of Antitrust Enforcement under Regulation 1/2003: Achievements and Future Perspectives' COM (2014) 453 Brussels, 9 July 2014 (hereinafter Commission Communication Regulation 1/2004, 2014); European Commission, Enhancing Competition Enforcement by the Member States Competition Authorities. Institutional and Procedural Issues, SWD (2014) 231, Brussels 9 July 2014, accompanying the Commission Communication 2014 (hereinafter Commission SWD Regulation 1/2003, 2014).

135 Commission SWD Regulation 1/2003, 2014 (n 134) para 4.

136 Wouter PJ Wils, 'Ten Years of Reg 1/2003' (2013) 4 Journal of European Competition Law & Practice 295. See, however, Monti (n 107) 15, on the possible discrepancy between envisaged and final decisions.

The positive assessment seems to be sustained more recently by a preliminary analysis of the responses to the latest consultation launched by the Commission in 2022 on evaluating Regulation 1/2003.[137]

Concerning participation and engagement of NCAs and the functioning of enforcement cooperation more generally, the Commission reports describe a harmonious relationship between NCAs, a smoothly functioning mechanism of case allocation and lack of conflicts between network members. The Commission underlines the permanent exchange of views, taking place within the Network, often in an informal manner, that "has established confidence and trust between network members, increased the expertise and promoted convergence". The ECN is presented as an achievement "widely recognised by the legal and business community". Despite non-insignificant divergencies in the institutional design and enforcement approach of NCAs, the Commission asserts that a common competition culture has indeed emerged through the network, something that has explicitly been the objective when launching the ECN.[138]

These Commission assessments are broadly confirmed by academic studies. According to a 2010 study by Cengiz, the statistical data on the enforcement activity of NCAs provide evidence of high and relatively equivalent engagement of national authorities in the application of EU competition law irrespective of agency size or jurisdiction.[139] Furthermore, empirical studies building on questionnaires and semi-structured interviews with representatives of NCAs in the ECN, document an almost uniform high appreciation for the work of the network, which is interpreted as a "testimony to shared ownership and the vision of the ECN as a joint enterprise".[140]

Still, when looking at the horizontal dynamic within the ECN, the empirical surveys of Vantagiatto et al. disclose a more complex picture, suggesting that participation in the activity of the Network is far from even. In particular, analysis of informal contacts between officials of NCAs has indicated different levels of engagement of different NCAs. The study finds that certain NCAs play a more active role in the Network than others, in terms of authorities actually instituting enforcement proceedings, but also authorities that are being sought by their peers for expert advice and experience-sharing. The authorities most often consulted appeared to be those with the highest level of resources and experience, which often coincides with number of cases handled. Most intense

137 Factual summary of the contributions received during the public consultation on the evaluation of Regulations 1/2003 and 773/2004, Ref Ares(2022)8359727 - 2 December 2022.

138 Commission Report Regulation 1/2003, 2009 (n 132) para 249, p. 74.

139 Cengiz (n 98) 668.

140 See Kassim and Wright (n 95) 14. The positive evaluation is confirmed by the more recent study of Francesca Vantaggiato, Hussein Kassim and Kathryn Wright, 'Internal Network Structures as Opportunity Structures: Control and Effectiveness in the European Competition Network' (2021) 28(4) Journal of European Public Policy 571, 583. To the question what could be improved in the Network, many respondents are reported to have replied "more of it". Vantaggiato, Kassim and Wright (n 140) 584.

outgoing contacts from NCAs were typically from agencies with an intermediate level of resources and experience, which is interpreted in the sense that the network is used as compensation for insufficient own resources.[141] Furthermore, recent analyses discern a trend of closer regional cooperation between NCAs based on geographic proximity.[142] This may signal a positive horizontal dynamic but also an emerging variable geometry of network cooperation.

One concern from the inception of the ECN has been the position of the NCAs from the new Member States from CEE. These states were admittedly lacking robust experience in market economy and competition law and policy and one objective with creating the Network was, in fact, to serve as a platform for socializing and learning for the public officials from these states.[143] At the same time, the authorities in these states were expected to be less active in the ECN, something that could arguably create a varied-speed cooperation. The initial study by Kassim and Wright did not seem to confirm these misgivings. The Network was highly appreciated by officials from both old and new Member States, by experienced agencies and competition law novices alike.[144]

However, subsequent studies focusing specifically on the CEE countries and their participation in the ECN reveal a less optimistic picture, suggesting that with few exceptions, the authorities in these Member States are passive and essentially on the receiving end of policy recommendations and guidance as to enforcement activity.[145] A different nuance is added by an insightful analysis into the ways NCAs from some CEECs are interpreting and applying the criterion of "effect on trade", which is the decisive trigger for applying EU competition law.[146] The study shows that in the New Member States from CEE, there is a practice of overly narrow interpretation of this requirement with the result of many cases being treated as national and therefore not EU law–relevant infringements. According to the authors, NCAs from the studied new Member States tended to "systematically avoid the application of EU competition rules, and thus avoid the scrutiny of the Commission and other NCAs within the ECN".[147]

141 Vantaggiato, Kassim and Wright (n 140) 584.

142 Maher and Hosseini report of such regional agreements between e.g. the Nordic countries. Imelda Maher and Mina Hosseini, 'Cooperation Between National Competition Authorities: An Overview of EU and National Case Law' [18 January 2024] e-Competitions.

143 See Cengiz (n 98) 664.

144 Kassim and Wright (n 95) 14 with reference to replies to question 29 of their survey.

145 Katalin Cseres, 'Competition Law Enforcement Beyond the Nation State: A Model for Transnational Enforcement Mechanisms?' in Hans-W Micklitz and Andrea Wechsler (eds), *The Transformation of Enforcement: European Economic Law in a Global Perspective* (Hart Publishing 2016) 338.

146 See Article 3 Regulation 1/2003.

147 Marco Botta, Alexandr Svetlicinii and Maciej Bernatt, 'The Assessment of the Effect on Trade by the National Competition Authorities of the "New" Member States: Another Legal Partition of the Internal Market?" (2015) 52(5) Common Market Law Review 1247, 1249, 1252.

In sum, the ECN has established itself as a highly appreciated enforcement network, improving the effectiveness of competition law enforcement and creating a sense of engagement of NCAs. The Network has been less successful in achieving equality of participation and there is certain evidence of a varied geometry of cooperation, whereby NCAs with less experience and resources are either marginalized, or alternatively deliberately stay 'under the radar' of EU competition law.

5.2 *Effectiveness and participation in the CPC Network*

When turning to the CPC Network, the picture that emerges is dramatically different. Under the CPC Regulation, the Commission was obliged to produce biennial reports based on periodic reporting by the Member States along specific indicators, including the number of mutual assistance requests issued, number of requests received and number of uses of the IT tool, developed to facilitate information exchange. A first Commission report published in 2009[148] acknowledged the contribution of the CPC Network for raising the level of enforcement of EU consumer protection law throughout the Union, but also noted a series of shortcomings. In particular, two years after the entry into effect of the Regulation, significant numbers of the notified national competent authorities were either not connected or not actively using the system, thus not issuing requests for mutual assistance. Not all authorities had gained access to the IT tool, and among those having access, one-third were still not actively using the tool.[149] Correspondingly, the number of mutual assistance requests was relatively low – a total of 317 in 2007 and 384 in 2008. The same, or largely similar, problems were identified in the second biennial report, showing that many authorities "rarely or never" used the CPC cooperation mechanisms. What is more, "some of the most active players of the first years had reduced their engagement".[150] The third (and last) biennial report showed results not much different than the preceding two reports with continued modest number of exchanges.[151] A similarly bleak picture of underdeveloped and poorly used mechanisms of mutual assistance was revealed in

148 See Report from the Commission to the European Parliament and to the Council on the application of Regulation (EC) No 2006/2004, COM(2009) 336 final, Brussels, 2 July 2009 (hereinafter: First Commission Report CPC Regulation).

149 First Commission Report CPC Regulation (n 148).

150 Report from the Commission to the European Parliament and to the Council on the application of Regulation (EC) 2006/2004, COM(2012) 100 final, Brussels, 12 March 2012 (hereinafter: Second Commission Report CPC Regulation) 12, 9.

151 Report from the Commission to the European Parliament and to the Council on the application of Regulation (EC) 2006/2004, COM(2014) 439 final, Brussels, 1 July 2014 (hereinafter: Third Commission Report CPC Regulation).

an external report in 2012,[152] broadly confirmed by a consumer programme evaluation in 2018.[153]

The other important indicator for the effectiveness of enforcement cooperation within the CPC Network is the timely handling of information and enforcement requests. The initially set time limit of 14 days[154] proved problematic, and the First Report concluded that mutual assistance requests were taking "longer and longer to be closed" with information requests being closed in an average of between 81 and 148 days in 2008.[155] Subsequent Operational Guidelines set more realistic benchmarks of three months for handling information requests and 9–12 months for enforcement measures requests.[156] Yet, even these exceedingly generous targets proved too ambitious and were not met.[157]

Apart from being a clear sign of deficient effectiveness of enforcement cooperation, low numbers of exchanges are certainly strong evidence of lacking engagement of national authorities in the activity of the Network. Furthermore, the biennial reports showed that informal contacts between case handlers were rather the exception than the rule.[158] Importantly, in contrast to the ECN, the competent authorities participating in the CPC Network, show lukewarm appreciation of the activities of the Network and the effects of the CPC-cooperation for increasing the effectiveness of enforcement.[159]

In terms of equality of participation, the first two biennial reports on the CPC Regulation provided tables with distribution of mutual assistance requests across Member States, showing a widely skewed pattern of engagement and use of the system. Although a formal analysis of intensity of use has not been performed, it is evident that among the countries least engaged in

152 (External) evaluation of the Consumer Protection Cooperation Regulation, Final Report submitted by the Consumer Policy Evaluation Consortium (CPEC), 17 December 2012 (hereinafter External Evaluation Report CPC Regulation).

153 European Commission, Ex-Post Evaluation of the Consumer Programme 2007–2013 and Mid-Term Evaluation of the Consumer Programme 2014–2020 – Final Report, Part 2 – Ex-post Evaluation of the Consumer Programme 2007–2013, 2018 <https://op.europa.eu/en/publication-detail/-/publication/3aefdcef-22af-11e9-8d04-01aa75ed71a1> accessed 2 November 2024.

154 Commission Decision 2007/76/EC implementing Regulation (EC) No 2006/2004 [2007] L 32/192; Cf. Commission Decision 2011/141/EU amending Commission Decision 2007/76/EC [2011] L 59/63.

155 First Commission Report CPC Regulation (n 148) 7.

156 Impact Assessment accompanying the document Proposal for a Regulation of the European Parliament and of the Council on cooperation between national authorities responsible for the enforcement of consumer protection laws, Brussels, SWD (2016) 164 final (hereinafter: Impact Assessment New CPC Regulation) 15.

157 See European Commission, Ex-Post Evaluation, Final Report, Part 2 (n 153) 56. The Results Are Similar for the Period 2014–2017, Final Report, Part 1 (n 118) 76.

158 Second Commission Report CPC Regulation (n 150) 10.

159 See a rate of 3.4 on a scale of 5 for the CPC Network, European Commission Ex-Post Evaluation Part 2 (n 118).

network cooperation are the countries with more limited resources or experience in consumer protection policy, or where the latter is not accorded political priority. Member States from CEE are systematically underrepresented in these statistics.[160]

A similar uneven pattern of participation transpires from the rate of attendance of network meetings, showing that certain Member States are systematically absent from CPC Committee meetings.[161] The impression is confirmed by the statistics from another form of participation in Network cooperation, namely exchanges of officials under the so-called Karolus programme. Here as well, participation is highly unbalanced, with a relatively low rate of participation of countries that were expected to be the prime beneficiaries of the programme, notably Member States from CEE.[162] Conversely, information in the periodic reports on coordinated enforcement action shows that a few authorities – those in the Netherlands, Italy, Sweden and UK (before Brexit) – have recurrently been in the lead of such initiatives.

In sum, the CPC Network has not fully delivered on the promise of increasing the effectiveness of EU consumer law enforcement. Moreover, it appears far from showing the same rate of engagement and approval as the ECN. In respect of the important horizontal dimension of the network, a picture emerges of uneven participation and engagement.

5.3 *Explaining the different outcomes*

Different explanations for the differential results from network cooperation through the ECN and the CPC Network have been advanced in evaluation reports and in the scholarly literature. Some see the strength of the ECN to derive foremost from the Commission's decision to share its monopoly over enforcement within a regime in which the Directorate-General for Competition (DG Comp) has been historically central.[163] The Commission's

160 See First and Second Commission Reports CPC Regulation (n 148, n 150). Starting from the Third Report such statistics is regrettably no longer presented, cf. Third Commission Report CPC Regulation (n 151).

161 This can be ascertained from a sample of attendance records from the CPC Committee meetings during the years 2009–2019. Such records are publicly accessible through the comitology register. The records are rather imperfect, since following the COVID-19 pandemic meetings take place chiefly online. But between 2009 and 2019 meetings took place in person in Brussels. A review of the summary records for this period shows that, for example, Greece was hardly ever present at meetings. Other countries such as Cyprus, Croatia, Lithuania and Romania, were often absent, or represented by their Permanent Representation, arguably indicating lower engagement with the Committee work.

162 Records on such exchanges are available in the reports of the executive agency CHAFEA, that used to provide funding for such exchanges. The rate of participation of CEE authorities as beneficiaries is higher in exchanges on the General Product Safety Directive compared to the CPC.

163 Kassim and Wright (n 95) 8.

retained power is in this view projected onto the NCAs, strengthening their self-confidence and appreciation for the Network.

The Commission itself sees the key to the "major success" of the ECN to lie in the possibility for network members to share knowledge and experiences in a confidential manner. This has, in the view of the Commission "triggered a very open and constructive dialogue with the national competition authorities which fosters the coherent application of Articles 81 and 82 EC".[164] In a similar vein Cengiz speaks of the "emergence of an extensive informal communication culture between the competition officials".[165] Related to this is the closed character of the Network and the limited number of officials that participate in the communication.[166]

On a deeper level, scholars point to the special character of competition law and its quasi-constitutional status in the EU. According to Cseres, competition law has become "deeply rooted in the economic constitutions of its Member States".[167] This arguably translates into greater commitment and a sense of a shared mission. Kassim and Wright also stress that what distinguishes the ECN from ERNs is "the perception of the network as a shared enterprise".[168]

These analyses feed into Peter Haas's theory of epistemic communities, which provides probably the most convincing explanation for the success of the ECN. Haas defines epistemic communities as networks "of professionals with recognized expertise and competence in a particular domain and an authoritative claim to policy-relevant knowledge within that domain or issue-area".[169] According to him, an epistemic community can consist of any kind of experts or professionals, who have (i) a shared set of normative and principled beliefs; (ii) shared causal beliefs; (iii) shared notions of validity and (iv) a common policy enterprise.[170]

Applying this definition to the area of competition policy, the existence of a strong epistemic community in competition law and policy becomes immediately apparent. Indeed, the prominent position of competition law in the EU integration project and the sheer volume of Commission and ECJ decisions in the field have been providing employment and intellectual occupation to a whole array of practitioners, public officials and academics, sharing the values and principles of EU competition law and building a tightly knit professional

164 Commission SWD Regulation 1/2003, 2009 (n 124) para 268; Commission Report Regulation 1/2003, 2009 (n 132) para 29.

165 Cengiz (n 98) 669.

166 See Imelda Maher and Oana Stefan, 'Competition Law in Europe: The Challenge of a Network Constitution' in OD Prosser and T Rawlings (eds), *The Regulatory States: Constitutional Implications* (OUP 2010) 187–88.

167 Cseres (n 145) 338.

168 Kassim and Wright (n 95) 14.

169 Peter Haas, 'Introduction: Epistemic Communities and International Policy Coordination' (1992) 46 International Organization 1, 3.

170 Haas (n 169).

community. This community has been informally existing already before the setting up of the ECN, but the Network provided a welcome platform, exacerbating the intensity of communication and the strong sense of common purpose of this community.[171]

Of course, one can ask whether the studies of Cseres and Botta et al., with a focus on NCAs in the CEE Member States of the Union, challenge these theoretical explanations. In my view, not necessarily. Some difference in outcome is probably due to differences in the design and focus of the individual studies. Thus, the results need not be incompatible. Furthermore, it is fully plausible that CEE members in the ECN are appreciative of their participation in the Network even if they are not playing the first fiddle. For them the ECN provides a way of being part of a powerful and respected professional community and institutional arrangement.[172] This does not necessarily stand in contradiction with their reluctance of having their enforcement activities monitored by the Commission, or by their peers in the Network.[173]

The CPC Network has been far less subject to scholarly scrutiny, but both internal and external reports and evaluations have sought to provide some explanations for the generally disappointing results from the functioning of the CPC Network.[174] Attention was initially directed foremost to practical impediments, such as insufficient resources at the national level and differences in competent authorities' capabilities. The "fairly broad scope of the CPC Regulation's annex" was brought up in several reports, as well as complex and diverging institutional frameworks and long communication lines, causing delays in the handling of requests and ultimately undermining confidence in the CPC Network.[175] The degree of 'fragmentation' with an excessive number of participating authorities was confirmed as a major barrier also in subsequent reports.[176]

More fundamentally, the reports highlighted that the CPC Network has not succeeded in developing a "corporate identity" and of gaining high profile.[177]

171 See van Waarden and Drahos (n 93); cf. Maher and Stefan (n 166) 188; Cengiz (n 98).

172 Based on relational analysis of the horizontal ties between NCAs within the ECN, Vantaggiato, Kassim and Wright suggest that there is "a mechanism of compensation, whereby NCAs use external informal network ties to compensate for lacking resources." Vantaggiato, Kassim and Wright (n 140) 584.

173 See Botta, Svetlicinii and Bernatt's testimony that NCA from CEECs "systematically avoid the application of EU competition rules, and thus avoid the scrutiny of the Commission and other NCAs within the ECN." Botta, Svetlicinii and Bernatt (n 147) 1249.

174 See the biennial reports on the CPC Regulation (n 148, n 150, n 151); cf. BEUC (n 85).

175 Second Commission Report CPC Regulation (n 150) 14. External Evaluation Report CPC Regulation (n 152) 76–77.

176 Civic Consulting, Ex-post evaluation of the Consumer Programme 2007–13 and mid-term evaluation of the Consumer Programme 2014–20 – Final report. Part 1, Mid-term evaluation Consumer Programme 2014–2020, 30 <https://op.europa.eu/en/publication-detail/-/publication/5e9ee253-22b0-11e9-8d04-01aa75ed71a1/language-en> accessed 2 November 2024. For transparency, it should be noted that the author of this chapter has participated as an expert in this evaluation.

177 First Commission Report CPC Regulation (n 148) 8.

The reports thus identify a potentially crucial difference between the two networks. The CPC Network cannot tap into a strong epistemic community in the same way as the ECN. This is prevented by the lower profile of consumer protection as a policy area, the broad and patchy scope of the policy domain with national institutional choices gravitating in different degree to public or private enforcement. The more limited role of the Commission in the enforcement of EU consumer law and in the CPC Network is also a likely explanation for the weaker commitment to cooperation of NCAs, something pointed out in some of the reports.[178]

As indicated, both the ECN and the CPC Network display some variation in the extent of participation and engagement of different national entities in enforcement cooperation. When studying cooperation in enforcement networks, Polak and Versluis distinguish between the categories "leaders" and "laggard" and note the corrosive effect divergent degrees of compliance and engagement can have for mutual trust.[179] The analyses of the networks in this chapter suggest a slightly different classification into three groups of typified roles in enforcement networks, namely: "activists", "followers" and "shirkers". Authorities in Member States with greater experience, resources and track record of effective enforcement, are recognized as leaders and acquire a more authoritative position in the network. They are the ones often entrusted with leading working groups or coordinated actions. These authorities are also the preferred hosts for exchange of officials. The second group, the followers, is made up of authorities that shy away from taking on the leadership role themselves, probably due to limited resources and experience, but are still interested in cooperation. For them the network could be a resource, strengthening their enforcement capacity. The third, and potentially most problematic group, the shirkers, consists of authorities that avoid and try to minimize their participation in the enforcement cooperation.

6. Exploring network dynamics: between horizontal and vertical empowerment

An important question posed at the outset is in what way the two enforcement networks influence the status of the national authorities that engage in enforcement cooperation, on the one hand, and the position of the Commission, on the other. Can we discern a dynamic of empowerment of participating national authorities? Or is there a pull of centralization and shift of power 'upwards' to the Commission?

178 See Third Commission Report CPC Regulation (n 151) 5; cf. BEUC (n 85).

179 Josine Polak and Esther Versluis, 'The Virtues of Interdependence and Informality: An Analysis of the Role of Transnational Networks in the Implementation of EU Directives' in Sara Drake and Melanie Smith (reds), *New Directions in the Effective Enforcement of EU Law and Policy* (Edward Elgar 2016) 117.

6.1 Dynamic of horizontal and vertical empowerment in the ECN

As has become clear from the previous discussion, the ECN represents an unusual example of actual divestment of powers from the Commission to national competition authorities and correspondingly of empowerment of national competition authorities. This was well acknowledged by national competition authorities, which according to Cengiz, "enthusiastically agreed with the enhancement of their enforcement powers under the new regime".[180] Likewise, Kassim and Wright conclude that "the evidence points to a strengthening of competition agencies (and national courts), where NCAs have been empowered, individually and collectively".[181]

Importantly, empowerment does not appear to constitute a one-time act, which is completed with the setting up of the Network. Rather it emerges as a continuous dynamic inherent in the logic and design of the enforcement cooperation mechanism. Its practical realization is enabled by the fact that the ECN quickly assumed a central role in the formulation of new competition policy, part of these policy-setting functions then being directed at strengthening the enforcement powers of the NCAs. Thus, a rather efficient mechanism for enhancement of NCAs' powers gradually takes shape, building on two components: first, gathering evidence about the diversity in enforcement competences, powers and procedures of NCAs, and second, calling for increased convergence of enforcement systems and upgrading of NCAs' powers. In combination, these two components have been used as a successful leverage of the position of NCAs.

This dynamic can be clearly discerned starting already from the First Report on the functioning of Regulation 1/2003, where the Commission draws attention to the divergence of national enforcement systems on aspects such as "fines, criminal sanctions . . . the power to impose structural remedies, as well as the ability of Member States' competition authorities to formally set enforcement priorities".[182] This divergence is singled out as the main reason for the suboptimal level of practical cooperation between NCAs.[183] Following this signal, the ECN quickly set up a designated Working Group on the powers of competition authorities, which in 2012 produced two reports: the Investigative Powers Report and the Decision-making Powers Report,[184] providing

180 Cengiz (n 98) 664, with reference to the summary of observations to the European Commission, White Paper on Reform of Regulation 17, Summary of the Observations, 29 February 2000.

181 Kassim and Wright (n 95) 17.

182 Commission Report Regulation 1/2003, 2009 (n 132) 7.

183 Commission SWD Regulation 1/2003, 2009 (n 124) para 200–7; cf. Cengiz (n 98) 670.

184 ECN Working Group on Cooperation Issues and Due Process, Report on Decision-Making Powers <https://competition-policy.ec.europa.eu/system/files/2021-07/decision_making_powers_report_en.pdf> and Report on Investigative Powers (31 October 2012) <https://competition-policy.ec.europa.eu/document/download/357ac0f6-92fb-41aa-b1ad-a906fcdd832d_en?filename=investigative_powers_report_en.pdfaccessed 2 November 2024.

detailed accounts of the enforcement powers of NCAs. Shortly thereafter, the ECN published a cluster of related Recommendations, covering almost all aspects of divergences identified in the First Commission Report of 2009, including investigative powers, enforcement measures and sanctions; setting priorities; imposing interim measures and imposing structural remedies.[185] The Working Group reports were then used as a basis for the second assessment report of Regulation 1/2003,[186] accompanied by a Commission document entitled "Enhancing competition enforcement by the Member States' competition authorities: Institutional and procedural issues".[187] A Commission proposal for a new legislative instrument harmonizing and enhancing the powers of NCAs was published in 2017.[188]

The final result, the so-called ECN+ Directive, declares its objective to be "to empower the competition authorities of the Member States to be more effective enforcers [of EU competition rules]"[189] and incorporates literally all proposals advanced within the auspices of the ECN (either as Working Group reports or recommendations). It establishes a common minimum of investigative and enforcement powers set at a high level, including powers to issue interim measures, to impose structural remedies, to set the size of the penalty at a sufficiently deterrent level with a common minimum set at 10% of the undertaking's total turnover.

Of particular significance in terms of empowerment is the strongly worded obligation that the ECN+ Directive stipulates viz. the Member States to ensure that NCAs have sufficient resources and qualified staff to perform their tasks effectively. This obligation is backed by a transparency duty, namely an obligation for NCAs to periodically report to a governmental or parliamentary body on their activities, funding and staff changes.[190] Arguably, most importantly, the ECN+ Directive sets out an unambiguous obligation for the Member States to provide fundamental guarantees of independence of competition

185 All recommendations are available on the webpage of the ECN (9 December 2013) <https://competition-policy.ec.europa.eu/antitrust-and-cartels/european-competition-network/documents_en> accessed 2 November 2024.

186 Communication from the Commission, 'Ten Years of Antitrust Enforcement Under Regulation 1/2003: Achievements and Future Perspectives' COM (2014)453 Brussels, 9 July 2014.

187 Commission SWD Regulation 1/2003, 2014 (n 134).

188 European Commission, Proposal for a Directive to Empower the Competition Authorities of the Member States to Be More Effective Enforcers and to Ensure the Proper Functioning of the Internal Market COM (2017) 142 final, 2017/0063 (COD) Brussels, 22 March 2017.

189 Directive (EU) 2019/1 of the European Parliament and of the Council of 11 December 2018 to empower the competition authorities of the Member States to be more effective enforcers and to ensure the proper functioning of the internal market [2019] OJ L 11/3.

190 On the issue of funding see also Resolution of the Meeting of Heads of the European competition authorities of 16 November 2010 'Competition authorities in the European Union – the continued need for effective institutions'.

authorities as one of the essential conditions for ensuring a "truly common competition law enforcement area" (Recitals 5 and 8; Article 4(1)). The concept of independence is defined in dual terms: independence from political influence, as well as from any other external influence, such as influence from market actors. Moreover, Member States are obliged to put in place clear, transparent and fair procedures for selection, recruitment, appointment and dismissal of NCA officials (Article 4(3)(4) Directive 1/2019).[191]

It appears plain that the transition from a centralized to decentralized enforcement has unleashed a dynamic of horizontal empowerment – and one can say self-empowerment – of NCAs. The question is whether such empowerment has been at the expense of loss of powers on the part of the Commission. Already from the inception of the ECN, many saw in this initiative a disguised attempt by the Commission to in fact increase its own powers, an Agency escape of sorts.[192] Initial empirical studies based on interviews with national representatives in the ECN did not confirm this thesis. Nevertheless, interviewees overwhelmingly describe the role of the Commission as still being "in the driver's seat".[193]

Indeed, the powers of the Commission in the network, as coded in the original set up of Regulation 1/2003 continue to be significant. Here only some leading principles will be mentioned briefly. The Commission occupies a central place in the system of case-allocation between competent authorities and is considered an authority "particularly well placed" to handle most cases of economic significance.[194] Importantly, the Commission has the power of taking over a case from an NCA and requiring the NCA to close its investigation or proceedings.[195] Furthermore, the Commission has a privileged position in cases involving "genuine uncertainty", presenting "novel or unresolved questions" or when new types of agreements and practices arise. In such situations, the Commission can either adopt a declaratory decision of non-application or provide informal guidance to individual undertakings.[196] This organization of the division of work within the ECN appears to foster the authority of the Commission.[197] The way information exchange is designed likewise puts the

191 Whereas strengthening the independence of competition authorities from national government has many advantages, its advancement as an unquestionable premise of the institutional set up of competition policy has been discussed. See Monti (n 107).

192 See Wilks, 'Agency Escape' (n 127).

193 Kassim and Wright (n 95).

194 If the allegedly anticompetitive agreement(s) or practice(s) "have effects on competition in more than three Member States". See para 14 Commission Notice on Cooperation.

195 See Article 11(6) Regulation 1/2003; Cengiz calls this provision "one of the central pillars of [the] previous centralised enforcement regime". See Cengiz (n 98) 644.

196 See Recital 14, Regulation 1/2003; Recital 38, Regulation 1/2003. See Vantaggiato, Kassim and Wright (n 140) 583.

197 Vantaggiato, Kassim and Wright (n 140) 583.

Commission in a position of oversight, if not control, over NCAs.[198] To be sure, analyses of the ECN show that the Commission has not used these powers so far, in particular the power under Article 11(6), or only infrequently.[199] Nevertheless, the very existence of Article 11(6) in particular is an unmistakeable marker of a hierarchical structure and the Commission's top position in it.

In terms of internal operation, it is again no question that the Commission and DG Comp are at the centre of ECN activity. DG Competition is the main contact point for the national competition authorities. The Commission sets the agenda for the plenary meetings and a representative of the ECN unit of DG COMP chairs the meetings. To be sure, NCAs are also consulted and involved in shaping the agenda of the Network. A recent empirical study finds that NCAs perceive they have sufficient opportunities to influence the work of the Network.[200] Nevertheless, based on analysis of ECN from the perspective of NCAs from CEE Member States, Cseres finds that the "ECN mechanisms are tilting towards hierarchical governance modes".[201]

A relevant question in this context is how the more recent legislative innovation, namely the ECN+ Directive, has impacted the vertical dynamic within the Network. As shown, the Directive strengthens the powers of NCAs and can therefore be seen as evidence of horizontal empowerment of NCAs rather than a shift of powers vertically to the Commission. Yet, in this respect, the effect is rather one of common, joint self-empowerment for both the Commission and the NCAs. The "power cake" is not redistributed between the Commission and the NCAs, it is increased for all participants in the Network. When the link of NCAs with their governments is weakened, the pull around the Commission can be expected to increase. Therefore, with enhanced independence and resources for NCAs, the Commission can see itself as the centre of a more powerful institutional conglomerate. If there is any loss of power, it would potentially be for national governments (both at the national level and in the Council) as locos for defining competition policy. Seen from the earlier discussion, the dynamic within the ECN seems to work towards empowerment on both the horizontal and vertical plane.[202]

198 See Article 11(3) Regulation 1/2003. On these information exchanges as "monitoring channels" for the Commission see Cengiz (n 98) 667. For a similar point see Poncibó (2010) 181.

199 For possible explanations for this self-restraint see Kassim and Wright (n 95) 15–16.

200 Kassim and Wright (n 95). Vantaggiato, Kassim and Wright claim that the ECN internal structure is open and therefore does not allow domination by the Commission. Vantaggiato, Kassim and Wright (n 140) 572.

201 Cseres (n 145) 338.

202 According to Sauter, "it is clear that the Commission is profiting from the new system, but also that the NCAs are empowered both by modernization and by collaborating in the ECN". See Wolf Sauter, *Coherence in EU Competition Law* (OUP 2016) 169. Cf. Cengiz (n 98) 670.

6.2 *Dynamic of horizontal and vertical empowerment in the CPC Network*

Although the CPC Network has clearly proven far less successful than its competition counterpart, what is remarkable is that it appears to have triggered a broadly similar horizontal dynamics towards empowerment of NCAs. The original CPC Regulation 2006/2004 set out certain minimum powers that national authorities needed to have in order to ensure the effective enforcement of EU consumer law in cases of cross-border infringements, but these were not particularly demanding.

As seen, the first reports on the functioning of the CPC Network saw the main reasons for the suboptimal performance of the Network to lie foremost in practical barriers to cooperation, such as large number of national competent authorities and insufficient resources. However, the attention was soon redirected to legal barriers to cooperation and in particular to the diversity in national enforcement systems and in national authorities' enforcement powers. In subsequent reports, diversity surfaced as the most important reason for the deficient performance of the Network,[203] which prompted further studies in the same direction.[204] Thus, in a manner similar to the ECN, diversity in the powers and status of national authorities is pressed on as a major explanation for the inefficiency of the system for enforcement cooperation and used as justification for new legislative initiatives seeking to harmonize and upgrade national authorities' powers.

Following a Commission proposal in 2016, a new Regulation 2017/2394 was indeed adopted on 12 December 2017.[205] The Commission in its press release described the new Regulation as giving "sharper teeth for EU consumer protection".[206] In a subsequent and related move, the powers of national authorities were additionally enhanced by the modernization reform of EU consumer law following the New Deal for Consumers through the Enforcement and Modernisation Directive.[207] The details in the new instruments cannot be presented in detail here for reasons of space. It suffices to say that the

203 See Third Commission Report CPC Regulation (n 151).

204 See Studio Grimaldi, Study on Enforcement Authorities' Powers and National Procedural Rules in the Application of Regulation 2006/2004/EC on Consumer Protection Cooperation, 2014; see also Support study for the Impact Assessment on the review of the CPC Regulation 2006/2004/EC, Final report submitted on 4 November 2015 by the Consumer Policy Evaluation Consortium (CPEC).

205 See Commission Proposal for a new Regulation on cooperation between national authorities responsible for the enforcement of consumer protection laws, Brussels, COM(2016) 283 final; cf. Impact Assessment New CPC Regulation (n 156).

206 European Commission, 'CPC Factsheet – Sharper Teeth for EU Consumer Protection' (17 January 2020) <https://commission.europa.eu/law/law-topic/consumer-protection-law/consumer-protection-cooperation-regulation_en>.

207 Directive (EU) 2019/2161 as regards the better enforcement and modernisation of Union consumer protection rules [2019] OJ L 328/7 (Omnibus Directive).

main direction of empowerment is parallel to that in the ECN. The New CPC Regulation defines in much stronger and exacting terms than the original Regulation the investigative powers to be granted to competent authorities.[208] Concerning enforcement powers, the arsenal of sanctions and remedies at the disposal of competent authorities is substantially expanded, including penalties and fines for infringements covered by the Regulation,[209] which following the Enforcement and Modernisation Directive, can reach up to 4% of traders' annual turnover in cases of widespread infringements.[210]

Still, there are aspects in which the reforms propelled by the two networks differ significantly. In contrast to the ECN+ Directive, the New CPC Regulation, while mentioning the need for sufficient resources, formulates this rather vaguely.[211] Most importantly, there is nothing in Regulation 2017/2394 about the status of the competent consumer protection authorities. Whereas the ECN+ Directive makes a very strong point about NCAs' independence, the New CPC Regulation remains silent on the position of competent authorities in the system of government of the Member State.[212] Apparently, consumer protection does not have the same political clout as competition policy and is not seen to warrant comparable guarantees of agency independence.[213]

Summing up, as a result of the reform, national consumer protection authorities could see themselves empowered and emboldened in their task as national watchdogs. In this, the logic of empowerment is similar in the CPC Network as in the ECN. As stated in the BEUC report "the CPC-Network is a chain which is as strong as its weakest link". Consequently, strengthening the component parts of the Network, i.e. national consumer CPC authorities, strengthens the whole network and EU consumer law enforcement in general.[214]

In respect of vertical empowerment, given the very different origin and background of the CPC Network, a relevant question is whether it has developed in a different way from the ECN. After all, in the case of the CPC Network, the Commission has no enforcement powers of its own. The setting up of the CPC Network did not formally change this. Therefore, in contrast

208 Article 9(3)(a)-(d) New CPC Regulation. Special powers are accorded for investigations and enforcement in the context of digital markets, see Article 9(4)(g).

209 Under the old Regulation the power to impose penalties was only required for violation of an injunctive order and not as a direct sanction of an infringement.

210 See Articles 1, 3 and 6 Omnibus Directive, amending Directives 93/13/EEC; 2005/29/EC and 2011/83/EU.

211 See Recital 4, Article 5(4) New CPC Regulation. This prompts the European Consumer Organization BEUC, in a report on the New CPC-Regulation, to suggest that the Commission should carefully monitor budgetary allocations to CPC authorities. See BEUC (n 85) 26.

212 BEUC (n 85) 23–24.

213 For a critique in this respect see BEUC (n 85) 23–24.

214 BEUC (n 85) 22.

to the ECN, observers describe the CPC Network mostly as a decentraliszed cooperation system where the Commission has "a limited role".[215]

Indeed, the original CPC Regulation envisaged mainly horizontal exchange of information and requests for enforcement measures between national competent authorities, where the Commission was to act chiefly as a moderator (Article 9(2) Regulation 2006/2004). Competent authorities could invite the Commission to participate in the coordinated action, but this possibility was formulated in weak terms.[216] Nevertheless, a closer look at the operation of the CPC Network shows that the Commission has with time come to assume a more central role than apparent at first sight, and this role has arguably been expanding. Probably due to the variation of national authorities participating in the Network and the broad diversity of their portfolios, design and working modes, bringing some operational efficiency into the Network would essentially be impossible without the Commission's disciplining role.

Partly through the vehicle of the regular reports required under Article 21 Regulation 2006/2004, the Commission assumed a sort of pace-setting function within the Network, identifying flaws and proposing new initiatives. Given that the periodic reports revealed systemic deficiencies in the horizontal exchange between national authorities, relatively early on, calls for a more centralized and coordinated course of action were advanced, where the role of the Commission would naturally become stronger. Cautious steps in this direction were indeed undertaken through experimentation with joint actions, in particular in the form of so-called sweeps.[217] In parallel, the reports sent a strong signal suggesting enhancement of the Commission's powers and position in the CPC Network.[218]

In response, the New CPC Regulation 2017/2394 formalized the practice of 'sweeps'[219] and decisively made a clear step towards centralization with new provisions on coordinated investigation and enforcement in cases of so-called widespread infringements and widespread infringements with Union dimension (Chapter IV Regulation 2017/2394). These are, in the first category, infringements that harm the collective interests of consumers in at least three Member States, and in the second one, infringements harming consumer

215 BEUC (n 85) 7.

216 See Article 9(3) and Article 10 Regulation 2006/2004.

217 The First Commission Report on the CPC Regulation, defines 'sweeps' as "a concerted investigation of consumer markets through simultaneous coordinated control actions to identify infringements of Union laws that protect consumers' interests". See, First Commission Report CPC Regulation (n 148) 4.

218 The Third Commission Report on the CPC Regulation emphasized that respondents to the public consultation were "generally supportive for the Commission to have a more active role in the CPC Network". See Third Commission Report CPC Regulation (n 151) 6.

219 The evolution of this instrument supports theories of experimentalist governance, demonstrating that network governance can work as 'incubator' for innovatory regulatory techniques. Sabel and Zeitlin (n 7).

interests in at "least two-thirds of the Member States, accounting, together, for at least two-thirds of the population of the Union" (Article 4(3)). If the competent authorities in the case of widespread infringements cannot agree on one authority to act as a coordinator, they may ask the Commission to take on that role. The Commission can itself coordinate actions in case of widespread infringements with Union dimension, but after consulting with relevant competent authorities (Article 17(3) and (4)).

Interestingly, the original proposal for a revised Regulation (Section II) sought to grant the Commission independent power to launch coordinated action without having to consult national authorities in the states concerned. Moreover, it envisaged granting the Commission wide-ranging powers of adopting implementing acts on a number of points concerning the institutional design of the cross-border cooperation within the CPC Network.[220] Obviously, the Commission envisioned a more precise and juridified framework for the system of enforcement cooperation. These proposals were, however, bluntly rejected by the Council under the label of "simplification of the enforcement mechanism".[221] It appears that while Member States in principle agree on the need for more effective tools to counteract widespread cross-border consumer law infringements, they are reluctant to vest too broad powers in the hands of the Commission.

As a result of this trimming of the original Commission proposal, the new CPC Regulation leaves essentially the responsibility for public enforcement to the EU Member States. The Commission still cannot itself launch a coordinated action and must rely on the investigative and enforcement powers, and on the engagement, of national authorities. Decisively, the Commission lacks adequate resources to effectively engage in the cooperation mechanism set up by the Regulation. The outcome is a fragmented enforcement landscape which is criticized as not particularly effective in curbing serious and widespread cross-border consumer law infringements.[222]

In sum, like the ECN, the CPC Network has generated both horizontal and vertical dynamics towards strengthening the Commission's role in the Network. In both dimensions, diversity is a crucial factor. Diversity of national authorities' enforcement powers is used as an argument for harmonization and ratcheting up of those powers. At the same time, the plurality and excessive diversity of participating NCAs creates internal fragmentation, which naturally calls for stronger leadership and coordination. The Commission has tried to procure a more formalized legal framework for exercising such a leadership

220 See Draft Articles 10, 11(5), 12(5), 13(6), 15(7), 20, 27, 31(3), 31(4), 34(6), 35(5), 36(2), 37(4), 39(3), 43(4), 46(2), Commission Proposal for a New Regulation (n 205).

221 See Council, General approach on the Proposal for a regulation on cooperation between national authorities responsible for the enforcement of consumer protection laws, 6187/17, Brussels, 10 February 2017, 4 <https://eur-lex.europa.eu/legal-content/EN/TXT/PDF/?uri=CONSIL:ST_6187_2017_INIT> accessed 2 November 2024.

222 BEUC (n 85) 10.

role, but these efforts have not resonated positively with the Member States. It appears that consumer protection does not command the same authority in the Union political spectrum and attempts to shift more powers to the supranational level meet with resistance.

7. Sideways dynamic

In the final section of this chapter, another type of dynamic arguably triggered by governance networks, and enforcement networks in particular, will be briefly highlighted, namely a tendency of networks to expand, spread and connect to other already existing networks, but also to spur the creation of new networks. What can be observed in the domains of both competition and consumer protection policy is how a network in one policy area often appears to work as a parent plant ('rootstock') on which new networks (or 'shoots') in the same area with different functions, different actors, or different geographical scope, are grafted. Thus, a policy network can serve as an instigation for the emergence of a separate but interlinked enforcement network, to which a dispute resolution network or a specialized judicial network can be added. Likewise, an international network can come on the waves of a European one, or vice versa. In addition to this 'propagation' of networks within one and the same policy field, the interlinking with networks in adjacent policy areas can also be observed. It is in this web of interconnected networks that Anne-Marie Slaughter sees the evolution of a new world order.[223] For lack of a better term, this dynamic can be dubbed 'sideways dynamic'.

A prominent example of such sideways dynamics, and of interaction between European and international networks in the field of competition law is the International Competition Network (ICN), which was founded in 2001; interestingly, exactly at the time when the Commission was contemplating its grand modernization reform and designing the ECN. Behind the initiative for the ICN was an informal group of competition law experts, convened by the US Justice Department with the task to provide recommendations for a global governance regime of competition law.[224] At the time of its inception in 2001, the ICN included top antitrust officials from 14 jurisdictions. Nowadays the Network encompasses representatives from 118 jurisdictions across the globe. Obviously, the immense experience of running a European network gives the Commission and the NCAs authority and leverage in the ICN.[225]

Similar dynamics in terms of global linkages can be observed in the area of consumer law. In fact, when the first ideas for the CPC Network were tested, inspiration was drawn from a recently founded informal cooperation network

223 See Slaughter, *A New World Order* (n 6) 135.

224 The group was named International Competition Policy Advisory Committee (ICPAC). See 'About' (*ICN Webpage*) <https://www.internationalcompetitionnetwork.org/about/>.

225 For a fascinating account on the flow of policy ideas across the globe, see David Gerber, *Global Competition: Law, Markets and Globalization* (OUP 2010). See also Wilks, 'Agency Escape' (n 127) 455.

in the area of marketing – the International Marketing Supervision Network (IMSN).[226] This network had been started by the Danish Consumer Ombudsman in 1992 and was in 2002 renamed International Consumer Protection Enforcement Network (ICPEN). Also in this context, the Commission acts as a liaison between the lead ICPEN members and the CPC Network.[227] Consequently, in a similar way as in competition policy, we can see a pattern of mutual reinforcement between European and international networks.

A particularly intense propagation of networks within one and the same areas, but with differing functions and constitutive units can be observed in the domain of EU consumer policy. In this policy area, an important precursor of the CPC Network has been the Consumer Policy Network (CPN) which is an informal policy network linking Member States representatives in higher official positions with responsibilities for consumer protection policy. The CPN operates as a platform for political dialogue, among others assisting the Commission in preparing legislative proposals and policy initiatives. Closer to the enforcement activity of the CPC Network is the network of European Consumer Centres (ECCs), the so-called ECC-Net.[228] This is a network of consumer advice centres co-funded in equal share by the Commission and the Member States. The national ECCs are hosted by either public or private consumer protection bodies depending on the institutional organization of consumer protection in the respective country. Finally, parallel to the CPN, ever since the 1970s, a network-like consultancy structure exists, initially called the European Consumer Consultative Group (ECCG)[229] and now replaced by the Consumer Policy Advisory Group (CPAG). This is an informal Commission expert Group,[230] "bringing together representatives from consumer organisations, civil society and industry in support of the consumer agenda".[231] It is thus a heterogenous network, including both private and public entities. In the New Consumer Agenda, the CPAG is described as a complement to the CPC Network and the ECC-Net. The reason for the greater proliferation of networks in consumer law in comparison to competition law is probably the more uncertain Community/Union competence in this policy domain. Networks represent therefore a governance mode paying due respect to subsidiarity.[232]

Finally, there are more recently visible efforts to formally link networks and network-like structures active in different policy domains, into common

226 See Commission Green Paper on European Union Consumer Protection, COM(2001) 531 final, Brussels, 2 October 2001.

227 Third Commission Report CPC Regulation (n 151) 15.

228 See European Consumer Centres (ECCs): Status Review and Future Challenges, Draft Final Report, 27 October 2017.

229 See Commission Decision 2009/705/EC setting up a European Consumer Consultative Group [2009] OJ L 244/21.

230 See Action 21, Communication from the Commission to the European Parliament and the Council, New Consumer Agenda. Strengthening consumer resilience for sustainable recovery, COM(2020) 696 final, Brussels, 13 November 2020, 21.

231 DG Justice and Consumers, Terms of Reference, 22 December 2022, para 4.

232 See Bourgoignie (n 80).

intersecting constructs. One can speak of networks of networks. This is partly prompted by new developments in technology that require innovatory policies, cutting across different sectors of economic governance and transcending rigidly delineated policy confines – and not least, the confines of legal sub-disciplines – thus overcoming what is perceived as the "silos" approach characterizing the current state of affairs. Most prominently, with the Digital Markets Act, the Commission commits itself to establishing a high-level group composed of various bodies and networks, notably the two networks studied in this chapter (the CPC Network and the ECN).[233] Imelda Maher speaks of a "thicket of actors" involved in the new enforcement design.[234]

Such a new 'cross-cutting' approach to enforcement may indeed be needed, especially in view of the fact that an increasing number of infringements, in particular those in the digital sphere, are multi-faceted and have consequences in multiple sectors of regulation.[235] Therefore, a joint and coordinated work between enforcement institutions and networks promises to enhance and strengthen enforcement.[236] At the same time, one lesson from the comparison between the ECN and the CPC Network carried out in this chapter should have become clear, namely a sharply delineated policy area is one factor that induces the creation of a tightly knit epistemic community, which in turn appears to be a well-proven guarantee for the successful operation of any enforcement and governance network.

8. Conclusion

The analysis of the two enforcement networks in this chapter testifies to the enduring importance of network governance in the European Union.[237] Despite a parallel movement towards agencification, governance through networks remains a lasting feature of the EU governance landscape. At the same time, the analysis suggests that the literature on transnational networks should pay closer attention to the specific characteristics of each network, particularly in terms of functions of the networks, policy domain, nature and diversity of the participating units and institutional design. Drawing parallels and seeking generalizations without considering the specificities of the analysed networks

233 These include "the body of the European Regulators for Electronic Communications, the European Data Protection Supervisor and European Data Protection Board and the newly created European Regulator Group of Audiovisual Media Regulators under the Digital Services Act". See Article 40 Digital Markets Act (EU Regulation 2022/1925). Cf BEUC (n 85) 19–20; cf. Recital 93 Digital Markets Act.

234 Imelda Maher, 'Regulatory Design in the EU Digital Markets Act: No Solo Run for the European Commission' [2024] Journal of Antitrust Enforcement 1–7.

235 BEUC (n 85) 11, 20.

236 BEUC (n 85).

237 Levi-Faur (n 4).

in these respects, might lead to misleading extrapolations, conclusions and recommendations.

The analysis in this chapter suggests that a clearly delineated policy field with narrow scope, coherent policy vision and strong legal basis in the constitutional framework of the Union is maybe the single most important condition for a strong network. Clear delineation and coherence allow for the emergence of an epistemic community, which pulls together like-minded professionals with common ideals, visions and practical experience. For such a community to emerge, the role of lawyers and legal professionals can hardly be overestimated. Enforcement networks are highly juridified networks, and they are much more smoothly organized around an easily identifiable legal discipline with basis in legal education and in professional communities. This is well illustrated by the differential success of the two networks.

An aspect that has not been sufficiently highlighted in the literature is the choice between public and private enforcement and the effect of network governance on this choice. In a contribution of 2007, Daniela Caruso drew attention to the position of private law in the European integration project, calling it aptly the "missing view on the Cathedral".[238] Indeed, the drive towards public enforcement that the two networks are a testimony to may appear natural from the perspective of trying to achieve maximum effectiveness of enforcement. However, as the case of the CPC Network has demonstrated, the need to align into the modalities of network cooperation may occasionally push enforcement away from reliance on private modes of governance and closer to a more hierarchical command-and-control model of enforcement, without taking into account long-term traditions and institutional settings in the Member States.

More generally, the chapter bears witness to the ambiguous relationship of governance networks, and enforcement networks in particular, to institutional diversity. On the one hand, the enforcement networks studied in this chapter are largely born out of perceived need to rein in diversity and cope with the existing plurality of regulatory bodies and approaches in the ever-expanding European context. Even when there is agreement and common view on regulatory objectives and legal rules, states differ significantly in their institutional solutions, both at the level of institutional choice and of institutional design. It is against this backdrop of institutional diversity that networks are brought forward as a more effective way to instil coherence and bring convergence than hierarchical forms of governance such as agencies or enforcement by the Commission.[239] This implies that diversity is approached normatively as an impediment to effective enforcement that has to be reduced or even withered away.

Yet, at the same time, nurturing respect for normative and institutional diversity and preserving national autonomy and institutional choices, were

238 Caruso (n 83).
239 Dehousse, 'Regulation by Networks' (n 4).

advanced as the most important advantages of the cooperative approach to enforcement launched with the Sutherland report in the beginning of the 1990s. This acceptance of diversity finds support in theories of experimentalist governance, seeing diversity as providing fruitful soil for innovatory institutional solutions and learning from difference. So, the question is, when does diversity go over from being a source of creative institutional experimentation to being an undesirable stumbling block and source of inefficiency? How much diversity is necessary and how much diversity can network architecture tolerate to remain sustainable?

This tension is to a certain extent resolved by Slaughter's normative concept of legitimate difference. According to Slaughter,

> legitimate difference is a principle that preserves diversity within a framework of a specified degree of convergence. It enshrines pluralism as a basis for, rather than a bar to, regulatory cooperation, leaving open the possibility of further convergence between legal systems in the form of mutual recognition or even harmonization, but not requiring it.[240]

The concept provides a positive interpretation of "difference" as a basis for learning and constructive experimentation and thus feeds into theories of deliberative supranationalism,[241] experimentalist governance[242] and adaptive efficiency.[243] As stated by Nicolaïdis in the context of the debate on mutual recognition, "any formal integration process [is] conditioned by the collective determination of where tolerable differences start and end between groups or nations".[244]

Interestingly, the chapter has revealed how diversity generates a dynamic of empowerment, both on the horizontal and the vertical level. The drive to overcome or even out diversity, creates pressure towards convergence through harmonization of national authorities' powers. This pressure seems almost unavoidably to lead to ratcheting up of the powers of public enforcers. The new instruments partly prepared and channelled through the two networks have equipped public authorities in their respective sector of regulation with stronger investigatory and enforcement powers. In the case of the ECN, the

240 Slaughter, *A New World Order* (n 6) 249. In her view transnational cooperation between regulators should start from "the premise that "difference" per se reflects a desirable diversity of ideas about how to order an economy or society." Slaughter, *A New World Order* (n 6) 248.

241 Joerges (n 8).

242 Sabel and Zeitlin (n 7).

243 Douglas North, *Institutions, Institutional Change and Economic Performance* (CUP 1990) 70.

244 Nicolaïdis (n 59) 688; in a similar sense, Christian Joerges, 'How Is a Closer Union Conceivable Under Conditions of Ever More Socio-Economic and Political Diversity? Constitutionalising Europe's Unitas in Pluralitate' (2018) 24 European Law Journal 257.

reforms have strengthened NCAs' independence from national government and have secured their financial position and adequate staffing. The parallelism in this dynamic is, however, not complete, the area of competition law clearly commanding more power and authority in the policy context.

The other dynamic, also partly spurred by diversity, is the vertical empowerment and shift of powers upwards towards the Commission. The strong position of the Commission is, however, not necessarily perceived as a threat by national authorities. Rather, at least in the context of competition law, it has had the effect of collective empowerment. In the CPC Network, the role of the Commission has likewise increased through greater emphasis on joint actions and coordinated enforcement. Yet, the Member States are not passive observers of this dynamic and are in full capacity of setting constraints.

What deserves reminding is the original philosophy behind the cooperative approach advanced in the Sutherland report, namely respect for difference, which in turn requires greater resistance to the siren songs of both horizontal and vertical empowerment. To be sure, empowering public enforcers at both the national and EU level is in many cases needed in order to ensure the effectiveness of EU law. However, this should not be an exercise of automatic 'ratcheting up', but rather a process that learns from and is attentive to legitimate difference.

Part IV

International, transnational, and global dimensions of representative democracy

10 Democracy and the rights of representation in the case law of the European Court of Human Rights[1]

Šejla Imamović

1. Introduction

Democracy as a form of government provides an environment for the protection and effective realisation of human rights. The European Court of Human Rights (hereinafter ECtHR or Court) has consistently held that democracy constitutes a fundamental element of the 'European public order'. The Preamble to the European Convention on Human Rights (hereinafter ECHR or Convention) establishes a clear link between democracy and the Convention rights and asserts that human rights and freedoms are best realised and maintained by an effective political democracy and by a common understanding of human rights. This is similarly reflected in the system of the European Union, which is founded on the core values of fundamental rights protection, democracy and the rule of law as set out in Article 2 of the Treaty on European Union.

While it is generally linked to representative institutions such as governments and parliaments, democracy also rests on the rule of law, which is in the hands of judges charged with ensuring that no one is excluded from the democratic process and intervening when there is democratic degradation, decay or backsliding.[2] Indeed, judges are there to protect – not perfect – democracy.[3] They can also have a preventive role in anticipating and, where they can, slowing down erosion of democracy. This means that, in a democracy, the role of

1 This chapter is produced as part and funded by the European Union-NextGenerationEU, through the National Recovery and Resilience Plan of the Republic of Bulgaria, project No bg-rrp-2.004-0008.

2 Jean-Paul Costa, 'The Links Between Democracy and Human Rights Under the Case-Law of the European Court of Human Rights' Speech of the (then) President of the European Court of Human Rights, Helsinki, 5 June 2008 <https://www.echr.coe.int/documents/d/echr/Speech_20080605_Costa_Helsinki_ENG> accessed 3 June 2024. See also European Court of Human Rights, ' Judges preserving democracy through the protection of human rights', Strasbourg, 29 November 2022.

3 David Prendergast, 'The Judicial Role in Protecting Democracy from Populism' (2019) 20 German Law Journal 245–62.

DOI: 10.4324/9781003610670-15

the judge is important. At the same time, one cannot ignore the fear of the 'government of judges',[4] which carries negative connotations relating to judicial activism and the exercise of power by non-elected individuals with no accountability to the people and therefore no legitimacy. Judicial restraint is thus also important in a democracy, along with an appropriate degree of deference to the elected government and legislature.[5] Finding the right balance between the two roles is not easy, and this goes as much for the ECtHR as for any other court.

However, many democracies appear to be eroding. In May 2021 the Secretary-General of the Council of Europe noted that Europe's democratic environment and democratic institutions have been in mutually reinforcing decline, which has been further exacerbated in the wake of the COVID-19 pandemic.[6] Indeed, over the past two decades democracy has seen a decline in various countries and regions, the prominent examples in Europe being Poland and Hungary. The latest Global State of Democracy 2024 Report shows that even traditionally stable European countries such as France and the Netherlands are seeing the rule of law deteriorate as voter turnout and democratic legitimacy decline worldwide.[7]

When it comes to the Convention system specifically, its values are also increasingly being called into question, both at the European and at the global levels.[8] The threats posed by inter alia terrorism, immigration, nationalist rhetoric and the rise of radical democracies have offered populism fertile ground to flourish.[9] In addition, and somewhat contra-intuitively, there seems to be an increasing tension between human rights and democracy in the ECtHR's case law. This has manifested itself in a number of ways, including in relation to the rights of representation and particularly in cases in which minorities challenge the political structure of a state. Indeed, important cases interfering with a

4 Michael H Davis, 'A Government of Judges: An Historical Re-View' (1987) 35(3) The American Journal of Comparative Law 559–80.

5 Jean-Paul Costa, 'The Links Between Democracy and Human Rights Under the Case-Law of the European Court of Human Rights' Speech of the (then) President of the European Court of Human Rights, Helsinki, 5 June 2008 <https://www.echr.coe.int/documents/d/echr/Speech_20080605_Costa_Helsinki_ENG> accessed 3 June 2024.

6 Council of Europe's Secretary General's 2021 Annual Report, 'State of Democracy, Human Rights and the Rule of Law – A Democratic Renewal for Europe' <https://www.coe.int/en/web/secretary-general/report-2021> accessed 3 June 2024.

7 International Institute for Democracy and Electoral Assistance (International IDEA), 'Global State of Democracy 2024 Report' <https://www.idea.int/publications/catalogue/global-state-democracy-2024-strengthening-legitimacy-elections> accessed 3 June 2024.

8 Richard Bellamy, 'The Democratic Legitimacy of International Human Rights Conventions: Political Constitutionalism and the European Convention on Human Rights' (2014) 25(4) European Journal of International Law 1019–42.

9 Armen Harutyunyan, 'The Future of the European Court of Human Rights in the Era of Radical Democracy' (2021) 2 European Convention on Human Rights Law Review 20–26.

state's constitutional structures have exposed the tension between 'rights' and the 'democracy' principles in ECHR case law.[10]

This chapter focuses on the role and potential of the ECtHR in upholding representative democracy. In that sense and due to the limited scope of this chapter, its focus is on the rights of representation as protected in Article 3 of Protocol 1 of the ECHR, but mention may be made of other (political) rights which are relevant when discussing ways of upholding democracy, such as freedom of expression and assembly. Under Article 3 of Protocol 1, European citizens are guaranteed free and democratic elections. Although the scope of this provision is reduced to the elections of the 'legislature' and does not afford an unlimited right, its relevance in the European legal space remains pertinent.

The chapter is structured as follows. Section 2 discusses the notion of democracy in the Convention system. In this context, a reference is made to the text of the Convention, including its Preamble and the right to free elections, freedom of expression and freedom of assembly. The next section analyses the case law of the ECtHR on the right to free elections which comprise the right to vote and the right to stand for elections, in order to reveal the tension between human rights and democracy that may exist at times and to provide a deeper understanding of the Court's reasoning. Special attention is devoted to the level of scrutiny the Court exercises in cases where the rights of representation are limited. Section 4 then reflects on the latter, particularly in comparison to the level of scrutiny the Court exercises in relation to other political rights. The conclusion gives a survey of the findings.

2. The concept of democracy in the convention system

Democracy, as a concept and as a normative principle, is both extremely broad and highly contested. It is not the purpose of this chapter to provide a comprehensive account of democracy, but merely to indicate some key points that will be helpful in framing the discussion of the rights of representation in the ECHR.[11]

According to the Preamble to the Convention, European countries have a common heritage of political tradition, ideals, freedom and the rule of law, which are the principles of political democracy and the underlying values of the Convention itself. Moreover, the Preamble asserts that fundamental human rights and freedoms are best maintained by 'an effective political democracy'. It can therefore be said that the Convention was designed to maintain and promote the ideals and values of a democratic society. The ECtHR has confirmed this vision repeatedly in its jurisprudence, maintaining that democracy is the

10 Stefan Graziadei, 'Democracy v Human Rights? The Strasbourg Court and the Challenge of Power Sharing' (2016) 12 European Constitutional Law Review 54–84.

11 For a comprehensive analysis of the concept of democracy and its different variations see Herman Cappelen, *The Concept of Democracy: An Essay on Conceptual Amelioration and Abandonment* (OUP 2023).

only system of government contemplated in the Convention and the only one compatible with it.[12] Another obvious link with the idea of democracy in the text of the Convention is the 'necessary in a democratic society' part included in some provisions, which guides the Court when assessing whether a restriction on a certain right can be justified. It demonstrates that the framers decided to explicitly incorporate the concept of democracy into the provisions themselves and give it a prominent role in the balancing of individual rights against the needs of the community as a whole.[13]

The concept of democracy in the case law of the ECtHR is primarily concerned with representation and participation. It must be understood as participatory democracy showing respect for pluralism of opinion through the exercise of civic and political freedoms and not as democracy in the strict sense, i.e. exclusively relying on the majority rule.

The ECtHR has adjudicated many cases in which the notion of democracy within the framework of the Convention was considered, as well as the rights of different actors in a liberal democracy. In particular, political rights, such as freedom of expression, the right to vote and the freedom of assembly, are understood as vital for establishing and maintaining the foundations of an effective and meaningful democracy governed by the rule of law.[14] Specifically, in the context of Article 3 of Protocol 1, the Court has emphasised that the rights of representation comprising the right to vote (the 'active' aspect) and to stand for election (the 'passive' aspect)[15] are crucial to establishing and maintaining the foundations of an effective and meaningful democracy governed by the rule of law. Moreover, the Court has consistently maintained that full participation of all the citizens of the High Contracting Parties is at the heart of the notion of democracy. At the same time, however, the Court interprets this right with caution, particularly cases concerning the passive right to run for elections or when questions of electoral design are raised. It is indeed not often that we find a judgement where the Court has found a state in violation of the Convention because of the choices it has made in designing its electoral system.

Furthermore, democracy must also be understood as requiring the protection of other human rights, in particular the freedom of expression and assembly. In its interpretation of Article 10 of the Convention, the Court has held that "freedom of expression constitutes one of the essential foundations of [democratic] society, one of the basic conditions for its progress and for the development of every man".[16] Indeed, the Court has considered

12 See inter alia *United Communist Party of Turkey and Others v Turkey* App No 19392/92 (ECtHR, 30 January 1998) para 45; *Ždanoka v Latvia* App No 58278/00 (ECtHR, 16 March 2006) para 98.

13 Conor Gearty, 'Democracy and Human Rights in the European Court of Human Rights: A Critical Appraisal' (2000) 51 Northern Ireland Legal Quarterly 381–96.

14 *Yumak and Sadak v Turkey* App No 10226/03 (ECtHR, 30 January 2007) para 65.

15 *Mathieu-Mohin and Clerfayt v Belgium* App No 9267/81 (ECtHR, 2 March 1987) paras 48–51; *Ždanoka v Latvia* App No 58278/00 (ECtHR, 16 March 2006) para 102.

16 *Handyside v The United Kingdom* App No 5493/72 (ECtHR, 7 December 1976) para 49.

that it is crucial in a democracy to allow diverse political programmes to be proposed and debated, even those that call into question the way a State is organised, provided that they do not harm democracy itself.[17] When it comes to Article 11 of the Convention, the Court has held that the state of democracy in the country concerned can be determined inter alia by the way in which freedom of association is secured under national legislation and the way in which the authorities apply it in practice. On numerous occasions the Court affirmed the direct relationship between democracy, pluralism and the freedom of association and has established the principle that only convincing and compelling reasons can justify restrictions on that freedom. All such restrictions are subject to a rigorous supervision by the Court.[18]

The ECtHR also often connects its analysis of Articles 10 and 11 ECHR, highlighting their combined importance for the protection of democracy. This is not surprising since freedom of association and the right to peaceful assembly, guaranteed by Article 11, are the extension of political speech and public debate protected by Article 10. The Court's reading of Article 10 may thus influence its interpretation of Article 11, and the principles it has developed under Article 10 are generally transposable to Article 11.[19] As with political speech, the Court submits any restrictions on political association to strict scrutiny. This is because any restrictions on political parties affect not only their freedom of expression and association, but also democracy as a whole in the State concerned. It is evident that any group which rejects democratic values and/or advocates violent means to achieve their political ends is excluded from the protection of Convention, by virtue of Article 17 ECHR concerning prohibition of abuse of rights. The threat that such groups pose to the democratic system and institutions of a State provides the justification for the State to restrict and even completely prohibit their activities.

Additionally, implementation of the principle of pluralism, which is inherent in democracy and can be defined as diversity of values, opinions and social groups, is impossible without an association being able to express freely its ideas and opinions. Indeed, the Court has recognised that the protection of opinions and the freedom of expression within the meaning of Article 10 of the Convention is one of the objectives of the freedom of association.[20] Article 3 of Protocol 1 is also closely linked to freedom of expression and assembly, as it guarantees respect for pluralism of opinion in a democratic society.

The most important democratic principles highlighted in the case law of the ECtHR are indeed pluralism, which has already been mentioned, and the

17 *Socialist Party and Others v Turkey* App No 21237/93 (ECtHR, 25 May 1998) para 47.

18 See, among many, *United Communist Party of Turkey and Others v Turkey* App No 19392/92 (ECtHR, 30 January 1998) para 42 et seq.; *Refah Partisi (the Welfare Party) and Others* App Nos 41340/98, 41342/98, 41343/98 and 41344/98 (ECtHR, 13 February 2003) para 86 et seq.

19 Costa (n 4). See also ECHR Guides on Articles 10 and 11 of the Convention.

20 See, for instance, *Refah Partisi (the Welfare Party) and Others* App Nos 41340/98, 41342/98, 41343/98 and 41344/98 (ECtHR, 13 February 2003) para 88.

related principles of tolerance and broadmindedness.[21] These three principles, with the principle of pluralism at the forefront, are considered hallmarks of the Court's conception of democracy.[22] Although individual interests must on occasion be subordinated to those of a group, democracy for the Court does not mean that the views of a majority must always prevail; instead, a balance must be achieved which ensures a fair treatment of people from minorities and avoids any abuse of a dominant position. Further on this point, pluralism and democracy must also be based on dialogue and a spirit of compromise which necessarily entail various concessions on the part of individuals or groups of individuals in order to maintain and promote the ideals and values of a democratic society.[23] In other words, most rights and freedoms can be restricted when the limitation is 'necessary in a democratic society'. The latter essentially means that the measure is proportionate to the legitimate aim pursued, which can be a general interest (e.g. public health, national security, prevention of crime) or the rights and freedoms of others. In the words of the Court, "it is precisely this constant search for a balance between the fundamental rights of each individual which constitutes the foundation of a 'democratic society'".[24]

Furthermore, it is important that the states offer the possibility to resolve any political or societal issues through dialogue and without recourse to violence.[25] Even in a state of emergency, the Contracting States must bear in mind that any measures taken should seek to protect the democratic order from the threats to it, and every effort must be made to safeguard the values of a democratic society.[26]

It becomes clear that multiple ECHR rights, and most prominently Article 3 of Protocol 1, Article 10 and Article 11 of the Convention, encapsulate the concept of democracy.[27] However, they are all qualified rights and, as already mentioned, they can be restricted when such restrictions pursue one (or more) of the accepted legitimate aims, there was a 'pressing social need' for the restriction and it was proportionate to the aim pursued. Despite the word not appearing in the Convention text, proportionality is at the heart of how the Court assesses what is necessary in a democratic society. This means that even if an action or policy pursues a legitimate aim, it is not permissible if the means used are excessive, arbitrary or unfair. Essentially, the Convention

21 For further analysis on the concept of pluralism see Aernout Nieuwenhuis, 'The Concept of Pluralism in the Case-Law of the European Court of Human Rights' (2007) 3 European Constitutional Law Review 367–84.

22 Alistair Mowbray, 'Contemporary Aspects of the Promotion of Democracy by the European Court of Human Rights' (2017) 20 European Public Law 469–98.

23 *SAS v France* App No 43835/11 (ECtHR, 1 July 2014) para 128.

24 See inter alia *Chassagnou and Others* App Nos 25088/94, 28331/95 and 28443/95 (ECtHR, 29 April 1999) para 113; *SAS v France* App No 43835/11 (ECtHR, 1 July 2014) para 128.

25 *Manole and Others v Moldova* App No 13936/02 (ECtHR, 17 September 2009) para 95.

26 *Şahin Alpay v Turkey* App no 16538/17 (ECtHR, 20 March 2018) para 180.

27 Other rights that could be mentioned are the procedural rights such as Article 6 (fair trial) and Article 13 (the right to effective remedy, which come into play in electoral disputes, as well as the non-discrimination clause found in Article 14 of the Convention.

requires national authorities to balance the individual's rights against the public interest; it may also be a matter of striking a balance between competing individual rights. However, Article 3 of Protocol 1 is worded differently from Articles 10 and 11 of the Convention, as will be explained in the following section, and it is also applied in a somewhat different way by the ECtHR.

3. Article 3 of Protocol 1 ECHR

3.1 The scope of application

Article 3 of Protocol 1 requires Contracting States to hold democratic and free elections, based on universal suffrage and secret ballot, at reasonable intervals. The ECtHR has always stressed the importance of rights under Article 3 Protocol 1 for establishing and maintaining the foundations of an effective and meaningful democracy governed by the rule of law. Indeed, free elections are a condition for the 'effective political democracy' referred to in the Preamble, and for the concept of democratic society which runs through the Convention. Moreover, this provision is to be regarded as an additional Article to the Convention and all the other provisions, including Articles 13 (effective remedy) and 14 (non-discrimination), apply to it.[28] However, it was not included in the original text due to some difficulties that arose during the drafting period, which ultimately resulted in a differently worded text when compared to most provisions that are in the main text of the Convention.[29] The full recognition of this right has also provoked considerable resistance from national governments in the period after its entry into force.[30] Nevertheless, the ECtHR has aligned the right to free elections with other Convention rights holding that the different wording of Article 3 of Protocol 1 does not reflect any difference of substance from the other substantive clauses in the Convention and Protocols.[31]

Most of the cases under this provision concern the holding of elections: applicants have complained of being excluded from the vote, candidates have complained of (permanent) disqualification and of no access to elected offices. However, there have also been cases in which the elections system as a whole was challenged. This section analyses a selected number of judgements in order to provide insights into the ways in which the ECtHR contributes to protecting the rights of representation.

In defining the scope of Article 3 of Protocol 1, the Court has emphasised the role of the state as ultimate guarantor of pluralism and its obligation to adopt positive measures to arrange democratic elections "under conditions which will ensure the free expression of the opinion of the people in the choice

28 Article 5 of Protocol 1 to the European Convention on Human Rights.

29 B Rainey, E Wicks and C Ovey (eds), *Jacobs, White, and Ovey: The European Convention on Human Rights* (8th edn, OUP 2020).

30 Yannick Lécuyer, *The Right to Free Elections* (Council of Europe Publishing 2014) 9.

31 *Mathieu-Mohin and Clerfayt v Belgium* App No 9267/81 (ECtHR, 2 March 1987) para 50.

of the legislature".[32] In clarifying this further, the Court used a textual interpretation – considering its ordinary meaning as well as its object and purpose[33] – and held that the text of the provision clearly suggests that its ambit is limited to elections determining the choice of the legislature. However, the choice of the legislature is not confined to the national parliament. Instead, 'the constitutional structure' of the State in question must be examined.[34]

This kind of restrictive interpretation excludes consideration of other forms of participation and consultation which is highly problematic.[35] More specifically, the wording of Article 3 of Protocol 1 in principle excludes local elections (municipal or regional) as well as referendums. Indeed, this approach was adopted recently in *Moohan and Gillon*,[36] concerning the Scottish independence referendum. The Court rejected the argument that the referendum, albeit of vital importance for an effective political democracy, fell within the scope of Article 3 of Protocol 1. Nevertheless, the Court takes into account the diversity of electoral systems in the various states. It has thus not completely excluded the possibility that a democratic process described as a 'referendum' or local elections in a particular context could potentially fall within the ambit of Article 3 of Protocol 1. In terms of requirements concerning elections, the text of the provision only provides that elections should be free, by secret ballot, and that they must be held at reasonable intervals. The Contracting States have a broad margin of appreciation in determining what exactly this means in the national context.

As mentioned before, Article 3 of Protocol 1 is somewhat different from other rights guaranteed in the Convention and Protocols, as it is phrased in terms of the obligation of the High Contracting Parties to hold elections which ensure free expression of the opinion of the people rather than in terms of a particular right or freedom. Nonetheless, having regard to *travaux préparatoires* to Article 3 of Protocol 1 and the interpretation of the provision in light of the objectives and purpose of the Convention as a whole, the Court has established that it guarantees individual rights, including the right to vote and to stand for election.[37] In establishing these individual rights the Court also referred to the Preamble of Protocol 1, which provides that the Protocol is meant to ensure "the collective enforcement of certain rights and freedoms other than those already included in Section I of the Convention". In the ECtHR's words, the particular phrasing of Article 3 of this Protocol does not reflect any difference in substance from the other substantive clauses in the Convention and other Protocols but rather highlights the fact that the primary

32 *Yumak and Sadak v Turkey* App no 10226/03 (ECtHR, 8 July 2008) para 105.
33 Articles 31–33 of the Vienna Convention on the Law of the Treaties.
34 *Timke v Germany* App No 27311/95 (ECtHR, 11 September 1995).
35 Rory O'Connell, *Law, Democracy and the European Court of Human Rights* (CUP 2020).
36 *Moohan and Gillon v the UK* App no 22962/15 and 23345/15 (ECtHR, 13 June 2017).
37 *Mathieu-Mohin and Clerfayt v Belgium* App No 9267/81 (ECtHR, 2 March 1987) paras 46–51.

obligation here is not negative, i.e. one of abstention or non-interference, as with the majority of the civil and political rights, but one of adoption of positive measures to hold democratic elections.[38] The latter cannot be done without the individual right to participate in an election as a voter (the 'active' aspect) and the right to stand as a candidate for election (the 'passive' aspect). Such 'active' electoral rights enjoy higher level of protection than the 'passive' ones, as further discussed in the following sections.

3.2 *The right to vote*

The proportionality analysis relating to this active aspect of Article 3 Protocol 1 has generally been stricter than the analysis relating to the passive aspect. Most cases decided by the Court concern statutory provisions in national law disqualifying a person or a group of persons from the right to vote. Usually, such individuals or groups of individuals are part of a vulnerable group of society – such as a member of a minority, an individual with mental or physical disability or persons deprived of their liberty – which results in the Court being more attentive in its assessment. Indeed, the wide(er) margin of appreciation afforded to States cannot, for example, have the effect of prohibiting certain individuals or groups from taking part in the political life of the country.

When it comes to the impossibility for certain groups or individuals to vote in parliamentary elections because they are part of a minority, the Court is particularly careful. In 2022, in *Bakirdzi and E.C. v. Hungary*,[39] the Court assessed the system of national minority voting in Hungary finding a violation of Article 3 of Protocol 1. It concluded that the system that had been put in place to ensure the political representation of national minorities in Hungary in fact limits their political effectiveness and is liable to reduce, rather than enhance, diversity and the participation of minorities in political decision-making. This was due to inter alia the fact that the voters were only able to vote for their respective national minority lists and had no choice between candidates presented on those lists. Similarly, in *Kovačević v. Bosnia and Herzegovina* the Court held that elections in Bosnia and Herzegovina are undemocratic since main ethnic groups enjoy a privileged position.[40] The case concerned a distinction that is made in the Bosnian Constitution between different categories of the population: the so-called constituent peoples (Bosniacs, Croats and Serbs) and others (members of ethnic minorities and those who do not declare affiliation with any ethnic group). This distinction has generated various consequences in the Bosnian legal system. Regarding elections, only persons declaring affiliation with one of the three dominant ethnic groups are entitled to run for the House of Peoples and the presidency. Moreover,

38 *Mathieu-Mohin and Clerfayt* (n 36) para 50.
39 *Bakirdzi and EC v Hungary* App Nos 49636/14 and 65678/14 (ECtHR, 10 November 2022).
40 *Kovačević v Bosnia and Herzegovina* App No 43651/22 (ECtHR, 22 August 2023).

and to complicate matters further, only the voters residing in a particular entity are able to participate in the election of the members from that entity to the House of Peoples (through indirect elections) and the presidency (direct elections). In contrast, no ethnic requirements apply in elections to the House of Representatives (the first chamber of the Parliament). In the present case, the applicant with no affiliation to any particular ethnic group alleged that the candidates best representing his political views were not from the 'right' entity and/or of the 'right' ethnic origin, so he had not been able to vote for them in the 2022 legislative and presidential elections. In deciding this case the Chamber reaffirmed the earlier landmark judgement in *Sejdić and Finci*,[41] in which the ECtHR had found a violation of Article 3 Protocol 1 as well as Article 1 of Protocol 12, which is the general non-discrimination clause, taken in conjunction with the right to vote. Remarkably, *Sejdić and Finci* was the first case in which the Court had found that a country's constitution violated the Convention. In *Kovačević v. Bosnia and Herzegovina*, the Chamber reiterated that this complicated system and distinction between different groups and entities is a result of the Dayton Peace Agreement reached in 1995. However, while such mechanism was necessary at the time to ensure peace it was no longer needed and/or justifiable. As the Court had found that this combination of territorial and ethnic requirements amounted to discriminatory treatment in the context of the right to participate in elections to the House of Peoples of the Parliamentary Assembly of Bosnia and Herzegovina, it considered that the same was true in respect of the right to vote.[42]

With respect to restricting or removing the right to vote for persons with mental or physical disability, the Court has been clear that any measure amounting to a blanket ban would not be proportionate. *Alajos Kiss v. Hungary* provides a good illustration of this.[43] The Court accepted the legitimate aim invoked by Hungary of ensuring that only citizens capable of assessing the consequences of their decisions could take part in public affairs. However, it stressed that it could not accept a blanket ban on the right to vote affecting all persons under protection regardless of their actual mental faculties, thus finding a violation of Article 3 of Protocol 1. In 2022, in the case of *Anatoliy Marinov v. Bulgaria*,[44] the Court held that there had been a violation of Article 3 of Protocol 1 because the indiscriminate removal of the applicant's voting rights – without individual judicial review and solely because he had been

41 *Sejdić and Finci v Bosnia and Herzegovina* App Nos 27996/06 and 34836/06 (ECtHR, 22 December 2009). See also the decision of the Committee of Ministers of the Council of Europe of 7 June 2023, in which it had examined the state of implementation of the Sejdić and Finci Group of Judgments <https://search.coe.int/cm/pages/result_details.aspx?objectid=0900001680ab7001> accessed 3 June 2024.

42 *Kovačević v Bosnia and Herzegovina* has been referred to the Grand Chamber on 14 December 2023 at the request of the Government of Bosnia and Herzegovina.

43 *Alajos Kiss v Hungary* App No 38832/06 (ECtHR, 20 May 2010).

44 *Anatoliy Marinov v Bulgaria* App No 26081/17 (ECtHR, 15 February 2022).

placed under partial guardianship – had not been proportionate to the legitimate aim for restricting the right to vote. In that case, the applicant had lost his right to vote as the result of an automatic, blanket restriction on the franchise of those under partial guardianship with no individual judicial evaluation of his capability to express his vote. The Court reiterated that such blanket treatment of all those with intellectual or psychiatric disabilities was questionable, and the curtailment of their rights must be subject to strict scrutiny.

At the same time, however, the Court was willing to accept limitations of the right to vote when domestic authorities conducted an individualised assessment in light of the legitimate aims pursued without looking too much into other details. In the recent case of *Caamaño Valle v. Spain*,[45] the ECtHR concluded that the disenfranchisement decision had been individualised and hence proportionate to the aim pursued, namely ensuring that only citizens capable of assessing the consequences of their decisions and making conscious decisions should participate in public affairs. It also found that the disenfranchisement in this case did not hinder "the free expression of the opinion of the people", which is the exact wording of the text of the provision.[46]

In the context of the deprivation of voting rights as part of a criminal investigation, the Court agreed that suspending the voting rights for a period of time of persons against whom there was evidence of criminal activities pursued a legitimate aim. It observed, however, that it would not be proportionate to maintain such suspension after the person in question was acquitted because the evidence of the applicant's guilt had been rebutted during the trial. Concerning the rights of convicted persons (i.e. prisoners) to vote, the Court has repeatedly reaffirmed that a prisoner does not lose the rights under the Convention merely because of the status as a person detained following conviction and the rights guaranteed by Article 3 of Protocol 1, given their inherent importance to the democratic system, are no exception. The landmark case in this regard is *Hirst v. the UK* where the Grand Chamber held that there had been a violation of Article 3 Protocol 1 on account of the automatic and discriminate restriction on the applicant's right to vote due to his status as a convicted prisoner.[47] This measure affected approximately 48,000 prisoners in the UK and concerned all sorts of prison sentences, ranging from one day to life, and for various types of offences from the most minor to the most serious. In addition, there was no direct link between the offence committed by an individual and the withdrawal of his voting rights.

The Court reasoned that prisoners in general continue to enjoy all rights and freedoms guaranteed under the Convention except for the right to liberty, where lawfully imposed detention falls within the scope of Article 5 of

45 *Caamaño Valle v Spain* App No 43564/17 (ECtHR, 11 May 2021).

46 *Caamaño Valle* (n 44) at para 77.

47 *Hirst v the UK* App No 74025/01 (ECtHR, 6 October 2005). See also ECHR Guide on Article 3 of Protocol No 1.

the ECHR. Furthermore, the Court considered that under the Convention system, where pluralism and tolerance are the acknowledged cornerstones of democratic society, automatic disenfranchisement based purely on what might offend public opinion could not be accepted. However, Contracting States are not precluded from taking steps to protect themselves against activities intended to destroy the rights or freedoms set forth in the Convention. Hence, Article 3 of Protocol 1, which enshrines the individual's capacity to influence the composition of the legislative power, does not exclude that restrictions on electoral rights could be imposed on an individual who has, for example, seriously abused a public position or whose conduct threatened to undermine the rule of law or democratic foundations.[48] The severe measure of disenfranchisement must not, however, be used easily or quickly and the principle of proportionality requires that a discernible and sufficient link between the sanction and the conduct and circumstances of the individual concerned is established. As in other contexts, an independent judicial authority constitutes a strong safeguard against arbitrariness.

Contracting States are not, however, prevented from implementing measures that are designed to enhance civic responsibility and respect for the rule of law and to ensure the proper functioning and preservation of the democratic regime. In *Scoppola v. Italy*,[49] the applicant had been sentenced to life imprisonment for having committed several crimes. Under Italian law, his life sentence required a lifetime ban from public office, which in turn meant the permanent loss of his right to vote. The Court noted that the ban applied only to persons convicted of certain well-determined offences or to a custodial sentence exceeding a statutory threshold. The legislature, the Court considered, had been careful to adjust the duration of this measure according to the specific circumstances of each case. It had also adjusted the duration of the ban depending on the sentence imposed, and therefore, indirectly, on the gravity of the sentence. Consequently, many of the convicted prisoners had retained the possibility of voting in legislative elections. In addition, this system had been complemented by the possibility for convicts affected by a permanent ban to recover their voting rights. Hence the Italian system did not violate Article 3 of Protocol 1.

3.3 *The right to stand for elections*

In a case concerning the right to stand for elections, the former president of Lithuania Rolandas Paksas was precluded from running for Parliament after the law was changed to stop any official who had been removed from office by impeachment from standing in elections.[50] Despite his removal from office,

48 *Hirst v the UK* (n 46) at para 71.

49 *Scoppola v Italy (No 3)* App No 126/05 (ECtHR, 22 May 2012).

50 *Paksas v Lithuania* App No 34932/04 (ECtHR, 6 January 2011). See also the ECHR Guide on Article 3 of Protocol No 1.

Paksas decided to stand in new presidential elections. But before those elections were held, Parliament changed the law to stop any official who had been removed from office from being elected president initially until at least five years had passed, which later turned into a permanent ban. The Grand Chamber of the ECtHR ruled that this permanent ban violated Paksas's right to stand for elections as protected in Article 3 of Protocol 1. Before any change was introduced in Lithuania in order to remedy the violation, the Lithuanian Supreme Administrative Court requested an Advisory Opinion from the ECtHR under Protocol 16 of the ECHR.[51] The request arose in the context of proceedings where the applicant challenged the Central Electoral Commission's refusal to register her as a candidate in the Seimas elections of October 2020 because in 2014 she had been removed from her position as a member of the Seimas in impeachment proceedings. As with Paksas, the legal ban preventing her registration was the direct consequence of the Lithuanian constitutional and statutory regulations on impeachment, which the Court had found to be in breach of Article 3 of Protocol 1 on the ground that a life-long disqualification, due to its permanent and irreversible nature, amounted to a disproportionate sanction. The execution of this judgement was still pending before the Committee of Ministers on the date of adoption of the advisory opinion. Hence, the Court used the opportunity to reiterate once more that when assessing the proportionality of a general measure restricting the exercise of the rights guaranteed by Article 3 of Protocol 1, decisive weight should be attached to the existence of a time limit and the possibility of reviewing the measure in question. The need for such a possibility was linked to the fact that the assessment of that issue must have regard to the evolving historical and political context in the state concerned. While states enjoy considerable margin of manoeuvre to establish in their legal order rules governing the status of parliamentarians, these rules should not be such as to exclude permanently some persons or groups of persons from participating in the political life of a country. The Court has also considered that, with the passage of time, general restrictions on electoral rights had become more difficult to justify, thus requiring restrictive measures to be individualised.

Lithuania executed the ECtHR's judgement in the *Paksas* case by changing the constitution to make the ban temporary. In April 2022, Lithuanian Seimas passed a constitutional amendment ensuring that any person removed from office would not face a permanent and irreversible ban from running in both parliamentary and presidential elections but would instead be able to stand after a period of at least ten years. Given the amount of time that has passed since he was removed from office, these changes mean Rolandas Paksas now has the right to stand as a candidate in future parliamentary elections.

51 Advisory opinion on the assessment, under Article 3 of Protocol No 1 to the Convention, of the proportionality of a general prohibition on standing for election after removal from office in impeachment proceedings, Request No P16-2020-002 (ECtHR, 8 April 2022).

However, states are allowed to implement measures restricting individuals' ability to stand for election when the measure in question is itself designed to protect the democratic order or to ensure the proper functioning of the public authorities. In *Etxeberria and Others v. Spain*,[52] the Court considered the case of Spanish nationals and electoral groupings whose candidatures had been annulled by the Supreme Court on the grounds that they were pursuing the activities of three political parties which had been declared illegal and dissolved on account of their support for violence and for the activities of the ETA, a terrorist organisation. The Court found that the national authorities had obtained considerable evidence enabling them to conclude that the electoral groupings in question wished to continue the activities of the political parties concerned. After an examination in adversarial proceedings, during which the groupings had been able to submit observations, the domestic courts had found an unequivocal link with the political parties that had been declared illegal. Lastly, the political context in Spain, namely the presence in the government bodies of certain autonomous communities (particularly in the autonomous community of the Basque Country) of political parties calling for independence, proved that the impugned measure was not part of a policy to ban any expression of separatist views. The Court thus found that the restriction had been proportionate to the legitimate aim pursued.

Similarly, in *Miniscalco v. Italy*,[53] the applicant was disqualified from standing as a candidate in the regional elections on account of his final conviction for abuse of authority. The Court found that the measure taken by the authorities corresponded to an urgent need and was compatible with the principle of the rule of law and the general objectives of the Convention. Having examined the existing legal framework, the Court concluded that the disqualification had been surrounded by guarantees. In particular, the disqualification was preconditioned on the existence of a final criminal conviction strictly defined by law, it was limited in time and its foreseeability fell within the wide margin of appreciation enjoyed by the state.

In some cases, the Court explicitly recognised that it exercises an even lower level of scrutiny when it comes to the passive aspect of the right to free elections. The case in point is *Ždanoka v. Latvia* where the applicant complained that she had been disqualified from running in parliamentary elections because of her continued active membership of the Communist Party after Latvia declared its independence from the Soviet Union.[54] The Grand Chamber underlined that the case law on the right to stand for election – the so-called passive aspect – was even more cautious than the case law on the right to vote. Restrictions on the passive right need only to pursue a legitimate

52 *Etxeberria and Others v Spain* App Nos 35579/03 and 3 others (ECtHR, 30 June 2009).
53 *Miniscalco v Italy* App No 55093/13 (ECtHR, 17 June 2021).
54 *Ždanoka v Latvia* App No 58278/00 (ECtHR, 16 March 2006).

aim and avoid arbitrariness in the relevant procedures. In other words, the scope of the Court's review in such cases is more limited and one could even say amounts to checking whether there are signs of a manifest breach. The Grand Chamber examined the proportionality of the restriction on the applicant's right to stand for election and held, having regard to the specific historical and political context of Latvia and to the fact that the ban was very limited in its application, it concluded that the state had remained within its wide margin of appreciation.

Finally, some cases can concern both active and passive aspect of Article 3 of Protocol 1. One of the prominent examples is *Aziz v. Cyprus*[55] regarding the rights of Turkish Cypriots in Cyprus to vote and to stand for elections. The applicant brought a claim regarding both aspects of Article 3 of Protocol 1 arguing they had been denied the opportunity to vote or stand as a candidate in parliamentary elections, solely on the ground that he was Turkish Cypriot. The Court noted that Contracting States enjoy considerable latitude to establish rules within their constitutional order governing parliamentary elections and the composition of the parliament, and that the relevant criteria may vary according to the historical and political factors peculiar to each state. However, these rules should not be such as to exclude some persons or groups of persons from participating in the political life of the country and, in particular, in the choice of the legislature, a right guaranteed by both the Convention and the Constitutions of all Contracting States. In the present case, Article 63 of the Cypriot Constitution provided for two separate electoral lists, one for the Greek-Cypriot community and one for the Turkish-Cypriot community, but the participation of the Turkish-Cypriot members of parliament was suspended as a result of the anomalous situation that began in 1963. Notwithstanding the fact that the relevant constitutional provisions have been rendered ineffective, there was a manifest lack of legislation resolving the ensuing problems. Accordingly, the Court concluded that the applicant, as a member of the Turkish Cypriot community living in the government-controlled area of Cyprus, was completely deprived of any opportunity to express his opinion in the choice of the members of the House of Representatives of the country of which he is a national and where he has always lived. This meant that the essence of the right to vote had been affected. Even though the Court did not explicitly rule on the passive aspect of the right in question, Cyprus changed its law following this judgement in 2006 giving Turkish Cypriots the right to vote and stand in elections; 270 Turkish Cypriots cast their ballot in the 2006 parliamentary election, while one member of the community ran as a candidate.

55 *Aziz v Cyprus* App No 69949/01 (ECtHR, 22 September 2004).

3.4 Integrity of election process as a whole

As previously emphasised, the Court has continuously held that Contracting States enjoy considerable margin to establish rules within their constitutional order governing parliamentary elections and that the relevant criteria may vary according to the historical and political factors peculiar to each state. However, the Court is also ready to intervene where such rules are in manifest violation of the Convention.

The Georgian Labour Party v. Georgia is a case concerning protection against the arbitrary exclusion of voters in elections. The matter at stake in this case was that voting stations failed to open on election day in a part of the country due to some irregularities. This meant that 60,000 people – around 2.5% of Georgia's electorate – were unable to vote. The Georgian Labour Party argued that the election could not be finalised without votes from the two districts in question.[56] The ECtHR found that Georgia breached a political party's right to stand for election by disenfranchising 60,000 voters it might have relied upon for support. The Court's judgement in the Georgian Labour Party's case led Georgia to change its election law, setting out clear criteria which must be met for the electoral authorities to annul results. Moreover, an effective mechanism to settle election disputes was promptly put in place.

In *Communist Party of Russia and Others v. Russia*,[57] the Court examined whether the state had a positive obligation under Article 3 of Protocol 1 to ensure that coverage by regulated media was objective and compatible with the spirit of 'free elections', even in the absence of direct evidence of deliberate manipulation. It found that the existing system of electoral remedies was sufficient to satisfy the state's positive obligation of a procedural nature. Indeed, the applicants' complaint about unequal media coverage was examined by an independent body in a procedure which afforded the basic procedural guarantees, and a reasoned judgement was given; the applicants did not clarify what other remedies or legal avenues could possibly be more effective.

As to the substantive aspect of the positive obligation and the allegation that the state should have ensured neutrality of the audio-visual media, the Court took the view that certain steps had been taken to guarantee some visibility to opposition parties and candidates on TV and to secure the editorial independence and neutrality of the media. Namely, the opposition parties were able to convey their political message to the electorate through the media that they controlled. Further, the applicants did obtain some measure of access to the nationwide TV channels: they were provided with free and paid airtime, with no distinction made between different political forces. These arrangements had probably not secured de facto equality, but it could not be established that the state had failed to meet its positive obligations in this area to such an extent as to amount to a violation of Article 3 of Protocol 1.

56 *The Georgian Labour Party v Georgia* App No 9103/04 (ECtHR, 8 October 2008).
57 *Communist Party of Russia and Others v Russia* App No 29400/05 (ECtHR, 19 June 2012).

Another case that deserves attention is ***Yumak and Sadak v. Turkey***, concerning the electoral threshold of 10% of the national vote imposed for the representation of political parties in Parliament.[58] The consequence of such a high threshold was that voting results from parliamentary elections showed that approximately 45% of voters in one province were not represented in the legislature. This is because they voted for the Democratic People's Party, which obtained approximately 45% of the vote (47,449 votes) in that province but secured only 6.22% of the vote nationally. The overall result was that out of the 18 parties which took part in the elections, only two succeeded in passing the 10% threshold and thus obtained seats in Parliament. The government argued that the election system was designed to reconcile representativity and stability, both of which are constitutional values, and that the previous system produced a series of unstable and ineffective governments. The case was first decided by a chamber and subsequently by the Grand Chamber.

The Grand Chamber considered that the threshold pursued the legitimate aim of avoiding excessive and debilitating parliamentary fragmentation and thus of strengthening governmental stability. Furthermore, the Court reasoned that the choice made by the legislature was not in itself incompatible with Article 3 of Protocol 1. Indeed, the latter does not in principle impose on Contracting States the obligation to adopt an electoral system guaranteeing parliamentary representation to parties with an essentially regional base irrespective of the votes cast in other parts of the country. At the same time, however, the Court noted that the electoral threshold used in Turkey is the highest among the Contracting States of the Council of Europe. While the Court agreed that an electoral threshold of about 5% corresponded more closely to the common practice, it also had to consider the specific context in which the elections happened, other aspects of the electoral system and the political evolution of the country concerned. In doing so, the Court first noted that a 10% electoral threshold appeared excessive and agreed with the organs of the Council of Europe that it should be lowered.[59] This is due to several reasons, including the fact that the high threshold compelled political parties to make use of tactics which did not contribute to and possibly even had negative effect on the transparency of the electoral process. However, the Court was not convinced that, when assessed in the light of the specific political context of the elections in question and accompanied by other guarantees which had limited its effects in practice, the threshold had had the effect of impairing the essence of the rights of the applicants protected by Article 3 of Protocol 1. Outside of that, the States enjoy a wide margin of appreciation when it comes to the design of their system of government. As the Court noted numerous times in the case law, there are many ways of organising and running electoral systems, and a wealth of differences, inter alia, in historical development, cultural

58 *Yumak and Sadak v Turkey* App No 10226/03 (ECtHR, 8 July 2008).

59 See, e.g., Resolution 1547 (2007) on the state of human rights and democracy in Europe.

diversity and political thought within Europe.[60] The choice is thus ultimately in the hands of the national authorities to make constitutional choices they deem appropriate and necessary in their own 'democratic vision'.

Finally, Article 3 of Protocol 1 also covers the post-election period, including the counting of votes and the recording and transmission of the results.[61] The States also have a positive obligation to ensure careful regulation of the process in which the results of voting are ascertained, processed and recorded.

4. The ECtHR's contribution to protecting representative democracy

The ECtHR has continuously repeated that democracy is the only political model that is compatible with the Convention. The previous case law analysis shows that the Court has made significant efforts to protect democracy. It has done so using different rights in the Convention, extending their scope and limiting the margin of appreciation of the Contracting States where possible and appropriate.

When it comes to the rights of representation specifically, the Court extended the scope of Article 3 Protocol 1 on free elections to include individual rights, including the right to vote and to stand for elections. Although those rights are central to democracy and the rule of law, they are not absolute and may be subject to limitations. The Contracting States have a wide margin of appreciation in this sphere, but it is for the Court to determine in the last instance whether the requirements of Article 3 of Protocol 1 have been complied with. In doing so, the Court ascertains that the imposed measures pursued a legitimate aim and were proportionate to the aims pursued. The latter is usually done by assessing whether imposed limitations of the rights in question are liable to impair their very essence and deprive them of their effectiveness.

Now, this is not a strict proportionality test. It is true that the Court employs a stricter scrutiny when it comes to the active aspect of Article 3 Protocol 1, namely the right to vote. It is also true that the Court has been vigilant against arbitrariness and indiscriminate measures and has found such instances disproportionate, as illustrated in the previous section. Nevertheless, the overall level of scrutiny remains rather limited. One of the reasons is that the margin of appreciation afforded to the States is broad, which necessarily lowers the level of scrutiny. This is in stark contrast to the Court's approach regarding some other rights, including freedom of expression and freedom of assembly where the Court exercises strict(er) scrutiny coupled with narrow(er) margin of appreciation. Indeed, the distinction becomes particularly clear when one compares how the ECtHR applies the proportionality test to those provisions. Under Articles 10 and 11, the ECtHR assesses whether the interference

60 See, e.g., *Hirst v the UK* App No 74025/01 (ECtHR, 6 October 2005) para 61.
61 See, e.g., *Kovach v Ukraine* App No 39424/02 (ECtHR, 7 February 2008).

pursued a legitimate aim and whether it was necessary in a democratic society. The legitimate aims that can be used are limited and spelled out in the second paragraph of both provisions. The 'necessary in a democratic society' part requires that the measure in question must answer a 'pressing social need' and be proportionate to the legitimate aim, and the reasons adduced by the national authorities to justify it must be 'relevant and sufficient'. The breadth of the margin of appreciation is assessed on a case-by-case basis, and it is more often than not that the margin afforded is narrow. In contrast, under Article 3 of Protocol 1, the ECtHR's application of the test is limited to examining whether the conditions imposed on the rights to vote or to stand for election do not curtail the exercise of those rights to such an extent as to impair their very essence and deprive them of their effectiveness. Moreover, the margin of appreciation afforded to the states is generally wide. Some scholars have argued that this essentially means that the normative basis of the measure itself – and its compatibility with the ECtHR's democratic society – is in fact not assessed in substantive terms.[62] They suggest that the Court should adopt the same necessity test in relation to this provision as it does in relation to other political rights.

Indeed, the concerns about democratic erosion and backsliding could perhaps be addressed more effectively if the Court would exercise stricter scrutiny, modify the necessity test and bring it in line with the test it uses for other political rights. Another way could be to focus more on the wider context in which certain restrictive measures are adopted, justifying stricter scrutiny on that basis. This would fit well with the Court's own rhetoric concerning evolutive and dynamic interpretation of Convention rights and the importance of the principle of effectiveness. It is questionable, however, how such an approach would be perceived at the national level given the distinct wording of this provision compared to others and the fact that these decisions touch on the core of their constitutional systems. While the Court can go beyond the textual interpretation of the Convention rights considering the living instrument doctrine, the latter has its limits too, particularly given the increasingly important principle of subsidiarity in the Convention system.[63] Lastly, one should not forget that the Convention system was largely devised in the 1940s and that even with these interpretative tools in mind the Court continues to operate within the broader limits of the Convention legal framework, which may simply not be suitable to properly address present concerns.[64]

Notwithstanding the criticism regarding the approach when it comes to Article 3 of Protocol 1, the ECtHR has also been commended for already

62 Alain Zysset, 'Freedom of Expression, the Right to Vote, and Proportionality at the European Court of Human Rights: An Internal Critique' (2019) 17(1) International Journal of Constitutional Law 230–51.

63 The principle of subsidiarity has been included in the text of the Convention with the entry into force of Protocol No 15 to the ECHR on 1 August 2021.

64 Rory O'Connell, *Law, Democracy and the European Court of Human Rights* (CUP 2020) 270.

broadening the scope of the right to free elections significantly and for strengthening democracy in many individual states and in Europe more broadly. When an individual or group has been deprived of the right to vote, the Court is particularly attentive and will step in where necessary. Deprivation of the right to vote must then pursue a legitimate aim but also pass a more stringent proportionality test. In cases in which deprivation of voting rights was part of a criminal investigation, the Court employed this stringent test. It found a violation where the loss of civic rights was imposed on individuals after their acquittal or after they have been subjected to police surveillance. The same can be said for cases in which depravation of voting rights did not concern criminal but civil procedures.

5. Conclusion

The concept of democracy is deeply entrenched in the Convention system. The ECtHR has consistently held that democracy constitutes a fundamental element of the 'European public order', of which the Court is the guardian. At the same time, the Court is sensitive to the boundaries of its competence when it comes to constitutional structures of Member States.

The ECtHR protects democracy through different ECHR rights. This is true for Articles 10 and 11, freedom of expression and assembly, but also Article 6 (fair trial), for example, in the cases of electoral disputes or judicial independence. When it comes to the rights of representation, Article 3 of Protocol 1 is the core provision and the backbone of the democratic system itself. It is, however, different from the other substantive provisions of the Convention and the Protocols as it is phrased in terms of the obligation of the High Contracting Party to hold elections which ensure the free expression of the opinion of the people rather than in terms of a particular individual right or freedom. Nevertheless, the Court has established that this provision does not have a different scope since it also implies individual rights, comprising the right to vote (the 'active' aspect) and the right to stand for election (the 'passive' aspect).

As with freedom of expression and assembly, the right to free elections is not absolute. As illustrated in the case law analysis, there is room for the so-called implied limitations, and the Court has held that Contracting States must be given a wide margin of appreciation in this sphere. The concept of 'implied limitations' under Article 3 of Protocol No. 1 is of major importance for the determination of the relevance of the aims pursued by the restrictions on the rights guaranteed by this provision. Given that Article 3 of Protocol No. 1 is not limited by a specific list of 'legitimate aims', such as those enumerated in Articles 8–11 of the Convention, the Contracting States are free to rely on an aim not contained in that list to justify a restriction, provided that the compatibility of that aim with the principle of the rule of law and the general objectives of the Convention is ascertained in the particular circumstances of a given case. This implies a less rigorous approach by the Court when it comes to the design of a state's democratic system, as it considers that every such system is unique, reflecting the historical experiences of the state, its values, traditions and its aspirations. As the Court has held many times, the role of an international human rights court cannot be to question and second-guess the choices made by the electorate or their representatives except for manifest breaches of the Convention. In other words, the extent to which the rights of representation can be safeguarded in Strasbourg is limited and the Court steps in only when there are signs of manifest breach. It is thus primarily a duty of the domestic authorities in every European State, both legislative and judicial, to ensure sufficient protection of the rights of representation. At the same time, the national and international supervision should remain in a mutually reinforcing relationship.

11 Global democracy

Between people's representation and participation

Maria Victoria Kristan[1]

1. Introduction

The current impact of globalization, coupled with the expansion of global regulatory instruments, poses a significant challenge to democracy and freedom. This scenario undermines the ideal of freedom as non-domination. It seems unlikely that we will ever be able to develop a global democracy if we fail in our attempt to address the problem of domination. What, if anything, can and should be done to solve this problem? There are at least two aspects we need to consider in order to find an answer.

The first consideration is the concept of authority, which plays a crucial role in understanding the dynamics of globalization. In a globalized world, traditional notions of absolute state sovereignty and authority are challenged by the increasing importance and influence of a multitude of actors at different levels, including local, national, international, and transnational bodies. This complex tapestry of actors often results in overlapping and sometimes conflicting claims of authority, which is where the idea of relative authority becomes particularly relevant.

Relative authority[2] acknowledges that in a global context, no single authority operates in isolation. Instead, the legitimacy and effectiveness of an authority are inherently tied to its relationships with other authorities. This interdependence is a key feature of globalization, where local, national, and international bodies must often interact and cooperate to address global challenges effectively.

The second consideration dwells with a global democratic account to be able to adequately explain the three aspects of authority mentioned earlier. Any account that cannot adequately explain them will not be able to provide a satisfactory account of a global democratic system, because it will not be

1 This chapter is produced as part of and funded by the European Union-NextGenerationEU, through the National Recovery and Resilience Plan of the Republic of Bulgaria, project No bg-rrp-2.004-0008.

2 Nicole Roughan, *Authorities: Conflicts, Cooperation, and Transnational Legal Theory* (OUP 2013).

DOI: 10.4324/9781003610670-16

able to explain the world as it is, nor the world as it ought to be. I believe that Pettit's work, along with the work of other neo-Republican scholars, is not only less vulnerable to the problems of a post-Westphalian world than most other proposals in political philosophy. I also believe that a neo-Republican theory of freedom as non-domination is best suited to offer a blueprint for global democracy, and one that strengthens participation, representation, and contestation. This chapter is guided by the normative vision of freedom as non-domination, our ideal of free people living in a world made up of legitimate actors. As Pettit mentioned,[3] we need some kind of moral compass to guide us on our way in this complex world, a compass that will allow us to rethink the foundations of republican cosmopolitan institutions. In general, any proposal to reform existing institutions or to create new institutions must aim to avoid those forms of government that lead to domination in order to secure freedom.

To this end, this work deals with the design of a global democracy that captures the consequences of a relative authority. It outlines the normative requirements for a global democratic account capable of avoiding domination. This chapter will argue for the value of deliberative democracy in the global context, and at the same time for individual participation, since it prevents domination by ensuring individual influence and direction on global issues, thus creating a global legitimate governance that is compatible with some forms of global representation and contestatory power.

2. Legitimizing global democracy: authority and plurality

Some years ago Joseph Raz published a paper titled 'The Future of State Sovereignty'.[4] In it, he acknowledges the growing number of international organizations and raises the question of whether state sovereignty has become obsolete. That paper marks a change in the understanding of political authority by recognizing the pluralistic nature of authority today. Of course, Raz is not the only, nor the first, scholar[5] that has changed his mind regarding the role of the state as sovereign. To be clear, this section will explore some novel

3 Philip Pettit, *Just Freedom: A Moral Compass for a Complex World* (WW Norton & Company 2014).

4 Joseph Raz, 'The Future of State Sovereignty' (King's College London Law School Research Paper 2017) 42. See also by the same author: 'Why the State?' (King's College London Law School Research Paper 2013).

5 See, e.g., Mattias Kumm, 'The Legitimacy of International Law: A Constitutionalist Framework of Analysis' (2004) 15(5) European Journal of International Law 907, S Besson and J Tasioulas (eds), 'The Philosophy of International Law' (OUP 2010); A Buchanan, 'The Legitimacy of International Law' in S Besson and J Tasioulas (eds), *The Philosophy of International Law* (OUP 2010); Miodrag Jovanović, 'Global/Transnational Law Challenges to Theorizing About Law' in *Jurisprudence in a Globalized World* (Edward Elgar Publishing 2020).

forms of authority in order to strengthen the theoretical foundations of a global public sphere.

In doing so, in this chapter I will engage with Nicole Roughan's notion of relative authority.[6] This notion has deep implications for understanding global democracy because it addresses the theoretical implications of interdependent and interconnected authority. I will argue that embracing a relative authority framework can facilitate the transition toward a global democracy characterized by comprehensive yet flexible global democratic governance, where public authorities maintain their integrity while functioning in a relative capacity. Her point of departure is the interaction between local, national, international, and transnational law and the overlapping and sometimes contradictory claims to authority that are associated with it. The question that the author pursues in her work is 'whether, and if so how, plurality of authority and relationships between authorities affect or even effect the existence and legitimacy of authority'.[7] She also argues that existing state-centric conceptions of authority cannot be maintained everywhere where there are multiple authorities sharing or competing for domains, which leads to difficulties of ranking or identifying authorities. In a pluralistic framework of sources of law, she explains that law is neither ordinary nor solitary, nor it is limited by the borders of modern states, that law is disordered and diverse and it nevertheless creates obligations for its subjects. Roughan also argues that procedural[8] and substantive[9] theories of legitimate authority are unsatisfactory in order to explain a world of plural authorities, that is, they cannot identify and rank plural legitimate authorities.

The idea of relative authority directs the focus of a theory of authority to the relationships that exist between interacting and/or overlapping authorities. Because of these characteristics, we should understand authority in pluralist circumstances as 'relative' and develop a theory of its legitimacy that goes along with this by revising the idea that law claims exclusive legitimate authority. Such an approach to relative authority aims at explaining interconnected authority, i.e., authority whose legitimacy is mutually constituted and mutually constrained between two persons or bodies who *prima facie* have the rank of authority but who, because of the existence of the other and the necessity of interaction, cannot alone have independent legitimacy.[10] The generator

6 See Roughan (n 2).

7 Roughan (n 2) 5.

8 See, for instance, A Buchanan, 'The Legitimacy of International Law' in S Besson and J Tasioulas (eds), *The Philosophy of International Law* (OUP 2010).

9 See, e.g., Joseph Raz, *The Morality of Freedom* (Clarendon Press 1986); Joseph Raz, *Practical Reason and Norms* (OUP 1999).

10 In a similar way, Hurrelman assesses the growing importance of relational legitimacy by stating that 'the legitimacy of institutions at multiple levels of governance should increasingly be assessed in interconnected ways. . . . [A] relational legitimacy assessment can then be defined as an evaluation of political institutions in one political system (or at one level of governance) that is systematically linked to the evaluation of institutions in another system (or at another level). This typology of legitimacy relations proposed by Hurrelman is meant to explain the

of all this relativity is, of course, the properties of the subjects of the authorities, which are either shared by the authorities or whose activities bring the authorities into interaction. The conception of relative authority explains that whenever authority is shared or intersects as a result of the properties of these subjects, that authority is not independent and its legitimacy cannot be evaluated as if it were.[11] To this end, Roughan, like other republican scholars such as Bohman and Braithwaite, explains that authority is relative to the authority of other interacting or overlapping authorities, whereby an institution at any level of law can only be authoritative if it is appropriately related to others with whom it intersects or overlaps.[12]

2.1 *Global individual influence, direction, and ultimate popular control*

To recognize that authority is plural and interconnected reveals that there are some peculiarities of the global realm that make any account of global government somewhat complex. To name but a few: states are still perceived as the main legitimate source of authority; there is no single demos in the global realm from which we might benefit as a unifying forum; and there is a plurality of dispersed and disaggregated actors – traditionally as states and non-traditionally as hybrid public-private actors – who exercise authority over individuals.

The realization of a global democracy inevitably requires the establishment of an institutional decision-making system of authority, a system which, in a republican conception of political freedom, is one of the keys to guaranteeing that freedom. In other words, it means establishing a decision-making system that ensures individual influence, direction, and ultimate popular control. Ensuring influence, direction, and ultimate popular control requires that individuals contribute to a decision-making system in a system constrained by the common good. In other words: if interference is not subject to adequate controls and checks and does not pursue what Pettit called 'commonly avowable interests' it will be arbitrary.[13] However, the reality of disaggregated authority makes electoral democracy a less useful ideal than contestatory democracy, so the realities of global governance should prompt us to return to a rediscovered usefulness of deliberative democracy, such as through the use of the World

relations between the European Union and its member states. In particular, he has described these relations as zero-sum, negative-sum, and positive-sum relations where 'each kind of relationship might come about as the result of more or less implicit and unintentional interpretations that underlie a person's legitimacy beliefs'. Achim Hurrelmann (ed), *Democratic Dilemmas of Multilevel Governance* (Palgrave Macmillan) 17, 20.

11 See Roughan (n 2) 138.

12 Roughan (n 2) 180–81.

13 Cecile Laborde, 'Republicanism' in M Freeden (ed), *Oxford Handbook of Political Ideologies* (OUP 2013) 1543.

Wide Web or mechanisms like CrowdLaw.[14] Deliberative democracy is an ideal that can be most fruitfully employed to enrich freedom as non-domination in global governance, because people need to have the opportunity to participate in global decision-making, but it is also necessary that they can secure direction to be non-arbitrary.

The famous case of Ulysses and the Sirens is a paradigmatic example of non-arbitrary influence. After all, despite being controlled, Ulysses remains free in spite of the Sirens' singing and his plea to his crew for release. His freedom was based on his capacity to track his interests. Following this line of argument, institutional decision-making must be constrained by the common good where individuals retain the ability to control, even if they have not consented to a certain interference.[15] Placing this argument in the current circumstances of global domination, democracy is avowed by the form that international actors have adopted. *The world as it is* does not allow individuals to act as contributors to global decision-making. At best, individuals can exercise contestation,[16] but I believe that they can do more as initiators and contributors to democratization than as just counterpublics, because counterpublics lack two basic characteristics, they do not rule or set the agenda.[17]

The influence that individuals should retain in order to ensure that it is not arbitrary, must be individualized, unconditioned, and efficacious. It is individualized when individuals have equal access to the system of popular influence, so that everyone can be expected to accept the direction imposed on the government; it is unconditioned when it does not depend on the good will of anyone to exercise it; and it is efficacious when it is clear that influence remains present even when government decisions run counter to the interests of particular groups or individuals.[18] It is important to note that influence and direction can diverge, and it is possible for individuals to influence political processes without that influence imposing any preferred direction on what that process entails. Indeed, popular control means that individuals have equal access to a system of popular influence over government to give direction through influence, and that direction should be equally acceptable to all individuals, regardless of the willingness of any other authority to let government go along with it (Pettit 2012: 172, 2014: 121–124).[19] To avoid arbitrary interference, an act, be it a norm, a standard, a regulatory act, or a decision of

14 <https://www.thegovlab.org/project/project-crowdlaw> accessed 6 January 2024.

15 Philip Pettit, *On the People's Terms: A Republican Theory and Model of Democracy* (CUP 2012) 235–38.

16 See John S Dryzek, 'Environmental Movements: Local, National and Global' (2000) 35(1) Australian Journal of Political Science 165; John S Dryzek, *Deliberative Democracy and Beyond: Liberals, Critics, Contestations* (OUP 2002); John S Dryzek, 'Two Paths to Global Democracy' (2008) 15(4) Ethical Perspectives 469.

17 James Bohman, *Democracy Across Borders: From Demos to Demoi* (MIT Press 2007) 62–64.

18 See Pettit (n 15) 209–38.

19 See Pettit (n 15) 172; Roughan (n 2) 121–24.

an international organization, should be formulated by tracking the interests and ideas of the person suffering the interference (Pettit 2012: 55).

3. Global democracy and the value of individual participation

As it was said, the aim of this chapter is to outline a legitimate global institutional design to shield our freedom from domination. In this sense, legitimacy can be defined as the 'right to rule' (Besson 2010, Christiano 2012, Martí 2017). Legitimacy gives us a path to determining who should make the public decisions and rules that govern us, and how. Importantly, the decisions made by an institution will be legitimate if freedom has been guaranteed in the decision-making process, understood as non-domination. Setting that a global democracy is desirable, the question that arises is how the institutions should be designed to pursue a system capable of avoiding domination.

The republican tradition attaches great value to civic virtue, public participation, and deliberation. There are various reasons why people's participation is valuable, such as epistemic reasons.[20] But the most important reason why people participate is because it prevents domination. In a global context, participatory democracy is an ideal that should be pursued because it recognizes the importance of individuals uniting their voices on those issues that affect their lives by empowering public reason. And that value lies in the fact that it enables people to influence, to impose direction effectively on public policy, and enables legislation to follow people's interests, opinions, and reasonings. In short, participation improves people's capacity for democratic direction and control and enriches freedom as non-domination.

Despite this, most advocates of both the state-centric and the cosmopolitan approaches have left public participation – in the form of direct democracy – aside when they design global democracy. They have done so for various reasons. Some believe that state representation is the best way to ensure non-domination, while others argue that public participation is not enforceable at the global level. Of course, those who consider the state as the center of the global order, such as Pettit[21] or Bellamy,[22] will ask why individuals would want the international order to be controlled by them if states are legitimate. Why would individuals want to have direct control rather than indirect control? However, as it was argued in this chapter, relying on representation only is problematic and should not be a regulative ideal to strive for in global democracy.

20 See, for example, José Luis Martí, 'The Epistemic Conception of Deliberative Democracy Defended Reasons, Rightness and Equal Political' in José Luis Martí & Samantha Besson (eds), (1st ed.). *Deliberative Democracy and Its Discontents* (Routledge 2006) 27.

21 Philip Pettit, 'Representation, Responsive and Indicative' (2010) 17 Constellations 426; Philip Pettit, *The State* (Princeton UP 2023).

22 Richard Bellamy, *A Republican Europe of States: Cosmopolitanism, Intergovernmentalism and Democracy in the EU* (CUP 2019).

One problem with representation when it is magnified in the global arena is its opacity. Let me provide an example: the day after the announcement of the results of the presidential election in the United States of America in 2016, a newspaper article revealed some of the reasons why citizens voted for Donald Trump. The article mentioned that Trump voters cited as one reason 'he is not a politician' and, in relation to international affairs, that they saw an open door to the kitchens of diplomacy that were normally closed to them.[23] Two years earlier, a comment from Emmanuel Macron about a telephone conversation with Trump summarized his policy of refraining from making off-the-record comments on his conversations with other world leaders:

> As Bismarck used to say, if we explained to people how sausages were made, it's unlikely they'd keep eating them. So I like it when people see the finished meal, but I'm not convinced the kitchen commentary helps with delivering the meal or eating it.[24]

Macron's words show very well how opaque international affairs are to the people. First and foremost, representation in the international and global context is carried out by unelected representatives. Diplomats are not part of the pool of representatives that a society could elect, and the chain of delegations between individuals, elected authorities, and diplomats obscures the possibility of accountability.[25]

On the other side, the world is not entirely democratic, so the executive power of non-representative states acting on behalf of the people in international organizations is not legitimized. Even if all states were democratic, the problem described earlier would persist and make representation inadequate, because international norms, standards, and regulations are negotiated by unelected government officials and unelected experts, making the link between voters and diplomatic officials insignificant. Also, to overcome the first and second points, states should have a monopoly on the production of international legal norms,[26] but due to the way the production of international norms is designed this is not always possible. These reasons show us why representation alone cannot be a model for global democracy.

23 Amanda Mars, 'Donald Trump, el perdedor que odiaba a los perdedores' (*El País Newspaper*, 2020) <https://elpais.com/internacional/elecciones-usa/2020-11-07/donald-trump-el-perdedor-que-odiaba-a-los-perdedores.html> accessed 8 November 2023.

24 See Rick Noack <https://www.washingtonpost.com/news/world/wp/2018/06/06/frances-macron-phone-calls-with-trump-are-like-sausages-best-not-to-know-what-is-inside/> accessed 8 November 2023.

25 Anne Peters, 'Dual Democracy' in J Klabbers, A Peters and G Ulfstein (eds), *The Constitutionalization of International Law* (OUP 2009) 294.

26 See Steven Wheatley, 'A Democratic Rule of International Law' (2011) 22(2) European Journal of International Law 525; Samantha Besson, 'The Authority of International Law – Lifting the State Veil' (2009) 31 Sydney Law Review 343.

In this respect, Nino[27] suggested that representation itself has a democratic value and is necessary in a large political community but that it should play a subordinate role in terms of people's participation. This is a purely representative model, as proposed by a large part of the theorists of global democracy, which does not offer the possibility of individual participation, under the form of influence and direction, is not sufficiently democratic and therefore cannot be considered the only valid institutional mechanism; on the contrary, good representation should be articulated with the mechanism of people's participation and see global democracy from a systemic viewpoint. Following this lead, in recent years, republican cosmopolitans have taken a turn toward representation, arguing that global democracy must not only improve representative institutions[28] but also include mechanisms to promote people's participation.[29]

3.1 Enhancing democratic participation in global governance

In the remainder of this section, this chapter will focus on sketching a participatory account of global democracy. The main reason for advocating participation in the circumstances of globalization, however, is that people must have a relevant say in the decisions that affect their lives. In republican terms, having a say in a decision-making process means exercising influence and imposing direction, that is, influencing the decisions that affect my life, and this in combination with contestation enriches freedom as non-domination. Participation in global decisions is a form of exercising direction over those decisions that will affect my life. I mention here the circumstances of global domination because the deficits that affect representation domestically are magnified in the global arena,[30] and giving people a significant opportunity to participate directly mitigates this deficit. In short, participation improves people's capacity for democratic direction and control, especially in a global context.

Moreover, in the global context, there are at least two conditions that speak for people's participation. The first is the *relevance criterion*. The most urgent conditions for people's lives occur in the global context, for example terrorism, ecological collapse, pandemics, and chemical and biological weapons, to name but a few. It could be argued that the relevance criterion is not easy to use to call for people's participation, that it is not worth holding public deliberations on complex global issues. This assertion leads me to my second point, *the capacity of control*. In representative democracies, citizens are expected to

27 Carlos S Nino, *The Constitution of Deliberative Democracy* (Yale UP 1996).
28 S Besson and JL Martí, 'Cities as Democratic Representatives in International Law-Making' in *Research Handbook on International Law and Cities* (Elgar Publishing 2021).
29 James Bohman, *Democracy Across Borders: From Demos to Demoi* (MIT Press 2007).
30 See Besson and Martí (n 28).

delegate political decisions to their representatives, officials, etc.[31] However, the chain of delegation in decision-making on global issues is so long[32] that people are not able to maintain control over representative institutions, and that conspires against non-domination.

To this end, people's participation in global decision-making contributes to its legitimacy, because (a) it reduces the gap between individuals and representative institutions, (b) it counteracts the fact that not every state is democratic, and (c) it also counteracts the imbalance of power among the representative states around the negotiating table of the international podium, which is due to the fact they do not have the same weight and it affects their capacity to influence international decision-making. People's participation contributes to alleviating the imbalance of power between states, since the interests of the people do not necessarily coincide with the interests of the state.[33]

People's participation has the capacity to promote global deliberation and gradually shift deliberation from the state to the global arena. Advocates of a state-centric approach will argue that there is sufficient deliberation in the global realm regarding global issues such as climate change or terrorism. However, as was already mentioned, debates conducted by states or international organizations lack transparency, are closed, and are mainly conducted by technocrats; in contrast, people's participation will bring more global deliberation and transparency and avoid an oscillation of state officials between national geopolitics and global decision-making, and will also potentially strengthen democracy within states. But if we recognize that democratic deliberation has value and that people need proper checks and balances to avoid arbitrary interference (sometimes this means setting the agenda), open participation processes in institutional decision-making will also contribute to the dispersion of power that an account of freedom as non-domination requires.

In this context, the question that arises is how the participation of people in global decision-making processes can help us to achieve the ideal of freedom as non-domination. One clarification first: advocating people's participation does not mean that I totally reject the mechanism of people's representation. I believe that an egalitarian representation of individuals is something valuable, but it cannot be the first nor the only option for individuals. For example, a global assembly, problematic as it might be, could be a valuable institution for channeling the representation of people, but it will only work if we think of that institution as being connected to others. For example, a Global

31 Cristina Lafont, *Democracy Without Shortcuts: A Participatory Conception of Deliberative Democracy* (OUP 2020).

32 Patrizia Nanz and Jens Steffek, 'Global Governance, Participation and the Public Sphere' (2004) 39(2) Government and Opposition 317.

33 For example, people's opposition in the United Kingdom and United States to military action against Iraq.

Parliament could act in connection with global mini publics[34] at the same time that social movements could act generating entry points for people's participation. Of course, as was mentioned earlier, representation is not an evil that needs to be excluded in a global democratic system. It rather should be combined with popular participation as a way to avoid people's domination. Regarding the feasibility of people's participating in a global democracy, technological changes in recent years mean that participation is no longer costly or factually impossible, especially at a global level, an example of which is CrowdLaw. Similarly, as happened during the COVID-19 pandemic, various mechanisms of participation and representation, both local and global, have been sustained thanks to technological progress, which also argues for the possibility of global deliberation with technological tools.

Bearing in mind that the regulative ideal that we want to pursue to avoid domination is people's participation, the institutional model that is better adapted to global governance is the participatory concept of deliberative democracy.[35] According to Bächtiger, Dryzek, Mansbridge, and Warren,

> a minimal definition of deliberation means a mutual communication that involves weighing and reflecting preferences, values, and interests on matters of common concern, while deliberative democracy is a concept that incorporates the requirements that deliberation take place in contexts of equal recognition, respect, reciprocity, and sufficiently equal power for communicative influence to function . . . [d]eliberative democracy is grounded in an ideal in which people come together, on the basis of equal status and mutual respect, to discuss the political issues they face and, on the basis of those discussions, decide on the policies that will then affect their lives.[36]

Deliberative democracy is an ideal. According to this ideal, in order to be legitimate, government decisions should be the result of a process of ongoing public deliberation. Throughout this process, people must be able to participate on an equal footing and under the condition of freedom to argue for their preferred political solution. This process of deliberation, under ideal conditions, should lead to large political consensus based on public reasons, and, as we saw, the outcome of deliberation may have an epistemic value.[37]

34 For a proposal along these lines see John S Dryzek and others, 'Global Citizen Deliberation on Genome Editing' (2020) 369 Science 1435–37.

35 See Lafont (n 31).

36 A Bächtiger and others (eds), 'Deliberative Democracy: An Introduction' in *The Oxford Handbook of Deliberative Democracy* (OUP 2019) 28.

37 Jon Elster, *Deliberative Democracy* (CUP 1998); David M Estlund, *Democratic Authority: A Philosophical Framework* (Princeton UP 2007); J Parkinson and J Mansbridge (eds), *Deliberative Systems: Deliberative Democracy at the Large Scale* (CUP 2012); Nino (n 27).

Habermas[38] and Elster[39] described deliberative democracy as a process leading 'by the force of the better argument, and not by the argument of force'. Elster points out that deliberative democracy is a two-part expression, a democratic and a deliberative part. The first part requires the full inclusion of all affected in public decision-making, while the second requires that the decision-making process gives everyone the opportunity to engage in a process of reciprocal argumentation by providing the opportunity to exchange reasons and arguments over certain positions, the aim being to convince the other by the force of the better argument. Deliberative democracy is a model of democracy that makes room for participation but also for representation, because of the characteristics that the global realm presents, such as an obscure change of representation.

In this section I have argued that a global democracy based only on a model of representation cannot be a regulative ideal. On the contrary, it is essential to provide for a participatory mechanism to connect those concerned with the decision-making process in order to avoid domination. This chapter would also point out that the model of democracy that better fits this need for participation is deliberative democracy. In the next section I will explain how we can link people's participation to global decision-making.

4. Connecting people's participation with the world, and the world with people's participation

People's connection with the world leads us to the question of how these people have a say that is different from that exercised by the consent of the state. Another question that is frequently asked concerns the state itself. Is a cosmopolitan approach that takes the individual as its starting point incompatible with assigning a role to states in a global framework? I would suggest that a cosmopolitan approach does not mean, as some proposals have suggested, discarding a role for states. Instead, states should be preserved, and they have a valuable role to play.[40] On the one hand, doing away with states would mean a single global community without the local aspect of governance, with more knowledge of local issues with global impact and the ability to act quickly. On the other hand, states are the only formally constituted political institutions representing identifiable groups; in the real world, states are intermediaries between six billion people and international and global institutions.[41]

To clarify my stance on the design of global participatory institutions, I pose the following question: How can a citizen of Tuvalu – an island nation

38 Jürgen Habermas, 'Tres modelos de democracia: Sobre el concepto de una política deliberativa' (1992) 39 Debats 18.

39 See Elster (n 37).

40 See Philip Pettit, *The State* (Princeton UP 2023); D Bello Hutt and MV Kristan, 'Philip Pettit: The State' [2024] Res Publica 1.

41 See Peters (n 25) 272.

sinking in the Pacific Ocean, whose residents are deeply concerned about the impact of climate change on their home – gain a voice within the international system? Imagine that she complains to the president of her state, the president of Tuvalu raises a voice against climate change at the COP28, but no agreement is possible without the consent of other states. In this – unfortunately real – scenario, the national and international system fails, and our citizen of Tuvalu wonders which other institution she could complain to. She is considering suing her government to oblige it to take action against climate change, because in 10 years the water level will be lethally high and her island at risk of being submerged. However, she is aware that climate change is a global problem and that, as a result, her government's own measures will not be sufficient to reverse it. She knows that there are actors like the INGOs – Greenpeace, for example – demanding that states and the international community act against climate change, but she still wonders whether this actor will be legitimized to act against climate change, whether in the end it will be representative of her concern and finally, and no less importantly, among the myriad of actors, she is confused about the path she should take.

This hypothetical scenario illustrates the increasing complexity of international law-making, as previously discussed through the concept of relative authority at the beginning of the chapter. The traditional sources – treaties, customs, and general principles – interact with the procedures established by INGOs, private actors, and hybrid regulators in determining international law. Two questions arise here. The first is related to legitimacy: who can speak on behalf of the citizen of Tuvalu and effectively represent her interests in international and global rule-making? The second refers to the nature of a system – that it is complex per se – capable of enabling participation. In the next steps of the argument, the chapter will focus on providing an answer to the second question by outlining the features that a system that enables participation and representation should have: a global institutional system must link the local levels with the global level; it should interconnect various levels of the system, and it need to be simple, otherwise it will be ineffective in achieving the participation of the people and, as a result, preventing domination. By simplicity I do not mean simplification. People are political actors in spaces such as cities, counties, or states, but a democratic system of global governance will consist of a multiplicity of actors, with many intersections and interactions. It will be complex 'from the inside', but from the perspective of the participants it is necessary to facilitate people's participation at a time when freedom of choice is promoted. In the end, the functioning of democracy depends on public debate, participation, and communication between citizens and institutions.[42]

Madison famously states that republican ideals work best on a small scale. But with globalization, it seems that crucial decisions for humanity must be made on a global scale. But large-scale decisions are not incompatible with

42 Peters (n 25) 308.

local deliberation. Think of climate change and the citizen of Tuvalu. Climate change does not affect all societies in the same way, and societies must also contribute in different ways to mitigate climate change. The cases of participation that link local levels with global problems can help to link small-scale deliberation with global problems. In this vein, for instance, cities are getting more and more involved in global politics. As global harms happen, mayors of several cities have positioned themselves in the discussion of a solution, even by advocating policies that go against their states' policies. In doing so, cities reveal themselves as global actors. Think of the Global Covenant of Mayors for Climate and Energy as a case in point. New York is included in that covenant, even though the USA formally withdrew from the Paris Agreement. Another illustration is provided by Besson and Martí:[43] as an example they mention the city of Rio de Janeiro negotiating a loan with the World Bank in 2010 without the consent of Brazil. This example is paradigmatic inasmuch as incurring public debt is one of the traditional powers of the state. The example reveals that cities can rise as actors in their own right independently of the goodwill of their states.

Let's turn the focus now on direct participation. One of the claims of this work is that people need the ability to have a voice in global decision-making; they should be able to play a significant role in global affairs. In this chapter I also assume that the people have a genuine interest in participating in global affairs. However, even if empirical evidence could argue against this, people are usually involved if (a) there are real spaces of participation and (b) they recognize that their involvement makes sense[44] so that global democracy still exists. In looking at one of the biggest global problems – climate change – we will see that even if there are no global spaces for participation, people are looking at how they can influence and trigger a discussion as, for example, the case of *Urgenda Foundation v. The State of the Netherlands*[45] shows or via younger or older generations, who are increasingly concerned about the consequences of climate change.[46]

In order to avoid domination, people must be able to exert influence and impose direction on the decision-making process. The inclusion of spaces of

43 See Besson and Martí (n 28).

44 See Peters (n 25) 313.

45 See <http://uitspraken.rechtspraak.nl/inziendocument?id=ECLI:NL:RBDHA:2015:7196> also see <http://www.lse.ac.uk/GranthamInstitute/litigation/urgenda-foundation-v-kingdom-of-the-netherlands-district-court-of-the-hague-2015/> both accessed 29 November 2023.

46 In 2018, 21 children sued the Washington State Department of Ecology to pursue a legal claim to a stable climate, while in Europe the School Strike for Climate, launched by the 15-year-old Greta Thunberg, is increasingly popular. As Greta Thunberg said at the United Nations Climate Change Conference, held in Katowice, Poland, in 2018: 'We cannot save the world by playing by the rules. Because the rules have to be changed'. See <https://medium.com/wedonthave-time/greta-thunberg-speech-to-un-secretary-general-antónio-guterres-362175826548> accessed 21 November 2023. See also <https://www.nytimes.com/2023/04/16/opinion/climate-change-grandmothers.html> accessed 22 January 2023.

participation in decision-making processes challenges the understanding of people acting merely as 'editors' of laws. According to the Pettit account of freedom, people should not be the direct authors of the laws that govern them, but their 'editors'.[47] People acting as editors of the norms that govern them implies that their interventions are contained in multi-layered and inclusive forums of 'contestatory democracy'. Democracy is a dual-aspect model: electoral and contestatory. While the first aspect (*ex ante*) correlates with the 'ideal of giving the people electoral control over government' (Pettit 2000: 105),[48] the second aspect (*ex post*), contestation, requires that individuals can contest those norms that they cannot reasonably accept and can contest those norms through reactive or proactive initiatives.

Neo-republicanism, then, advocates both for interest-identifying deliberation and for control of political decisions by the people. However, as was argued earlier, my claim here is that contestation alone is not enough, but that participatory deliberative democracy should be the ideal to be achieved. In this sense, the long republican tradition of active citizenry should be extended to cases (*ex ante*) of people's participation. Moreover, as Martí and Seleme[49] emphasize, Pettit's model of democracy

> does not say whether the dual-aspect model of democracy would favor the use of comprehensive and effective mechanisms of participatory democracy such as popular initiatives, citizens' assemblies, referendums, etc., and if so, what conditions these mechanisms would be subject to, neither does it provide concrete examples of how the dual-aspect model of democracy could be institutionalized.

And this omission supports the claim that the authorial aspect of global democracy should include individual direct participation by hosting a partial authorial role. This claim is especially important in the global context for the reasons given earlier and in the previous chapters: individuals cannot be expected to be blind to the political decisions that affect their freedom; moreover, it is essential that people have a say in the decisions that affect their life planning, that they identify with the political project in which they are involved and that they can support it as their own.

47 For Pettit, democracy has two dimensions, authorial and editorial. The authorial dimension however, which implies people's participation, is implemented by 'electoral institutions whereby policies and policy-making agencies are thoroughly discussed'. This authorial role, an indirect one, needs to be complemented by an editorial dimension of control over people's representatives. Philip Pettit, 'Democracy, Electoral and Contestatory' (2000) 42 Nomos 116–17.

48 Pettit (n 47) 105.

49 JL Martí and H Seleme, 'Three Comments on Philip Pettit's On The People's Terms' (2015) 5(2) Philosophy and Public Issues 37.

A participatory space means providing entry points to influence and control democratic decision-making. Lafont,[50] who, however, does not formulate a participatory account of the global context,[51] presents a participatory conception of deliberative democracy in which she explains that there are no justified exclusions from participation in this common task when the fundamental rights of everyone are equally important and their violation is everyone's concern. From this perspective, supporting the realization of this common task by creating and maintaining strong international institutions is not only the best antidote to populist threats to national democracies, but also the seed from which a global participatory democracy could grow. In this sense, Bohman[52] has argued that the ability to initiate deliberations is an essential characteristic in a global context, especially in terms of preventing domination. It is so, because in a context characterized by its complexity, the ability to set the agenda is a relevant characteristic, not only because it determines *ex-ante* deliberation, but also because it determines the course of deliberation. People should have the opportunity to play an active role in the decision-making process, a role that goes beyond the election and leads them from an editorial role to a partial authorial role.[53] As Besson and Martí[54] explain, a global public sphere as a condition for the democratic legitimacy of the international system must involve deep, sustained, and dynamic public debates fed by a vibrant global civil society. They also stress that:

> It is important, however, that global civil society actors be empowered to participate not only in an informal, non-institutional public deliberation, but also in more formal settings and procedures of international decision-making. In that sense, they should be allowed to interact with public actors as well as with international institutions. And they should be able to do it not only as watchdogs of the legitimacy of such institutions that can actually contest the decisions that have been made or the actions that have been taken, but also as active participants – and therefore as partial authors – of international law-making, especially in representation of the interests, views and claims of those people(s) who do not find adequate representatives among public actors.[55]

As we can see, in order to build a global, democratically legitimate system, it is important in expanding the role of people's participation to add entry

50 See Lafont (n 31) 161, 242.

51 M Victoria Kristan, 'Sovereign Schliberties: Where Pettit's International Protection of Individual Freedom Falls Short' (2022) 46 Revus: Journal for Constitutional Theory and Philosophy of Law.

52 John Bohman, *Democracy Across Borders: From Demos to Demoi* (MIT Press 2007) 25.

53 The role of people as authors will be partial, as there are also mechanisms of representation in place.

54 See Besson and Martí (n 28) 28–29.

55 Besson and Martí (n 28) 29.

points to the decision-making process. These proposals will strengthen people's capacity for democratic control by enabling them to identify with the policies to which they are subject. The value of people's participation is crucial to the legitimacy of global decision-making. The role of civil associations and organizations, social movements, and social protests should be able to influence relevant decision-making processes; following Wheatley,[56] the minimum requirement is that opinions emerging in the global public sphere are able to influence relevant decision-making processes. This weak form can become a strong form of the global public sphere through the introduction of institutionalized decision-making procedures with regularized opportunities for *ex-ante* inputs.

People's participation emphasizes informal actions over formal ones. The first is identified mainly with deliberation, while the other is identified with voting and elections.[57] Participation has an epistemological value that increases the chances of reaching well-informed and coherent decisions, but, more importantly, it is capable of preventing domination. If climate change is considered a paradigmatic case, people need and demand influence on it. Climate change mitigation policies are a source of domination, as decision-making on a global problem is carried out by 'islands of non-democracy'.[58] Climate change is a case in which its constituency is undoubtedly global, as its effects endanger the whole of humanity, but it does not affect everyone in the same way. Moreover, action against climate change requires the articulation of multiple levels of decisions, together with decisions based on people's deliberation and technical choices. For example, at the time of planning a policy against climate change, there are some decisions that belong to scientists and experts – technical decisions – that is, the level of CO_2 emissions allowed; others belong to the affected, for example, to open the agenda for the problems we are trying to solve and their possible solutions. In addition, mitigation of climate change requires fundamental changes in the economy, in the exploitation of resources, in living standards, etc., where people's participation will be vital.

People's participation is necessary to build a legitimate global democracy. I have also stressed that the proposal of a global democracy based on the people's participation does not mean that the representation of the people is excluded. But that representation must be reconsidered in order to avoid darkness and disconnection from the represented in decision-making. Mini publics and new representation rooms like the Global Parliament of Mayors are fulfilling the function of improving the representation rooms.[59] Even if the role of representation is reduced in this model, the link between people's

56 See Wheatley (n 26).

57 See Peters (n 25) 270.

58 This is how Charnovitz characterized international organizations. Steve Charnovitz, 'Two Centuries of Participation: NGOs and International Governance' (1996) 18 Michigan Journal of International Law 183.

59 See Dryzek and others (n 34).

participation and people's representation will improve the legitimacy of global decisions.

5. The transition to a global participation

Now that we have made it clear that the regulative ideal toward which a global democracy should tend is participation, we can ask how we envision the transition to it. In particular, and in line with the institutional structure that this chapter defends, the question is how we can establish a concrete transition strategy from current governance structures to a participative global governance. Two preliminary observations are in order. First, the idea behind this transition, as well as behind this work, is a cosmopolitan one, in which people perceive themselves as members of a single global community, with interest in and sensitivity for what is happening to other people, even in distant places. Secondly, as the example of the Urgenda case shows, participation already exists in global affairs, though it is contingent, sporadic, and spontaneous.

For this reason, we need to refine the question and ask ourselves how we can find ways to ensure participation and make contingent, sporadic, and spontaneous participation necessary, permanent, and relevant. Of course, this change in participation does not simply follow a recipe; it rather sets an agenda of transformations that falls on different actors. First and foremost, it is INGOs that have been most prominent and have increased in number in recent years. INGOs such as Greenpeace, the Urgenda Foundation, Human Rights Watch, Amnesty International, and the Oxford Commitment for Famine Relief (OXFAM) have enabled people both to participate in solving problems that are remote to them, and to be heard in decision-making processes. However, INGOs do not stop at the issues their directors deem relevant, and suffer from low levels of transparency and accountability, so a challenge is to make INGOs more horizontal and accountable. This challenge does not seem unattainable or far away, as many INGOs, aware of these shortcomings, are moving toward accountability, for example by joining the Accountable Now platform.[60]

Social movements can also play a relevant role in tracing a path to a global governance by setting the agenda but also by adopting a purposeful role.[61] A not too distant example of the power of social movements is of the ones that emerged in Iceland in 2009–2011 following the collapse of the Icelandic economy. The Icelandic people were protesting the government, and the political class at large, because they realized that they did not represent the people's interests and instead they were catering to the interests of the financial

60 See <https://accountablenow.org/> accessed 7 January 2024.

61 For the role of networks and activist see ME Keck and K Sikkink, *Activists Beyond Borders: Advocacy Networks in International Politics* (Cornell UP 1998); Manuel Castells, *The Rise of the Network Society* (John Wiley & Sons 2010) vol 1.

elite when the economic collapse happened. The pressure the people exercised by getting organized, especially using the Internet, and protesting every week led to the government enacting policies which led to economic recovery, the banks paying for the costs of the crisis, and proposing a transformation of the political system by elaborating a crowdsourced constitution proposal.[62] The Iceland example shows that ordinary citizens, through social movements and also individually, are capable of deliberating together and delivering good decisions, in this case, a constitutional project.

States can also play a role, they still hold value, even if they cannot prevent domination on their own. So when they act associatively and establish spaces like the European Parliament or participatory initiatives like the European Citizens' Initiative,[63] which works under the slogan 'Get a greater say in the policies that affect your lives', or even the Conference of the Future of Europe,[64] they provide an impetus to increase the participation of individuals in transnational affairs. This venue does not only mean to consider states as part of global governance, they can also play a role in helping international organizations reform themselves to be more democratic and participatory, as the European Citizens' Initiative shows. Archibugi,[65] for example, argues that states could support international organizations to become more participatory and democratic, and that even non-democratic states could play a role in this. In another vein, states could also support global participation from within, for example by allowing their own citizens to participate more directly in global politics, and by facilitating the social mobilization process driven by social movements, for example by allowing their citizens to form associations and networks with other citizens abroad.[66]

All of these spaces are valuable for transitioning to participation in global affairs, but initiatives on digital democracy – like, for instance, CrowdLaw[67] – need to be prioritized and replicated in number and scale. New digital technologies could have a positive impact for a global participative deliberative democracy. They could support and become a source of global democracy by enhancing the power of aggregation; they can strengthen our collective intelligence and our processes of political aggregation, deliberation,

62 The process of drafting a new constitution was the world's first 'crowdsourced' process that used Internet communications technology to involve the public directly in the drafting process.

63 <https://europa.eu/citizens-initiative/home_en> accessed 7 January 2024.

64 <https://commission.europa.eu/strategy-and-policy/priorities-2019-2024/new-push-european-democracy/conference-future-europe_en> accessed 22 December 2023.

65 Daniele Archibugi, *The Global Commonwealth of Citizens: Toward Cosmopolitan Democracy* (Princeton UP 2008).

66 D Archibugi, M Koenig-Archibugi and R Marchetti (eds), *Global Democracy: Normative and Empirical Perspectives* (CUP 2011).

67 Online public participation leveraging new technologies to tap into diverse sources of information, judgments, and expertise at each stage of the law and policymaking cycle to improve the quality as well as the legitimacy of the resulting laws and policies.

and collaboration.[68] As it is, it promotes participatory lawmaking. What is attractive about it is that it promotes direct engagement and participation, as well as enhancing the possibility of coordination and deliberation in social movements.[69]

6. Conclusion: from one day to another, achieving global democracy

While this chapter has emphasized that an effective response to preventing domination requires the unprecedented construction of a model of global democracy, the institutions that govern our present, as well as our future, should develop capacities such as long-term thinking, institutional reflexivity, and adaptation to content-based online deliberation. The development of these capacities should start where we are now, in order to make room for a new institutional framework capable of addressing the pressing issues that affect us. The choice of these capacities is not arbitrary, but it is not intended to be exhaustive. What it attempts to do is to open up some proposals to make feasible the step from an international system of states to a democratic global system.

- *Long-term thinking*

Global democracy is a long-term challenge. It is not possible to achieve it from one day to another. In other vein, we have seen that governments can be a part of a global democratic system, but they cannot continue to operate as they have done so far, and one of the things they must modify is the focus on the short term to instead articulate long-term thinking. Short-term thinking is a problem from at least two perspectives. The first is that it does not provide space for those problems that will impact us during the coming years or decades. The second is that those who are dealing in government will be not accountable for the future impacts of their policies, and sometimes their policies could violate government's obligations to future generations.[70]

Short-term thinking can be harmful,[71] think for example of disaster planning in the case of Hurricane Katrina, where the cost of reconstruction exceeded

68 See José Luis Martí, 'The Role of New Technologies in Deliberative Democracy' in G Amato, B Barbisan and C Pinelli (eds), *Rule of Law v Majoritarian Democracy* (Hart Publishing 2021).

69 V Alsina and JL Martí, 'The Birth of the CrowdLaw Movement: Tech-Based Citizen Participation, Legitimacy and the Quality of Lawmaking' (2018) 40(2) Analyse & Kritik 337–58.

70 See Simon Caney, 'Political Institutions for the Future: A Five-Fold Package' in I González-Ricoy and A Gosseries (eds), *Institutions for Future Generations* (OUP 2016). See also A Gosseries and LH Meyer, 'Introduction – Intergenerational Justice and Its Challenges' in *Intergenerational Justice* (OUP 2009).

71 Caney calls it harmful short-termism. Simon Caney, 'Climate Change and the Future: Discounting for Time, Wealth, and Risk' (2009) 40(2) Journal of Social Philosophy 163.

by 15 times the cost of efficient preparation,[72] ignoring the incalculable cost of lost lives. The failure to think with a long-term perspective is not only harmful at the local level, it also multiplies the capacity for damage in financial and human terms. Climate change is the most pressing example of the importance of long-term thinking, where past actions have determined our future and the future of generations to come. The delay in changing those policies that are harmful to the environment, together with the delay in implementing positive policies to mitigate climate change, is causing enormous costs for our future generations. Long-term thinking also implies thinking in plural terms beyond borders. In this sense, long-term thinking could be a driver of a global democratic system, since it could help to design a policymaking process which makes it difficult to ignore the common threats, and at the same time improve the democratic legitimacy of the decision-making process.

- *Institutional reflexivity*

If institutions are to respond to the threats posed by globalization, they must be flexible enough to respond to the feedback from public deliberation and context-changing conditions; they must strike a balance between agility and durability[73] while being stable enough to provide a framework for collective response.[74] There are various scholars working on the reflexivity of the institutions.[75] One of the more famous approaches to reflexivity belongs to Ulrich Beck.[76] He lays the focus of reflexivity over modernization, where reflexive modernization means 'the possibility of a creative (self)-destruction for an entire epoch: that of industrial society'. Scholte[77] provides a definition of reflexivity by understanding that it 'entails moving from negligence to vigilance about positionality'. Dryzek and Pickering,[78] however, stress this argument regarding what they call *ecological* reflexivity; the argument is broad enough to make it a general condition for institutions, and claims that states, or international organizations, are not suited to be part of a global democratic system in their current form. The attributes of flexibility, adaptation, and change are virtuous in reflexive institutions.

72 A Healy and N Malhotra, 'Myopic Voters and Natural Disaster Policy' (2009) 103(3) American Political Science Review 387.

73 Oran R Young, *Governing Complex Systems: Social Capital for the Anthropocene* (MIT Press 2017) 218–19.

74 JS Dryzek and J Pickering, *The Politics of the Anthropocene* (OUP 2018) 218.

75 See Jonathan W Kuyper, 'Designing Institutions for Global Democracy: Flexibility Through Escape Clauses and Sunset Provisions' (2013) 6(4) Ethics & Global Politics 19163.

76 Ulrich Beck, *Ulrich Beck: Pioneer in Cosmopolitan Sociology and Risk Society* (Springer International Publishing 2014).

77 Jan A Scholte, 'Beyond Institutionalism: Toward a Transformed Global Governance Theory' (2021) 13(1) International Theory 179.

78 See Dryzek and Pickering (n 74).

Institutions ought to avoid forms of 'lock-in' in unsustainable practices, such as those policies that are tied to useless structures such as traditional multilateralism, or a pathological path dependency. In this context, social movements and individual action will be vital for spurring the transition to more reflexive societies, but unless dominant institutions change, systemwide reflexivity will remain out of reach. According to Dryzek and Pickering, there are actions that can be taken toward an institution that could be less or more reflexive, for instance those institutions that provide for public inquiries, independent review bodies, procedural rights, requirements for periodic review of legislation, and institutions in light of performance, linking people with experts, having a global dissent channel, and so on. Such initiatives have the potential to initiate the deliberative processes that are required to initiate institutional changes. For instance, providing for a global dissent channel could enable people who are affected or are part of the decision-making institutions to express their dissent with a policy.[79]

79 As Dryzek and Pickering explain, they take this name idea from the US State Department's longstanding Dissent Channel. Dryzek and Pickering (n 74) 159.

Index